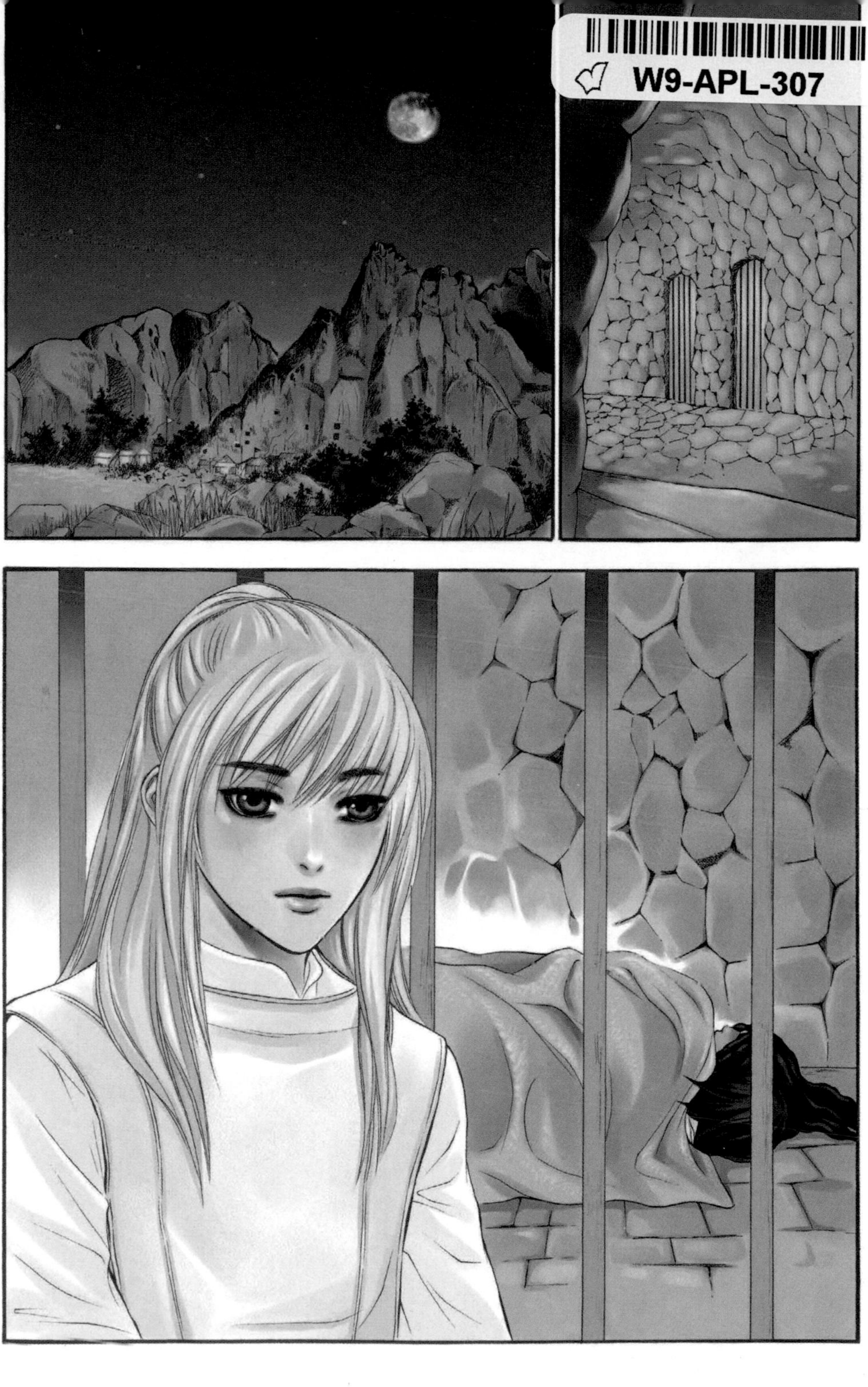

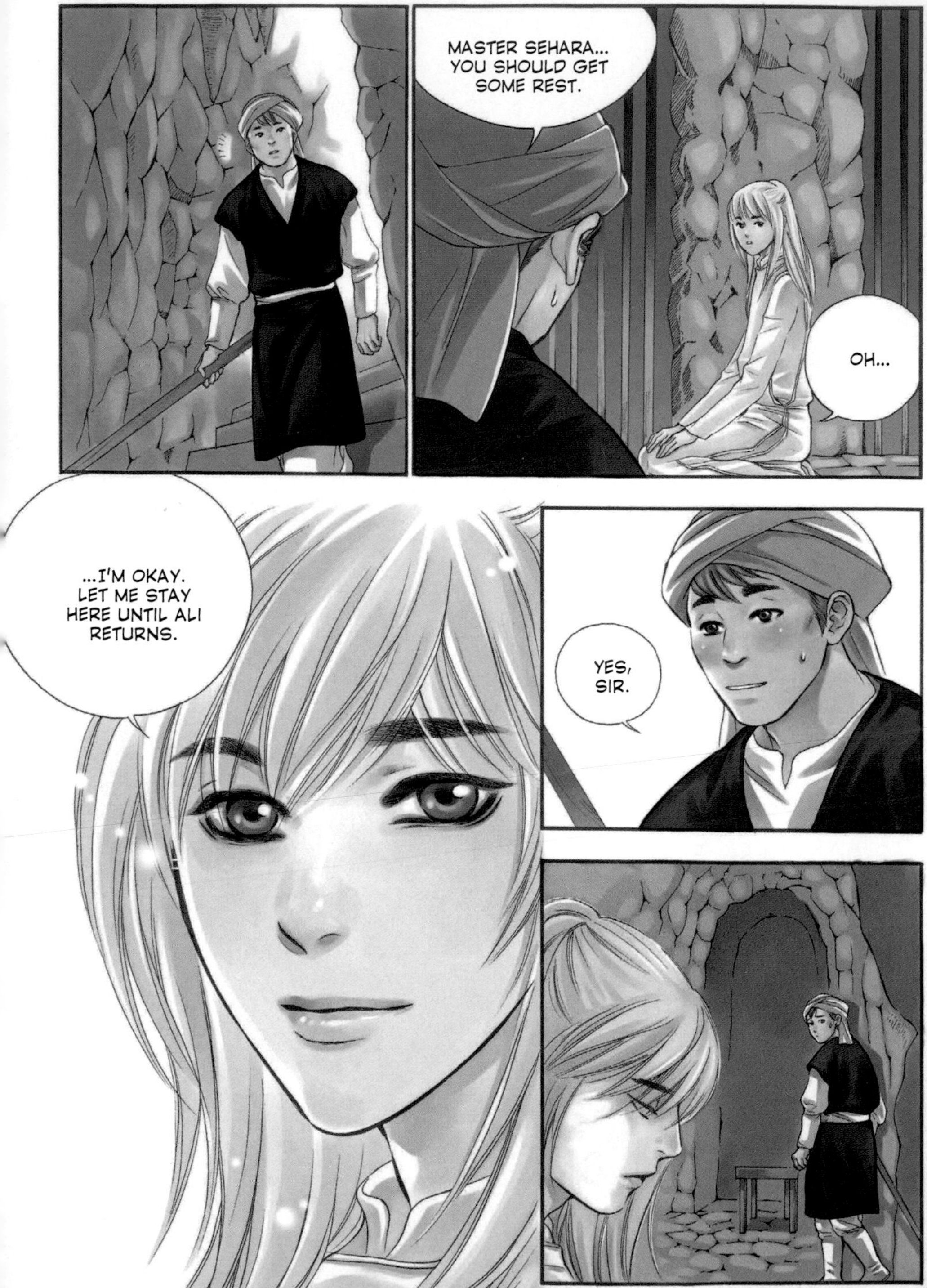
MASTER SEHARA... YOU SHOULD GET SOME REST.
OH...
...I'M OKAY. LET ME STAY HERE UNTIL ALI RETURNS.
YES, SIR.

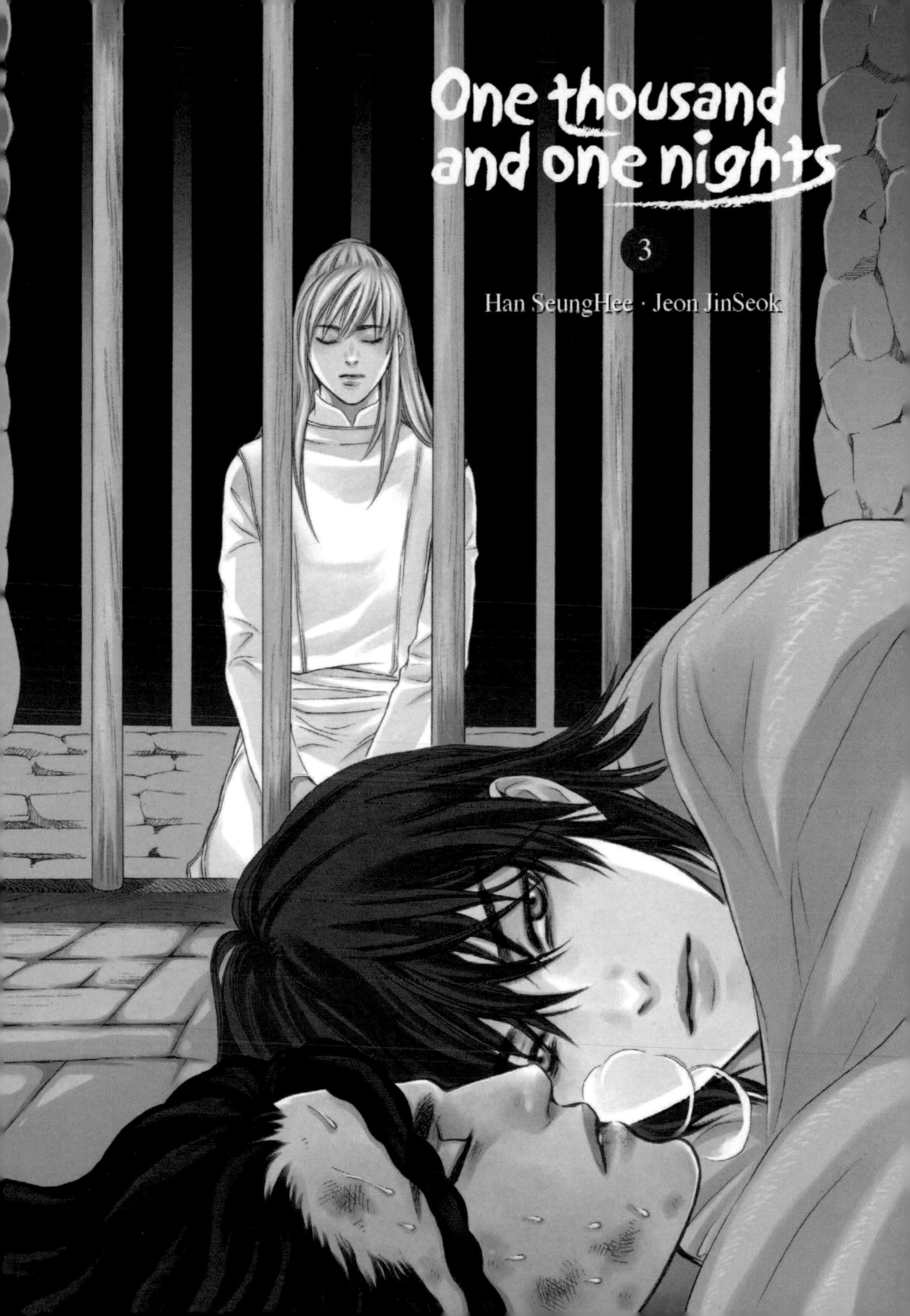
One thousand and one nights
3
Han SeungHee · Jeon JinSeok

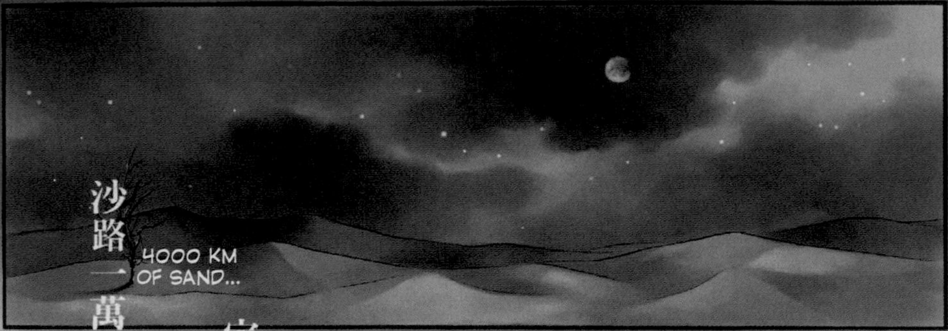
沙路一萬里
4000 KM OF SAND...

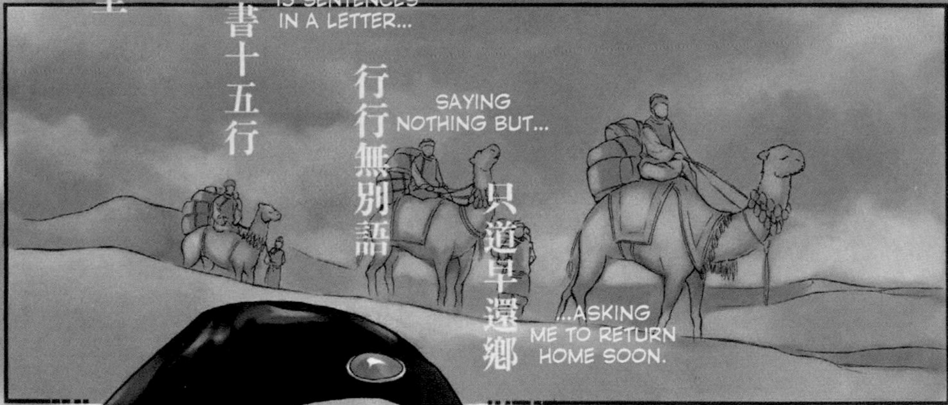
家書十五行
15 SENTENCES IN A LETTER...
行行無別語
SAYING NOTHING BUT...
只道早還鄉
...ASKING ME TO RETURN HOME SOON.

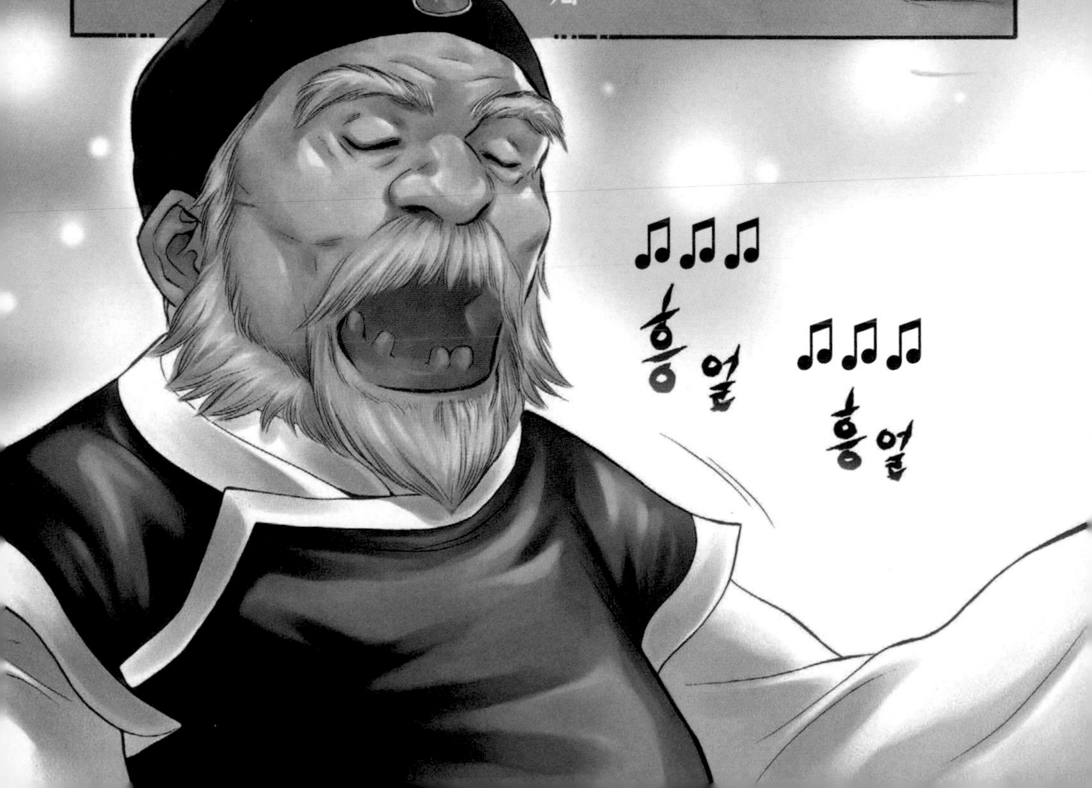
흥얼
흥얼

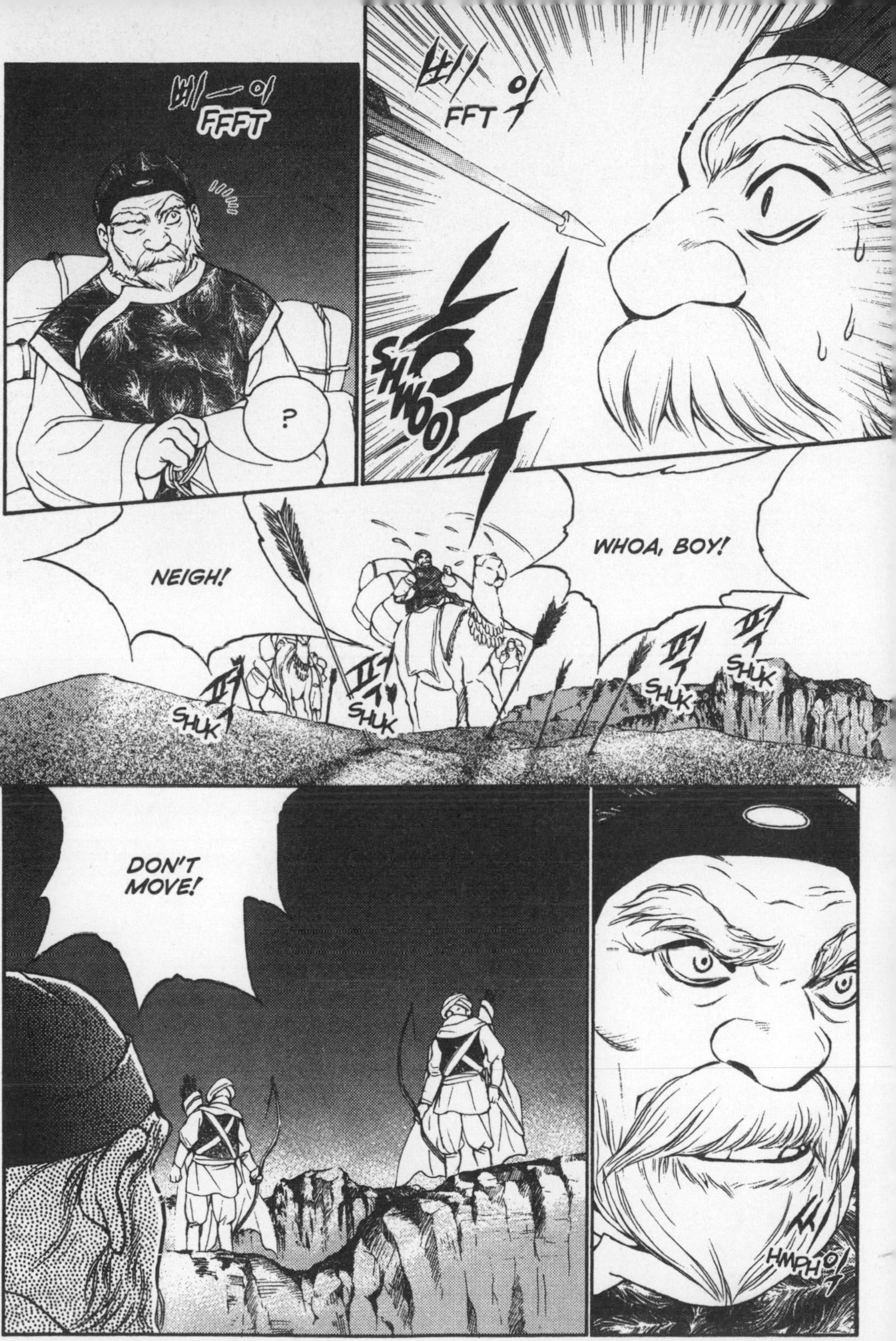
삐—이
FFFT
?
삐익
FFT
SHWOOO
NEIGH!
WHOA, BOY!
픽
SHUK
픽
SHUK
픽
SHUK
픽
SHUK
DON'T MOVE!
HMPH

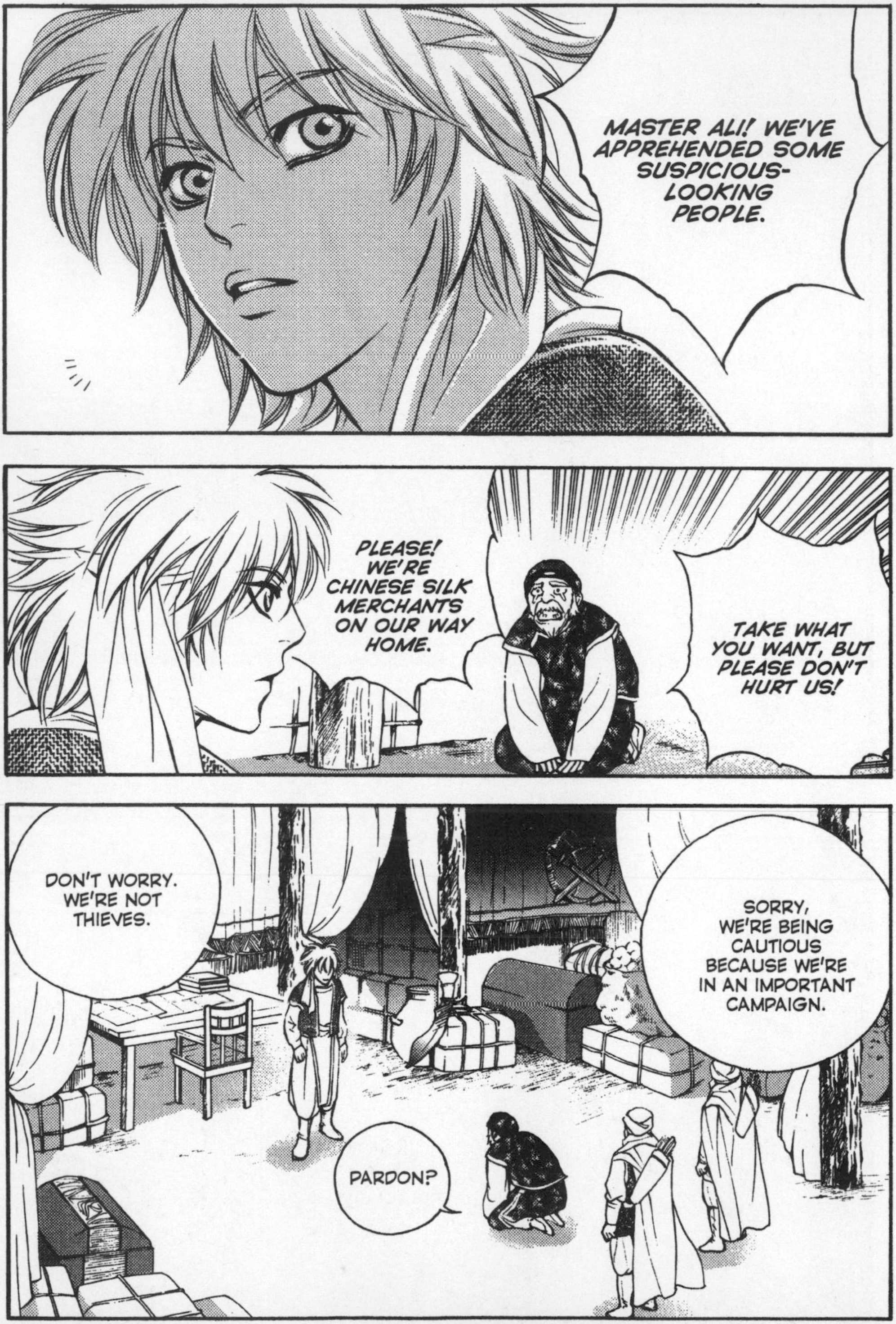
MASTER ALI! WE'VE APPREHENDED SOME SUSPICIOUS-LOOKING PEOPLE.
PLEASE! WE'RE CHINESE SILK MERCHANTS ON OUR WAY HOME.
TAKE WHAT YOU WANT, BUT PLEASE DON'T HURT US!
DON'T WORRY. WE'RE NOT THIEVES.
SORRY, WE'RE BEING CAUTIOUS BECAUSE WE'RE IN AN IMPORTANT CAMPAIGN.
PARDON?

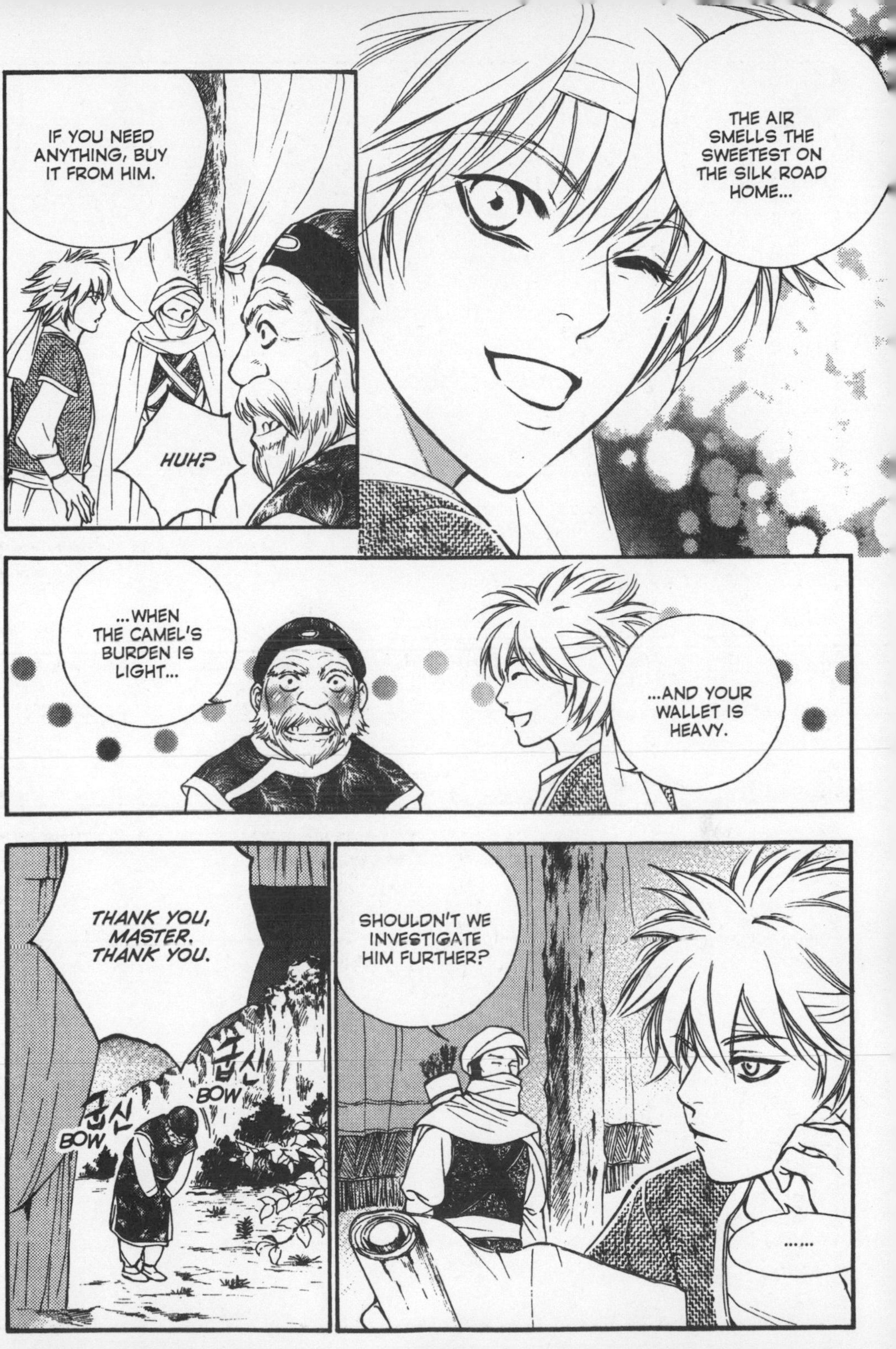
IF YOU NEED ANYTHING, BUY IT FROM HIM.
HUH?
THE AIR SMELLS THE SWEETEST ON THE SILK ROAD HOME...
...WHEN THE CAMEL'S BURDEN IS LIGHT...
...AND YOUR WALLET IS HEAVY.
THANK YOU, MASTER. THANK YOU.
굽신 BOW
굽신 BOW
SHOULDN'T WE INVESTIGATE HIM FURTHER?
......

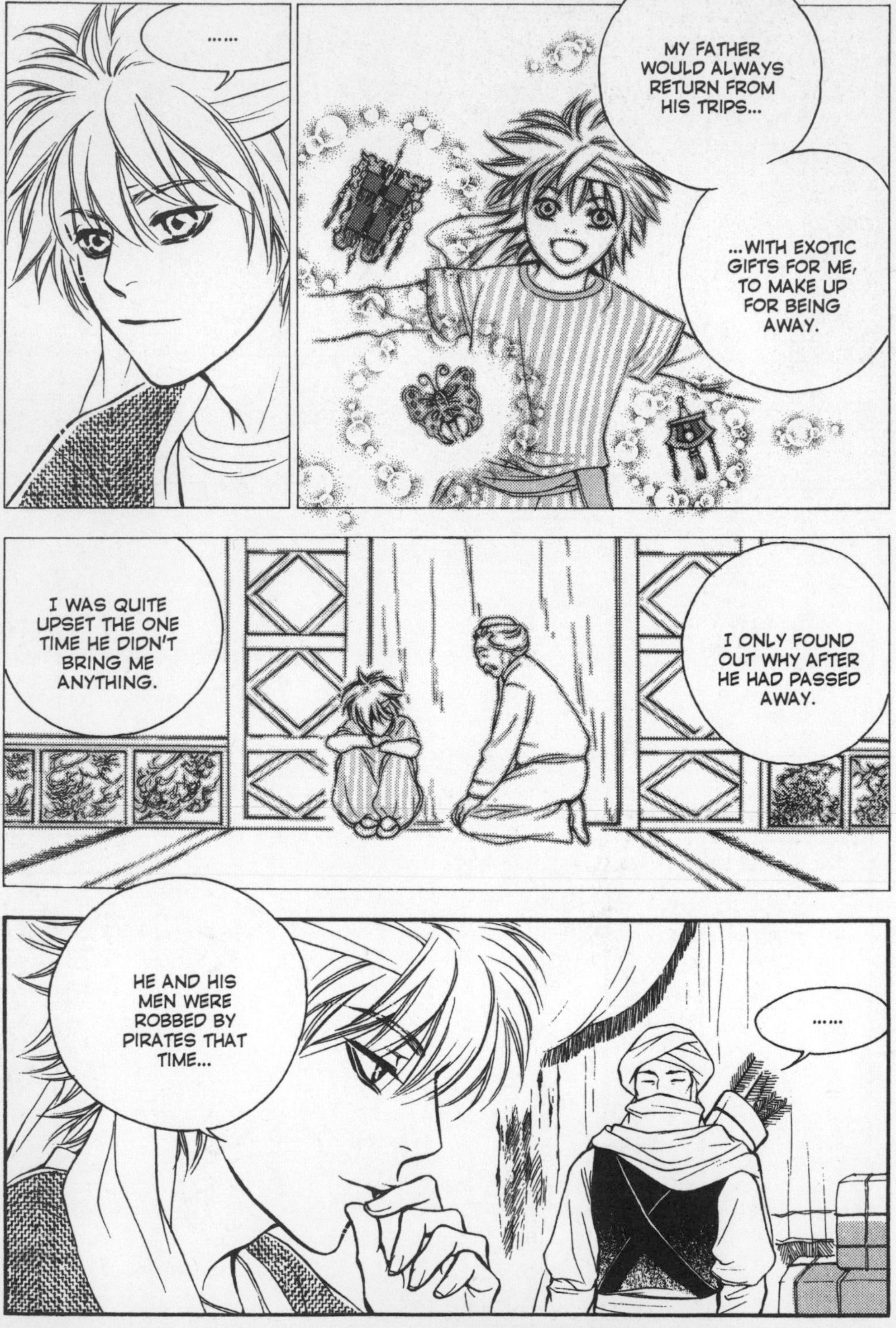
......
MY FATHER WOULD ALWAYS RETURN FROM HIS TRIPS...
...WITH EXOTIC GIFTS FOR ME, TO MAKE UP FOR BEING AWAY.
I WAS QUITE UPSET THE ONE TIME HE DIDN'T BRING ME ANYTHING.
I ONLY FOUND OUT WHY AFTER HE HAD PASSED AWAY.
HE AND HIS MEN WERE ROBBED BY PIRATES THAT TIME...
......

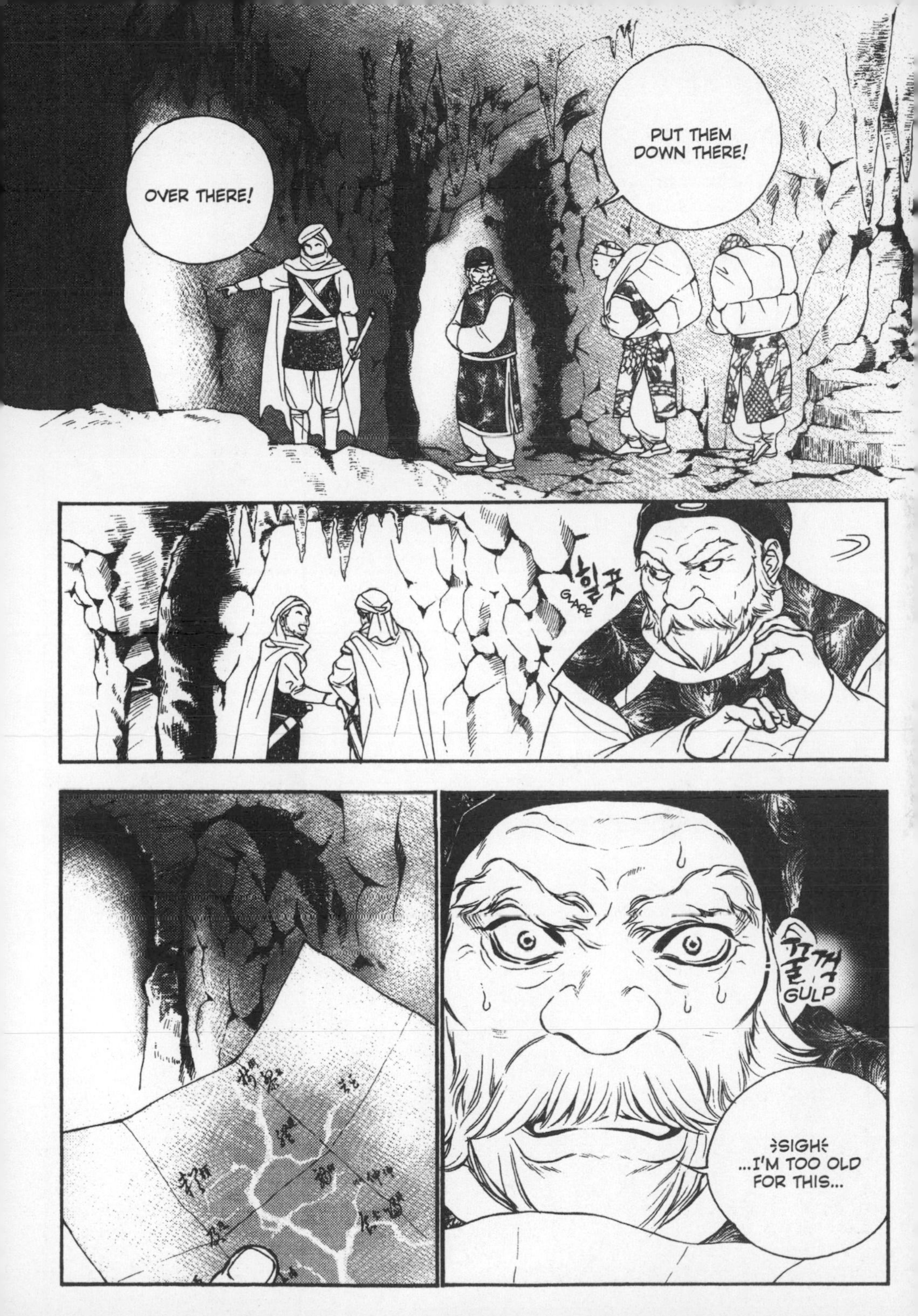
OVER THERE!
PUT THEM DOWN THERE!
힐끗
GLARE
꿀꺽
GULP
SIGH
...I'M TOO OLD FOR THIS...

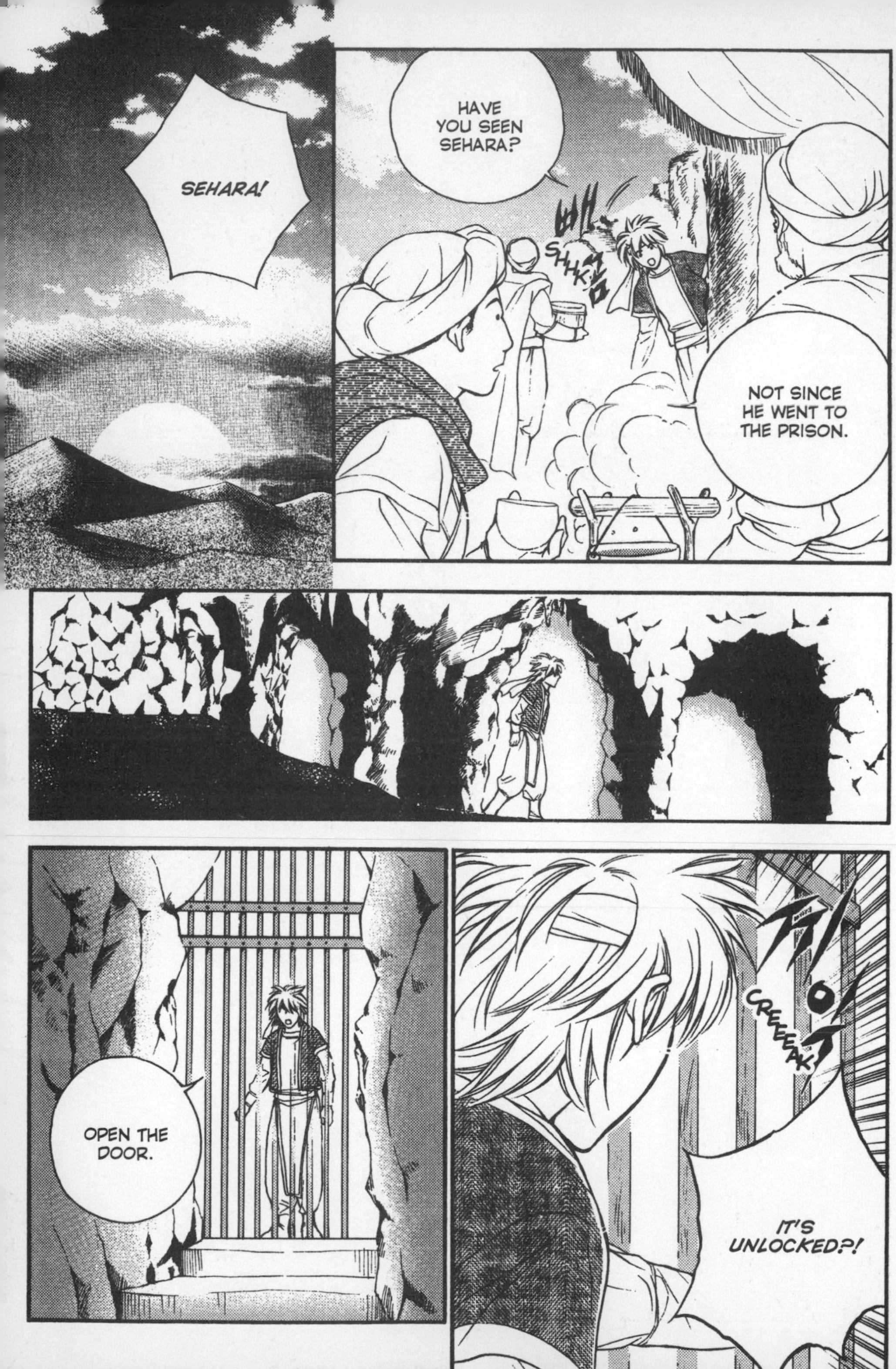
SEHARA!
HAVE YOU SEEN SEHARA?
SHHK
NOT SINCE HE WENT TO THE PRISON.
OPEN THE DOOR.
CREEEEAK
IT'S UNLOCKED?!

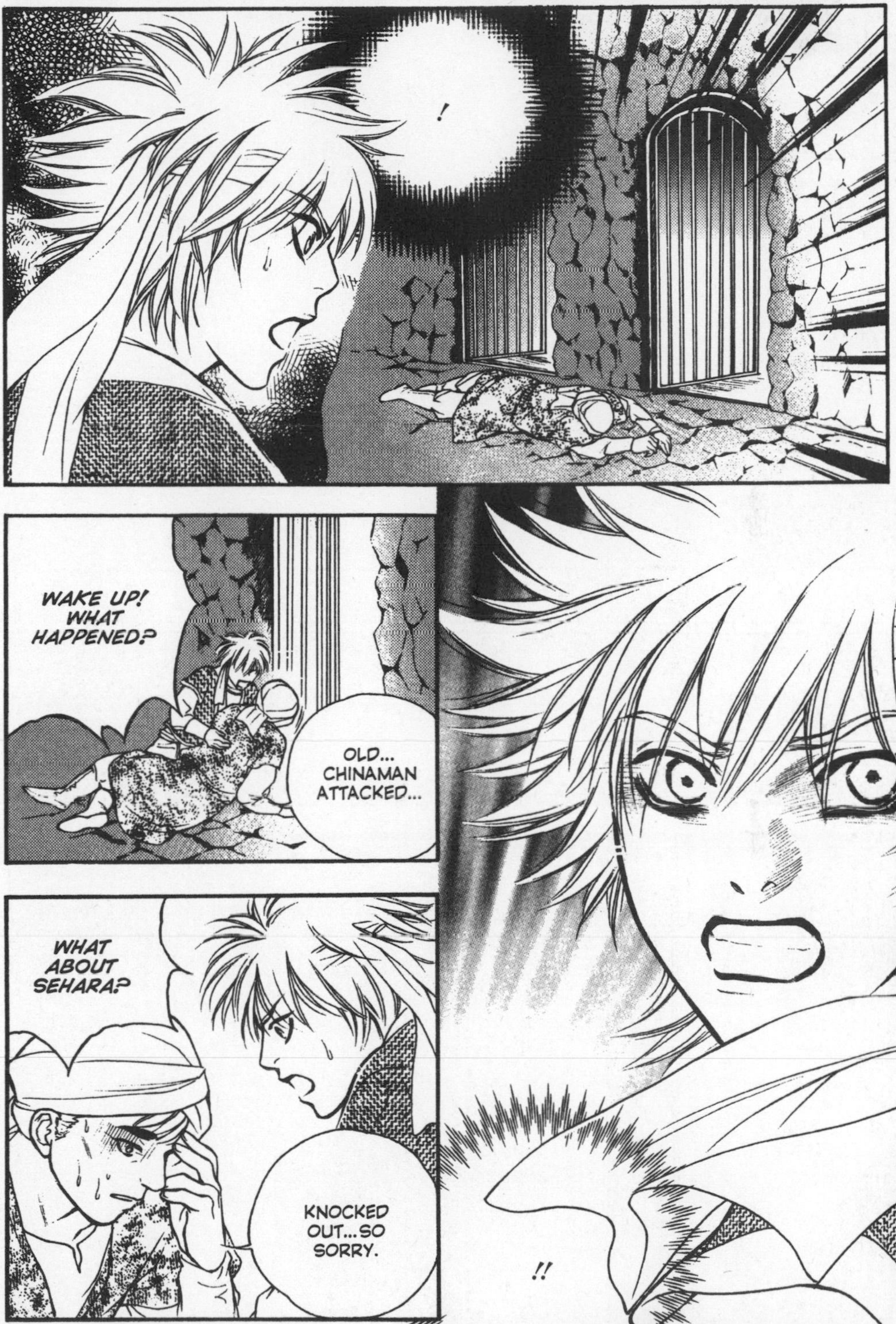
!
WAKE UP! WHAT HAPPENED?
OLD... CHINAMAN ATTACKED...
WHAT ABOUT SEHARA?
KNOCKED OUT...SO SORRY.
!!

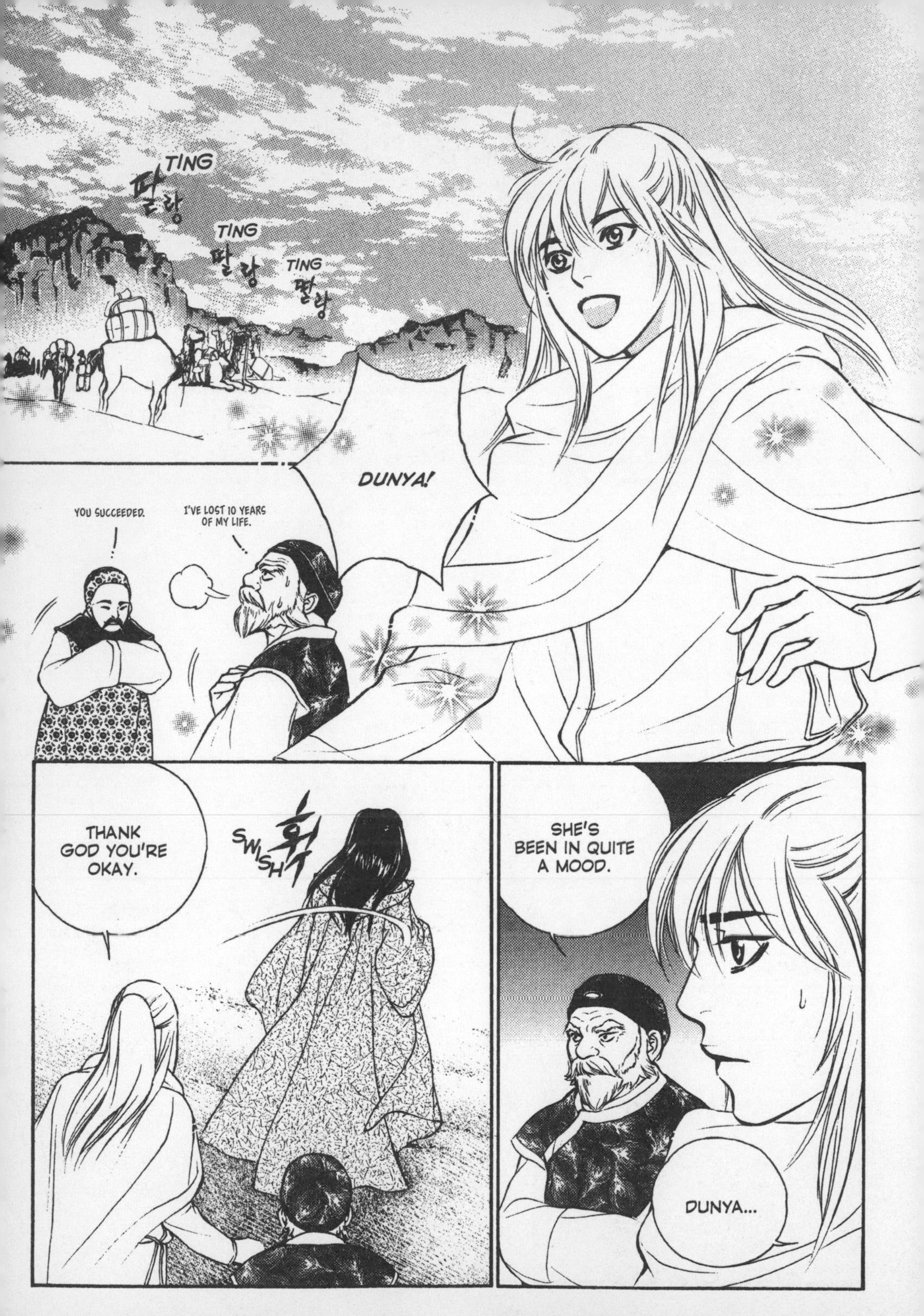

TING
팔랑
TING
팔랑
TING
팔랑
DUNYA!
YOU SUCCEEDED.
I'VE LOST 10 YEARS OF MY LIFE.
THANK GOD YOU'RE OKAY.
SWISH
휙
SHE'S BEEN IN QUITE A MOOD.
DUNYA...

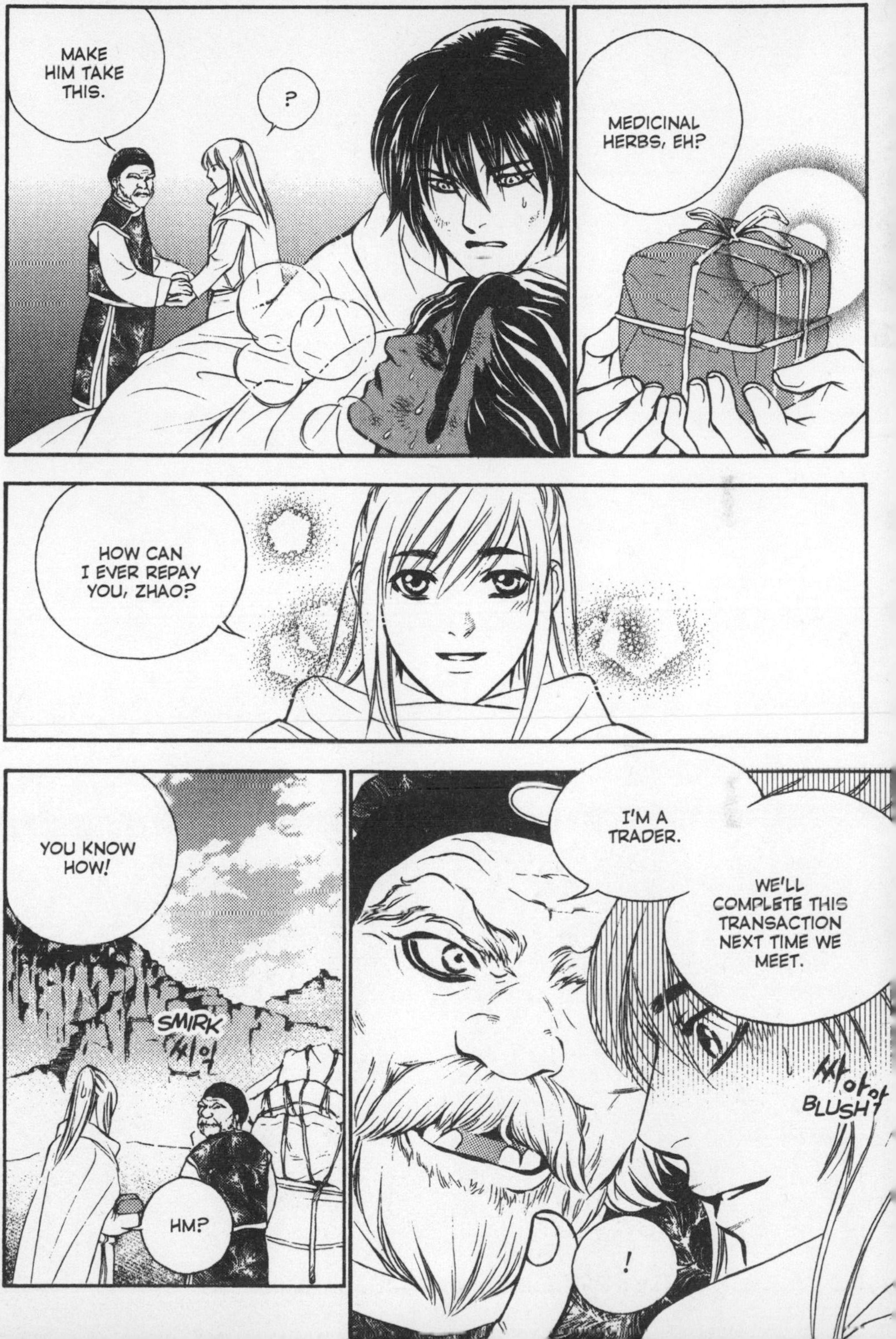
MAKE HIM TAKE THIS.
?
MEDICINAL HERBS, EH?
HOW CAN I EVER REPAY YOU, ZHAO?
YOU KNOW HOW!
SMIRK
씨익
HM?
I'M A TRADER.
WE'LL COMPLETE THIS TRANSACTION NEXT TIME WE MEET.
!
싸아아
BLUSH

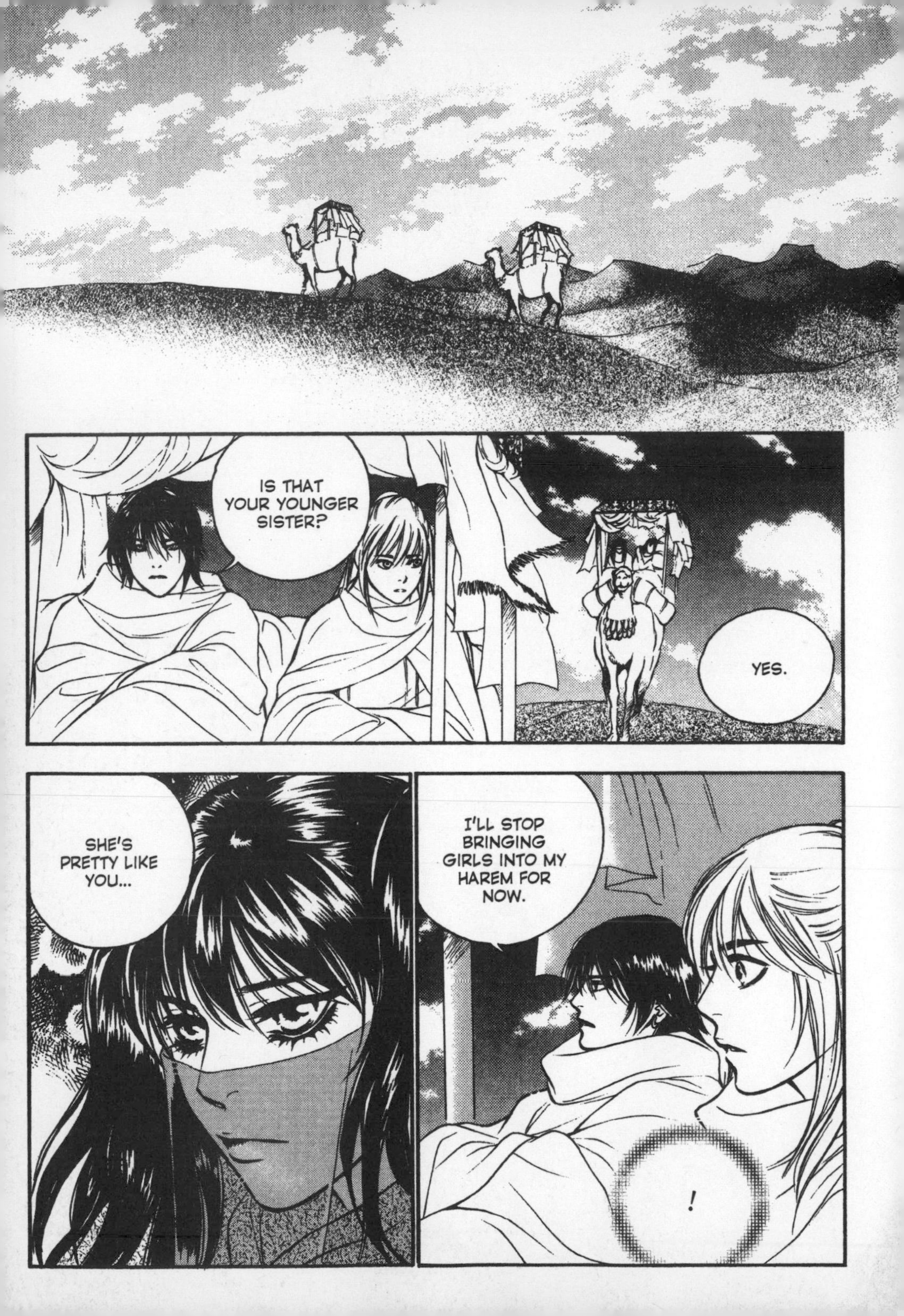
IS THAT YOUR YOUNGER SISTER?
YES.
SHE'S PRETTY LIKE YOU...
I'LL STOP BRINGING GIRLS INTO MY HAREM FOR NOW.
!

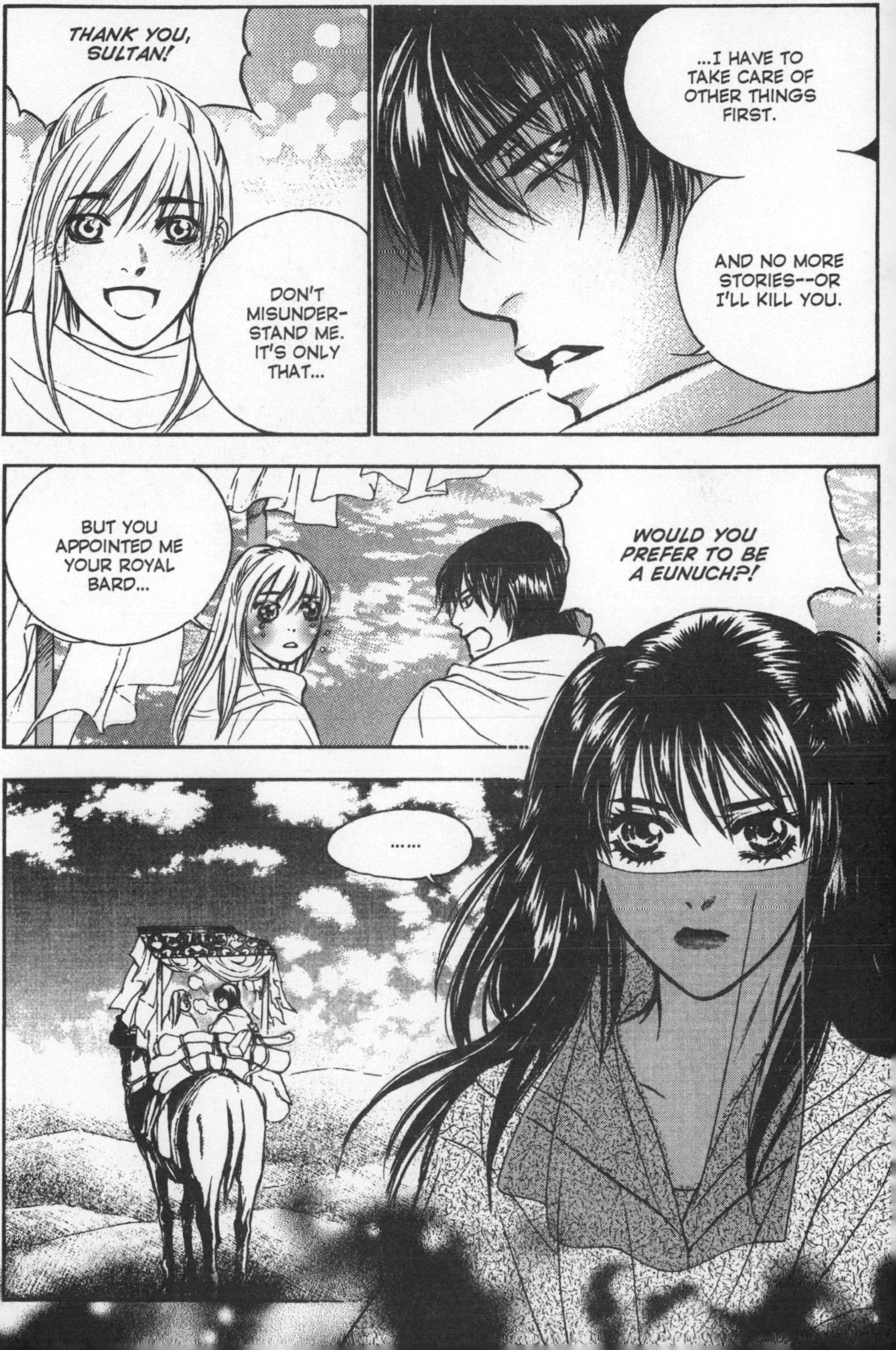
THANK YOU, SULTAN!
DON'T MISUNDER-STAND ME. IT'S ONLY THAT...
...I HAVE TO TAKE CARE OF OTHER THINGS FIRST.
AND NO MORE STORIES--OR I'LL KILL YOU.
BUT YOU APPOINTED ME YOUR ROYAL BARD...
WOULD YOU PREFER TO BE A EUNUCH?!
......

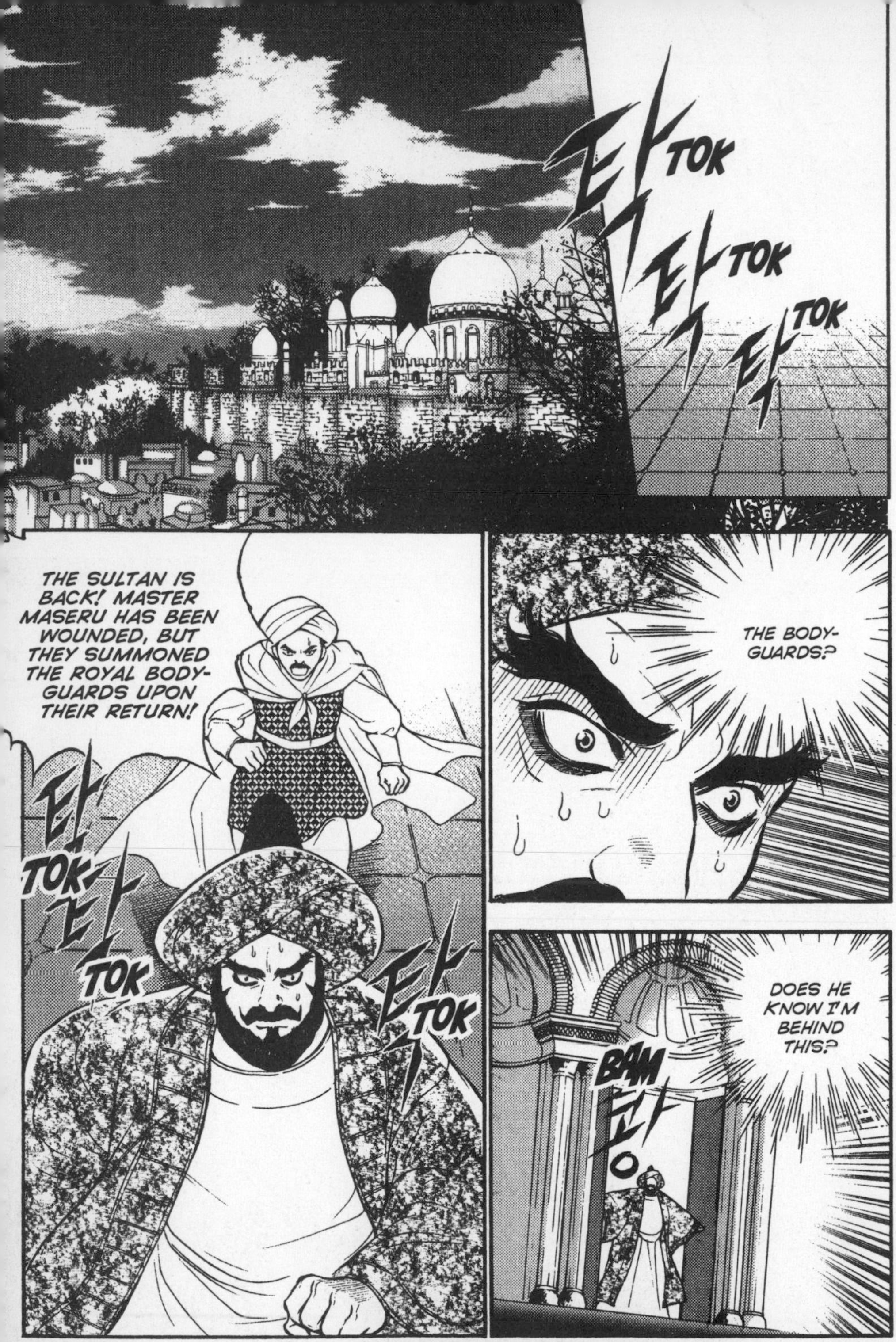
탁 TOK
탁 TOK
탁 TOK
THE SULTAN IS BACK! MASTER MASERU HAS BEEN WOUNDED, BUT THEY SUMMONED THE ROYAL BODY-GUARDS UPON THEIR RETURN!
탁 TOK
TOK
탁 TOK
THE BODY-GUARDS?
DOES HE KNOW I'M BEHIND THIS?
BAM

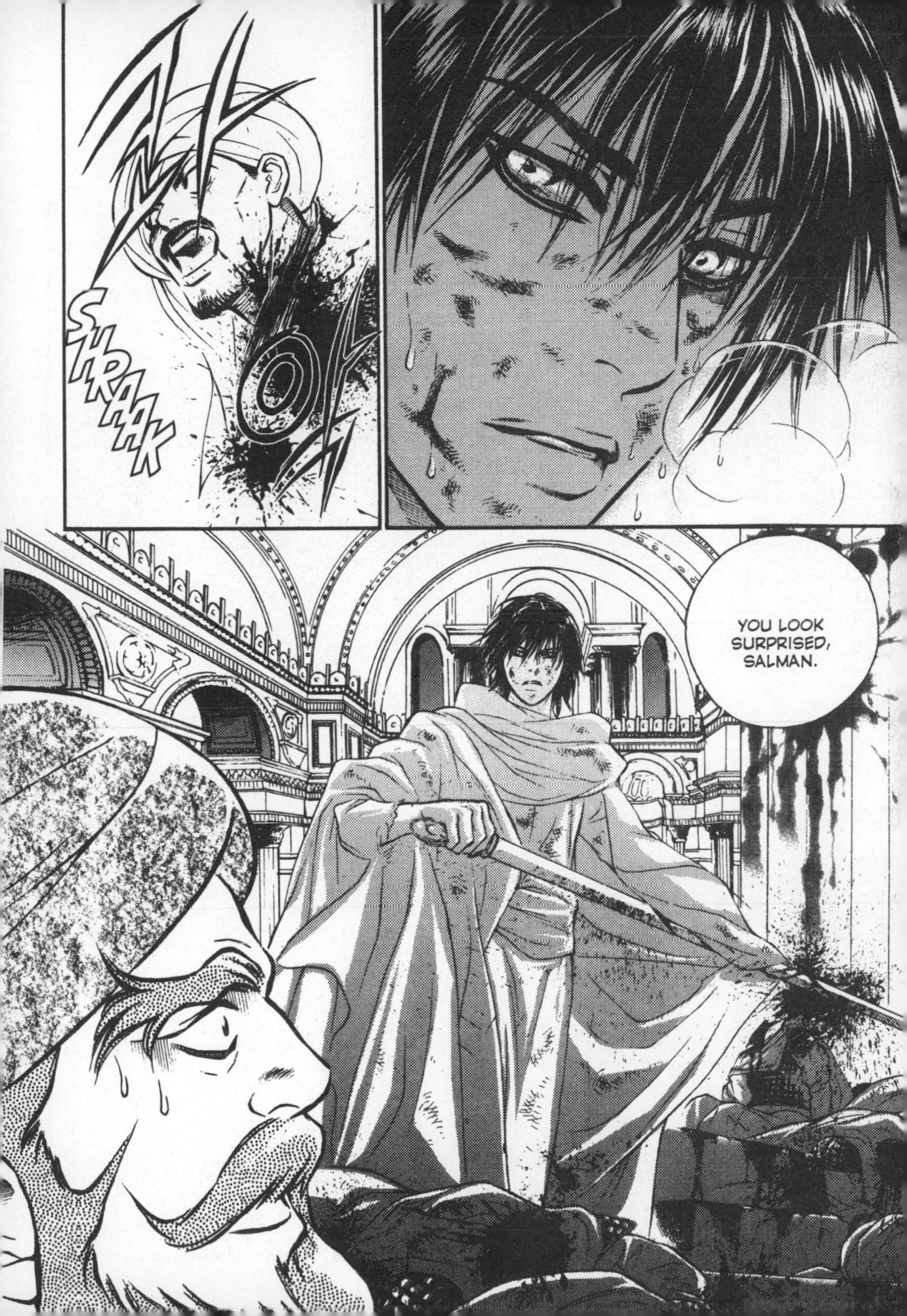
SHRAAK
YOU LOOK SURPRISED, SALMAN.

YOU... CAME BACK SAFELY...

TOK

TOK

IS THAT REALLY THE SULTAN?

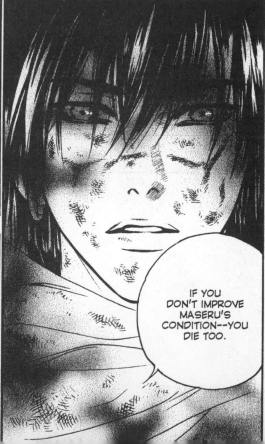

IF YOU DON'T IMPROVE MASERU'S CONDITION-- YOU DIE TOO.

CHUK

WAH!

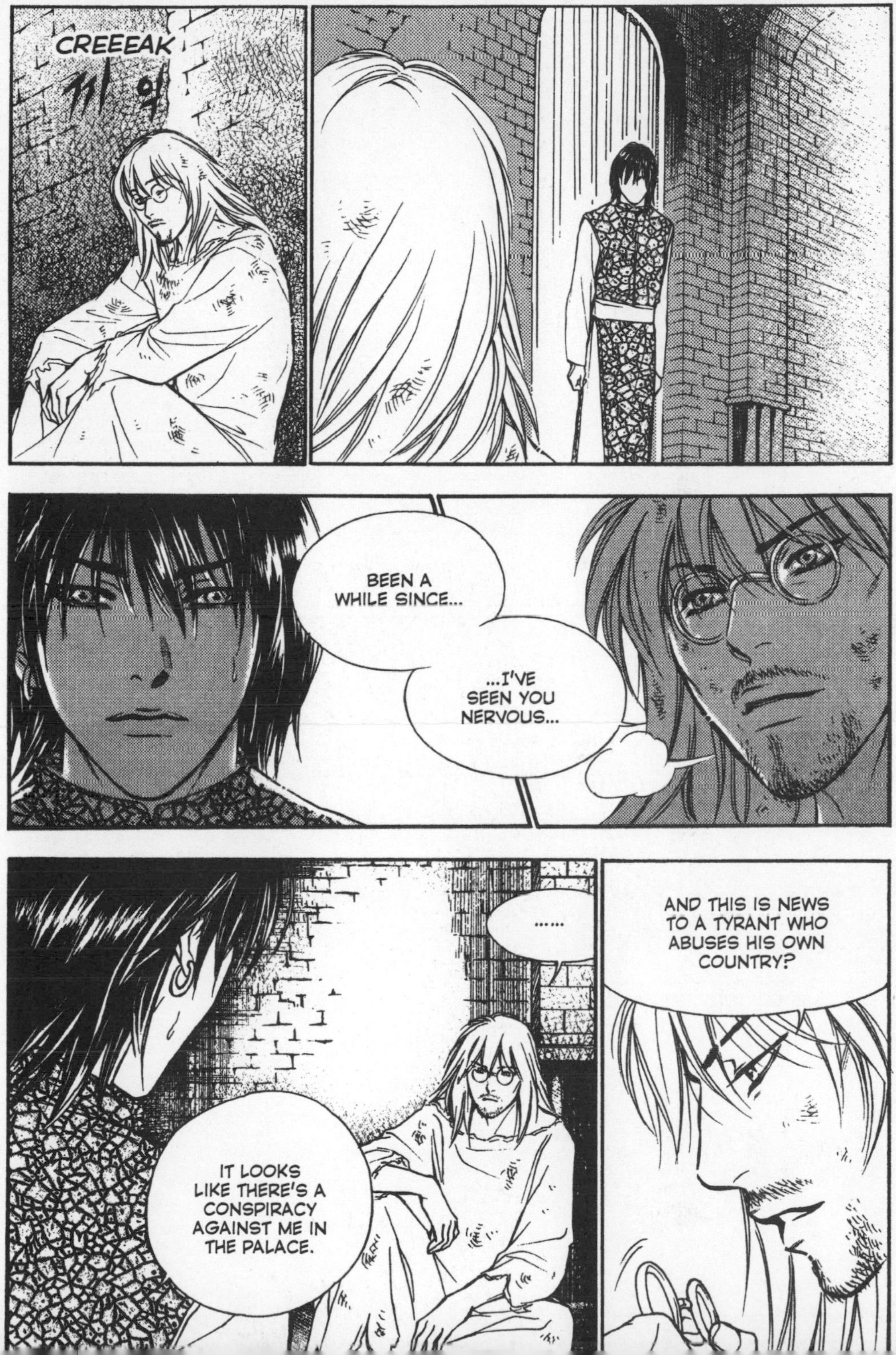
CREEEAK
끼익
BEEN A WHILE SINCE...
...I'VE SEEN YOU NERVOUS...
IT LOOKS LIKE THERE'S A CONSPIRACY AGAINST ME IN THE PALACE.
......
AND THIS IS NEWS TO A TYRANT WHO ABUSES HIS OWN COUNTRY?

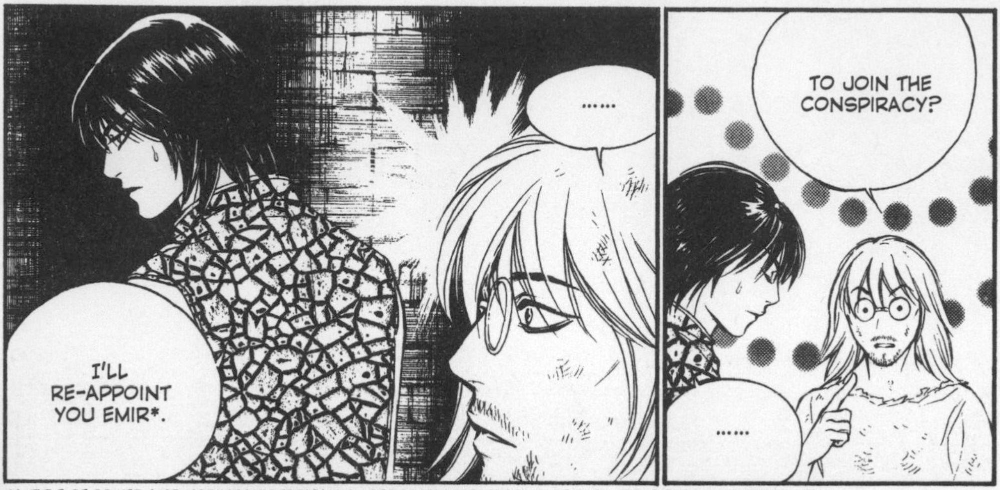
......
I'LL RE-APPOINT YOU EMIR*.
TO JOIN THE CONSPIRACY?
......

*A TITLE OF POWER AND NOBILITY HISTORICALLY USED IN ISLAMIC NATIONS OF THE MIDDLE EAST AND NORTH AFRICA.

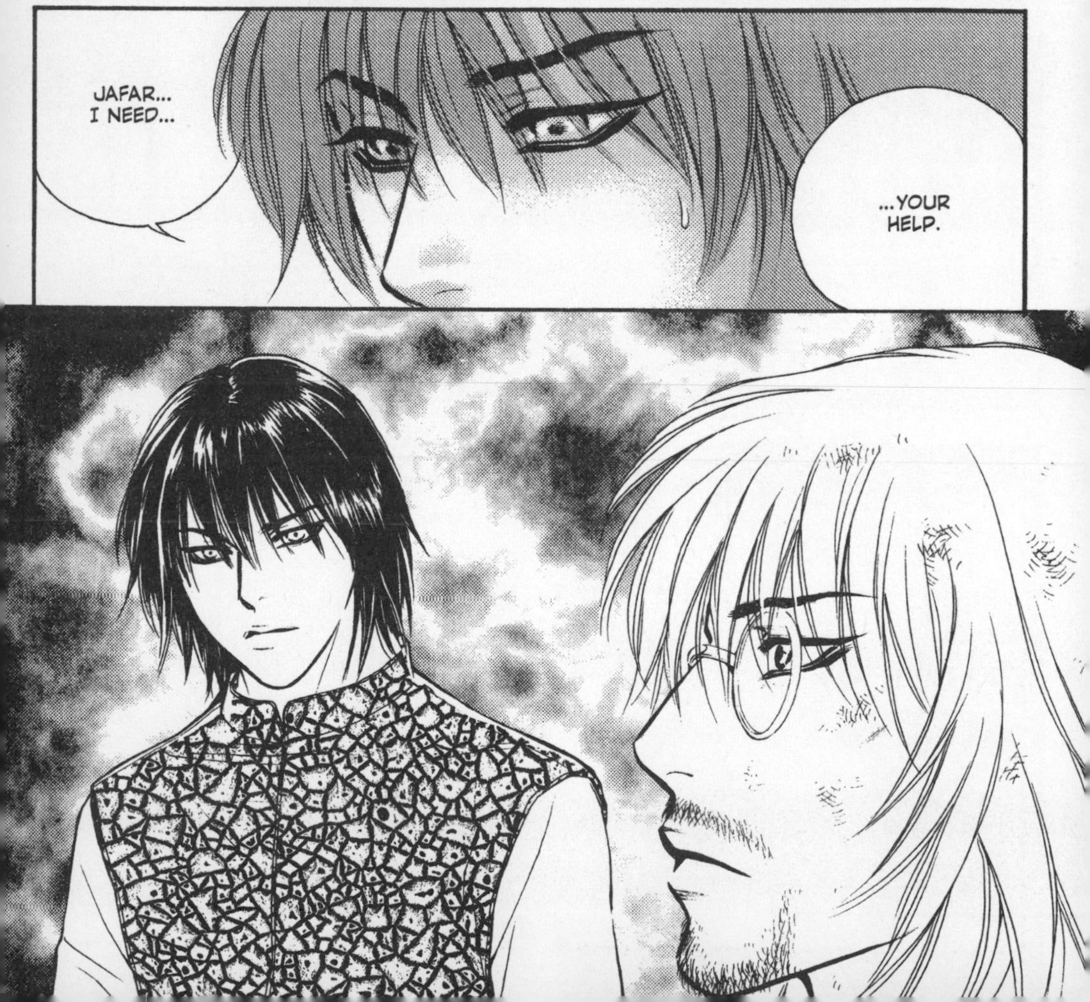
JAFAR... I NEED...
...YOUR HELP.

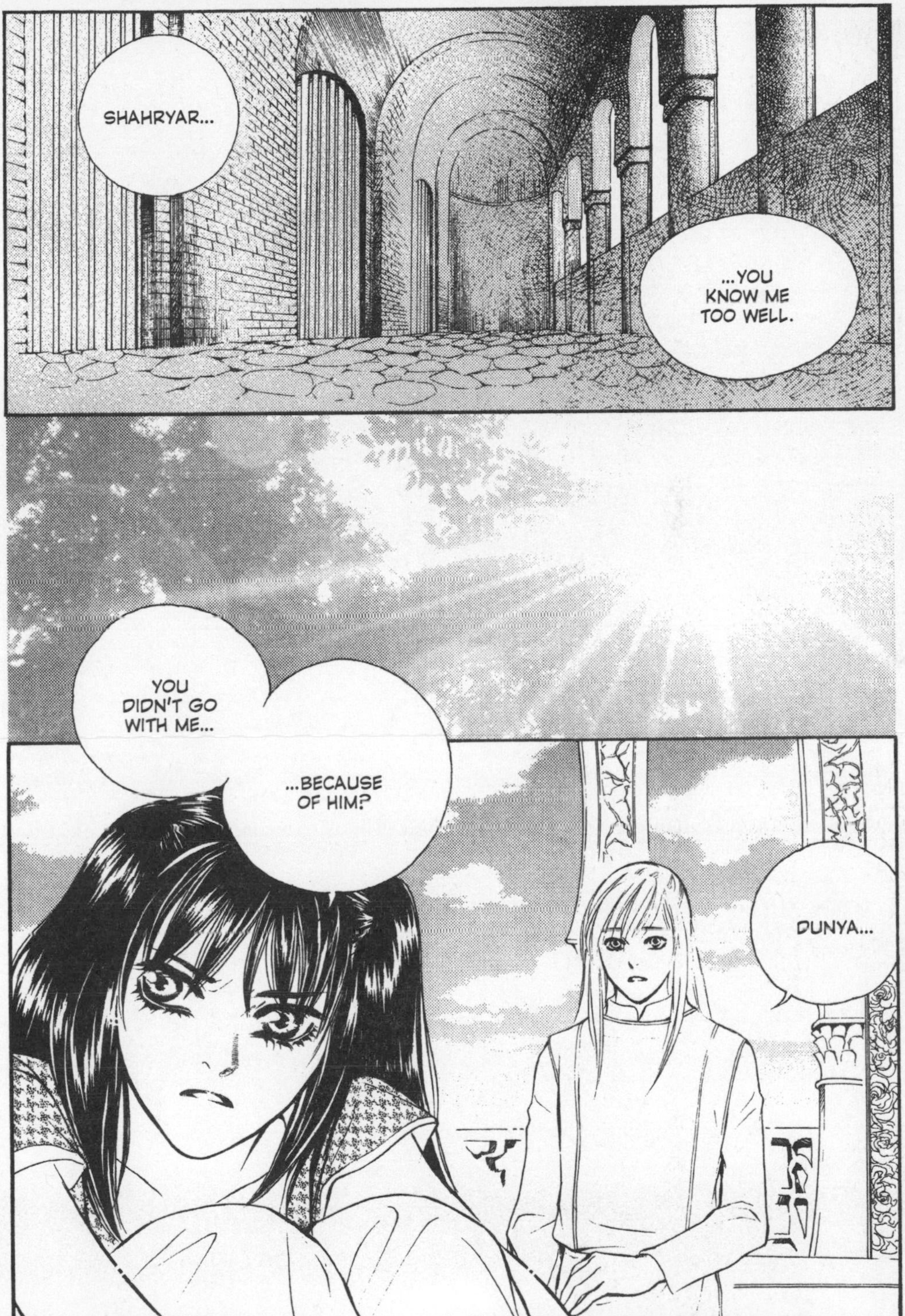
SHAHRYAR...
...YOU KNOW ME TOO WELL.
YOU DIDN'T GO WITH ME...
...BECAUSE OF HIM?
DUNYA...

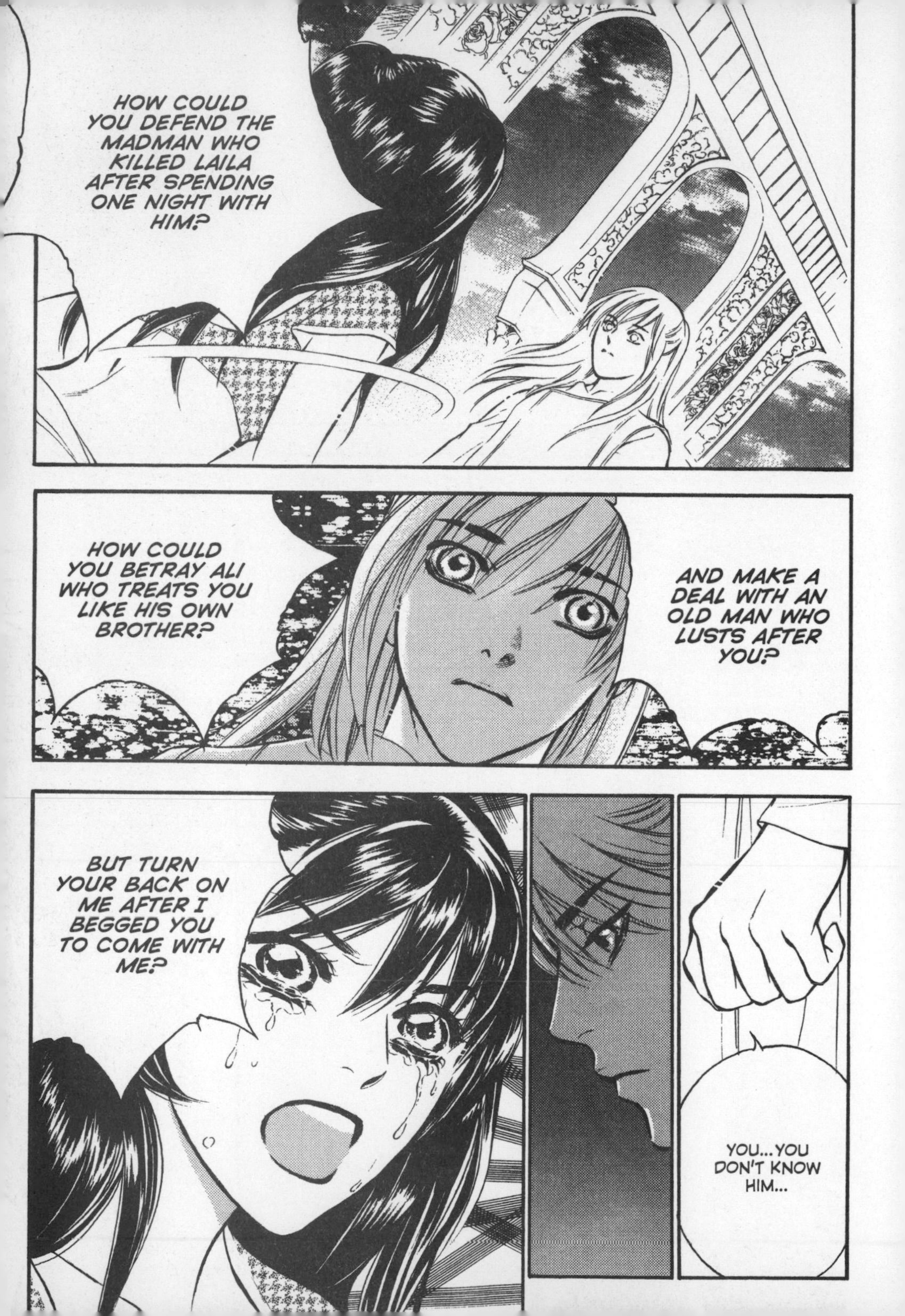
HOW COULD YOU DEFEND THE MADMAN WHO KILLED LAILA AFTER SPENDING ONE NIGHT WITH HIM?
HOW COULD YOU BETRAY ALI WHO TREATS YOU LIKE HIS OWN BROTHER?
AND MAKE A DEAL WITH AN OLD MAN WHO LUSTS AFTER YOU?
BUT TURN YOUR BACK ON ME AFTER I BEGGED YOU TO COME WITH ME?
YOU...YOU DON'T KNOW HIM...

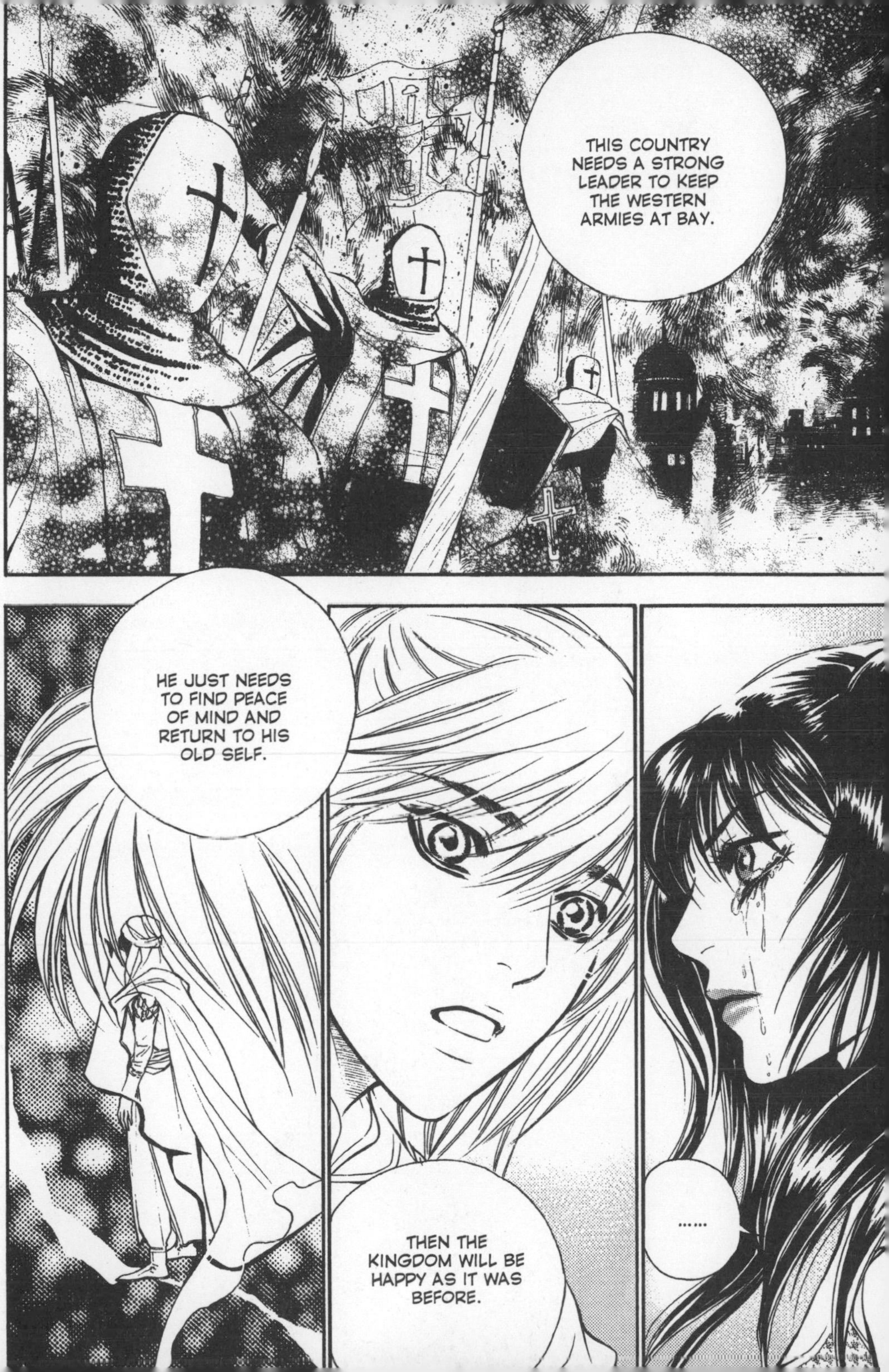
THIS COUNTRY NEEDS A STRONG LEADER TO KEEP THE WESTERN ARMIES AT BAY.
HE JUST NEEDS TO FIND PEACE OF MIND AND RETURN TO HIS OLD SELF.
THEN THE KINGDOM WILL BE HAPPY AS IT WAS BEFORE.
......

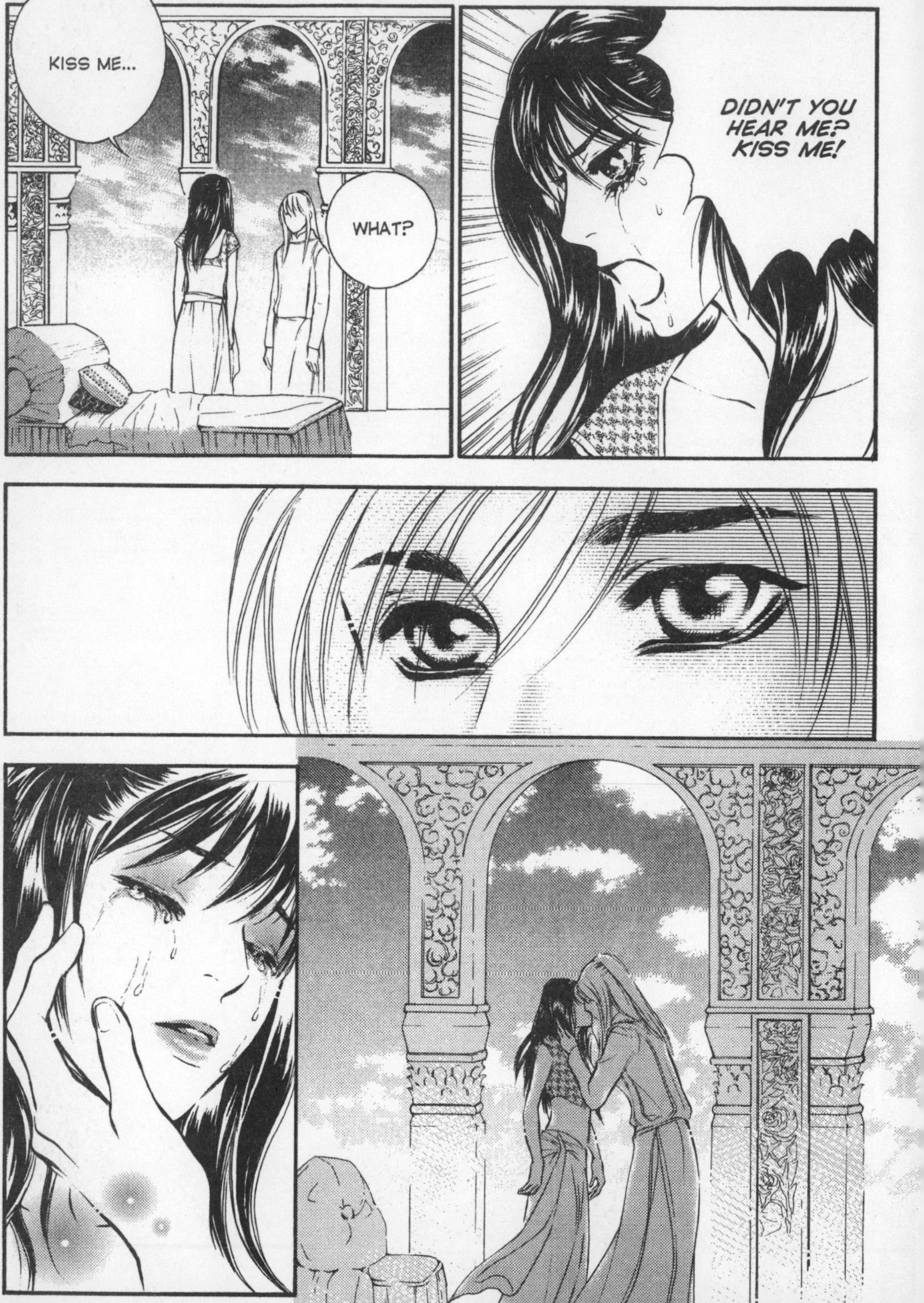
KISS ME...
WHAT?
DIDN'T YOU HEAR ME? KISS ME!

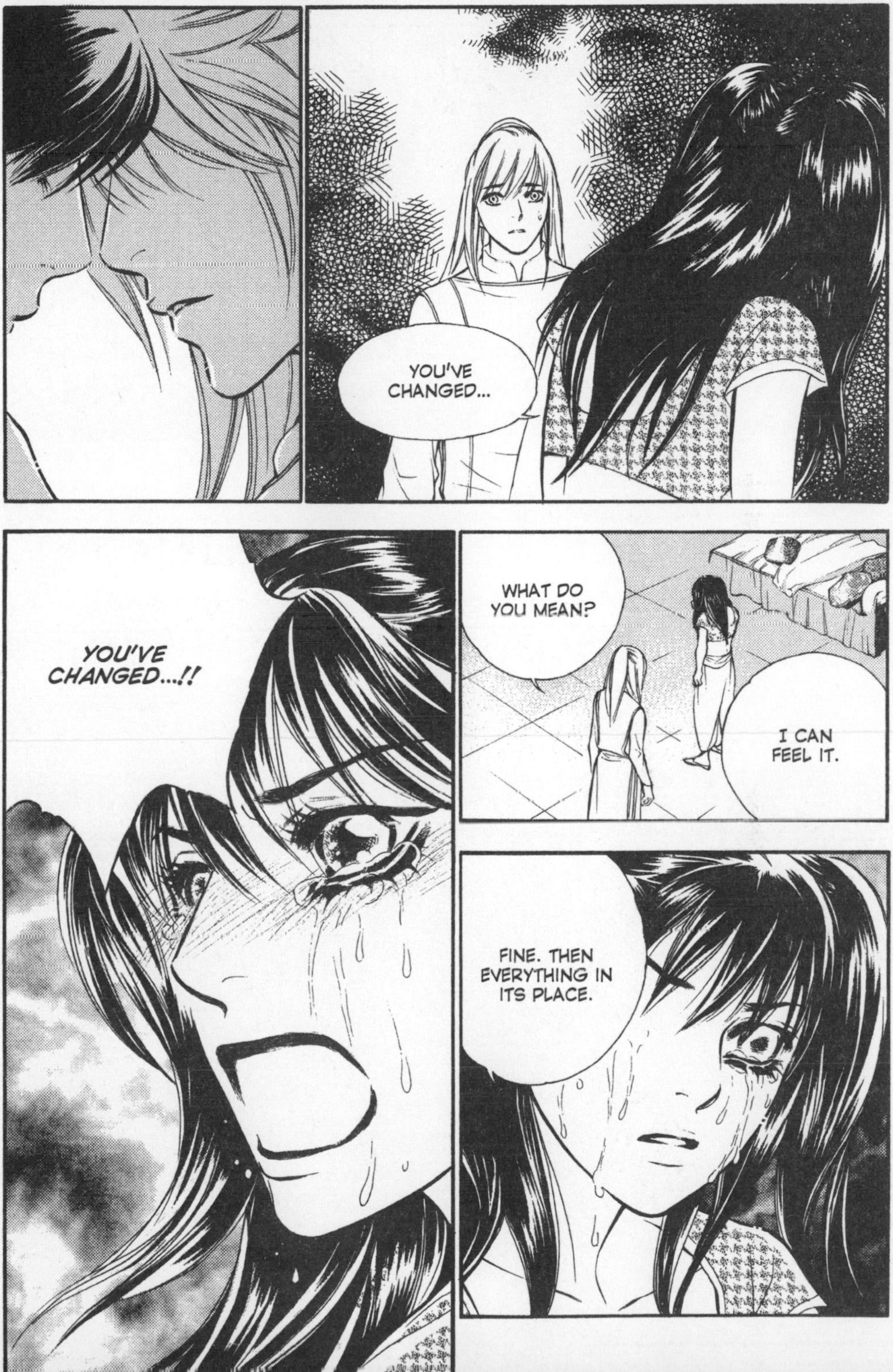
YOU'VE CHANGED...
YOU'VE CHANGED...!!
WHAT DO YOU MEAN?
I CAN FEEL IT.
FINE. THEN EVERYTHING IN ITS PLACE.

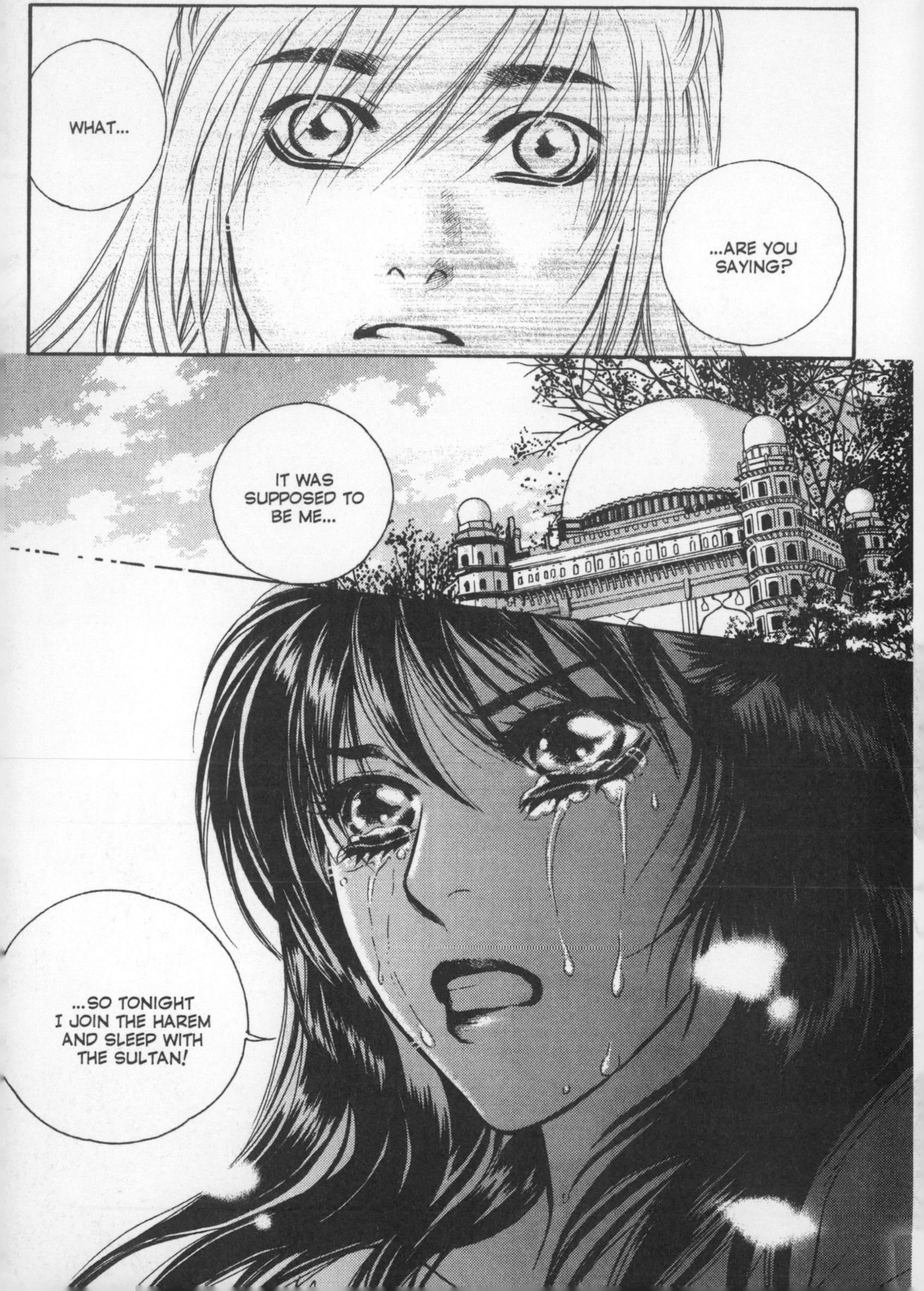
WHAT...
...ARE YOU SAYING?
IT WAS SUPPOSED TO BE ME...
...SO TONIGHT I JOIN THE HAREM AND SLEEP WITH THE SULTAN!

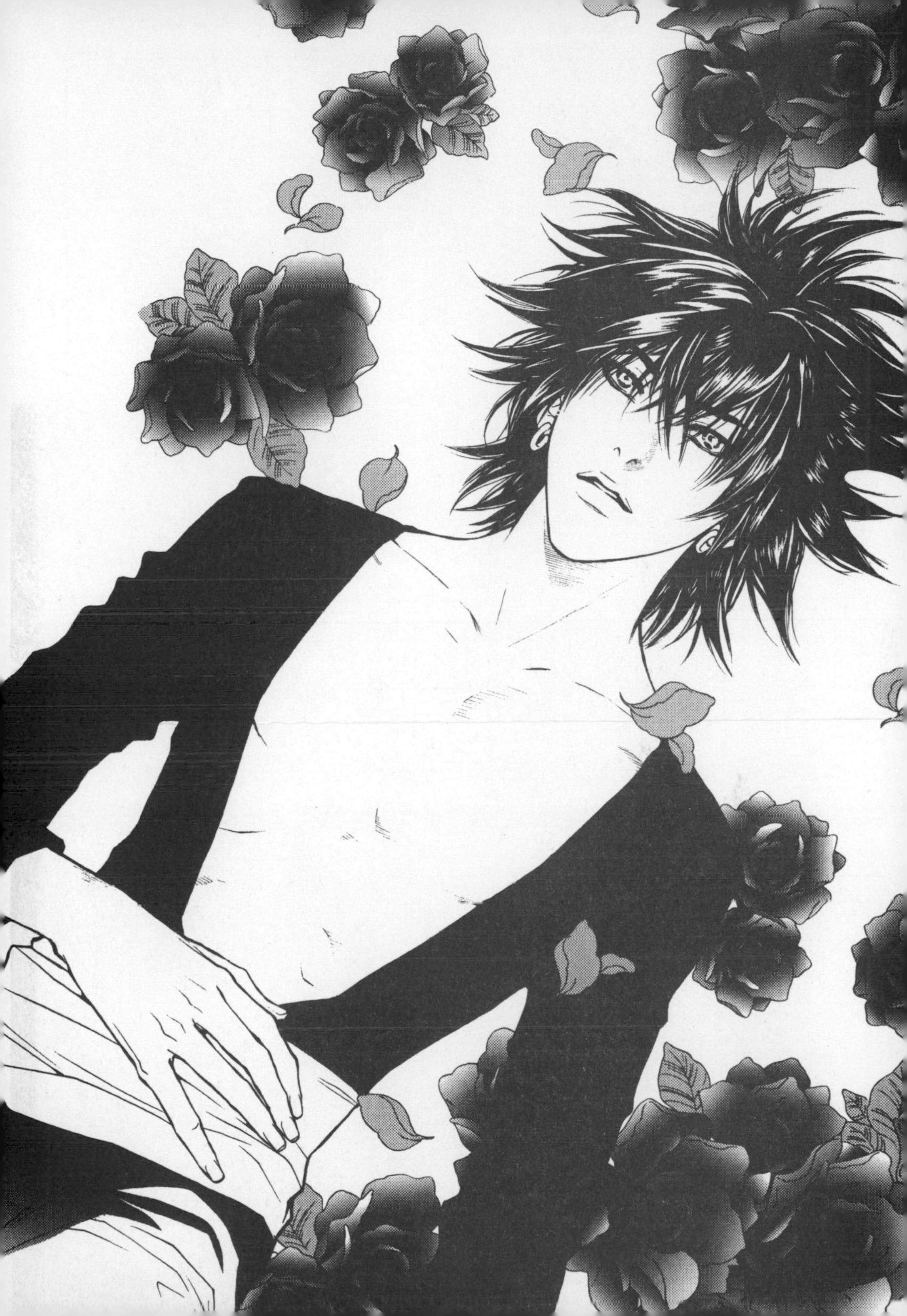

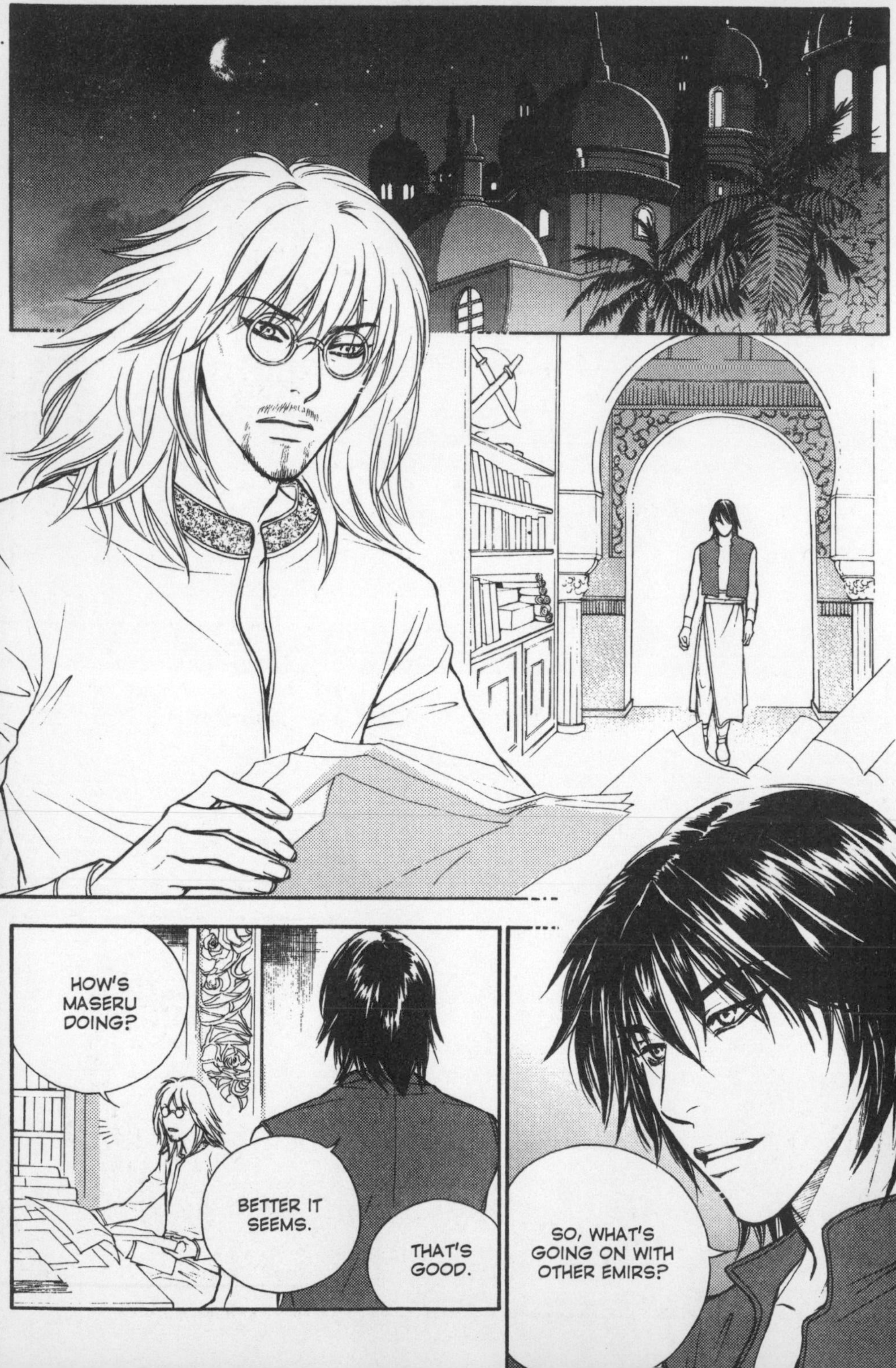
HOW'S MASERU DOING?
BETTER IT SEEMS.
THAT'S GOOD.
SO, WHAT'S GOING ON WITH OTHER EMIRS?

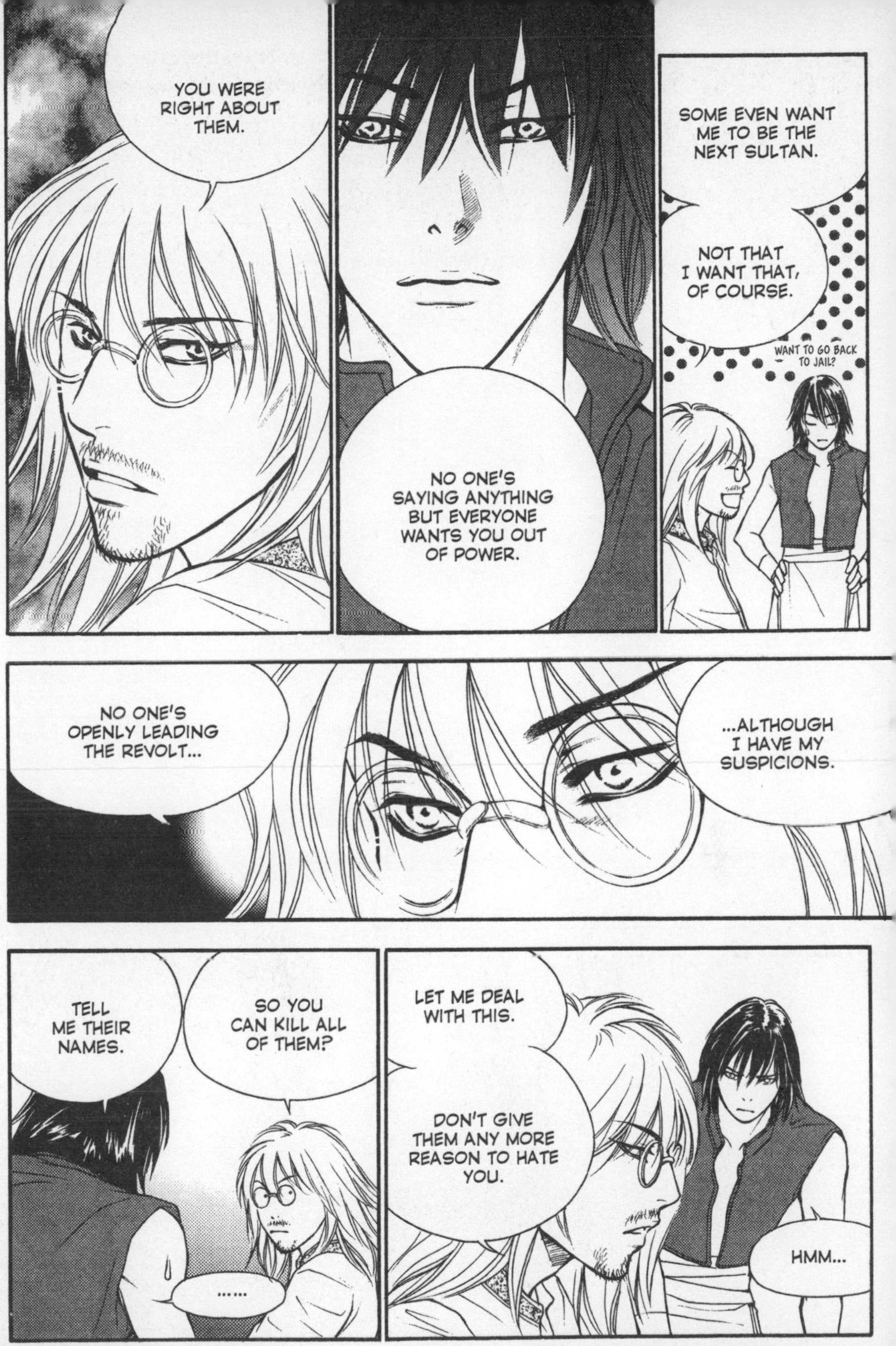
YOU WERE RIGHT ABOUT THEM.
NO ONE'S SAYING ANYTHING BUT EVERYONE WANTS YOU OUT OF POWER.
SOME EVEN WANT ME TO BE THE NEXT SULTAN.
NOT THAT I WANT THAT, OF COURSE.
WANT TO GO BACK TO JAIL?
NO ONE'S OPENLY LEADING THE REVOLT...
...ALTHOUGH I HAVE MY SUSPICIONS.
TELL ME THEIR NAMES.
SO YOU CAN KILL ALL OF THEM?
......
LET ME DEAL WITH THIS.
DON'T GIVE THEM ANY MORE REASON TO HATE YOU.
HMM...

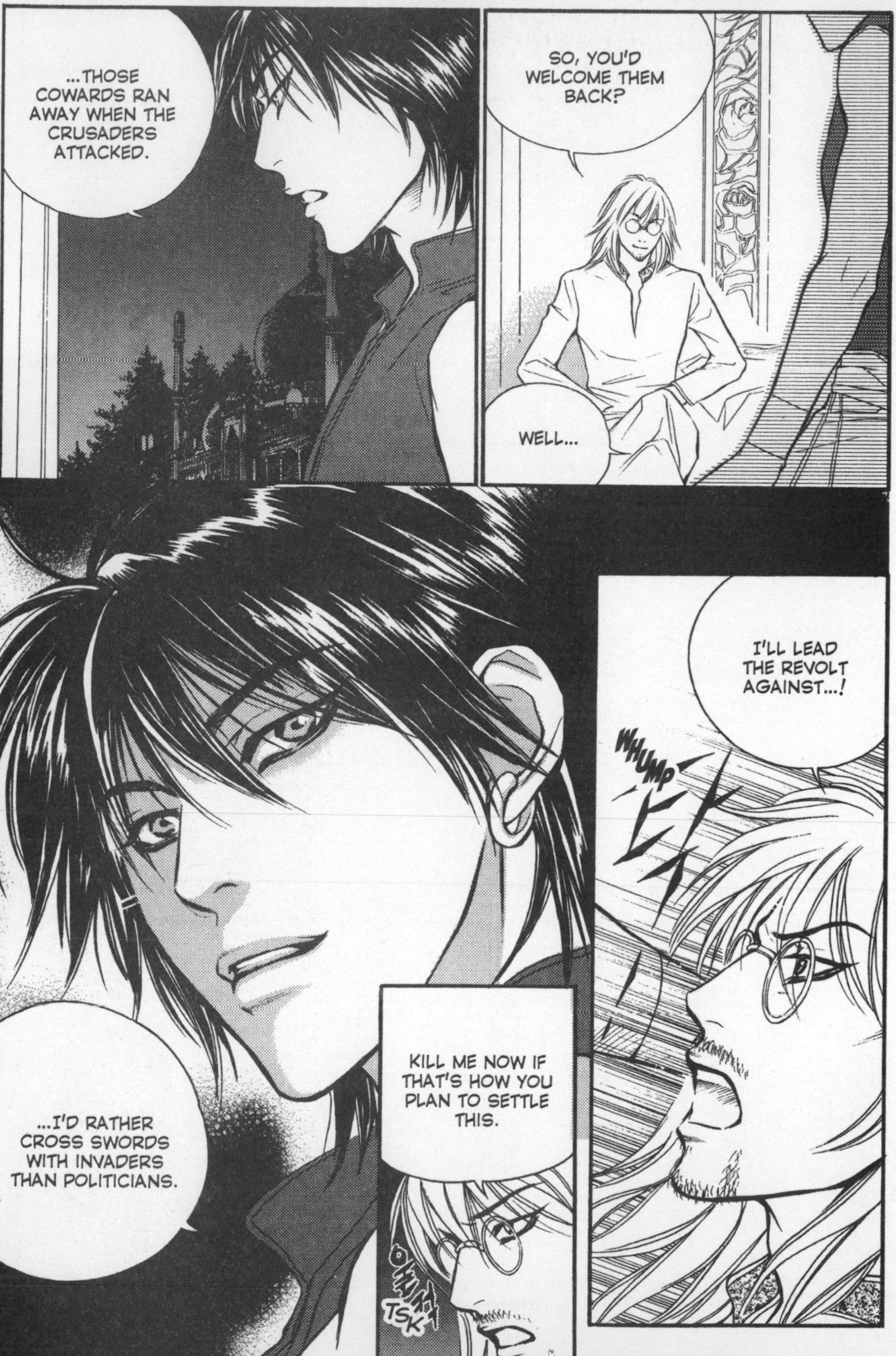
...THOSE COWARDS RAN AWAY WHEN THE CRUSADERS ATTACKED.
SO, YOU'D WELCOME THEM BACK?
WELL...
...I'D RATHER CROSS SWORDS WITH INVADERS THAN POLITICIANS.
I'LL LEAD THE REVOLT AGAINST...!
WHUMP
KILL ME NOW IF THAT'S HOW YOU PLAN TO SETTLE THIS.
TSK

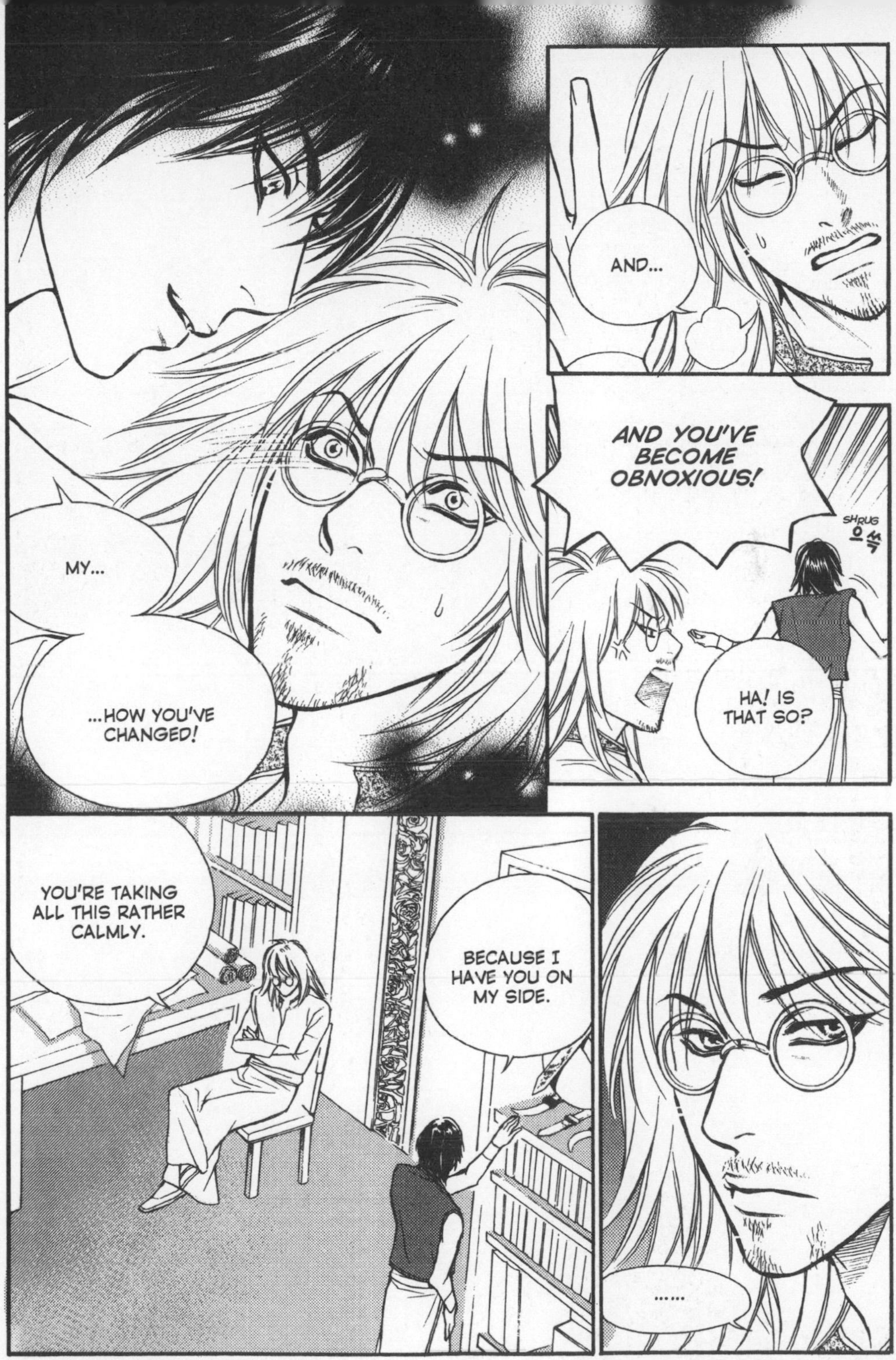
MY...
...HOW YOU'VE CHANGED!
AND...
AND YOU'VE BECOME OBNOXIOUS!
SHRUG
HA! IS THAT SO?
YOU'RE TAKING ALL THIS RATHER CALMLY.
BECAUSE I HAVE YOU ON MY SIDE.
......

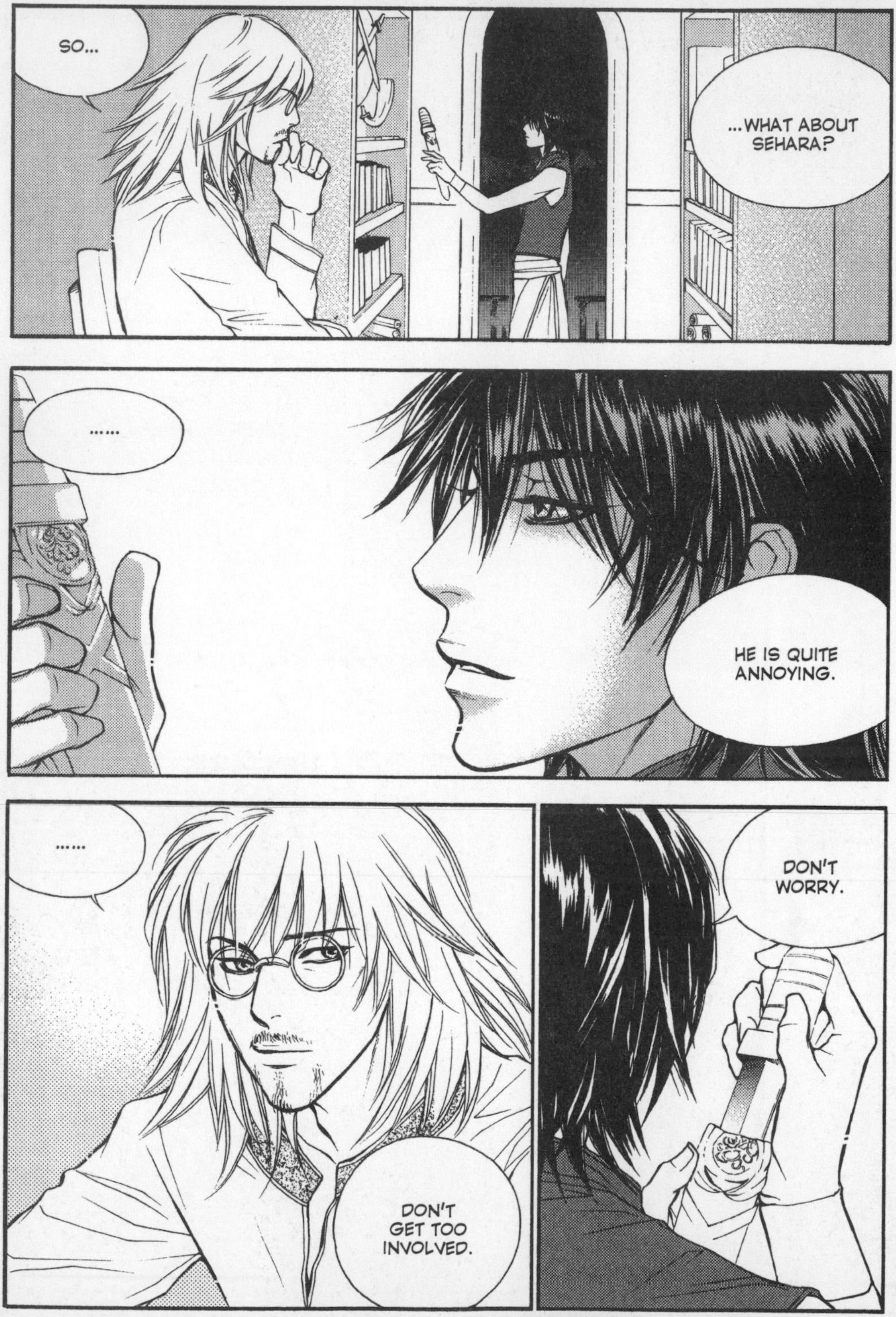
SO...
...WHAT ABOUT SEHARA?
......
HE IS QUITE ANNOYING.
......
DON'T GET TOO INVOLVED.
DON'T WORRY.

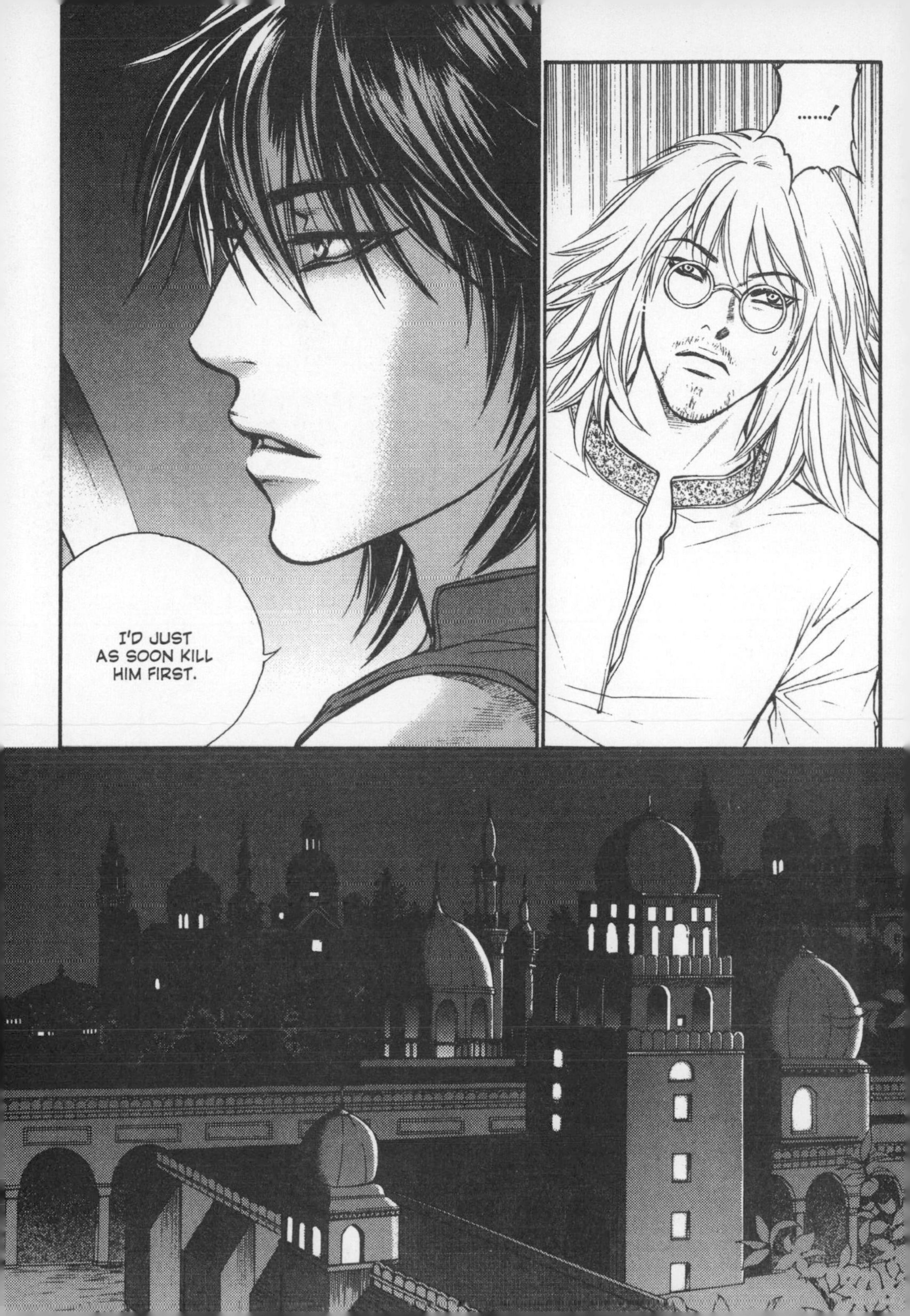

I'D JUST AS SOON KILL HIM FIRST.
......!

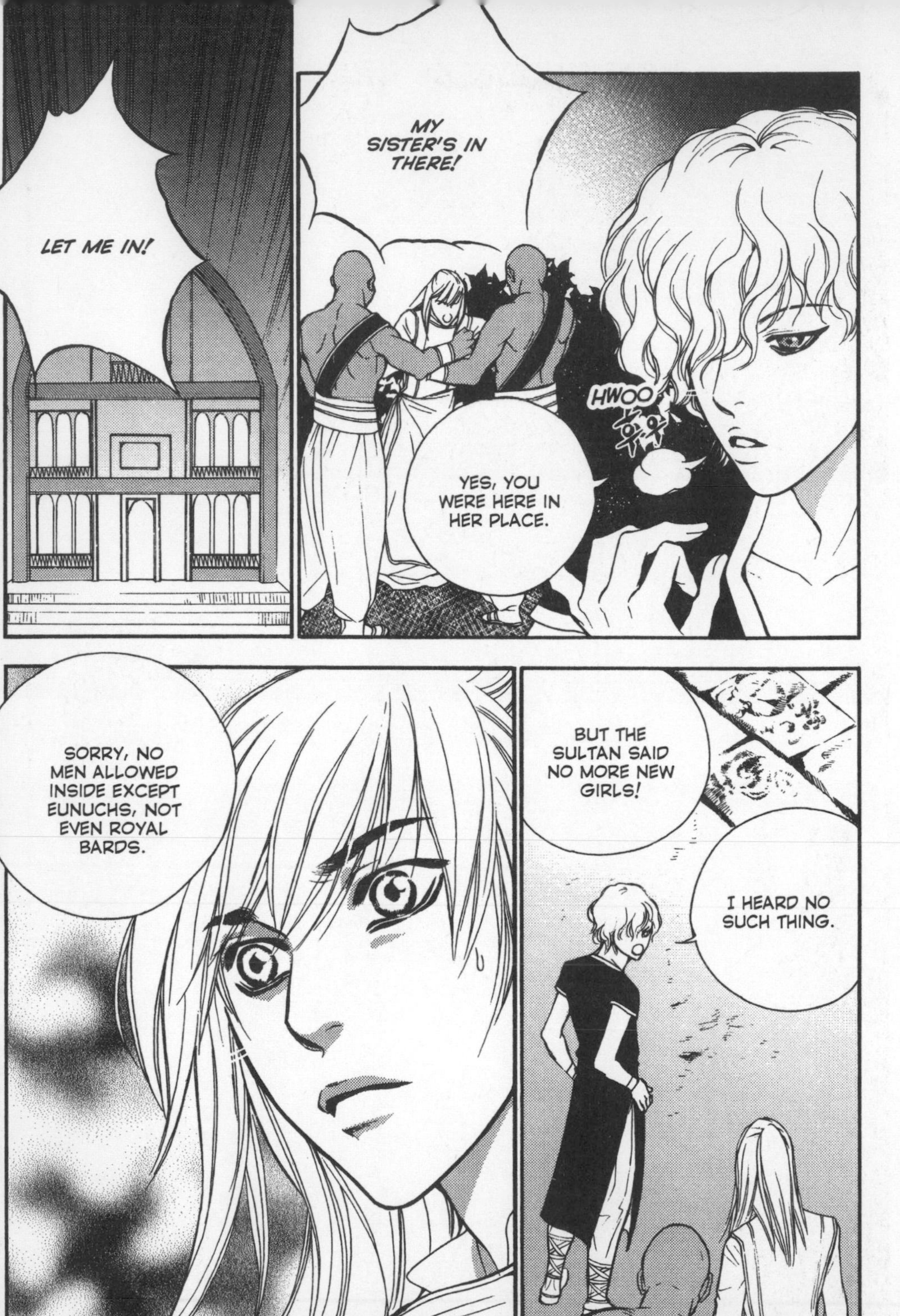
LET ME IN!
MY SISTER'S IN THERE!
HWOO
YES, YOU WERE HERE IN HER PLACE.
SORRY, NO MEN ALLOWED INSIDE EXCEPT EUNUCHS, NOT EVEN ROYAL BARDS.
BUT THE SULTAN SAID NO MORE NEW GIRLS!
I HEARD NO SUCH THING.

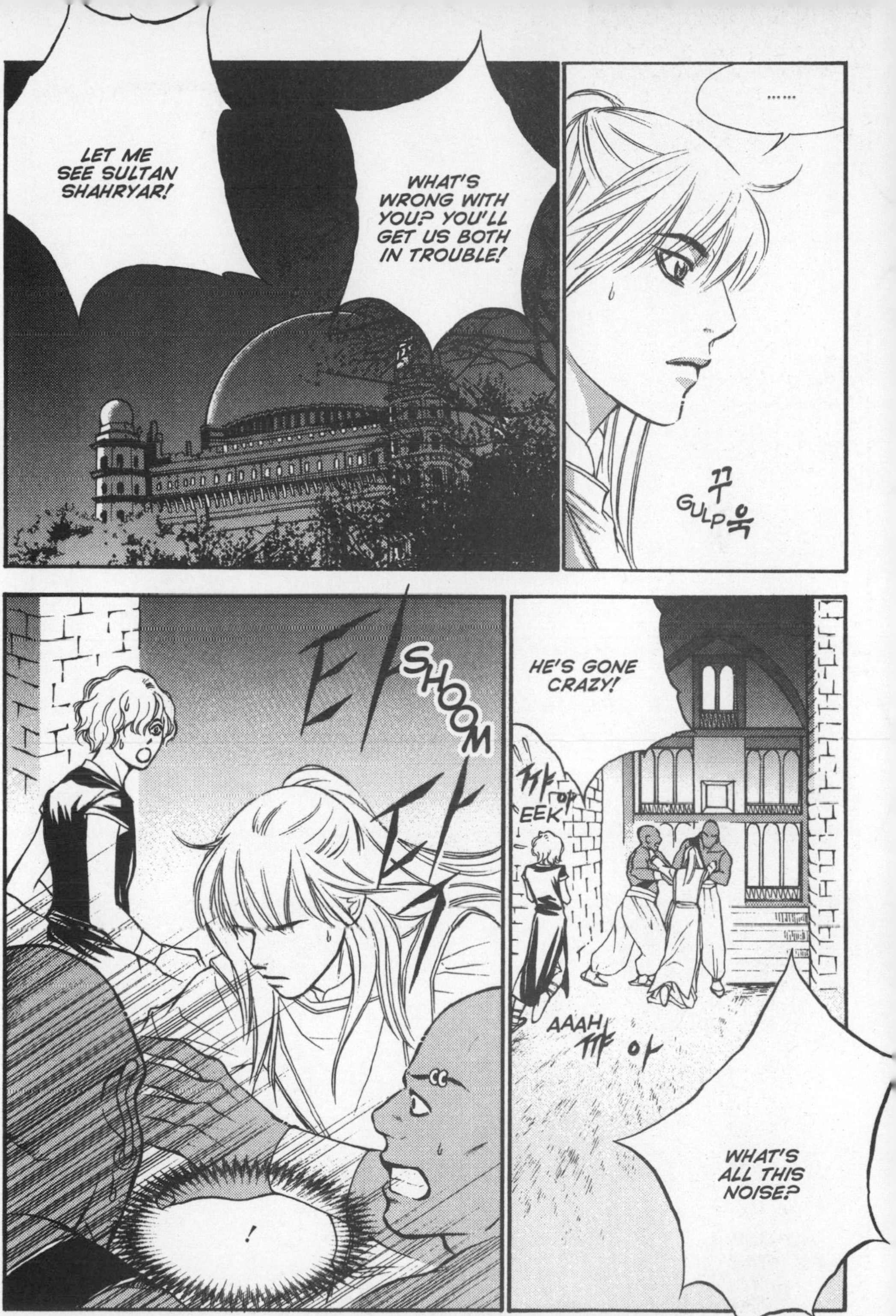
LET ME SEE SULTAN SHAHRYAR!
WHAT'S WRONG WITH YOU? YOU'LL GET US BOTH IN TROUBLE!
......
GULP
SHOOM
!
HE'S GONE CRAZY!
EEK
AAAH
WHAT'S ALL THIS NOISE?

MASTER JAFAR!

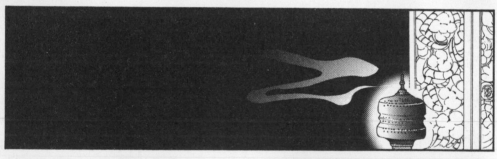

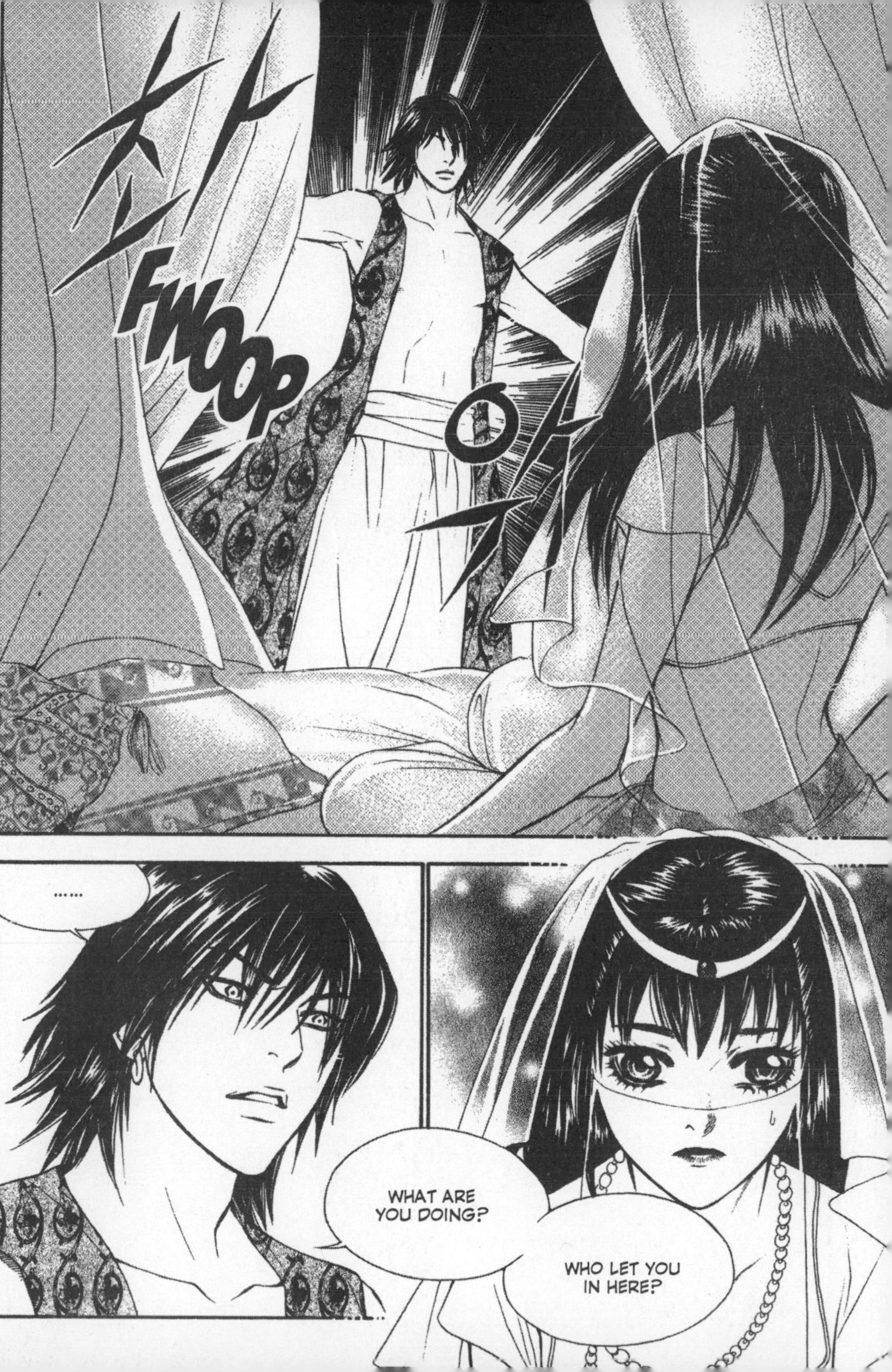
FWOOP
……
WHAT ARE YOU DOING?
WHO LET YOU IN HERE?

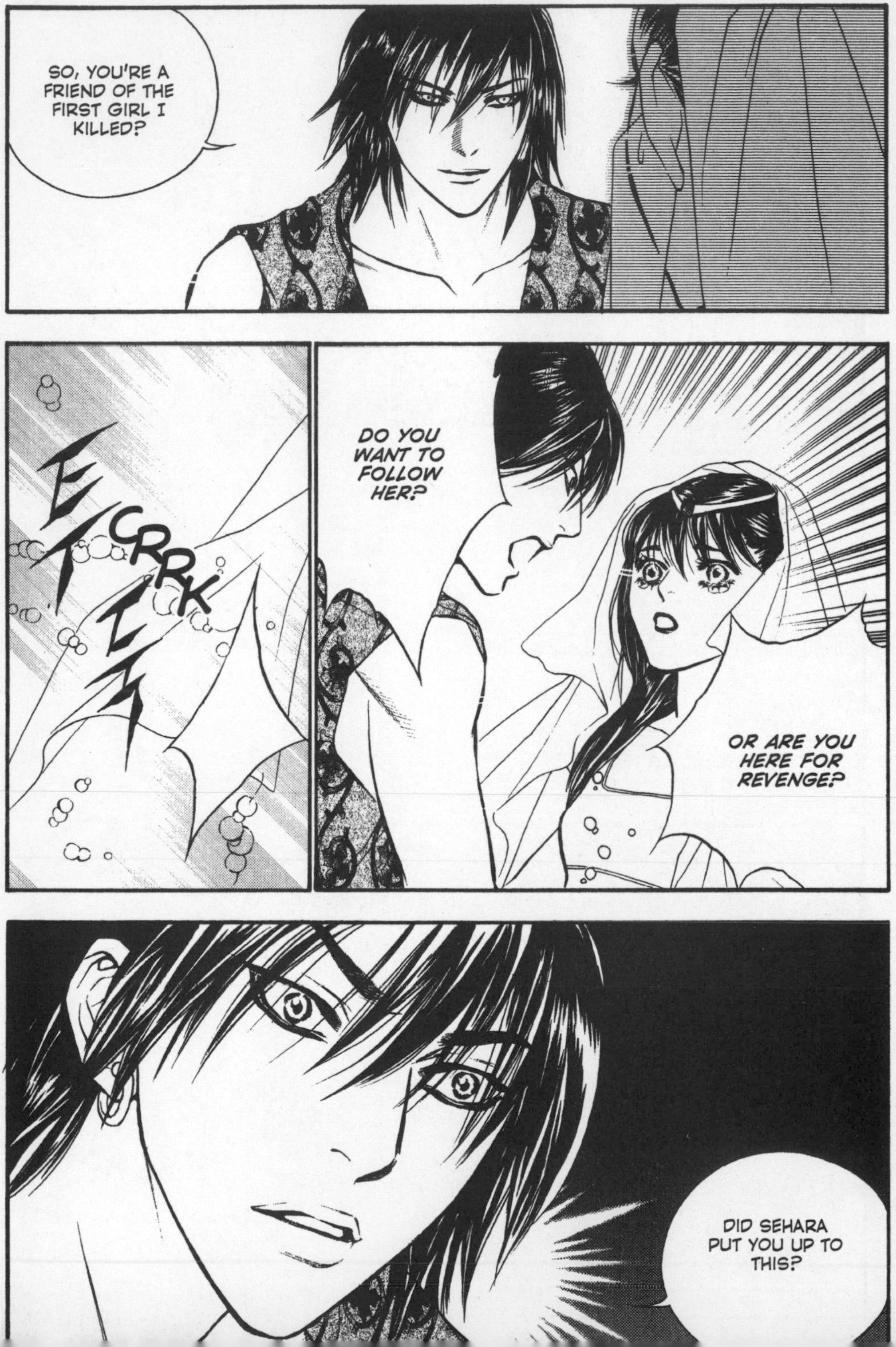
SO, YOU'RE A FRIEND OF THE FIRST GIRL I KILLED?
CRRK
DO YOU WANT TO FOLLOW HER?
OR ARE YOU HERE FOR REVENGE?
DID SEHARA PUT YOU UP TO THIS?

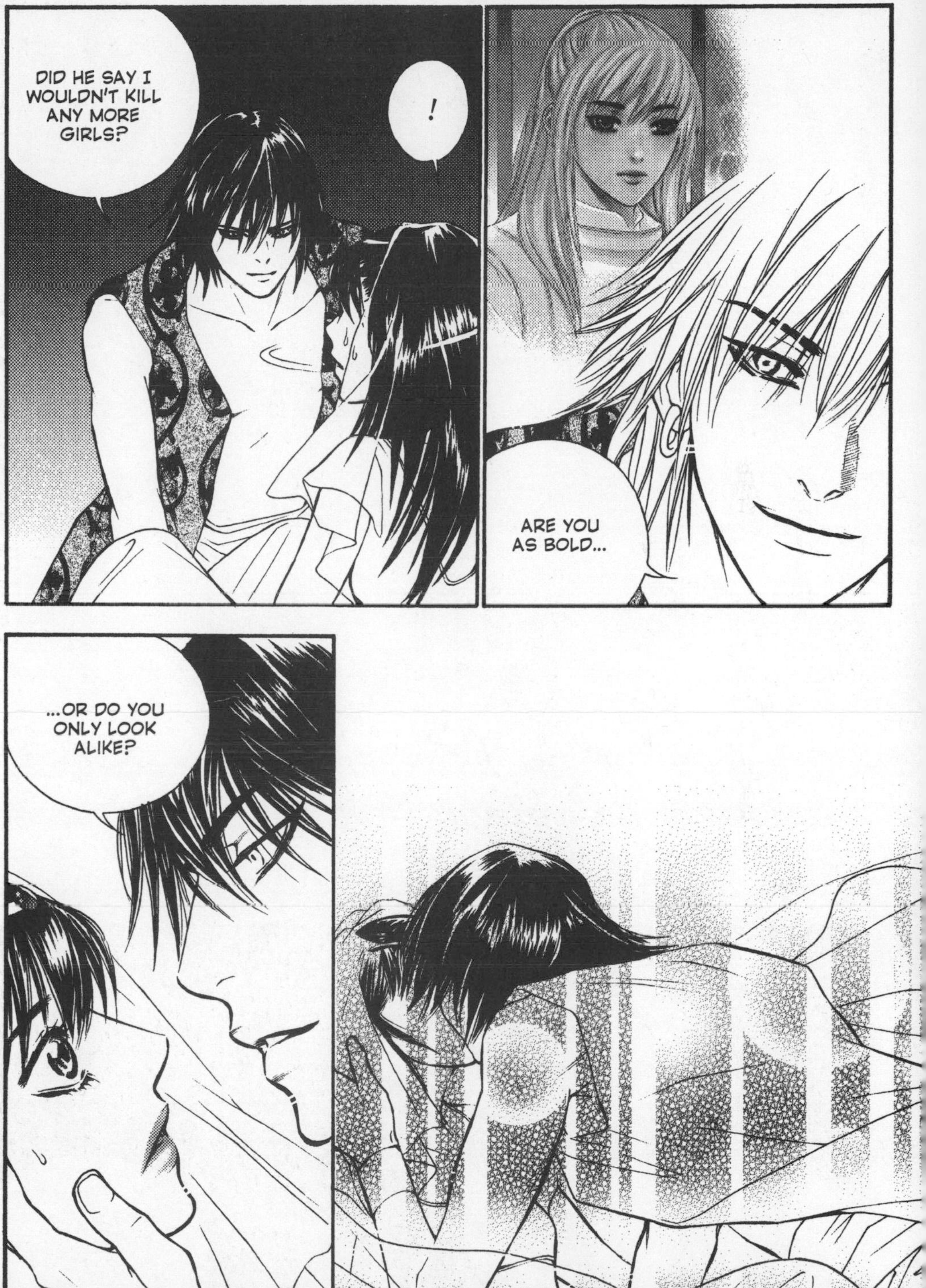
DID HE SAY I WOULDN'T KILL ANY MORE GIRLS?
!
ARE YOU AS BOLD...
...OR DO YOU ONLY LOOK ALIKE?

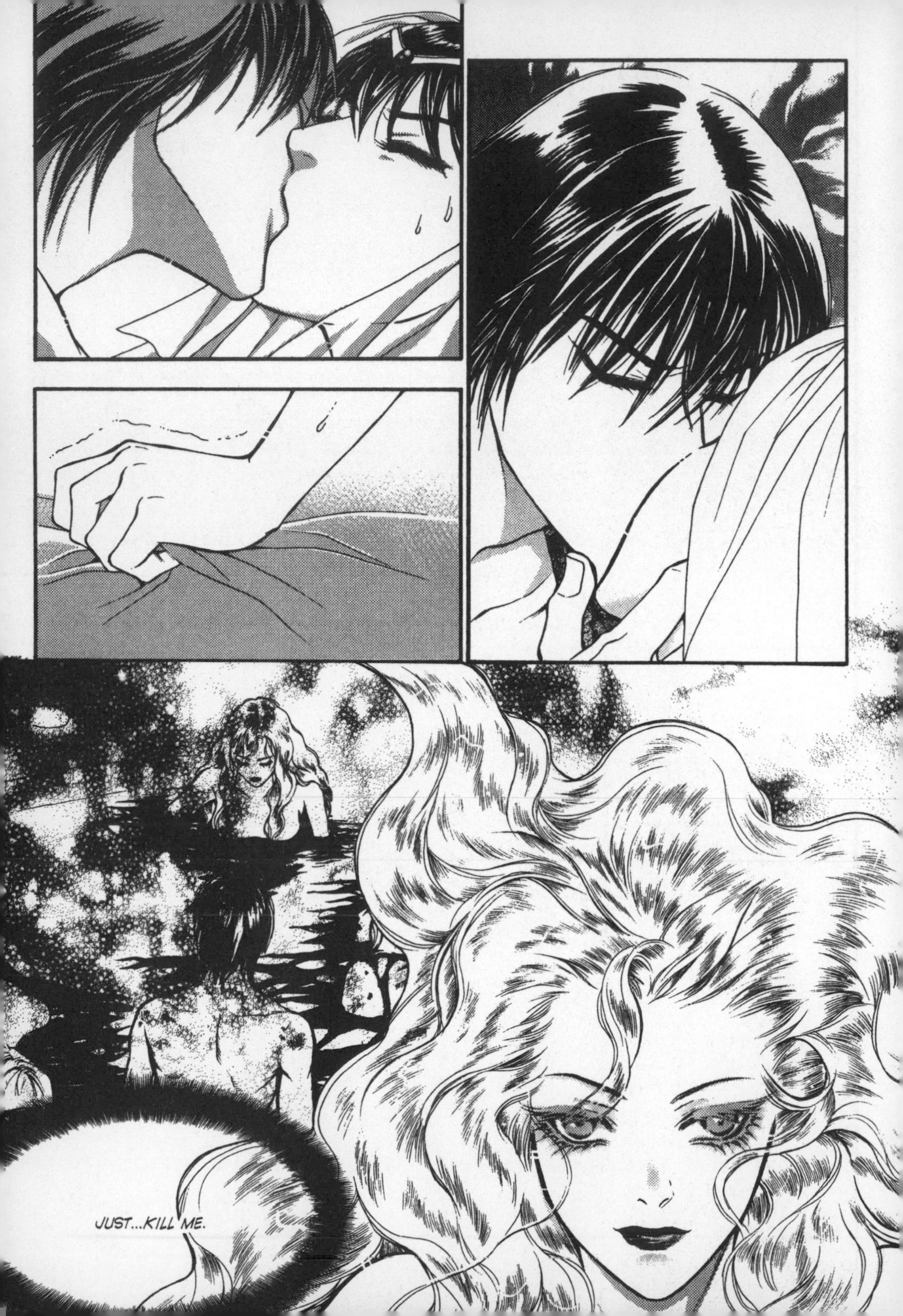
JUST...KILL ME.

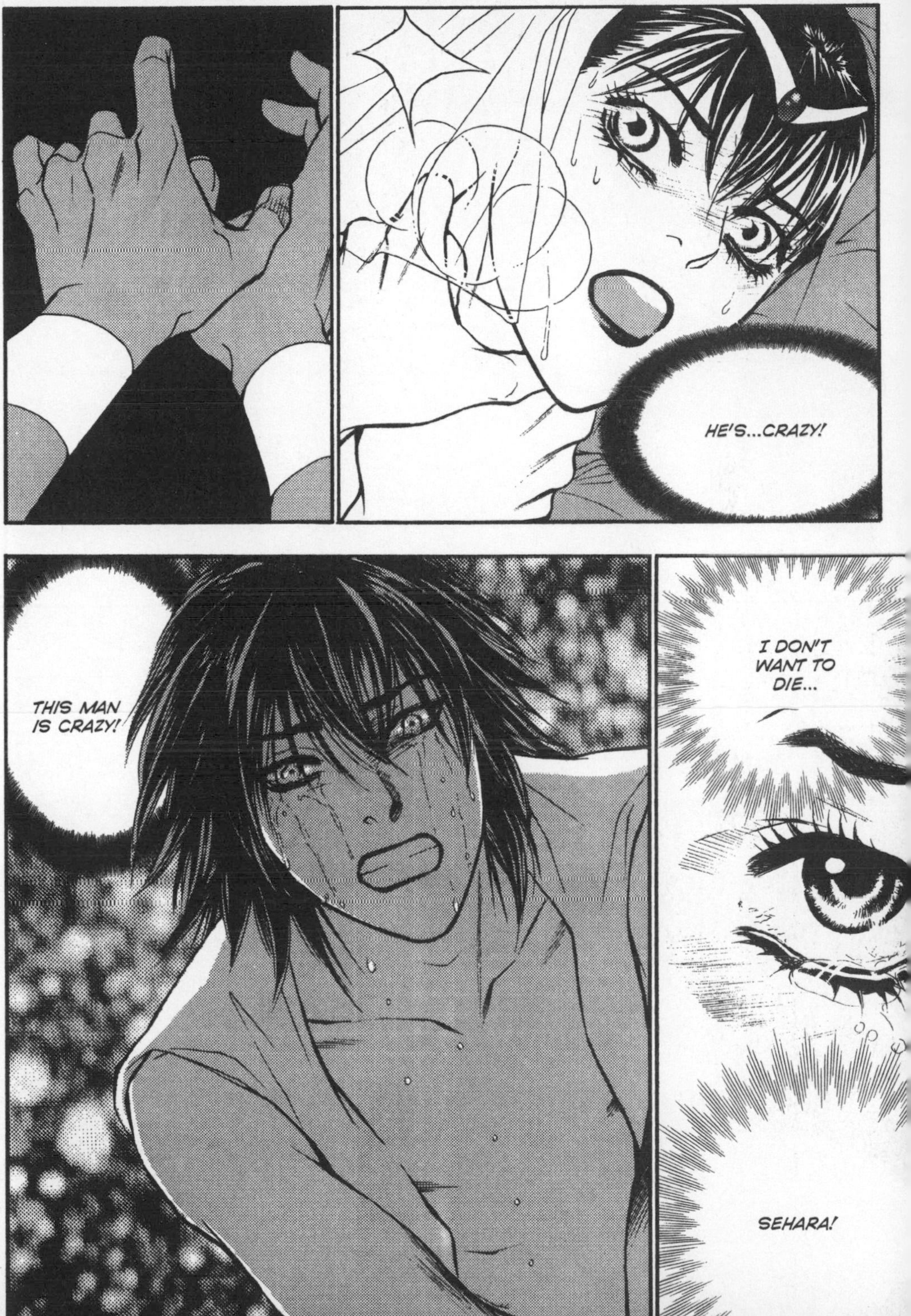
HE'S...CRAZY!
THIS MAN IS CRAZY!
I DON'T WANT TO DIE...
SEHARA!

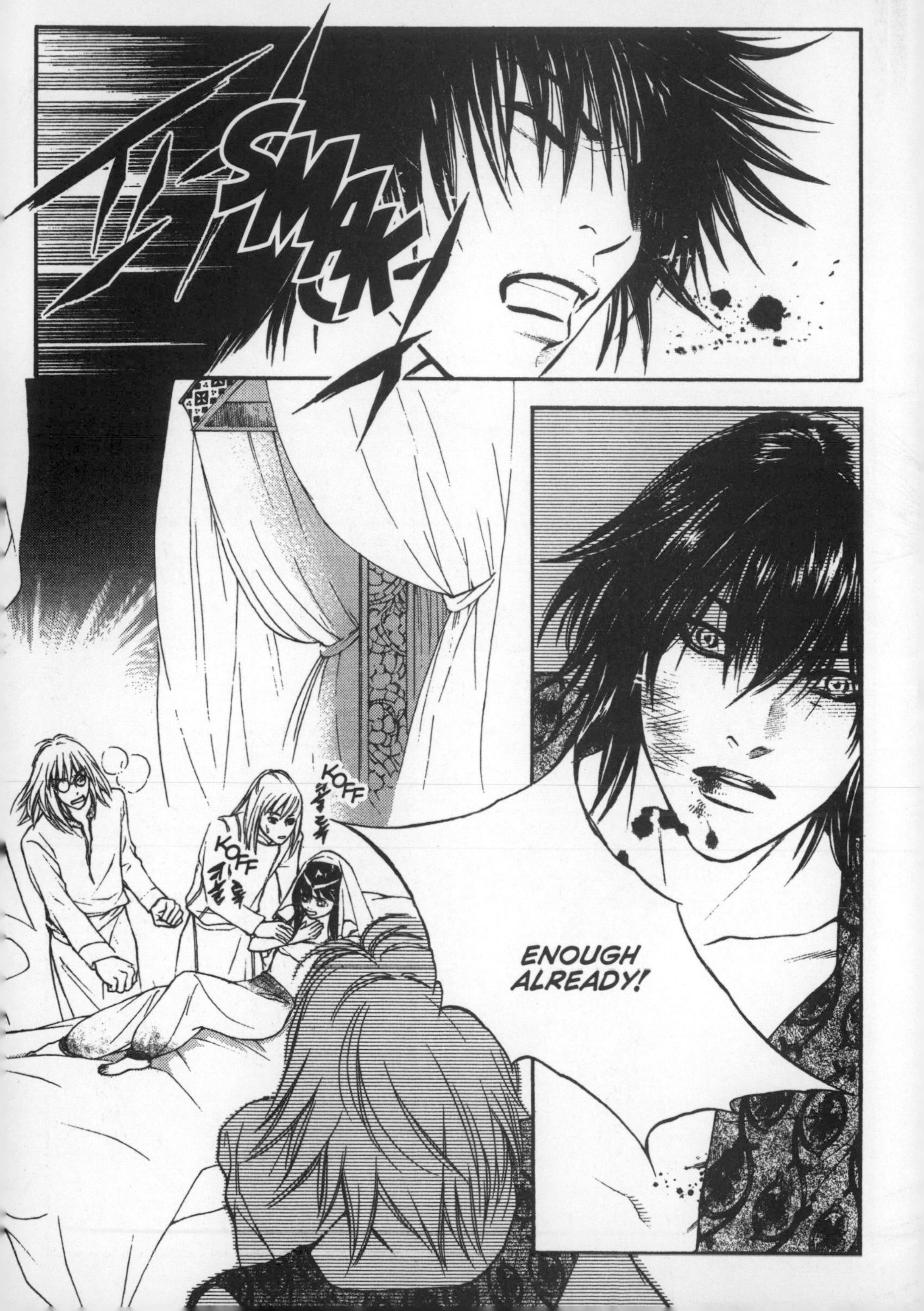
SMACK
KOFF
KOFF
ENOUGH ALREADY!

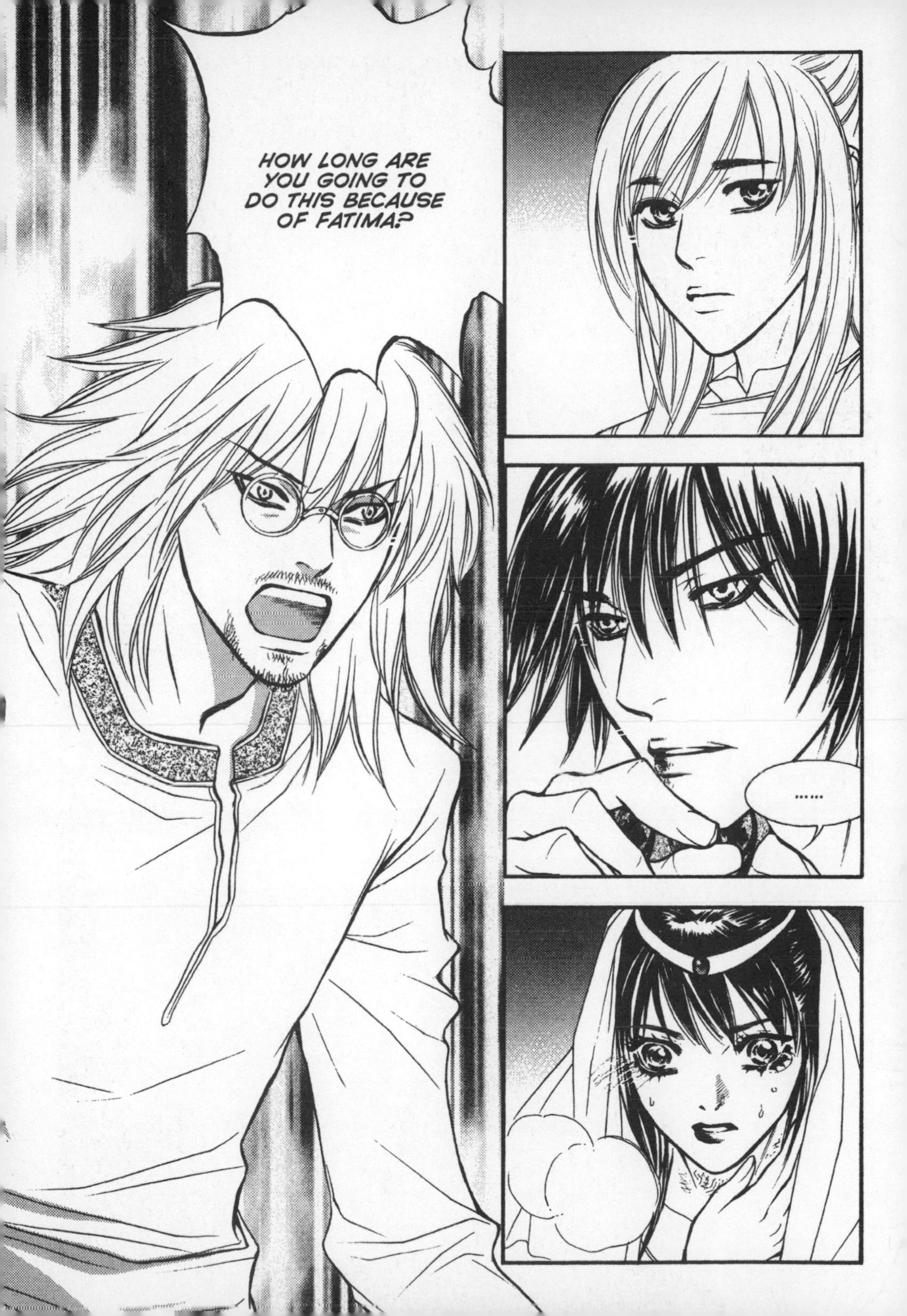
HOW LONG ARE YOU GOING TO DO THIS BECAUSE OF FATIMA?
……

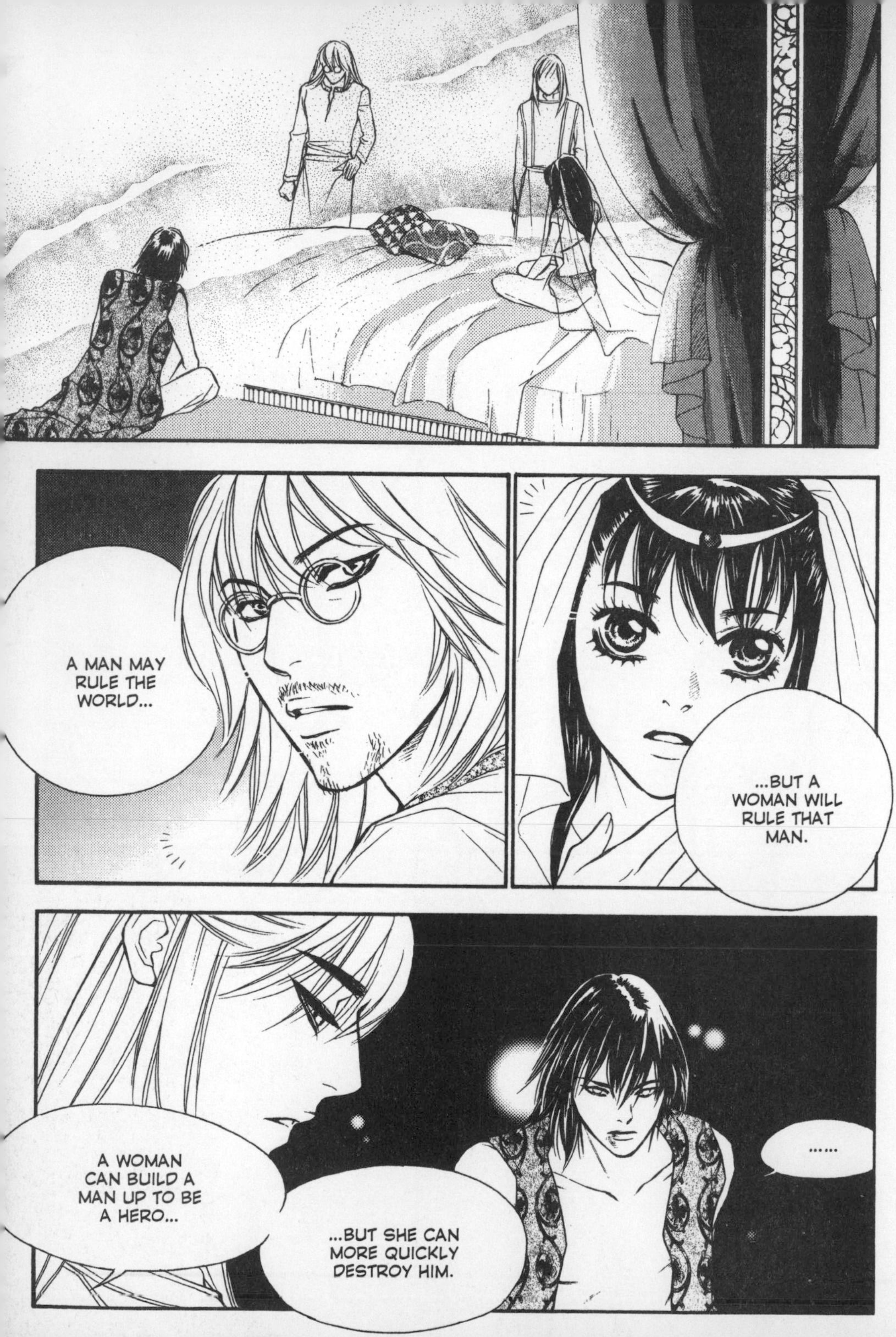
A MAN MAY RULE THE WORLD...
...BUT A WOMAN WILL RULE THAT MAN.
A WOMAN CAN BUILD A MAN UP TO BE A HERO...
...BUT SHE CAN MORE QUICKLY DESTROY HIM.
......

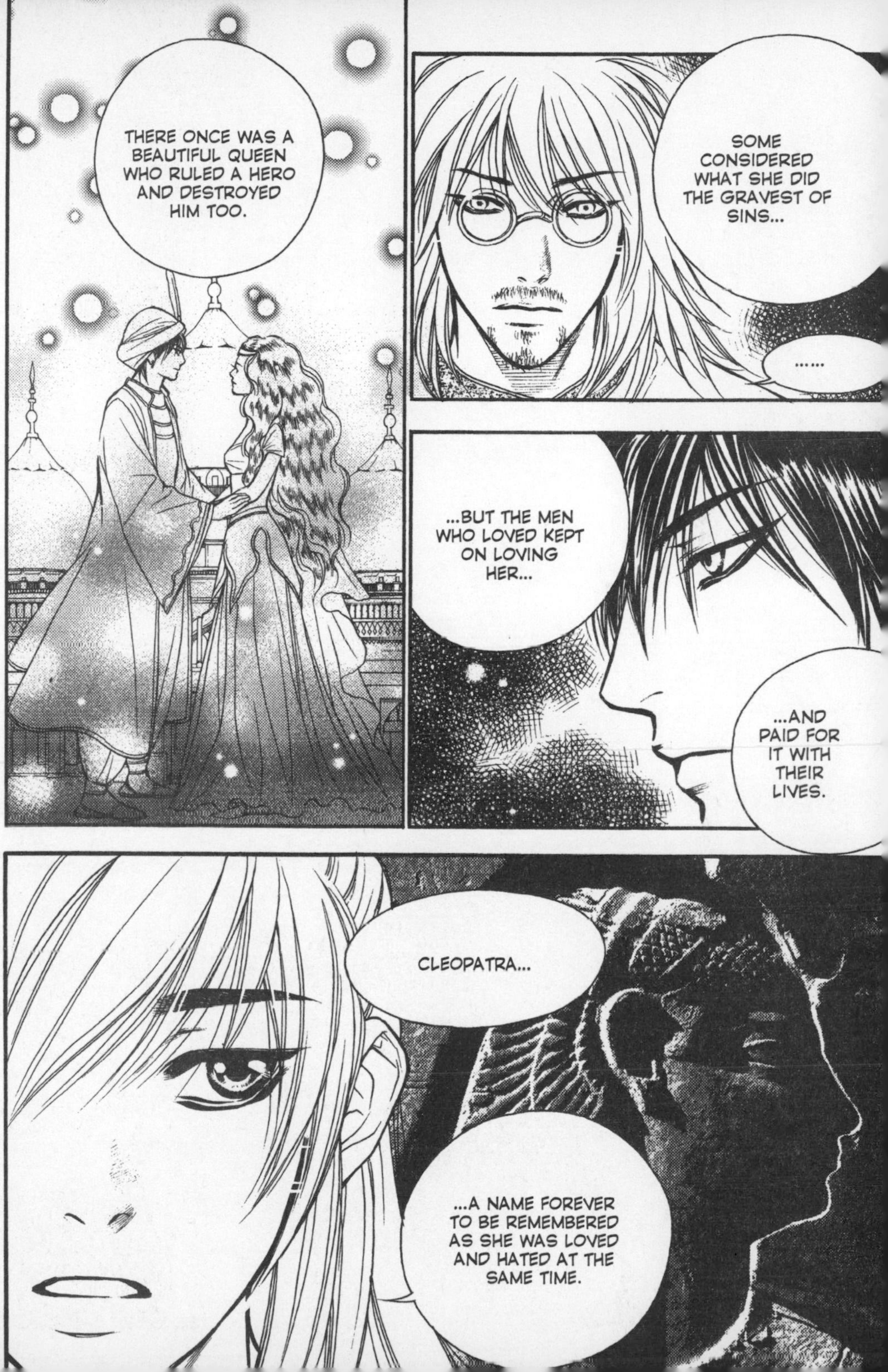
THERE ONCE WAS A BEAUTIFUL QUEEN WHO RULED A HERO AND DESTROYED HIM TOO.
SOME CONSIDERED WHAT SHE DID THE GRAVEST OF SINS...
......
...BUT THE MEN WHO LOVED KEPT ON LOVING HER...
...AND PAID FOR IT WITH THEIR LIVES.
CLEOPATRA...
...A NAME FOREVER TO BE REMEMBERED AS SHE WAS LOVED AND HATED AT THE SAME TIME.

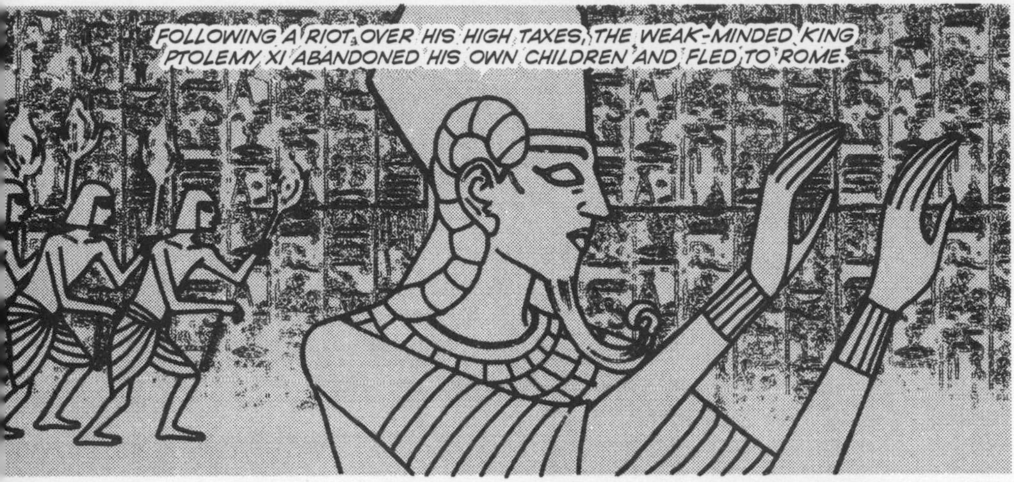
FOLLOWING A RIOT OVER HIS HIGH TAXES, THE WEAK-MINDED KING PTOLEMY XI ABANDONED HIS OWN CHILDREN AND FLED TO ROME.

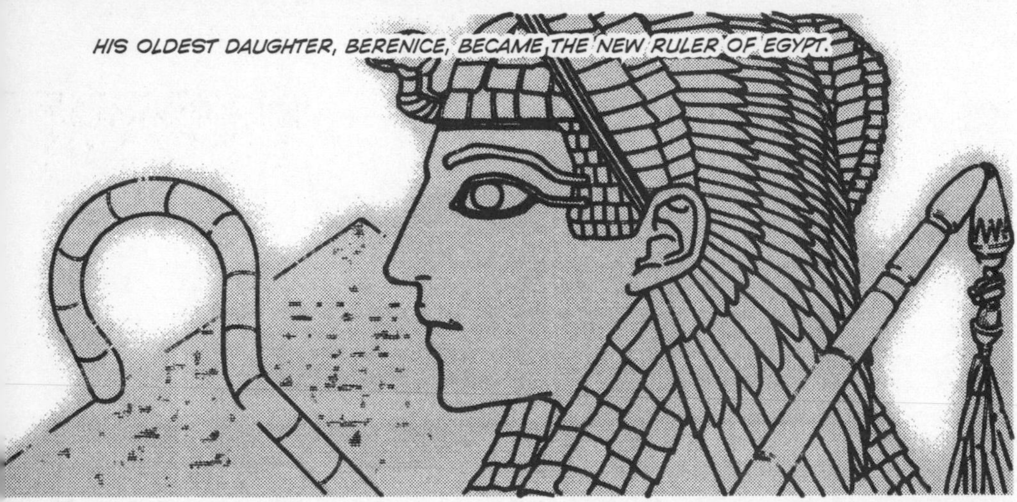
HIS OLDEST DAUGHTER, BERENICE, BECAME THE NEW RULER OF EGYPT.

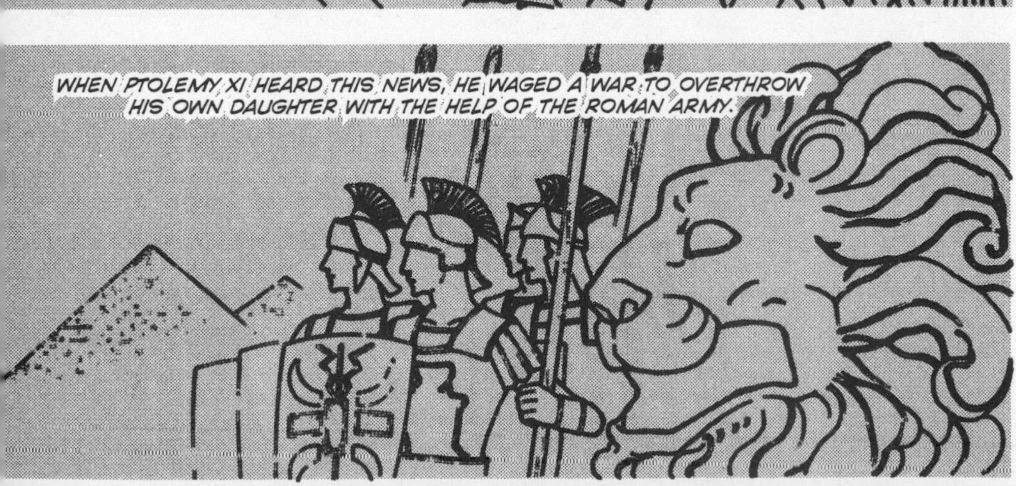
WHEN PTOLEMY XI HEARD THIS NEWS, HE WAGED A WAR TO OVERTHROW HIS OWN DAUGHTER WITH THE HELP OF THE ROMAN ARMY.

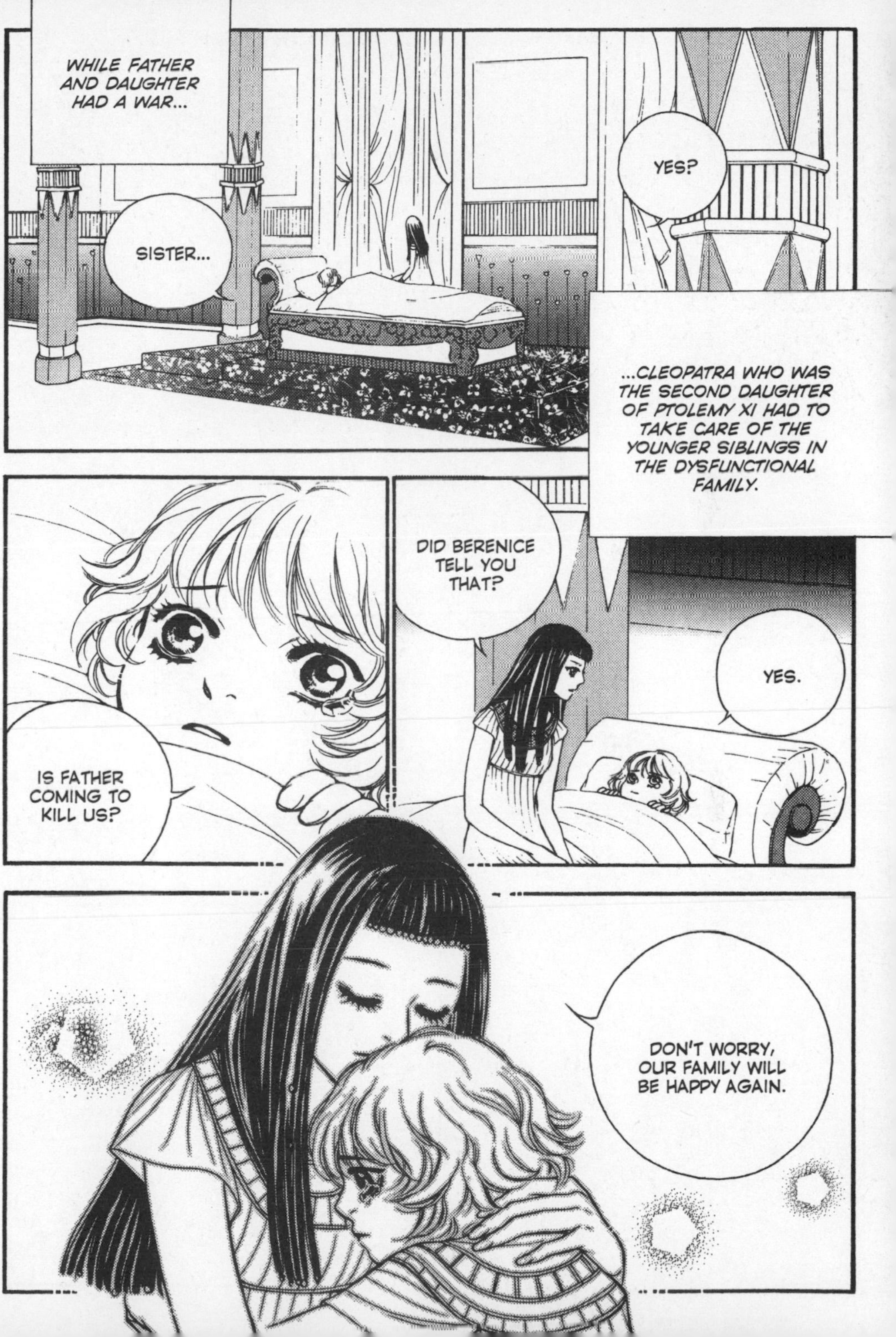
WHILE FATHER AND DAUGHTER HAD A WAR...
SISTER...
YES?
...CLEOPATRA WHO WAS THE SECOND DAUGHTER OF PTOLEMY XI HAD TO TAKE CARE OF THE YOUNGER SIBLINGS IN THE DYSFUNCTIONAL FAMILY.
IS FATHER COMING TO KILL US?
DID BERENICE TELL YOU THAT?
YES.
DON'T WORRY, OUR FAMILY WILL BE HAPPY AGAIN.

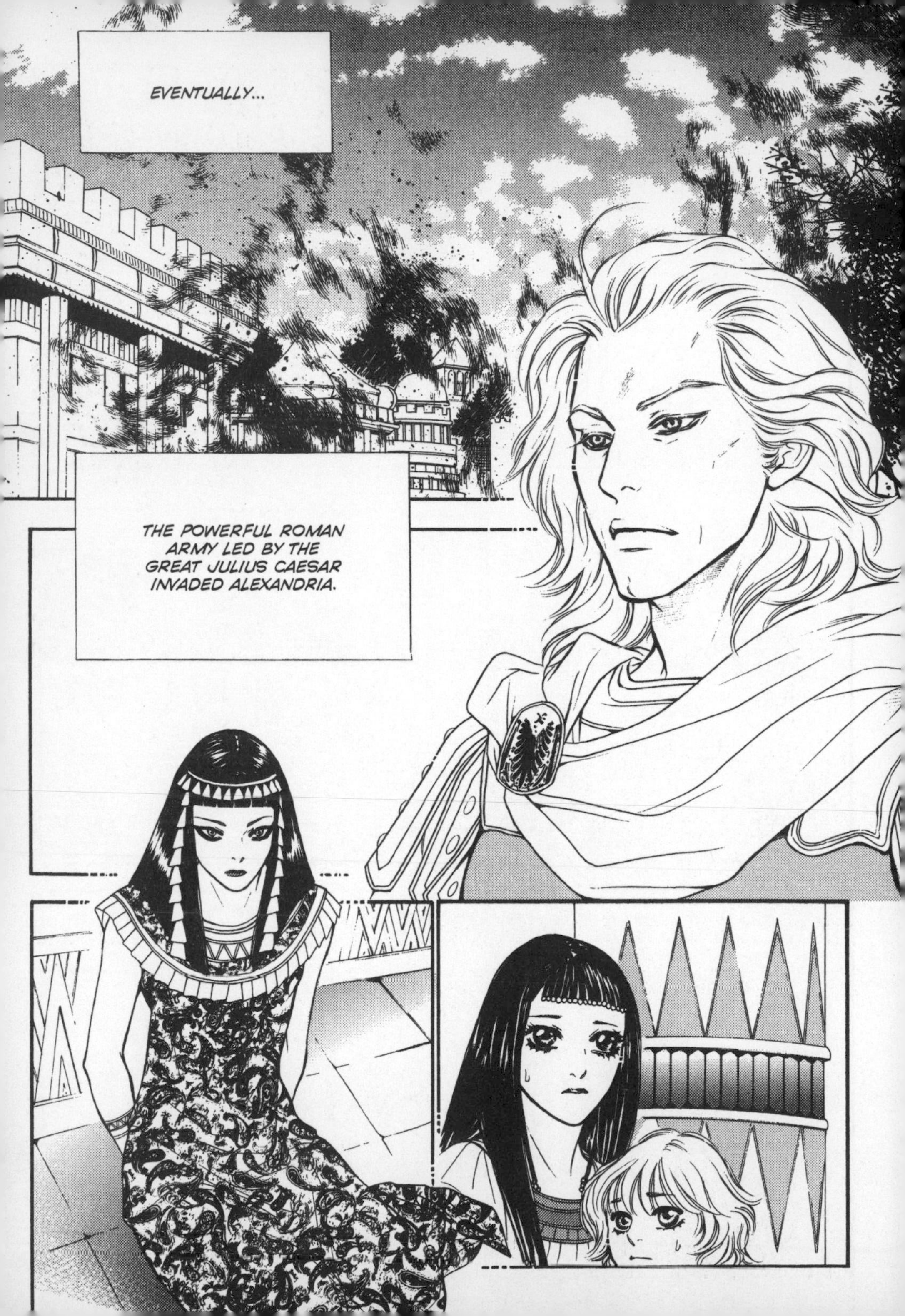
EVENTUALLY...
THE POWERFUL ROMAN ARMY LED BY THE GREAT JULIUS CAESAR INVADED ALEXANDRIA.

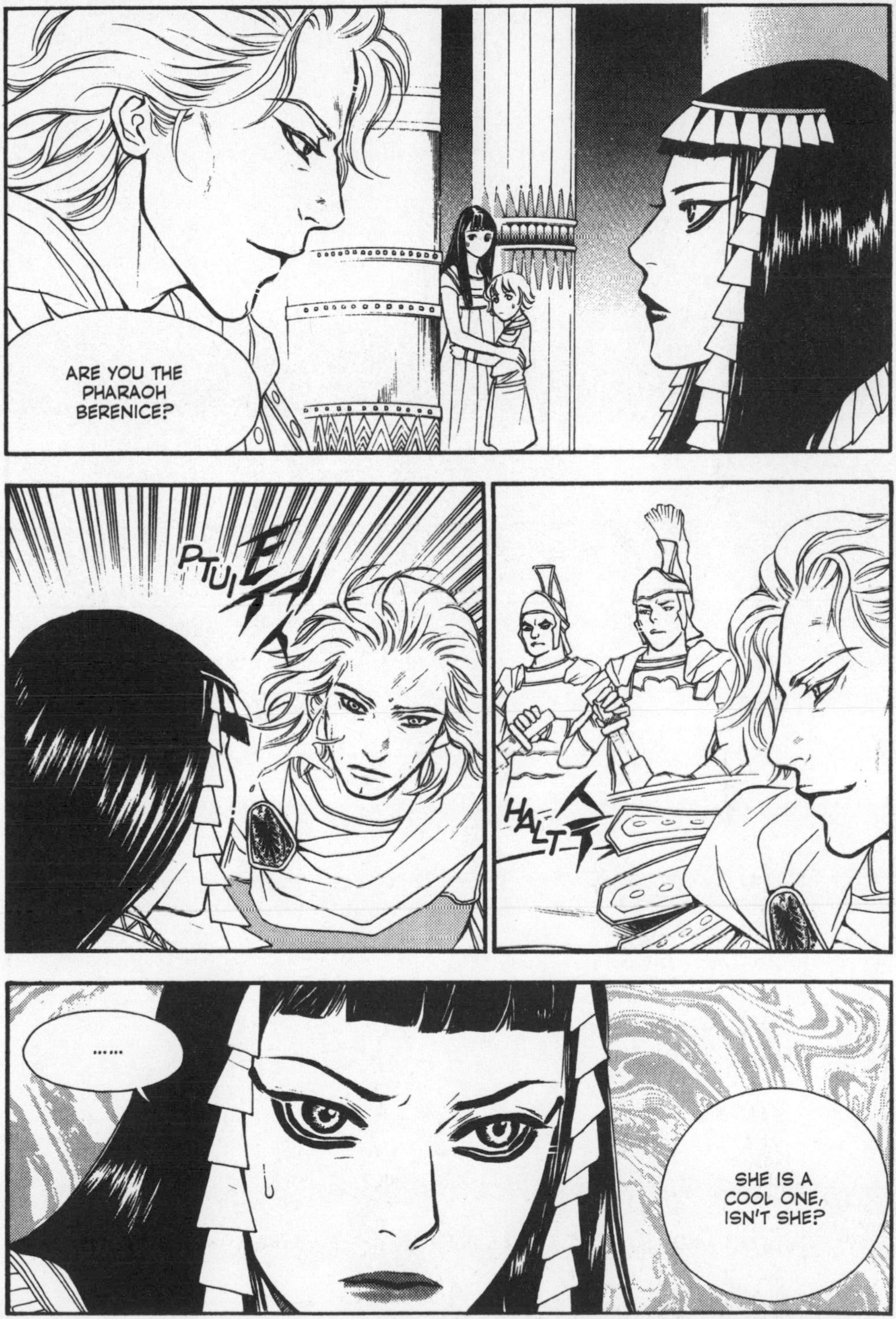
ARE YOU THE PHARAOH BERENICE?
PTUI
HALT
......
SHE IS A COOL ONE, ISN'T SHE?

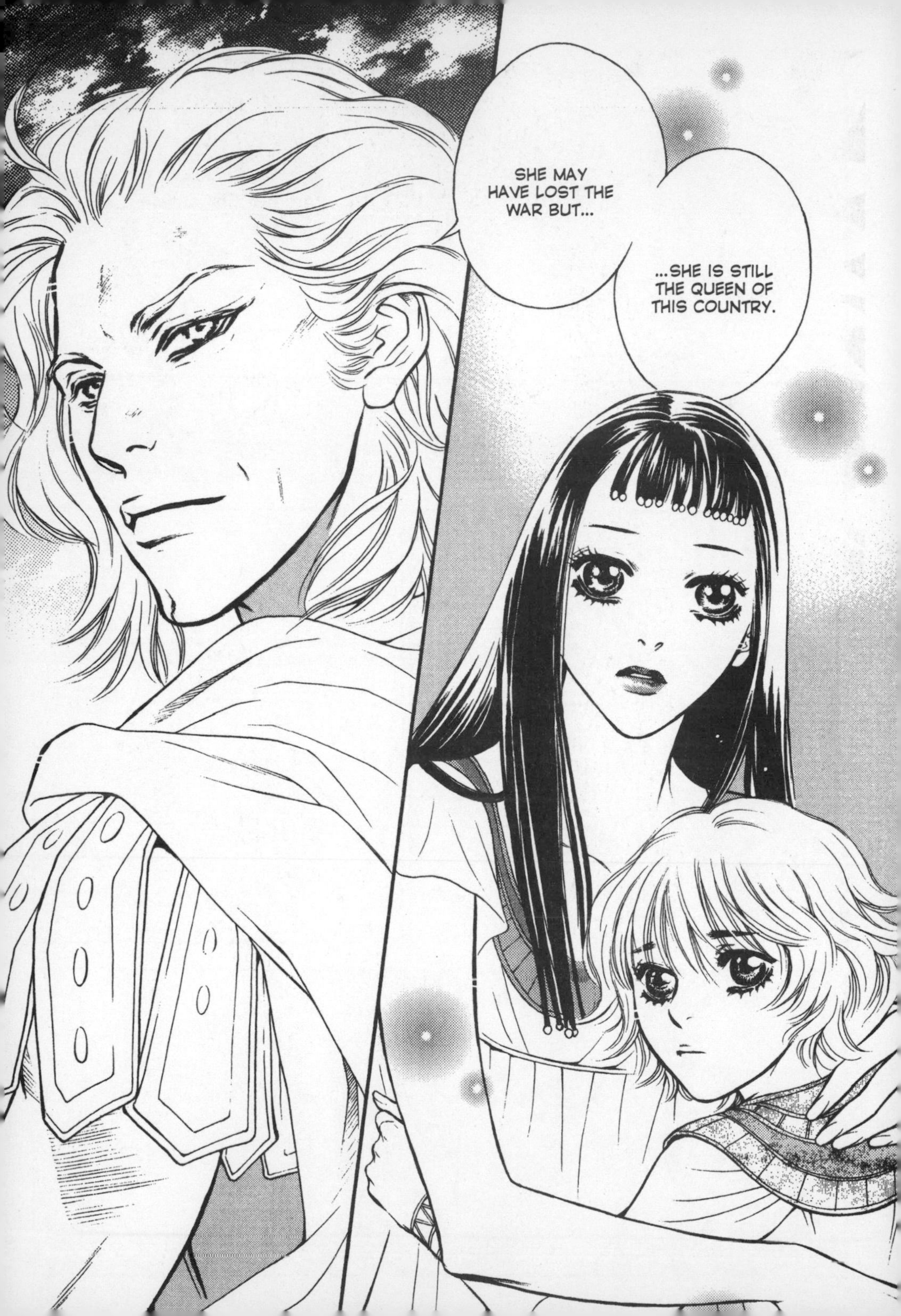
SHE MAY HAVE LOST THE WAR BUT...
...SHE IS STILL THE QUEEN OF THIS COUNTRY.

NIGHT STORY 3

FEMME FATALE

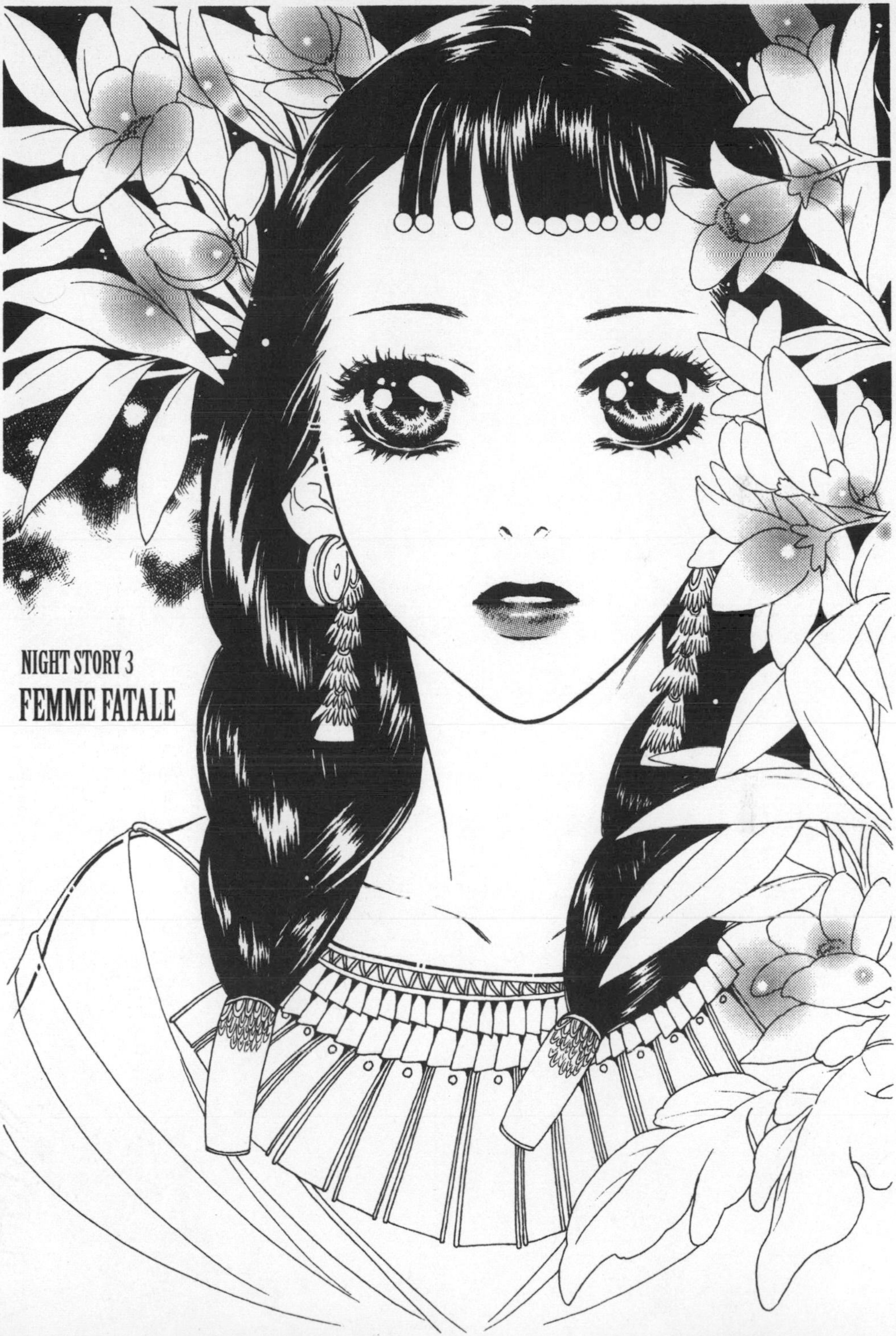

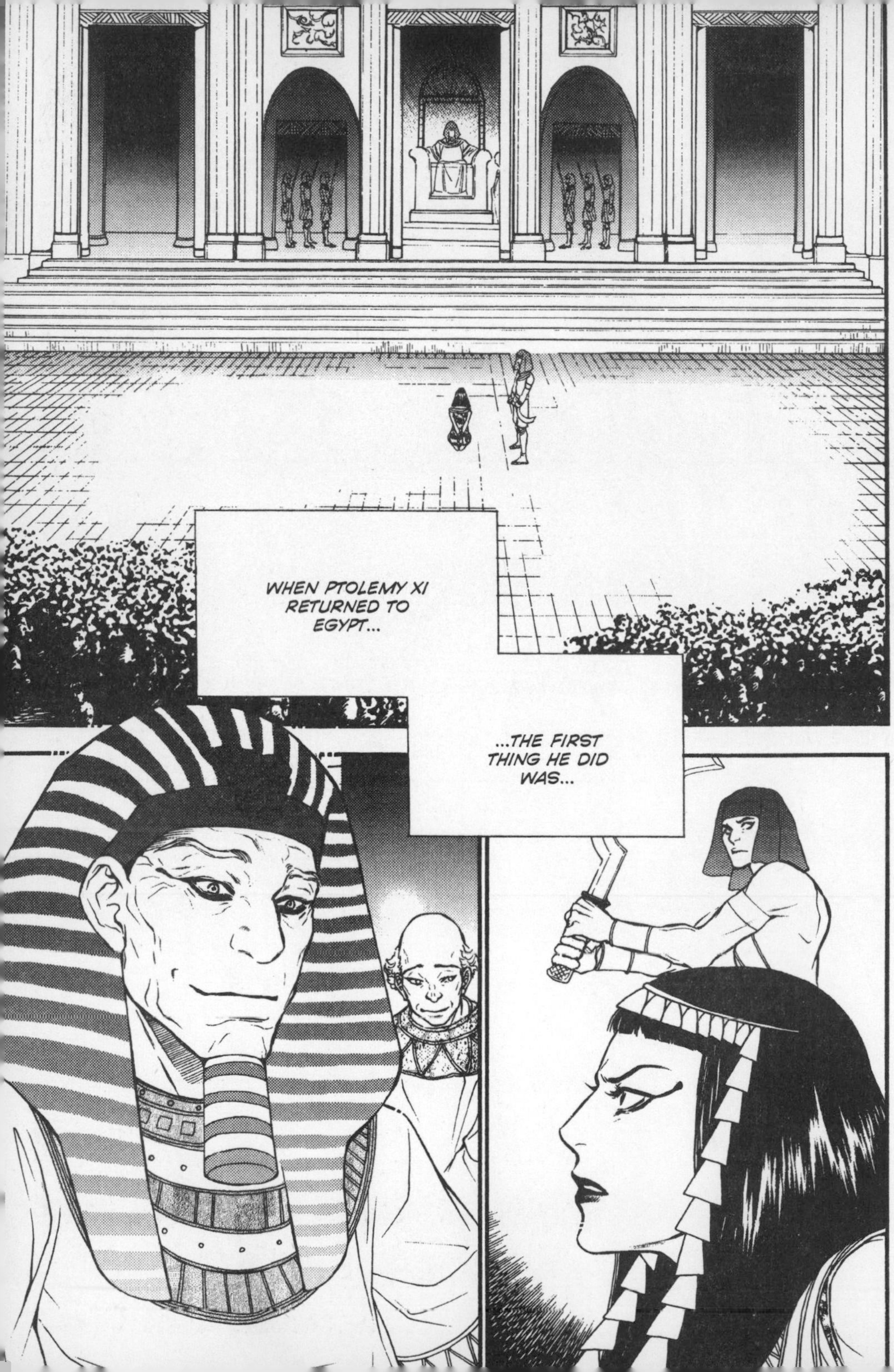
WHEN PTOLEMY XI RETURNED TO EGYPT...
...THE FIRST THING HE DID WAS...

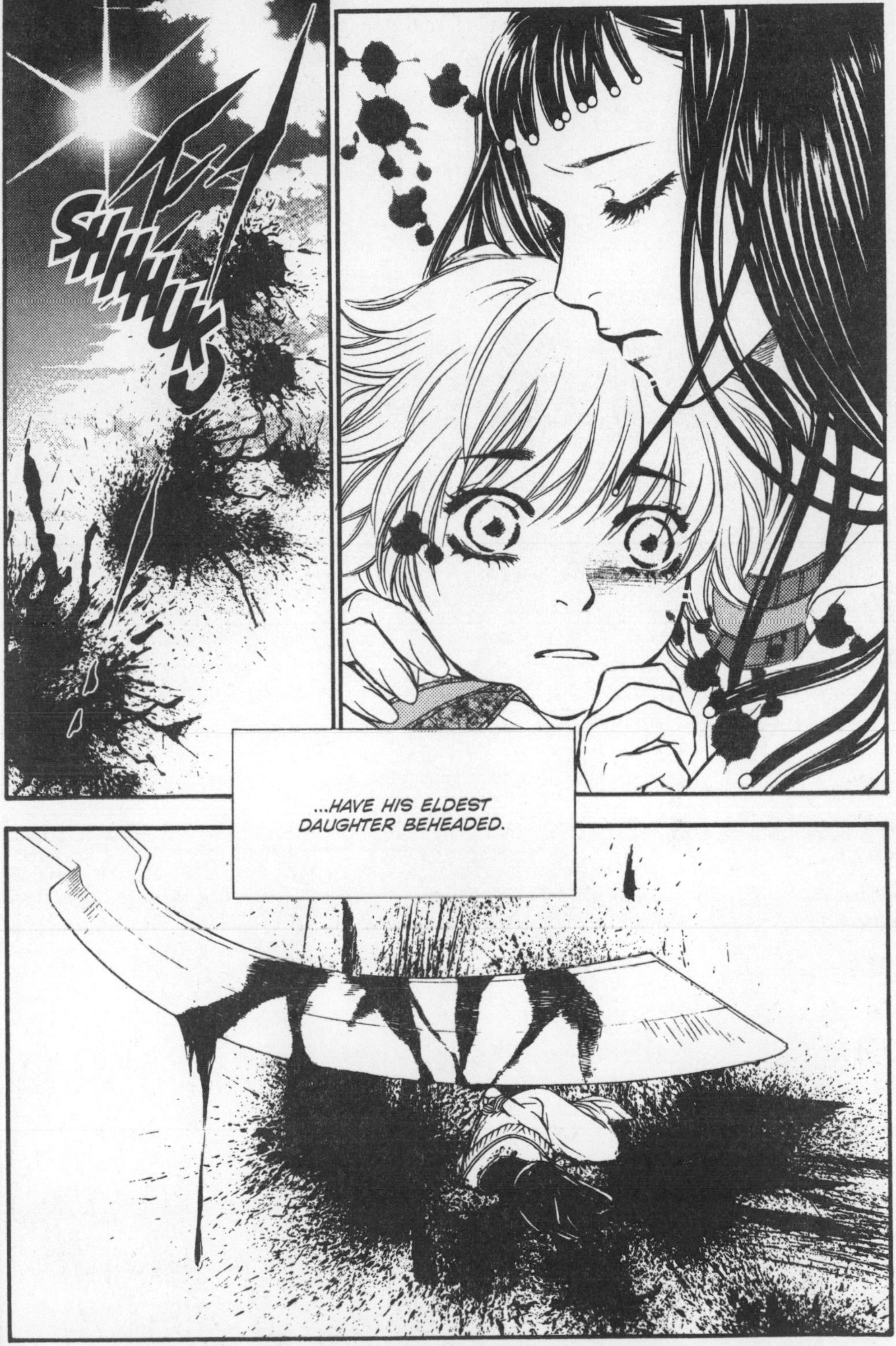
SHHHUK
...HAVE HIS ELDEST DAUGHTER BEHEADED.

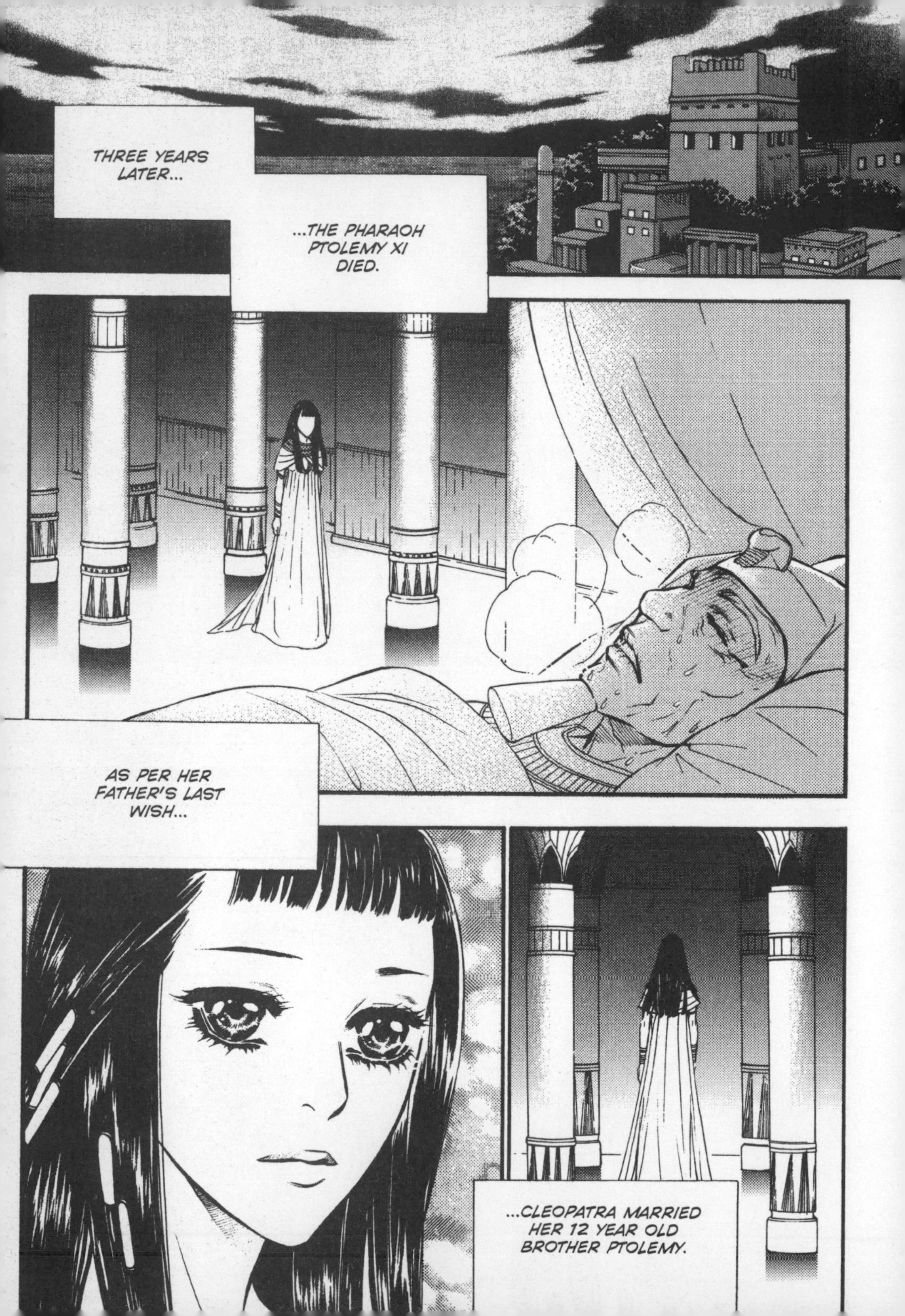
THREE YEARS LATER...
...THE PHARAOH PTOLEMY XI DIED.
AS PER HER FATHER'S LAST WISH...
...CLEOPATRA MARRIED HER 12 YEAR OLD BROTHER PTOLEMY.

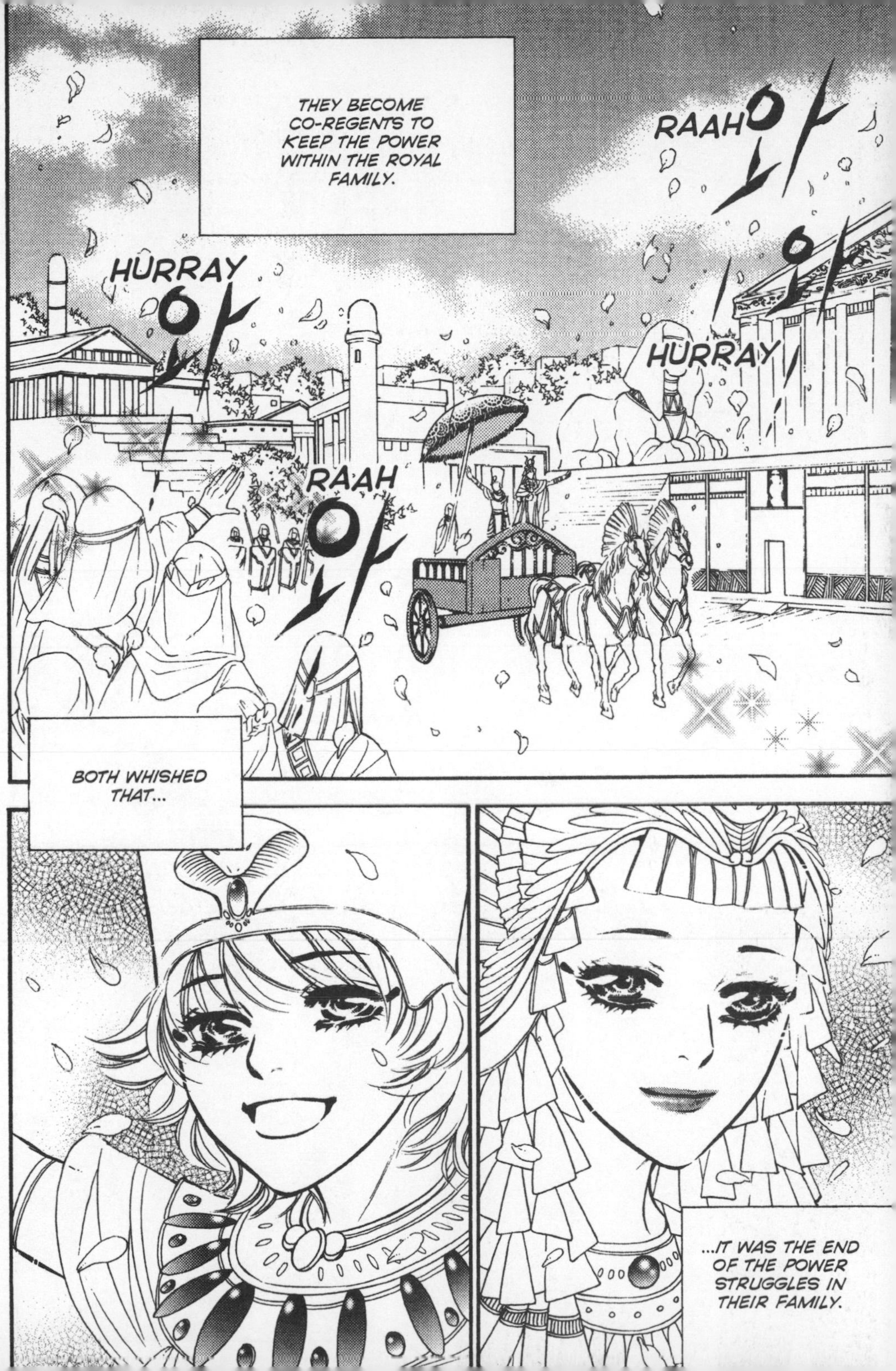
THEY BECOME CO-REGENTS TO KEEP THE POWER WITHIN THE ROYAL FAMILY.
HURRAY
RAAH
RAAH
HURRAY
BOTH WHISHED THAT...
...IT WAS THE END OF THE POWER STRUGGLES IN THEIR FAMILY.

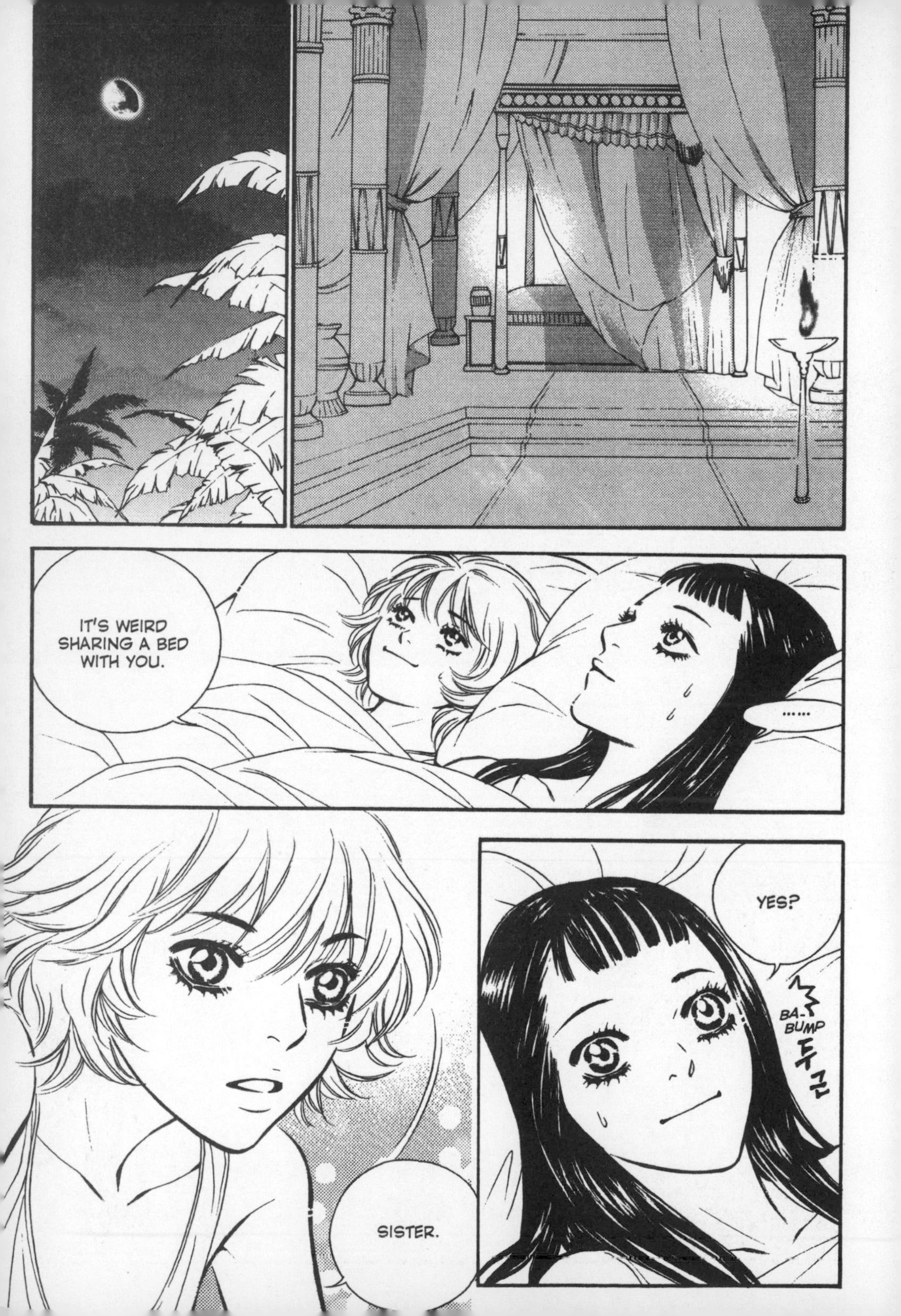
IT'S WEIRD SHARING A BED WITH YOU.
......
SISTER.
YES?
BA-BUMP

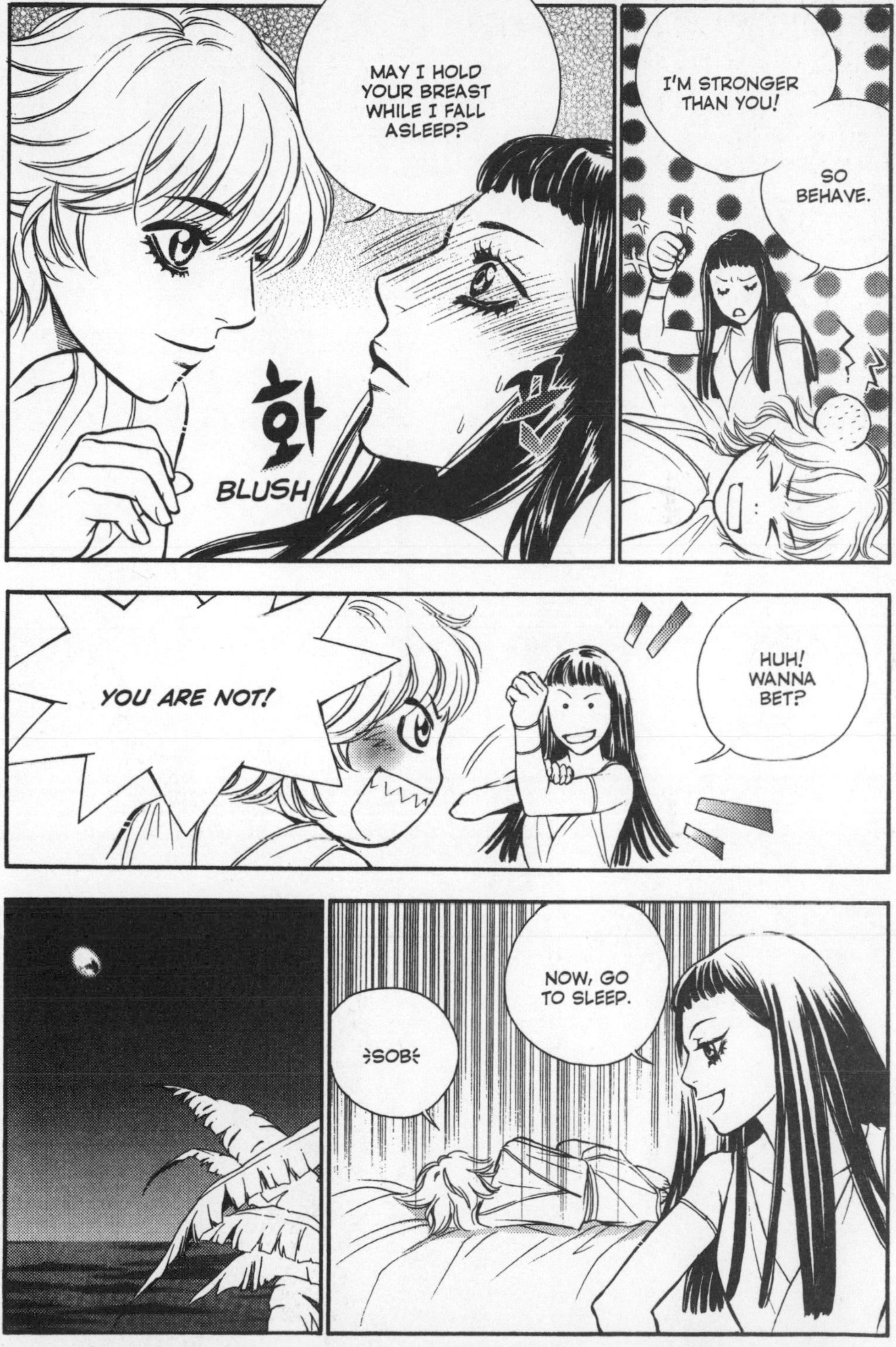
MAY I HOLD YOUR BREAST WHILE I FALL ASLEEP?
화
BLUSH
I'M STRONGER THAN YOU!
SO BEHAVE.
YOU ARE NOT!
HUH! WANNA BET?
NOW, GO TO SLEEP.
SOB

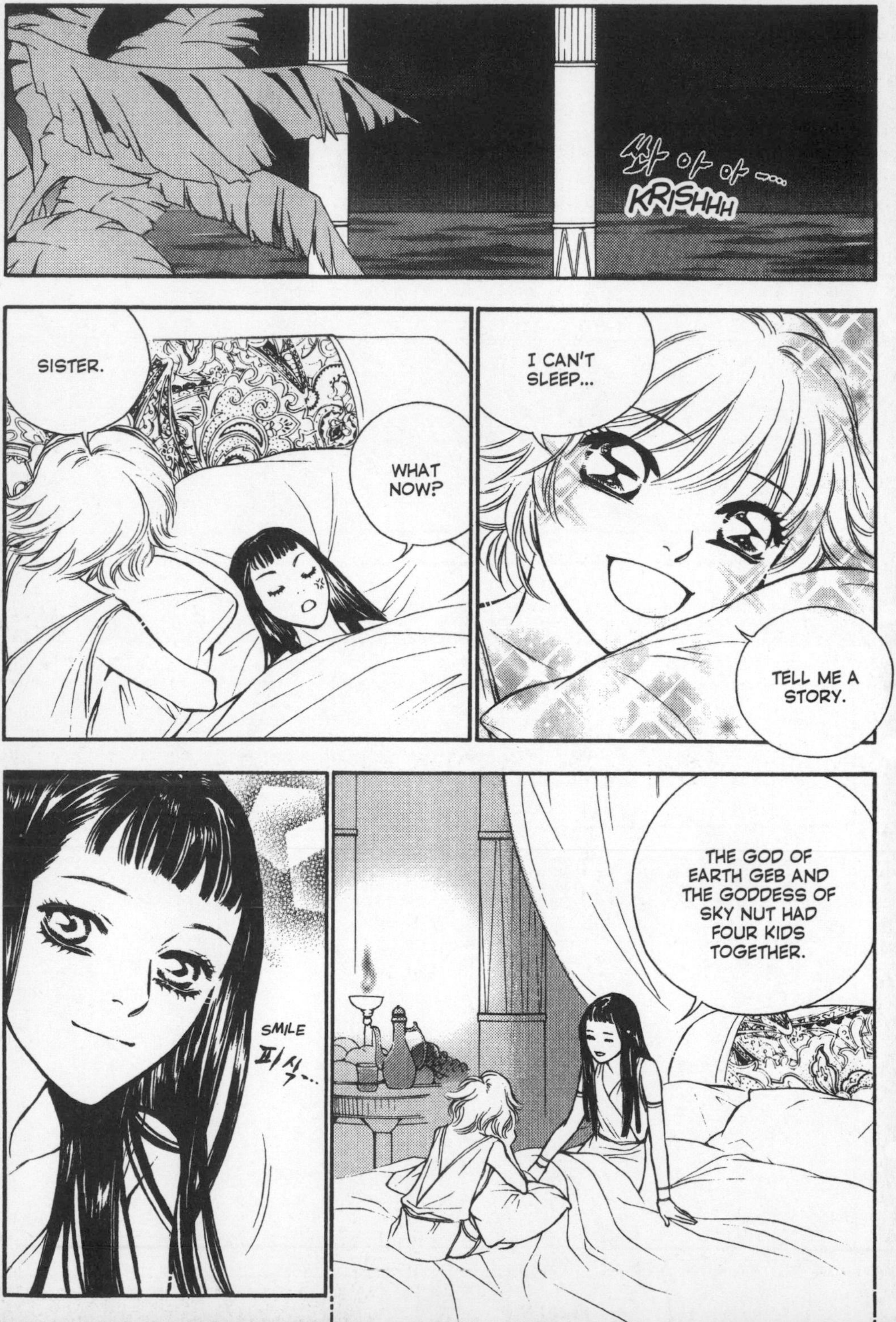
쏴 아 아 ~...
KRISHHH
SISTER.
WHAT NOW?
I CAN'T SLEEP...
TELL ME A STORY.
SMILE
피식~..
THE GOD OF EARTH GEB AND THE GODDESS OF SKY NUT HAD FOUR KIDS TOGETHER.

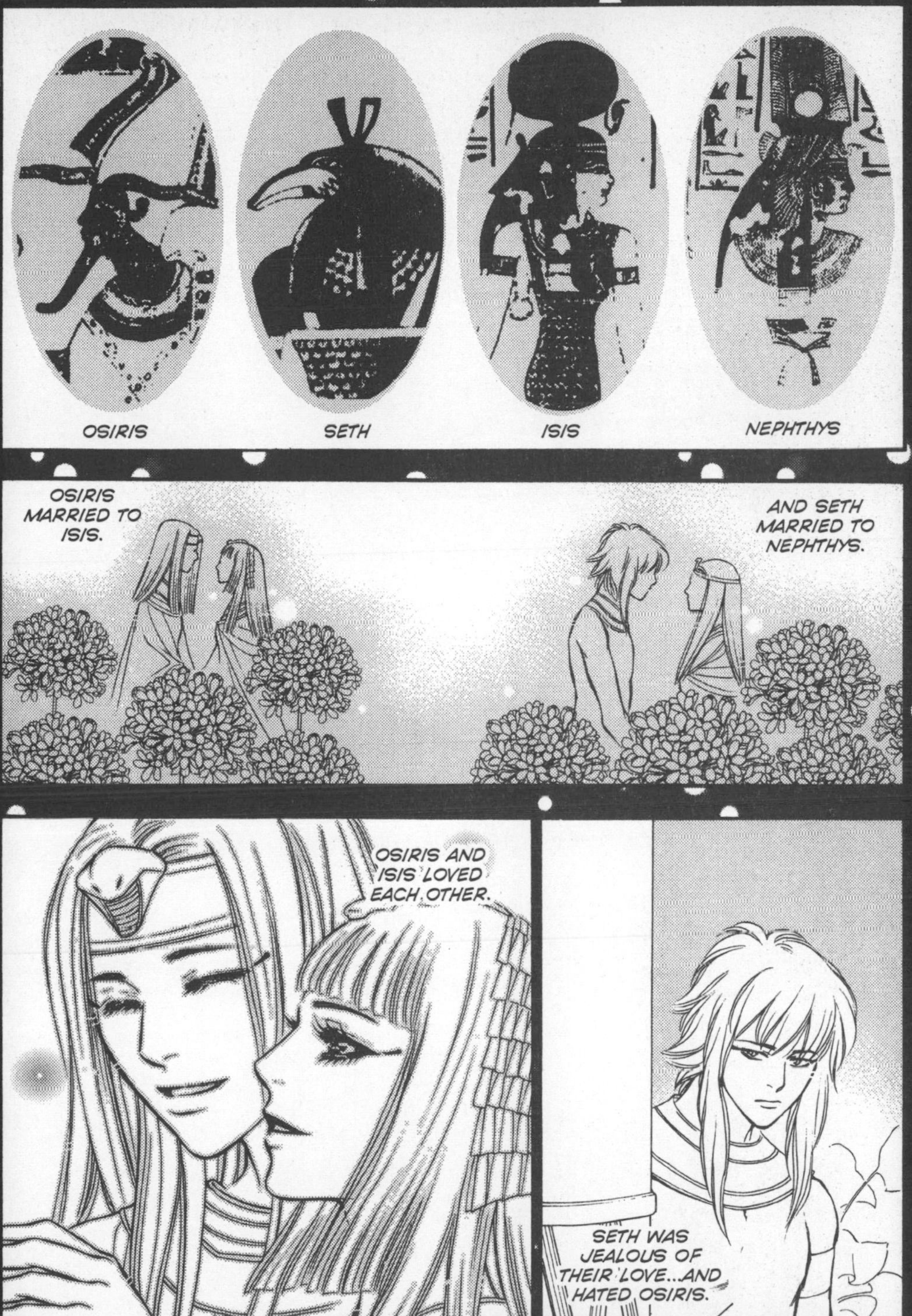
OSIRIS
SETH
ISIS
NEPHTHYS
OSIRIS MARRIED TO ISIS.
AND SETH MARRIED TO NEPHTHYS.
OSIRIS AND ISIS LOVED EACH OTHER.
SETH WAS JEALOUS OF THEIR LOVE...AND HATED OSIRIS.

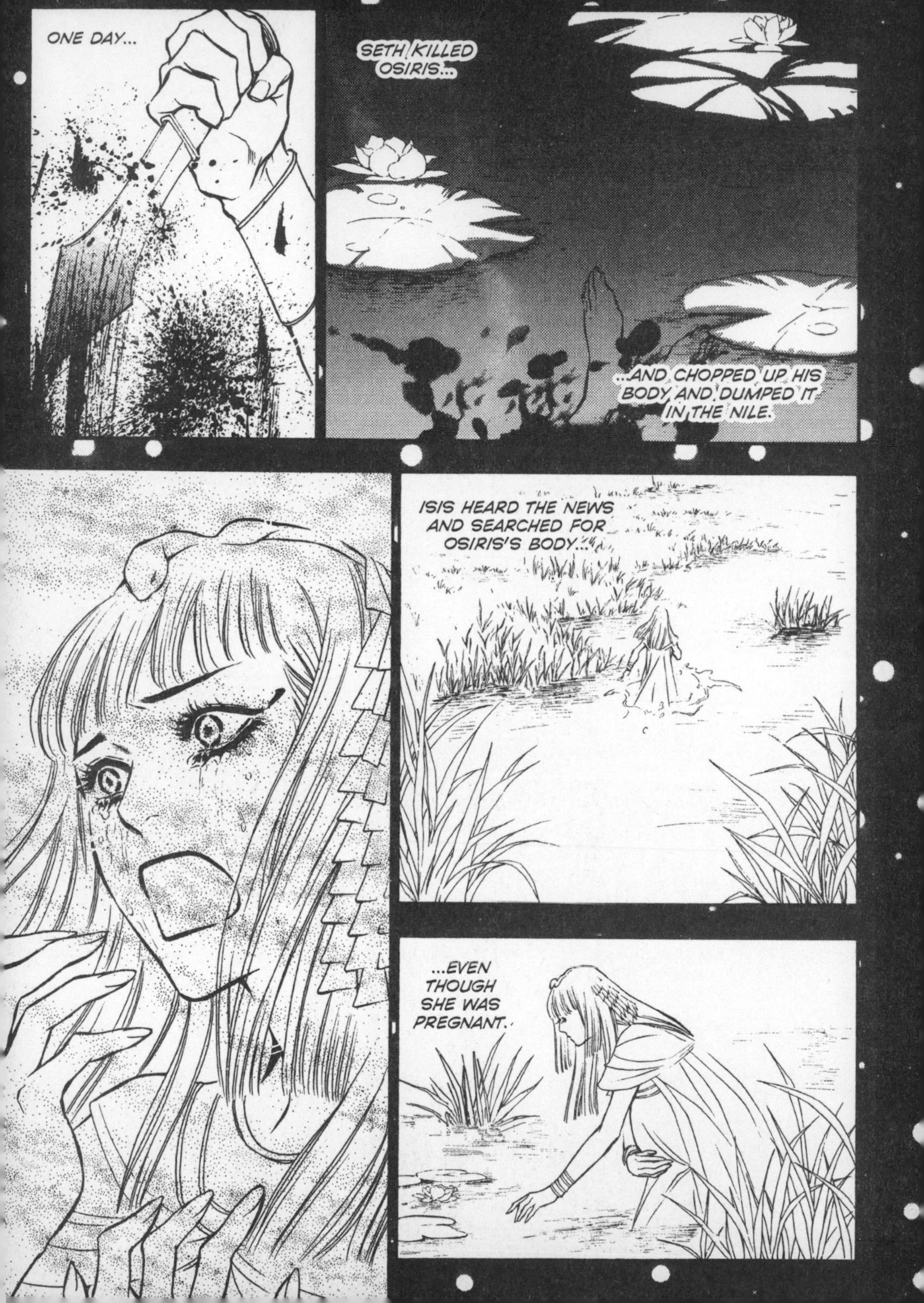
ONE DAY...
SETH KILLED OSIRIS...
...AND CHOPPED UP HIS BODY AND DUMPED IT IN THE NILE.
ISIS HEARD THE NEWS AND SEARCHED FOR OSIRIS'S BODY...
...EVEN THOUGH SHE WAS PREGNANT.

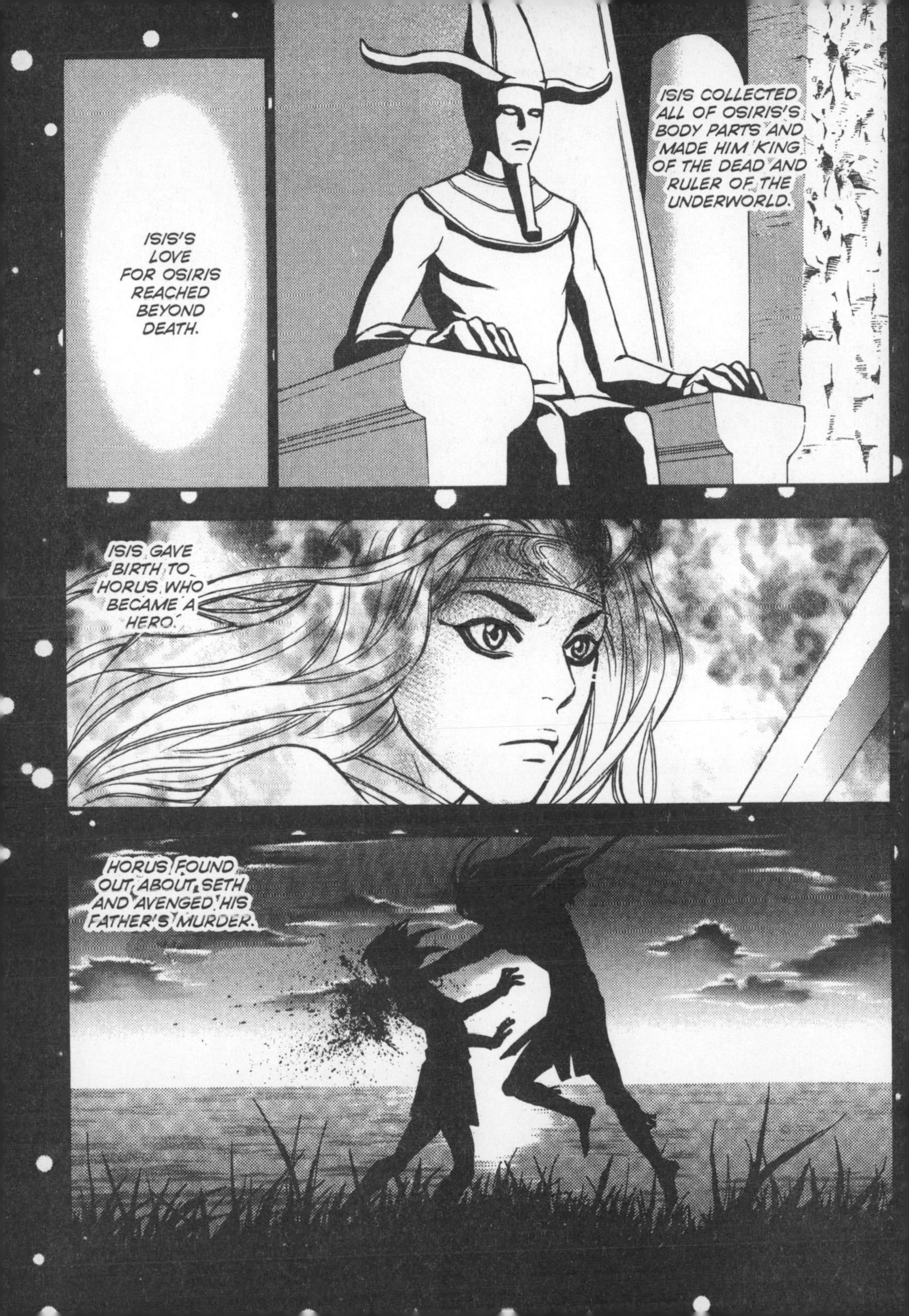
ISIS'S LOVE FOR OSIRIS REACHED BEYOND DEATH.
ISIS COLLECTED ALL OF OSIRIS'S BODY PARTS AND MADE HIM KING OF THE DEAD AND RULER OF THE UNDERWORLD.
ISIS GAVE BIRTH TO HORUS WHO BECAME A HERO.
HORUS FOUND OUT ABOUT SETH AND AVENGED HIS FATHER'S MURDER.

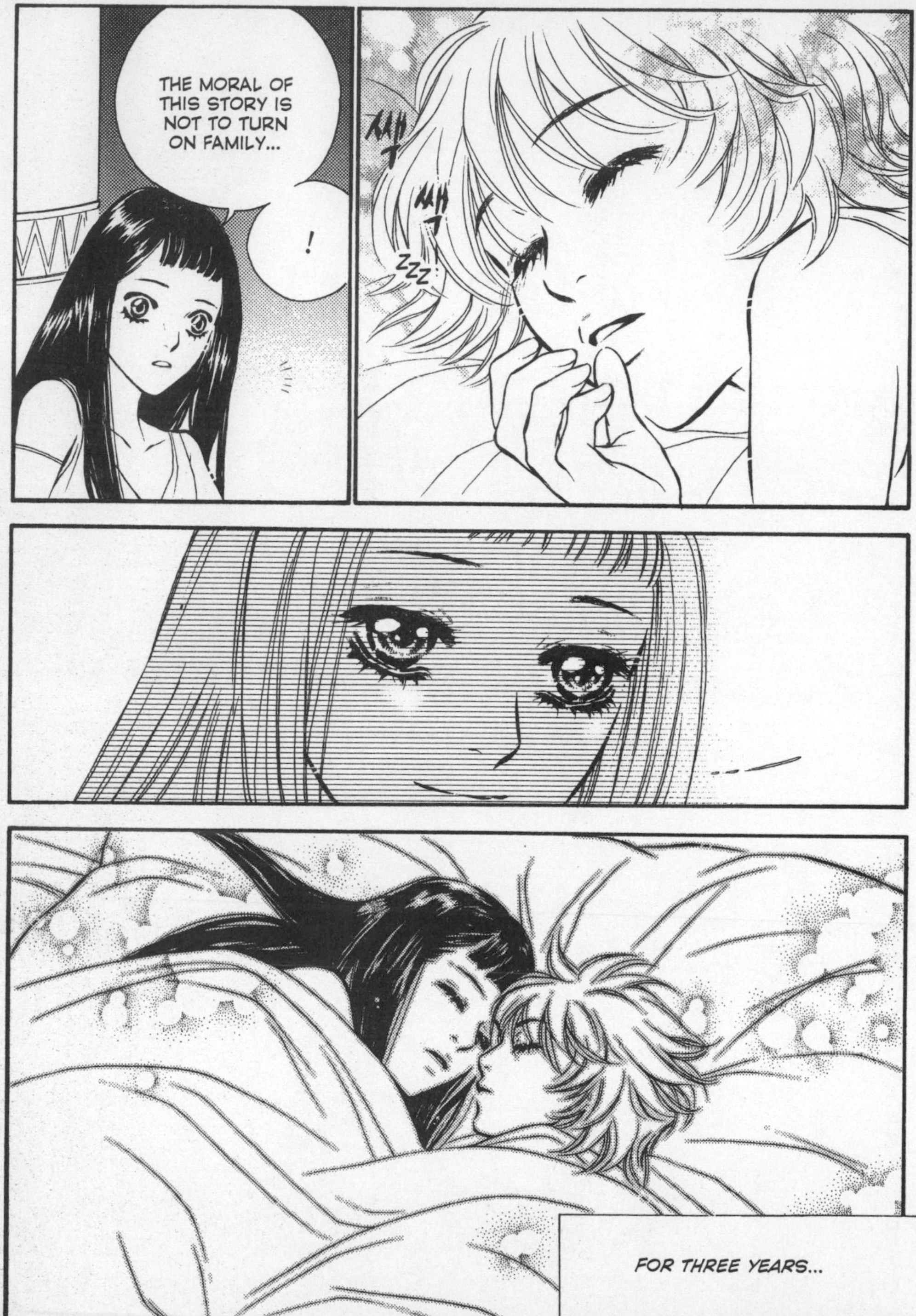
THE MORAL OF THIS STORY IS NOT TO TURN ON FAMILY...
!
ZZZ
FOR THREE YEARS...

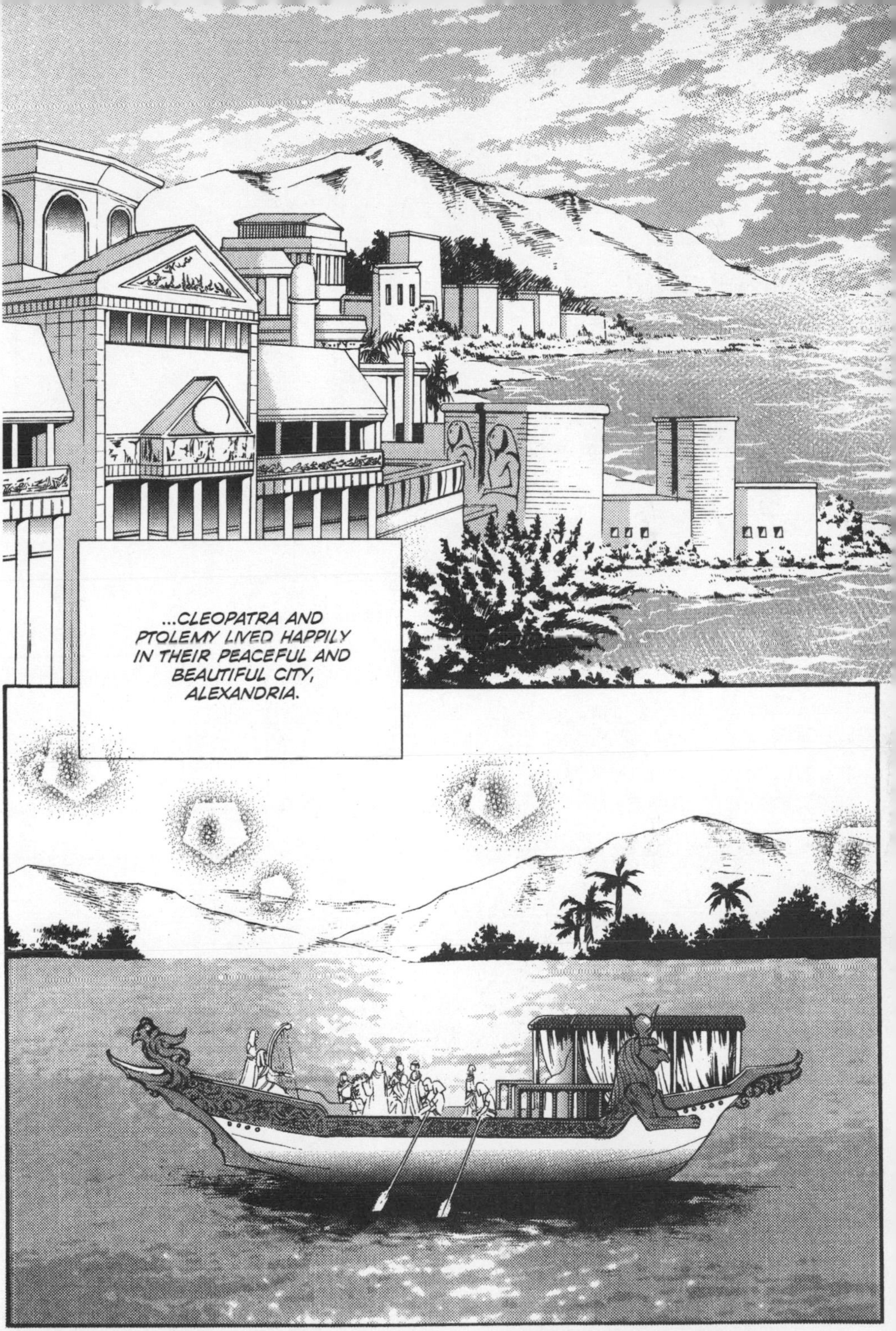
...CLEOPATRA AND PTOLEMY LIVED HAPPILY IN THEIR PEACEFUL AND BEAUTIFUL CITY, ALEXANDRIA.

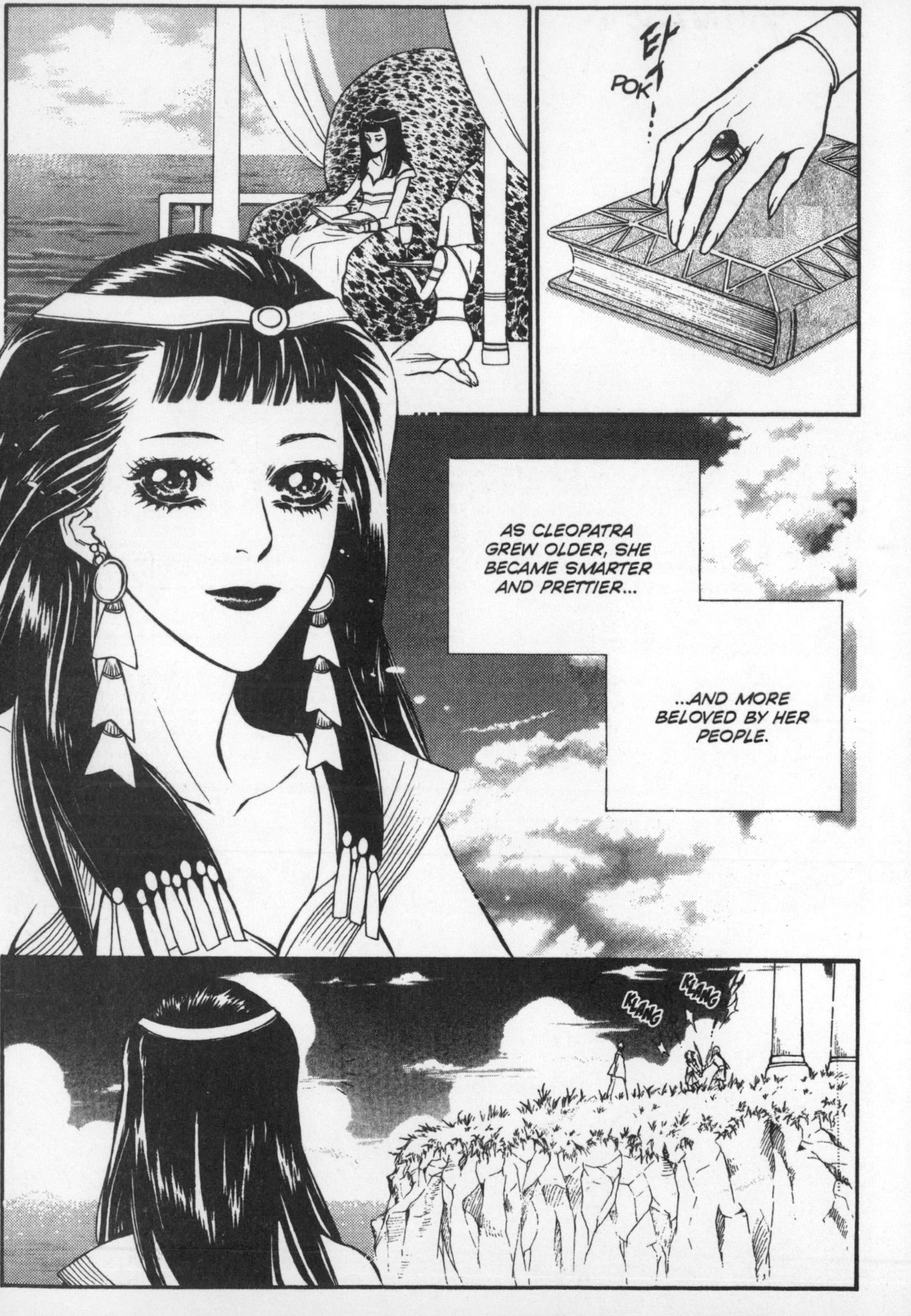
탁
POK
AS CLEOPATRA GREW OLDER, SHE BECAME SMARTER AND PRETTIER...
...AND MORE BELOVED BY HER PEOPLE.
KLANG
KLANG

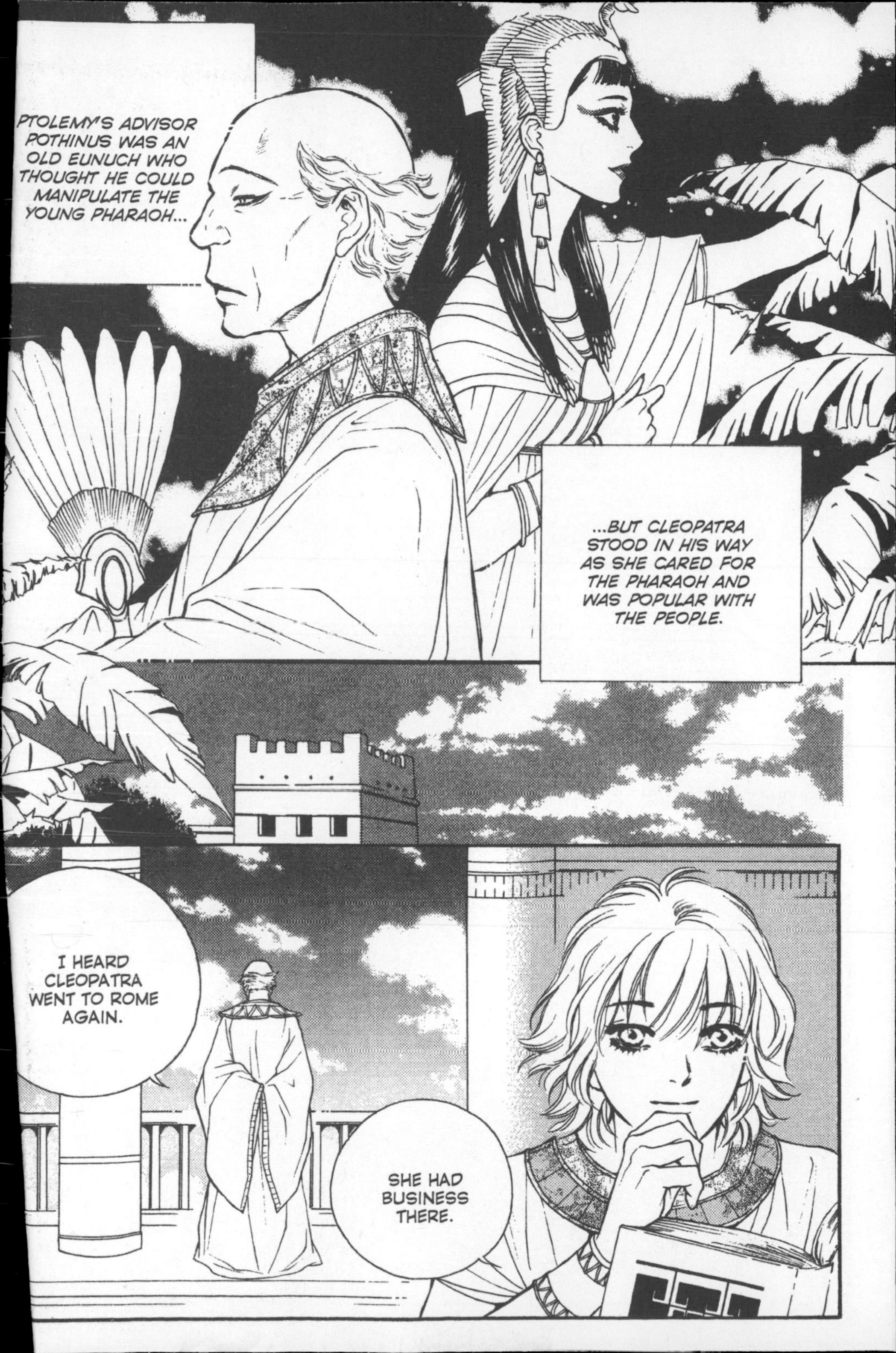
PTOLEMY'S ADVISOR POTHINUS WAS AN OLD EUNUCH WHO THOUGHT HE COULD MANIPULATE THE YOUNG PHARAOH...
...BUT CLEOPATRA STOOD IN HIS WAY AS SHE CARED FOR THE PHARAOH AND WAS POPULAR WITH THE PEOPLE.
I HEARD CLEOPATRA WENT TO ROME AGAIN.
SHE HAD BUSINESS THERE.

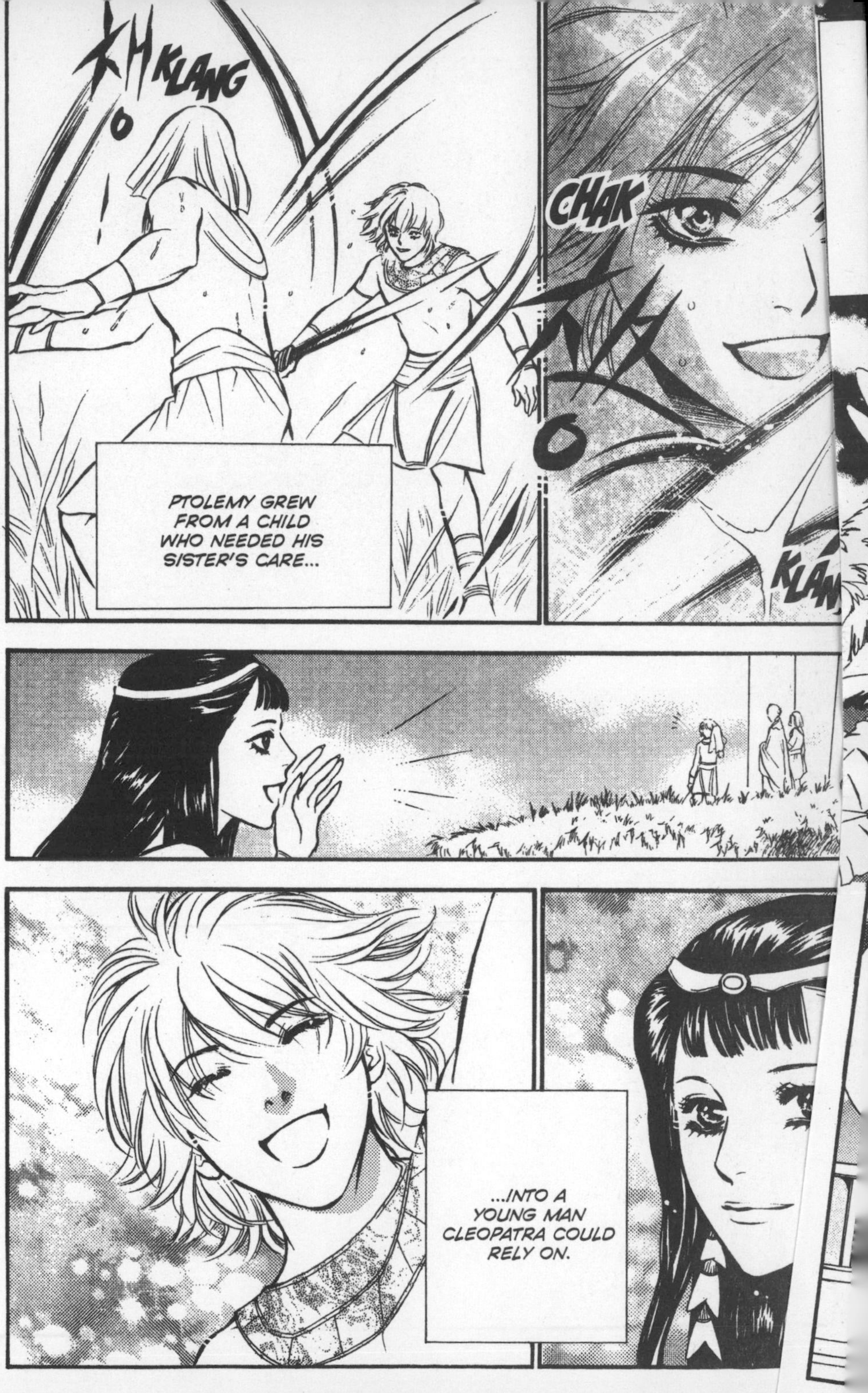
KLANG
PTOLEMY GREW FROM A CHILD WHO NEEDED HIS SISTER'S CARE...
CHAK
...INTO A YOUNG MAN CLEOPATRA COULD RELY ON.

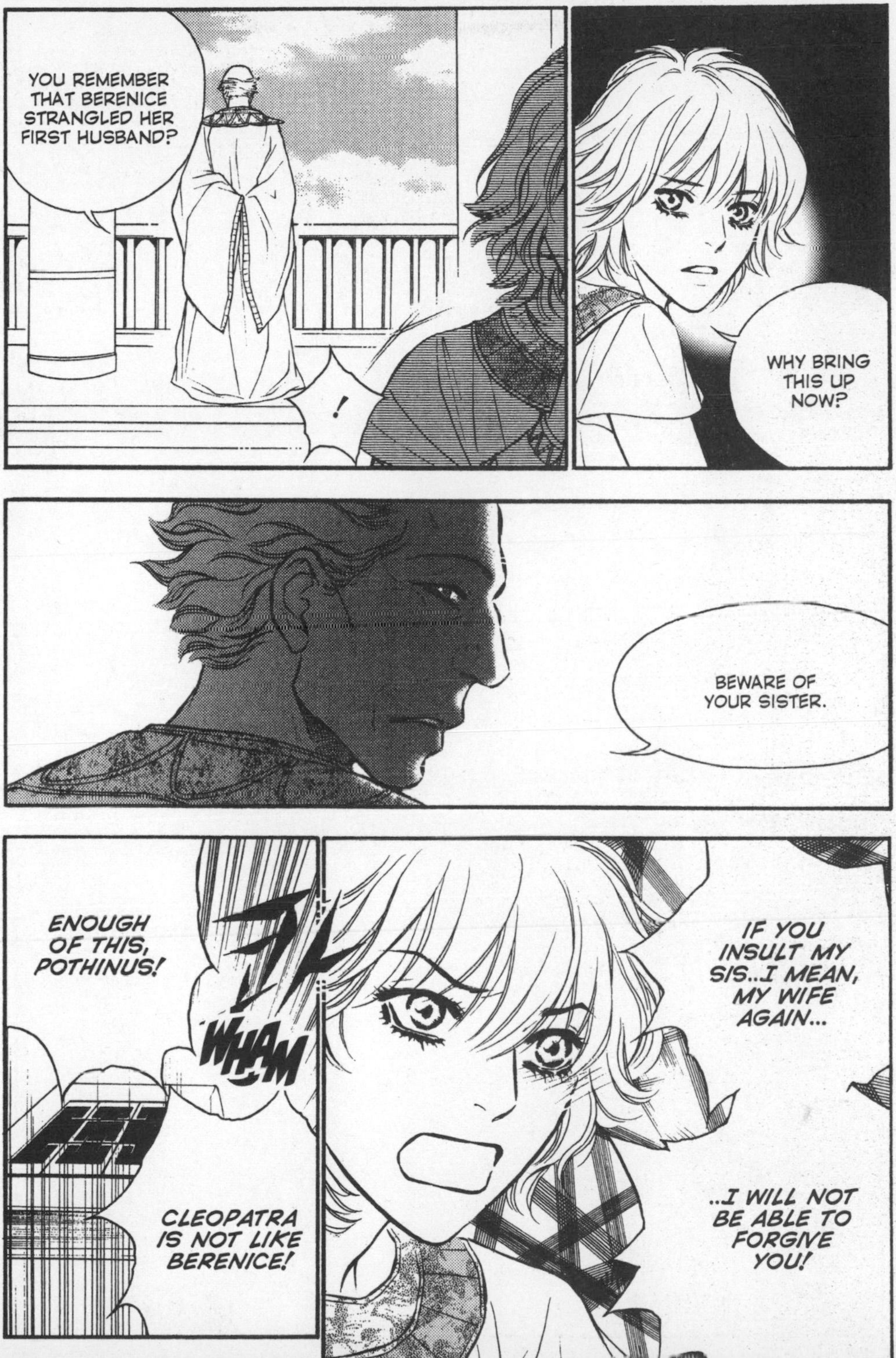
YOU REMEMBER THAT BERENICE STRANGLED HER FIRST HUSBAND?
!
WHY BRING THIS UP NOW?
BEWARE OF YOUR SISTER.
ENOUGH OF THIS, POTHINUS!
WHAM
CLEOPATRA IS NOT LIKE BERENICE!
IF YOU INSULT MY SIS...I MEAN, MY WIFE AGAIN...
...I WILL NOT BE ABLE TO FORGIVE YOU!

I SAW IT WITH MY OWN EYES.

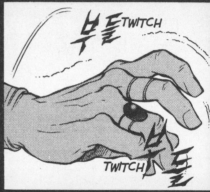

TWITCH

TWITCH

UNHH!

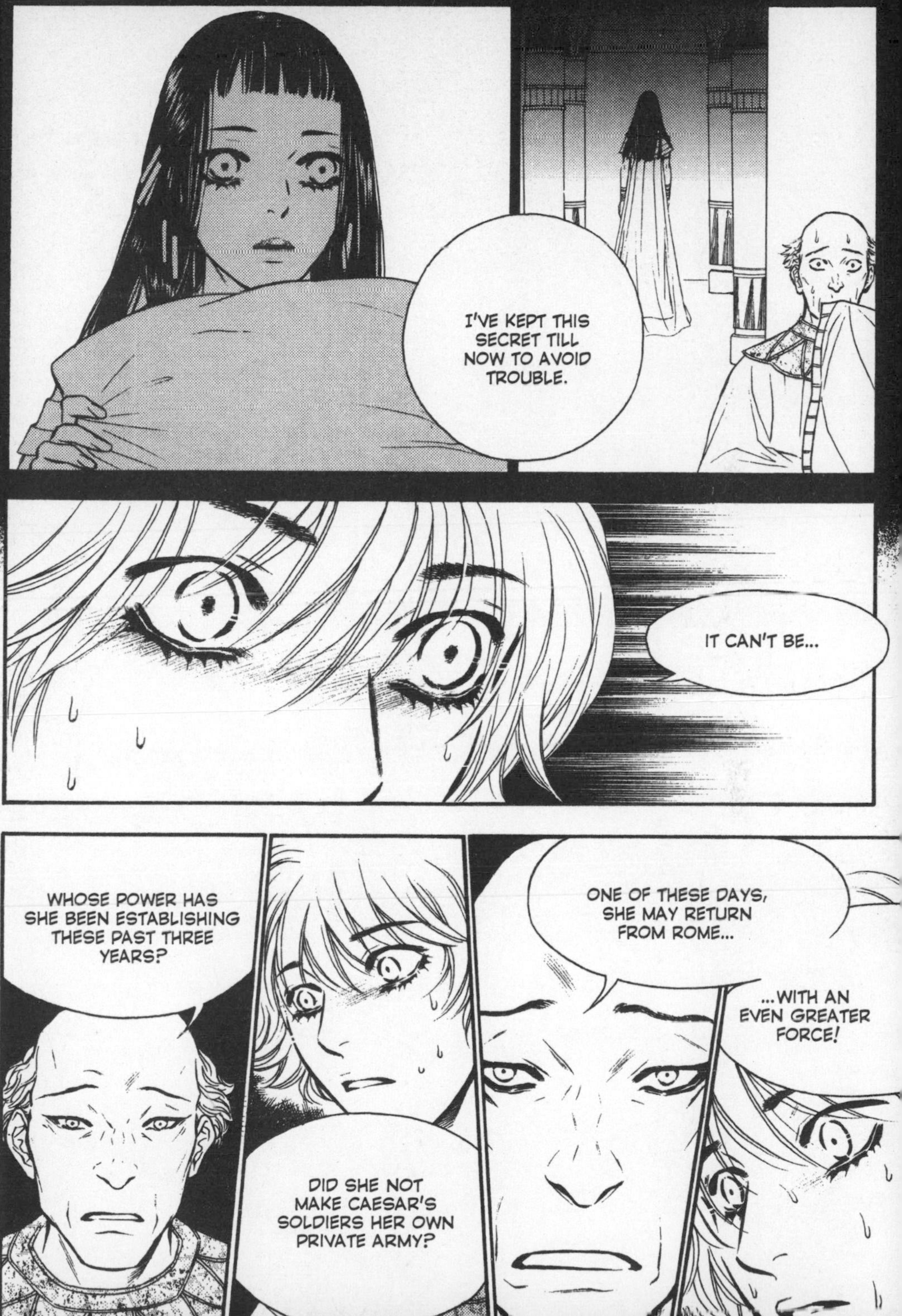

I'VE KEPT THIS SECRET TILL NOW TO AVOID TROUBLE.
IT CAN'T BE...
WHOSE POWER HAS SHE BEEN ESTABLISHING THESE PAST THREE YEARS?
DID SHE NOT MAKE CAESAR'S SOLDIERS HER OWN PRIVATE ARMY?
ONE OF THESE DAYS, SHE MAY RETURN FROM ROME...
...WITH AN EVEN GREATER FORCE!

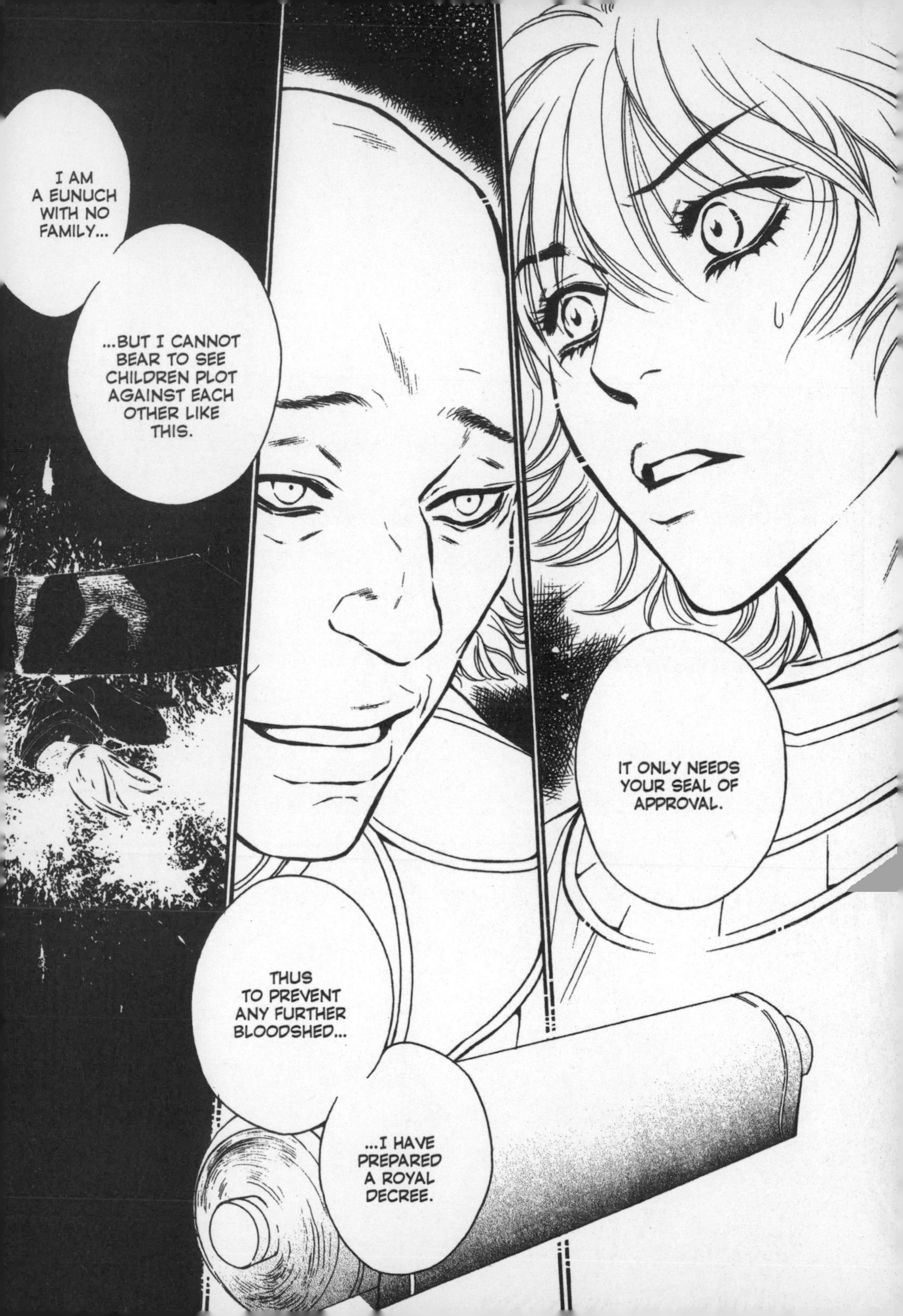
I AM A EUNUCH WITH NO FAMILY...
...BUT I CANNOT BEAR TO SEE CHILDREN PLOT AGAINST EACH OTHER LIKE THIS.
IT ONLY NEEDS YOUR SEAL OF APPROVAL.
THUS TO PREVENT ANY FURTHER BLOODSHED...
...I HAVE PREPARED A ROYAL DECREE.

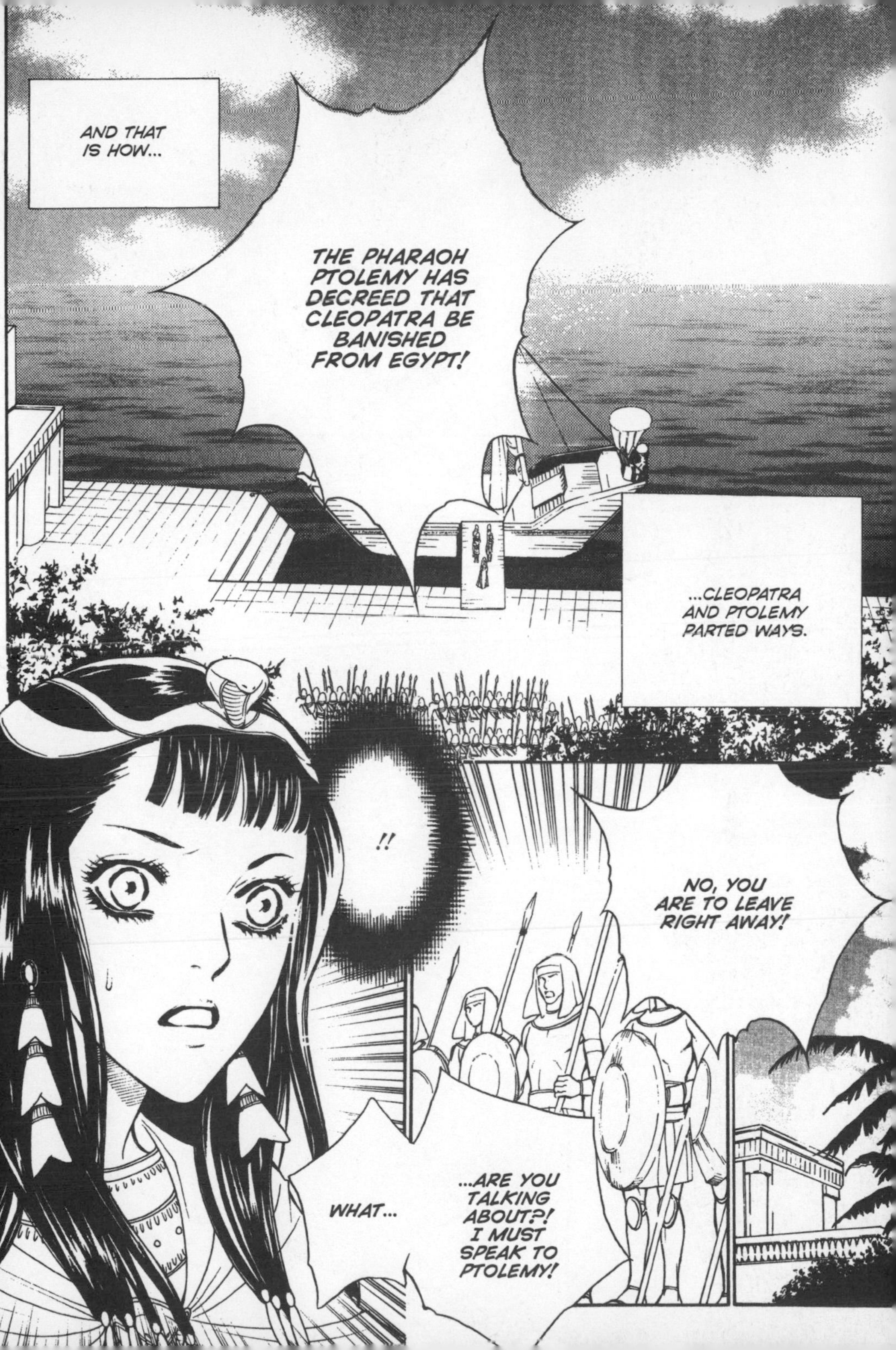
AND THAT IS HOW...
THE PHARAOH PTOLEMY HAS DECREED THAT CLEOPATRA BE BANISHED FROM EGYPT!
...CLEOPATRA AND PTOLEMY PARTED WAYS.
!!
NO, YOU ARE TO LEAVE RIGHT AWAY!
WHAT...
...ARE YOU TALKING ABOUT?! I MUST SPEAK TO PTOLEMY!

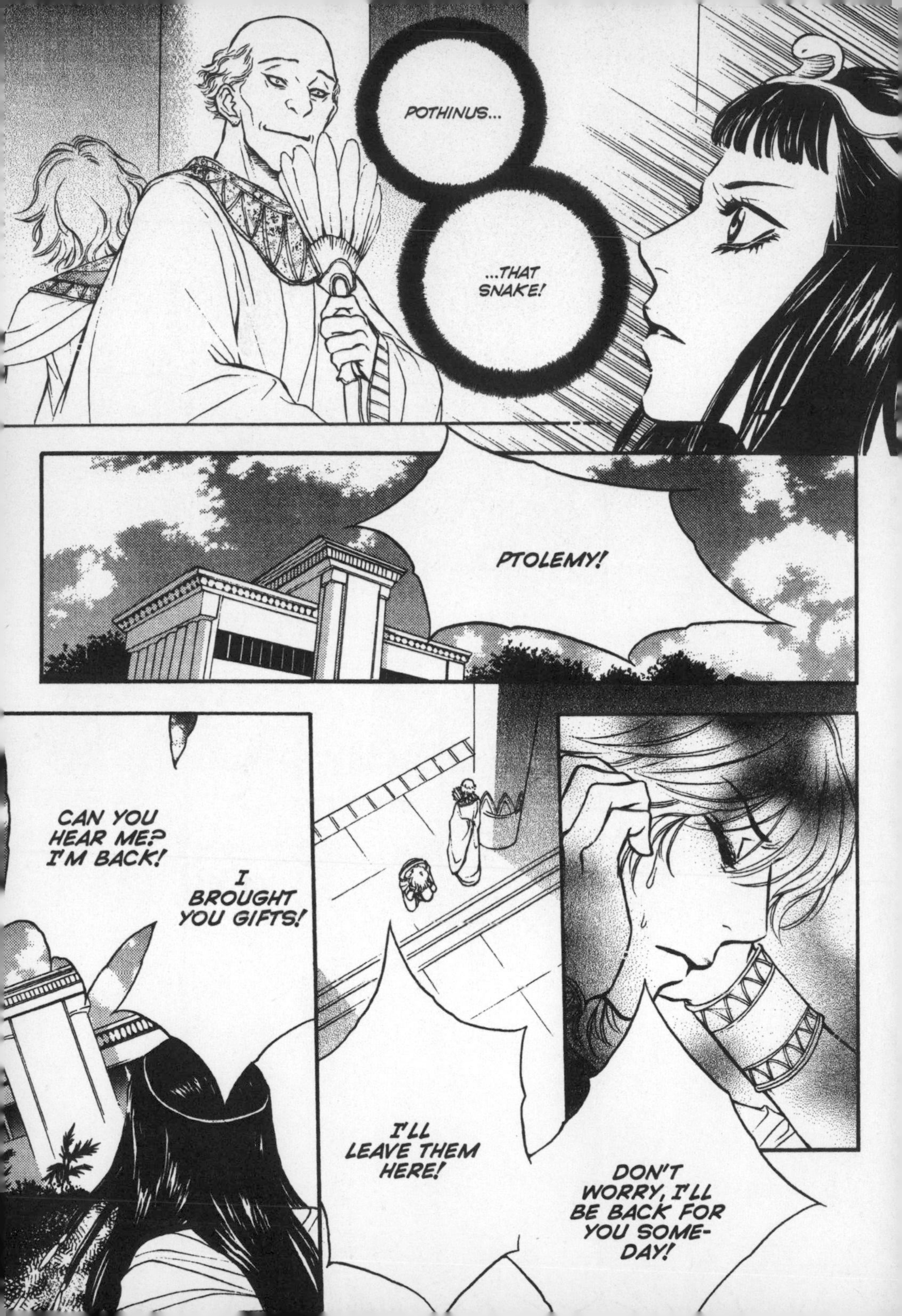
POTHINUS...
...THAT SNAKE!
PTOLEMY!
CAN YOU HEAR ME? I'M BACK!
I BROUGHT YOU GIFTS!
I'LL LEAVE THEM HERE!
DON'T WORRY, I'LL BE BACK FOR YOU SOME-DAY!

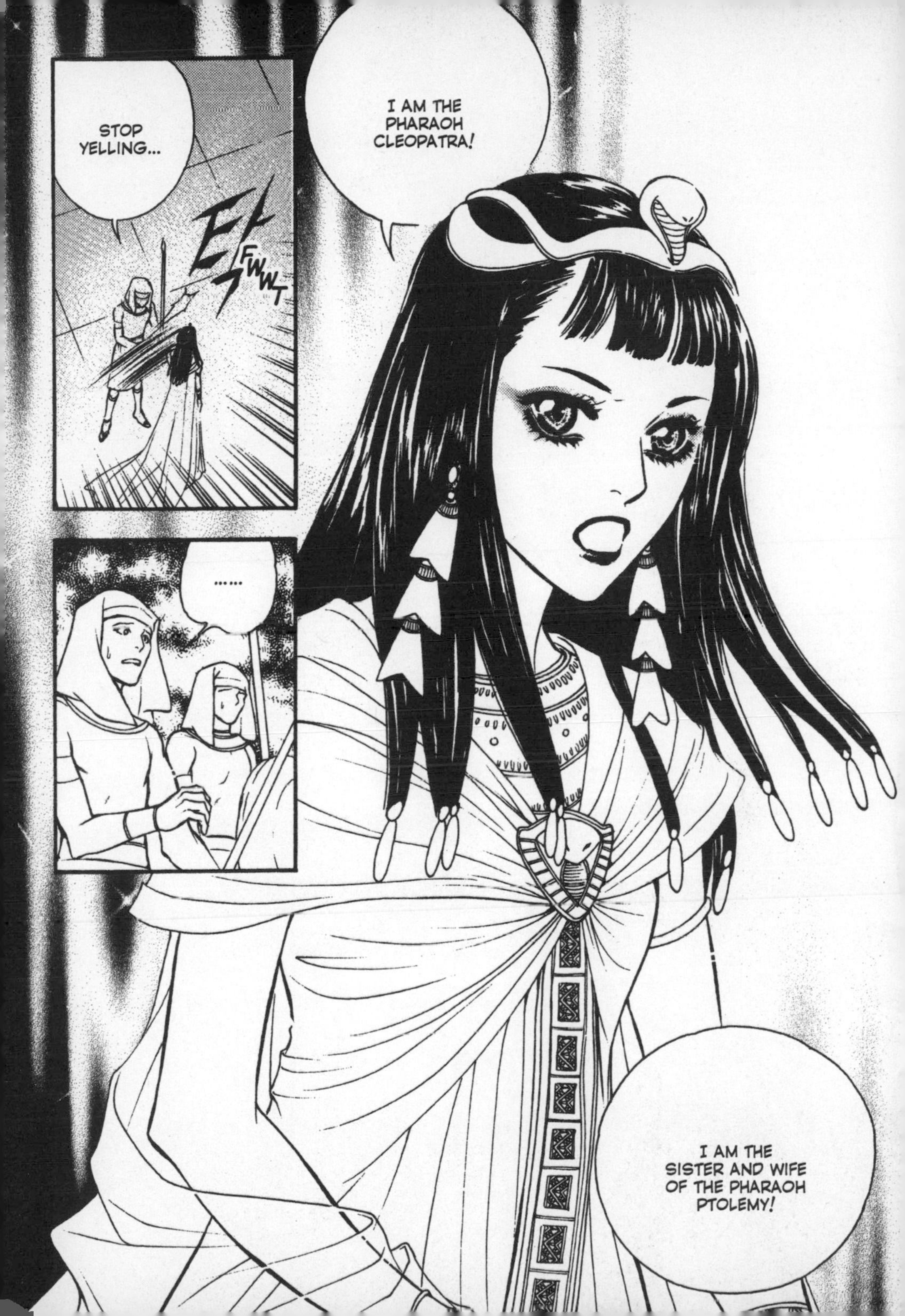
STOP YELLING...
FWWT
......
I AM THE PHARAOH CLEOPATRA!
I AM THE SISTER AND WIFE OF THE PHARAOH PTOLEMY!

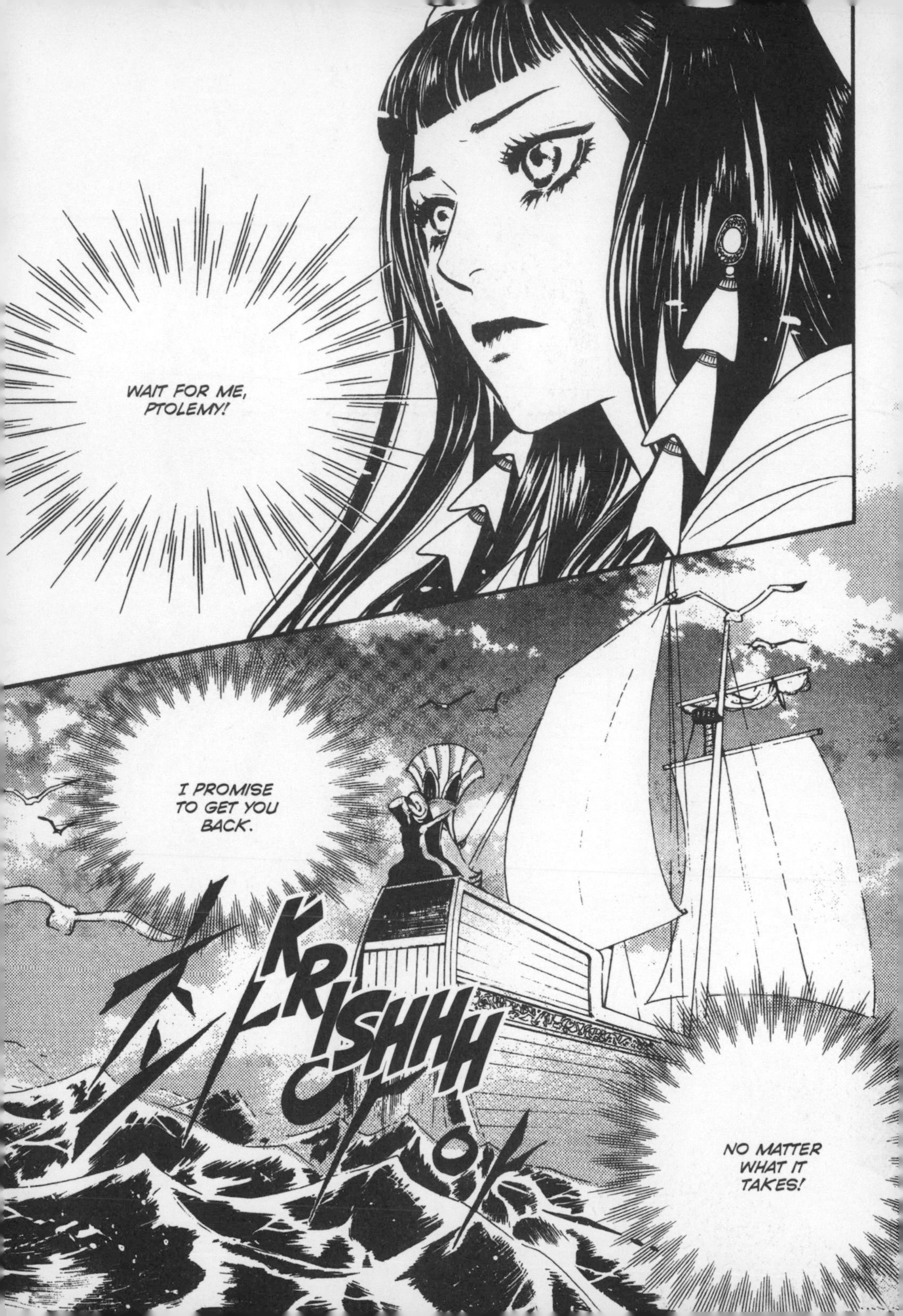
WAIT FOR ME, PTOLEMY!
I PROMISE TO GET YOU BACK.
KRISHHH
NO MATTER WHAT IT TAKES!

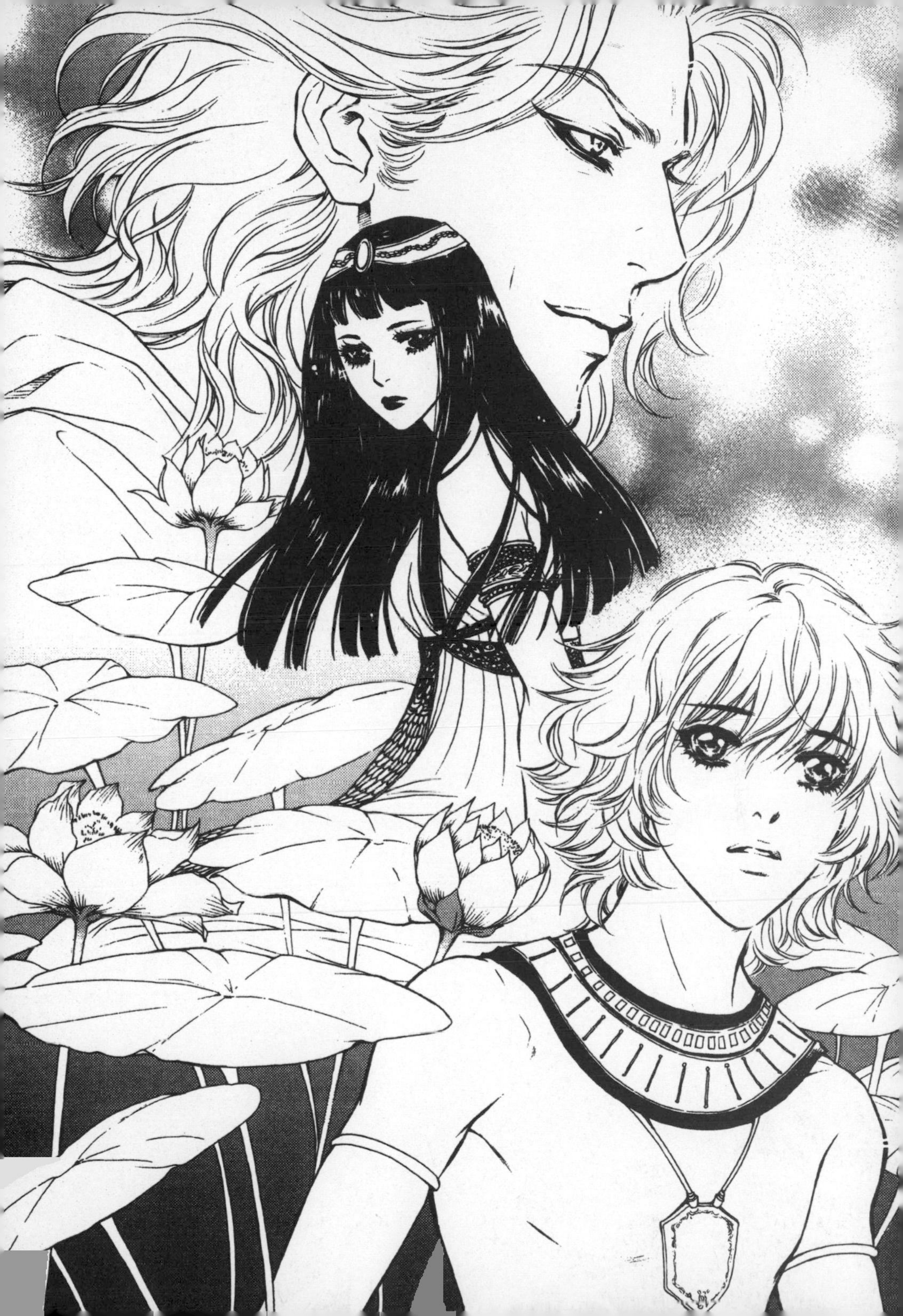

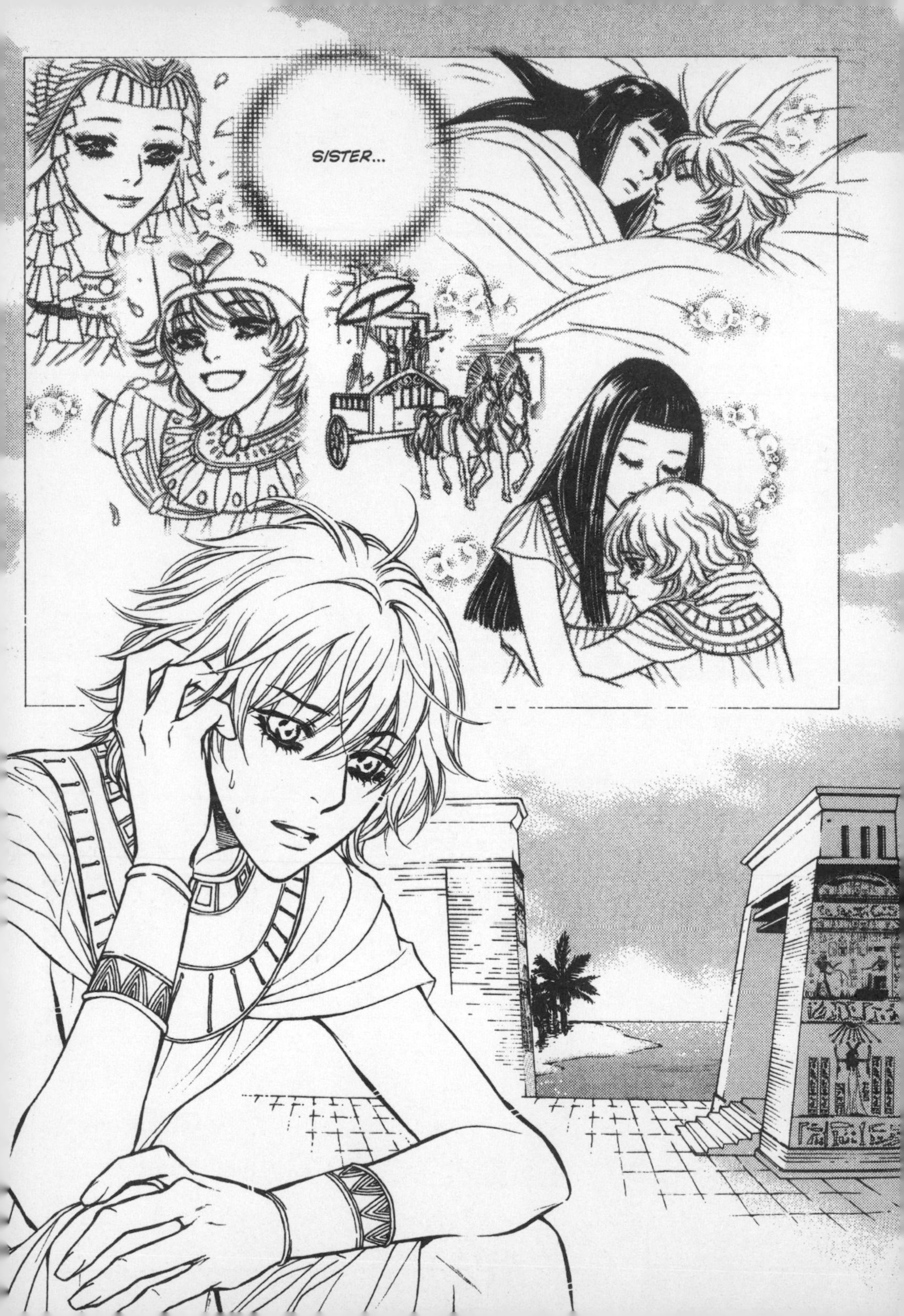
SISTER...

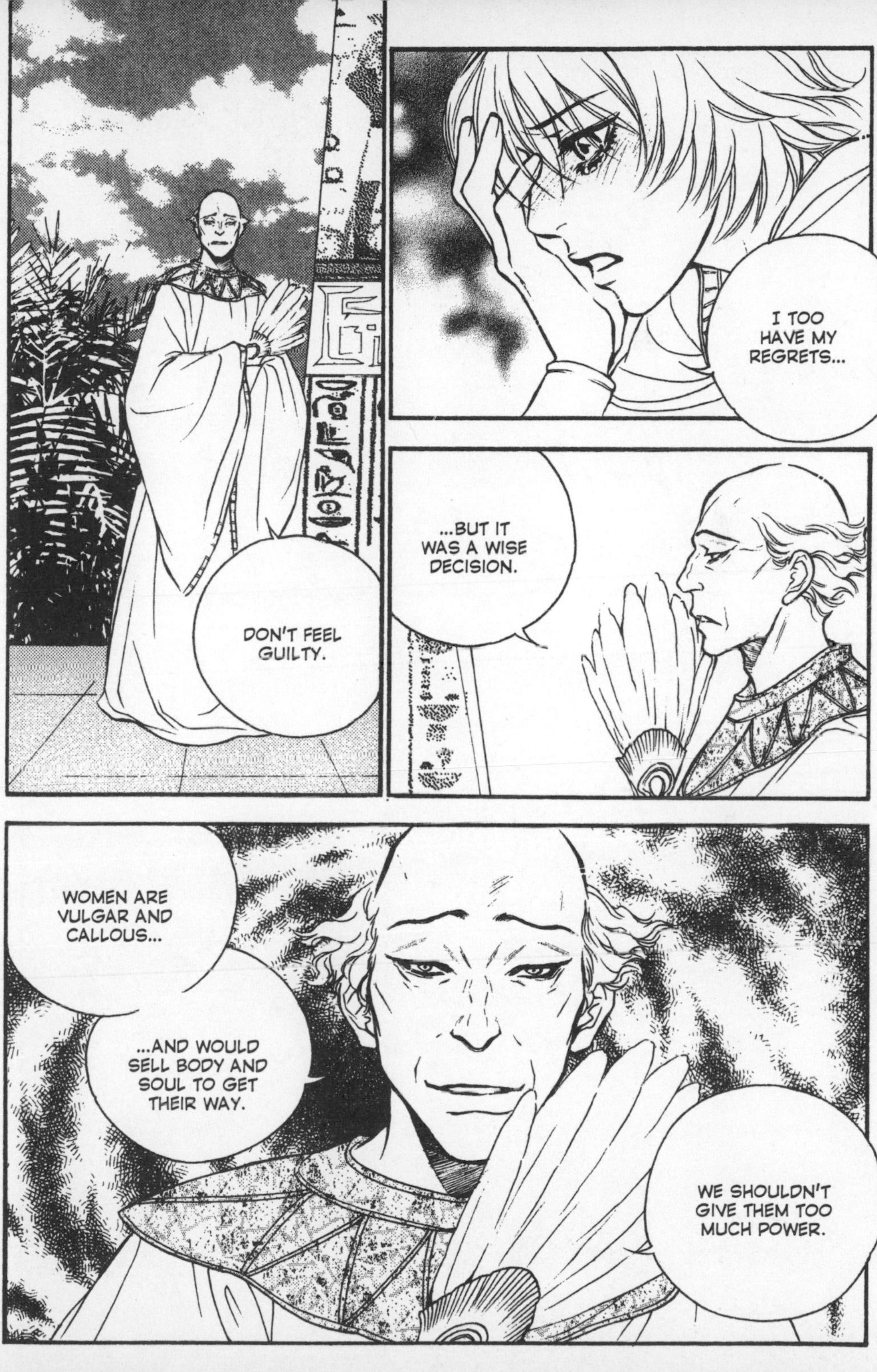
DON'T FEEL GUILTY.
I TOO HAVE MY REGRETS...
...BUT IT WAS A WISE DECISION.
WOMEN ARE VULGAR AND CALLOUS...
...AND WOULD SELL BODY AND SOUL TO GET THEIR WAY.
WE SHOULDN'T GIVE THEM TOO MUCH POWER.

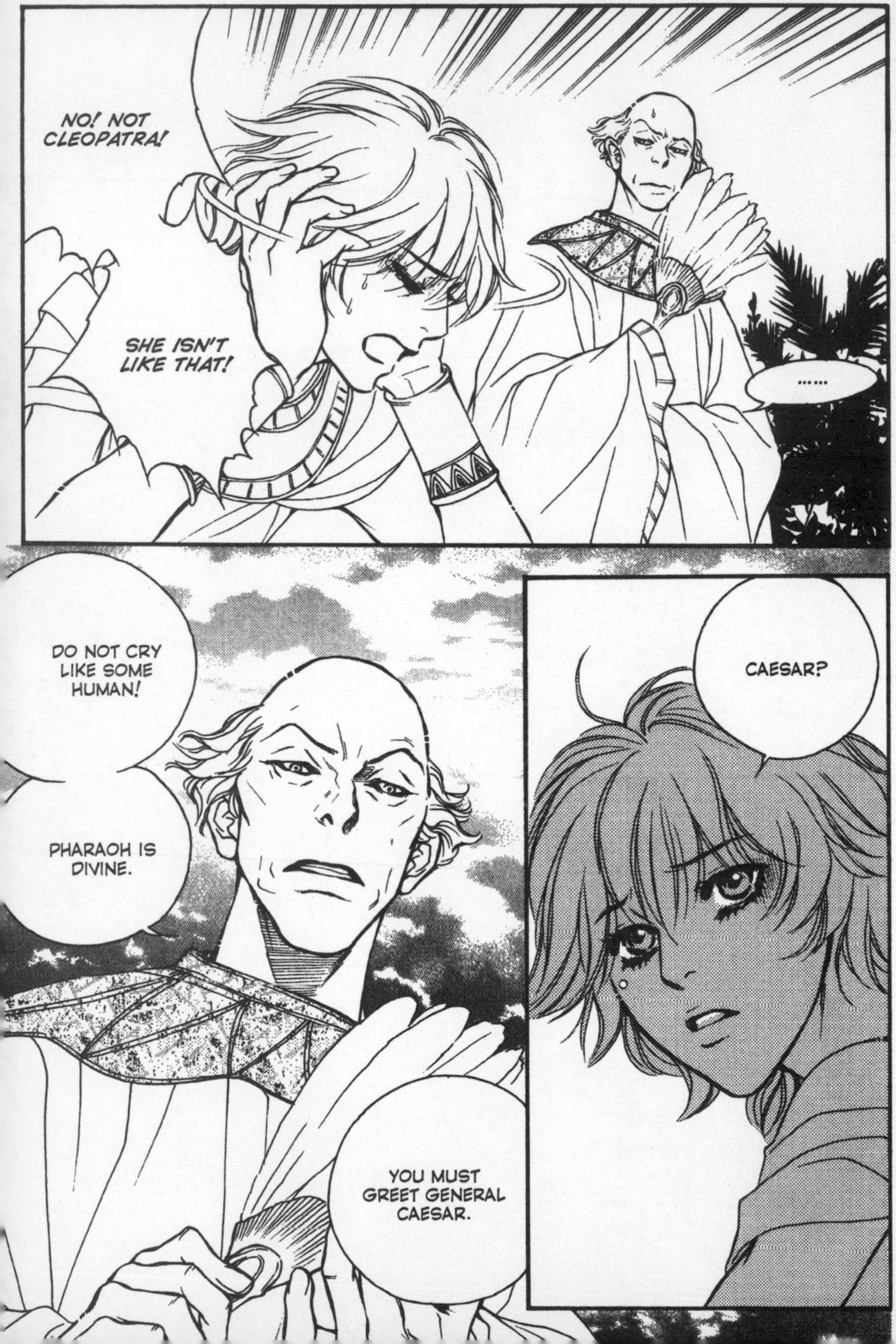
NO! NOT CLEOPATRA!
SHE ISN'T LIKE THAT!
......
DO NOT CRY LIKE SOME HUMAN!
PHARAOH IS DIVINE.
YOU MUST GREET GENERAL CAESAR.
CAESAR?

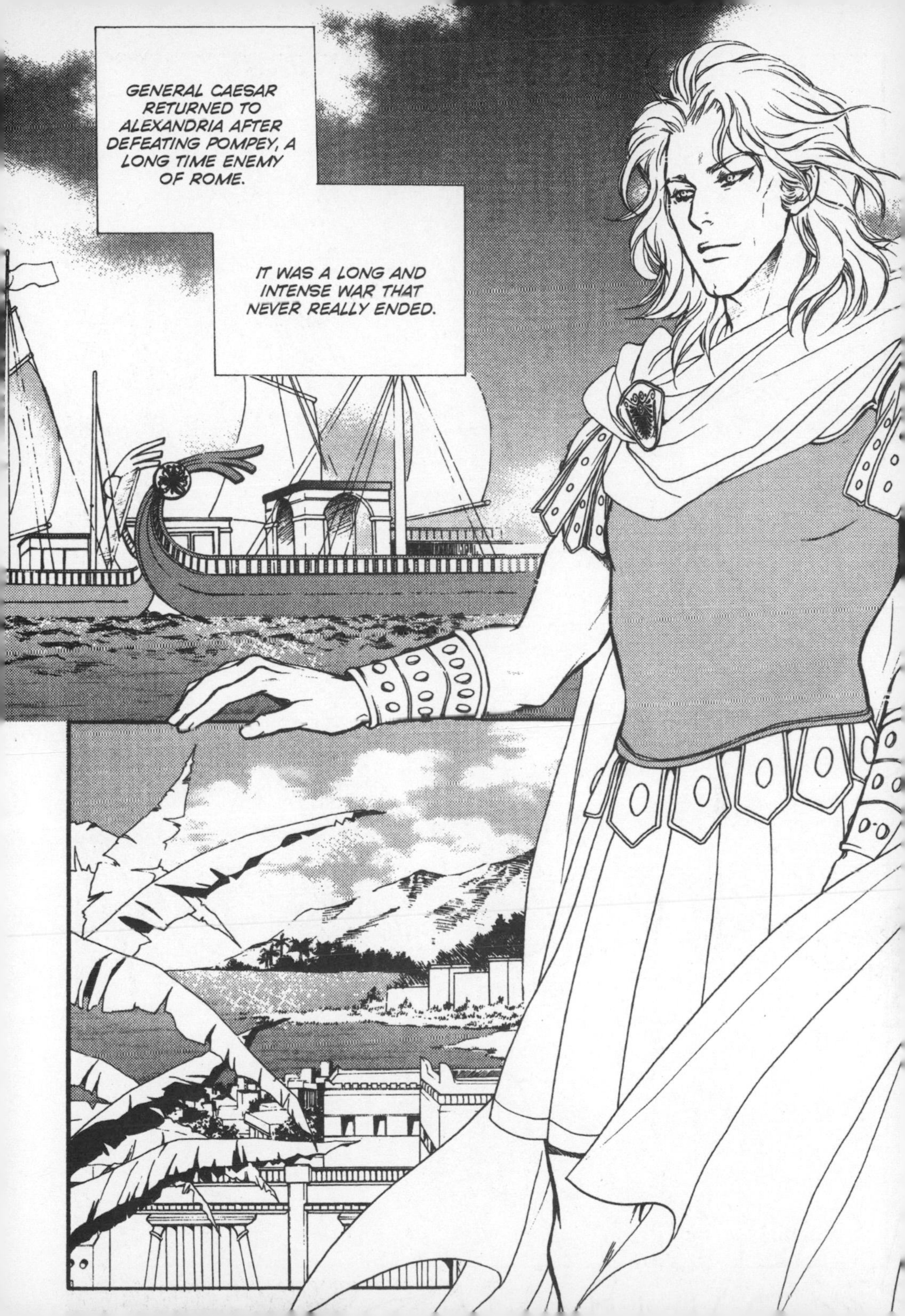
GENERAL CAESAR RETURNED TO ALEXANDRIA AFTER DEFEATING POMPEY, A LONG TIME ENEMY OF ROME.
IT WAS A LONG AND INTENSE WAR THAT NEVER REALLY ENDED.

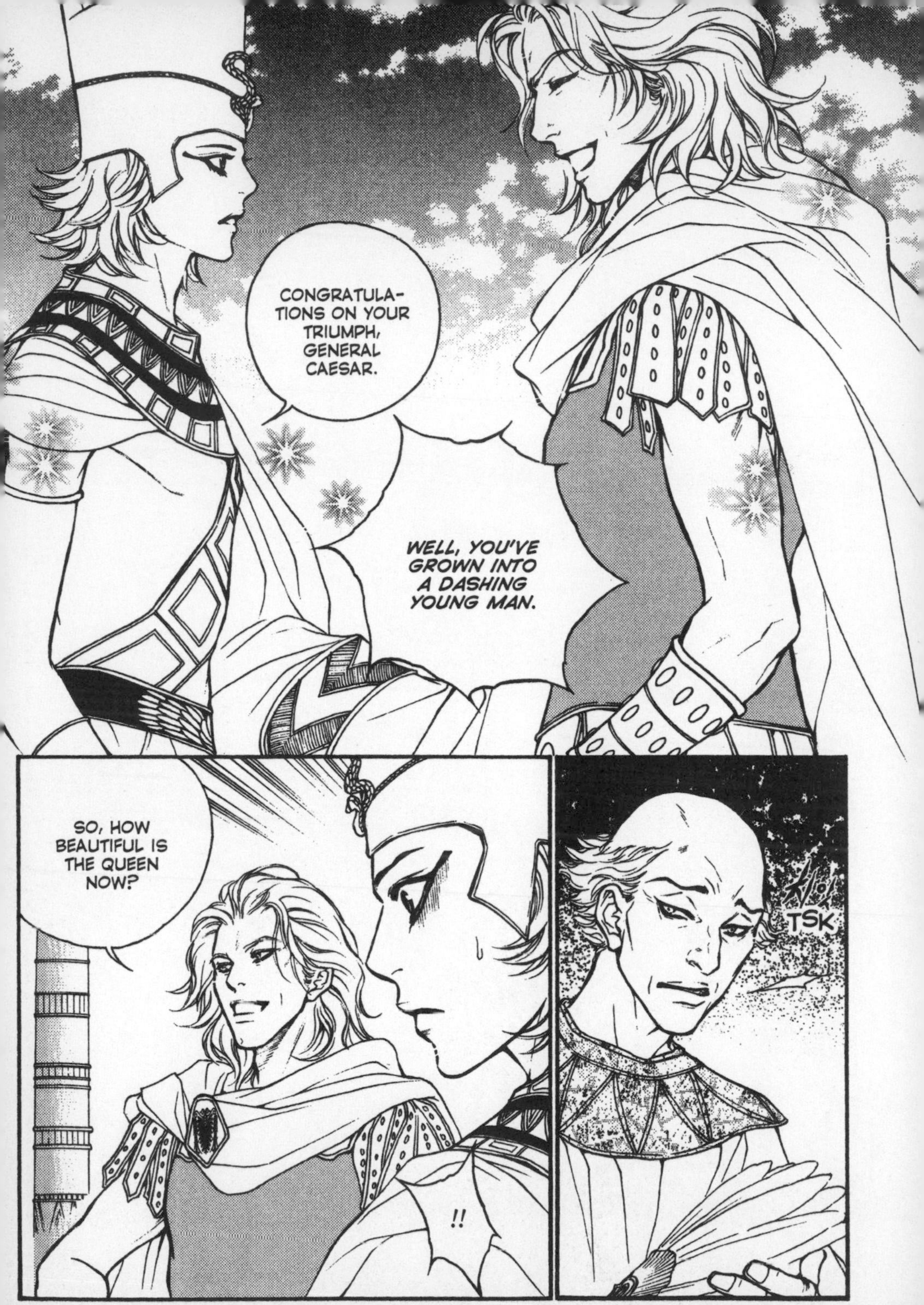
CONGRATULATIONS ON YOUR TRIUMPH, GENERAL CAESAR.
WELL, YOU'VE GROWN INTO A DASHING YOUNG MAN.
SO, HOW BEAUTIFUL IS THE QUEEN NOW?
!!
TSK

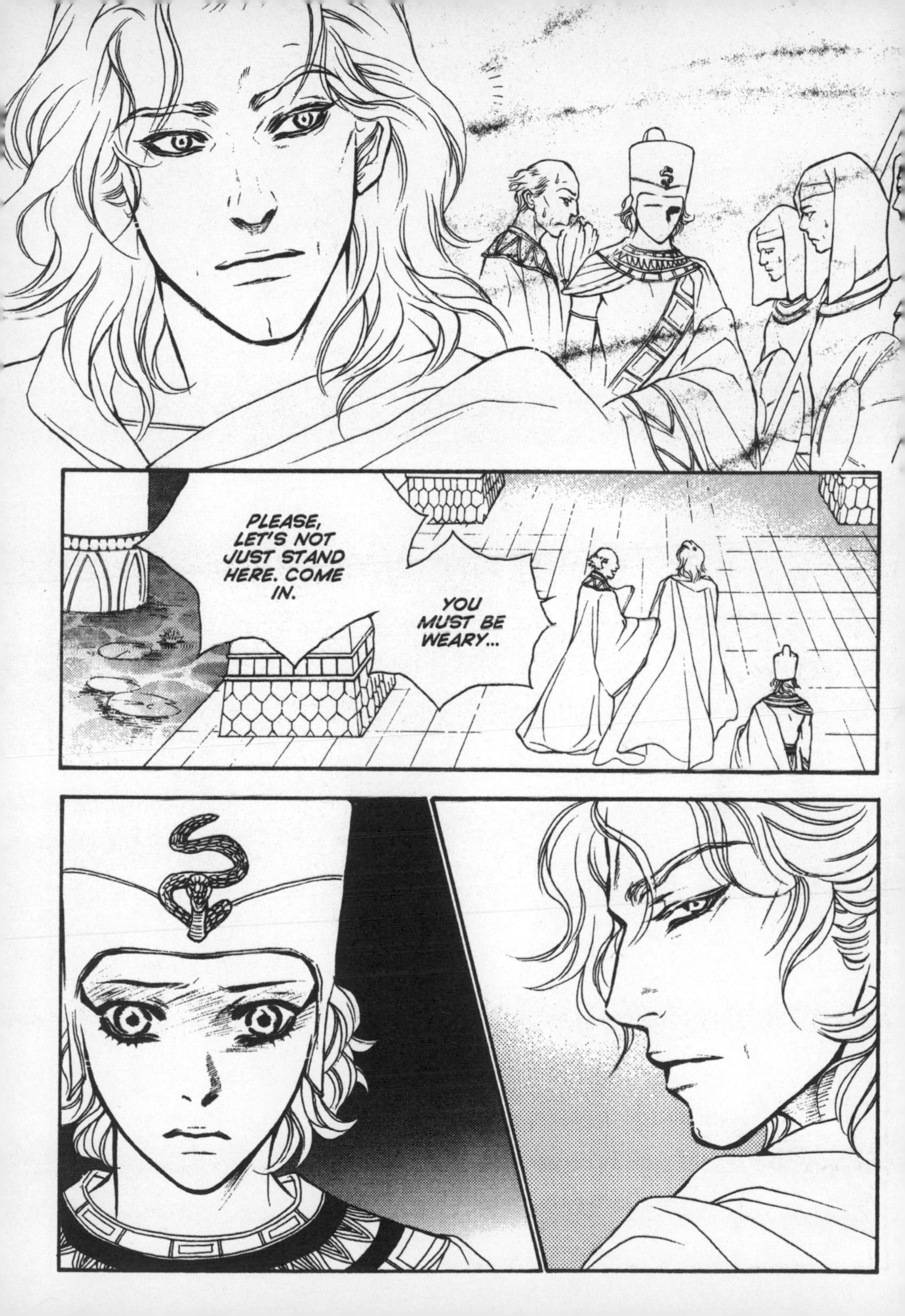
PLEASE, LET'S NOT JUST STAND HERE. COME IN.
YOU MUST BE WEARY...

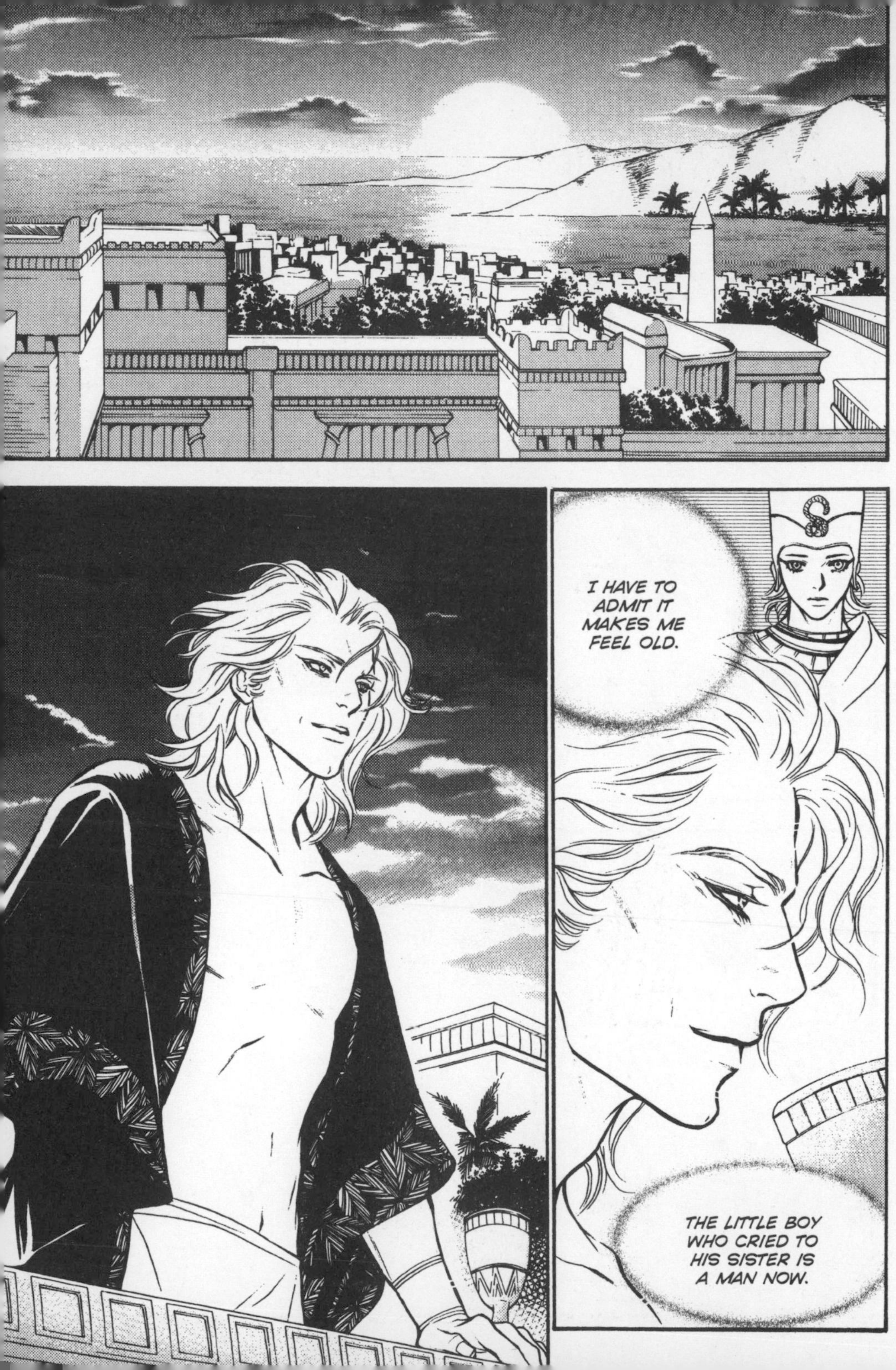
I HAVE TO ADMIT IT MAKES ME FEEL OLD.
THE LITTLE BOY WHO CRIED TO HIS SISTER IS A MAN NOW.

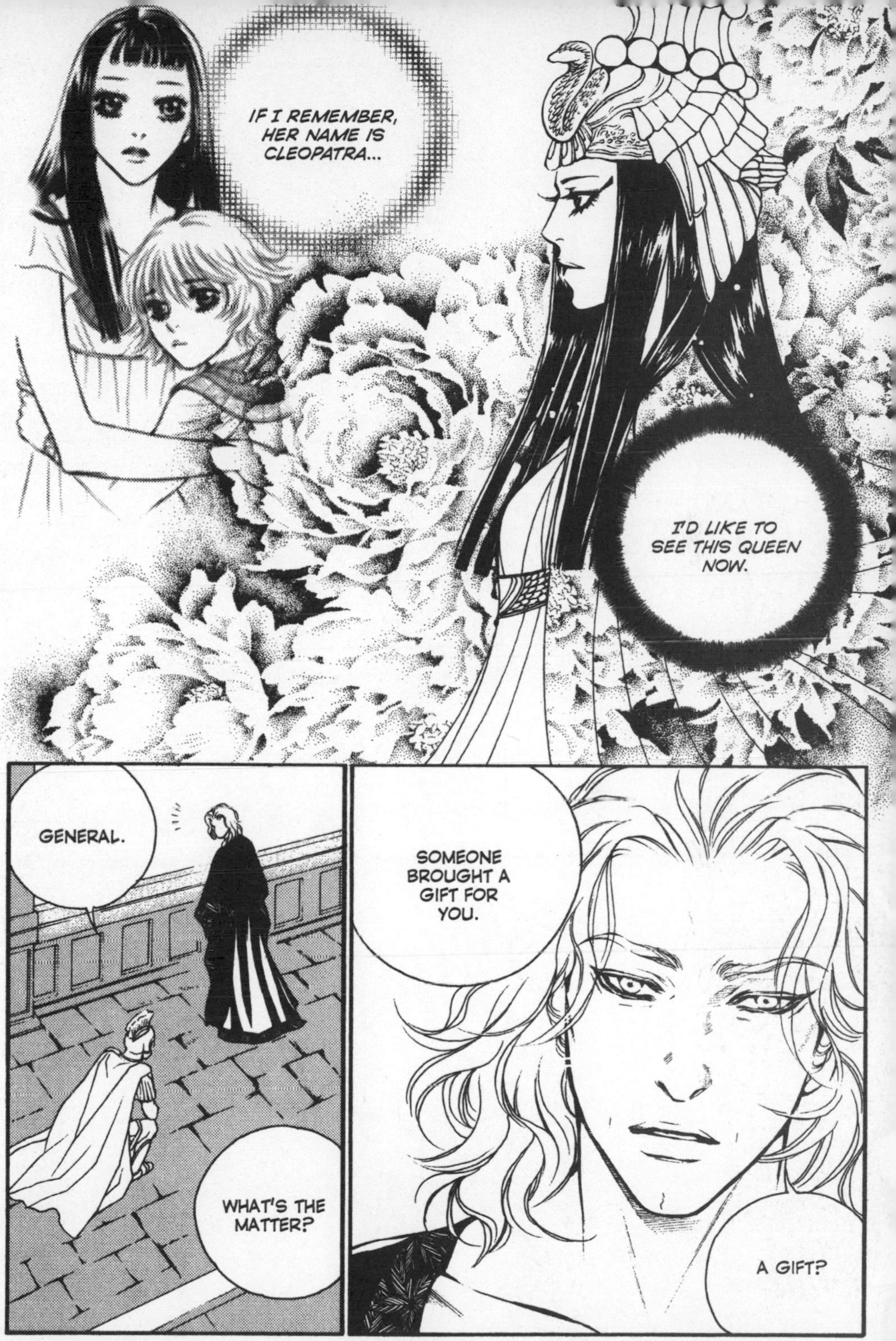
IF I REMEMBER, HER NAME IS CLEOPATRA...
I'D LIKE TO SEE THIS QUEEN NOW.
GENERAL.
WHAT'S THE MATTER?
SOMEONE BROUGHT A GIFT FOR YOU.
A GIFT?

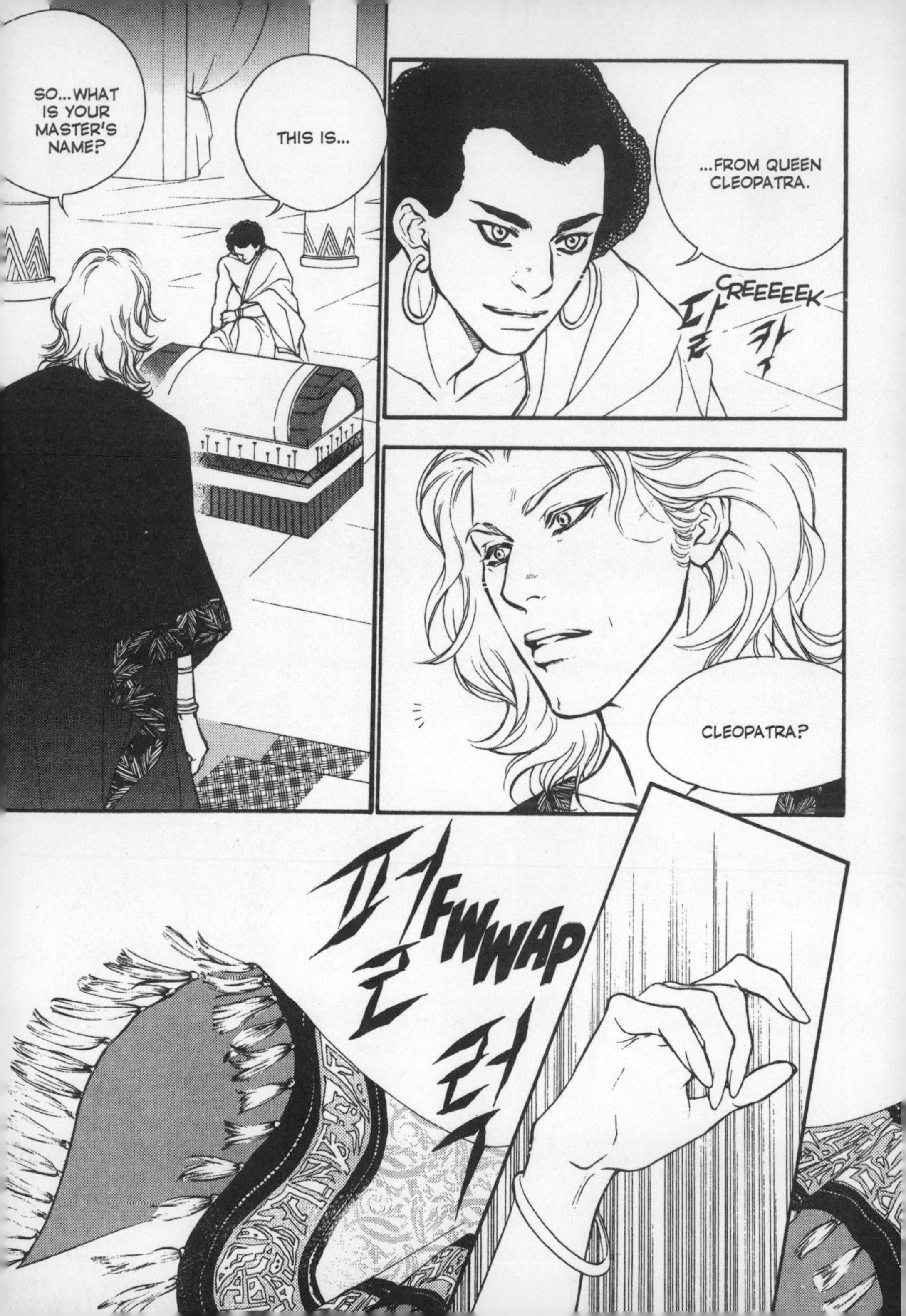
SO...WHAT IS YOUR MASTER'S NAME?
THIS IS...
...FROM QUEEN CLEOPATRA.
CREEEEEK
CLEOPATRA?
FWWAP

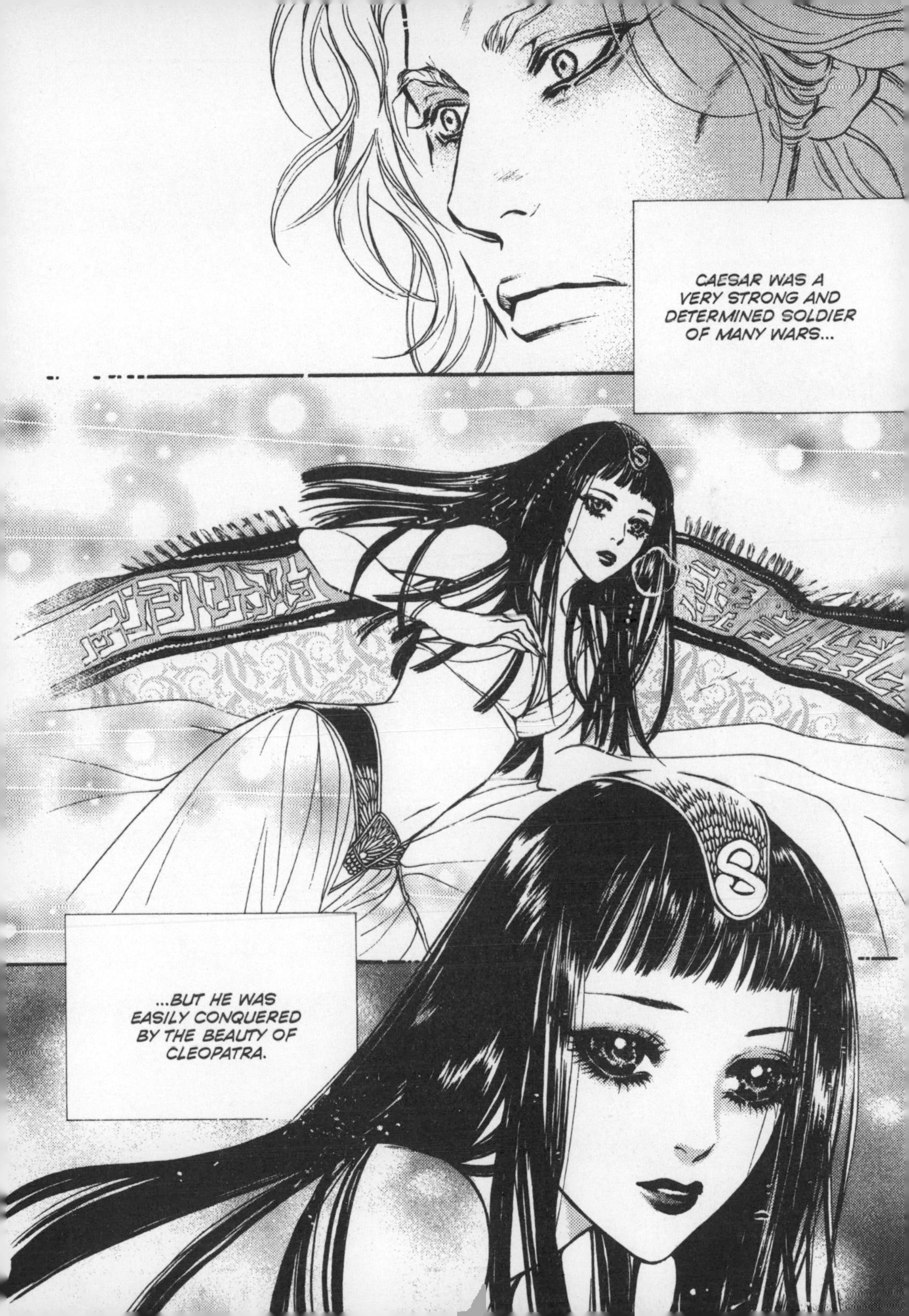
CAESAR WAS A VERY STRONG AND DETERMINED SOLDIER OF MANY WARS...
...BUT HE WAS EASILY CONQUERED BY THE BEAUTY OF CLEOPATRA.

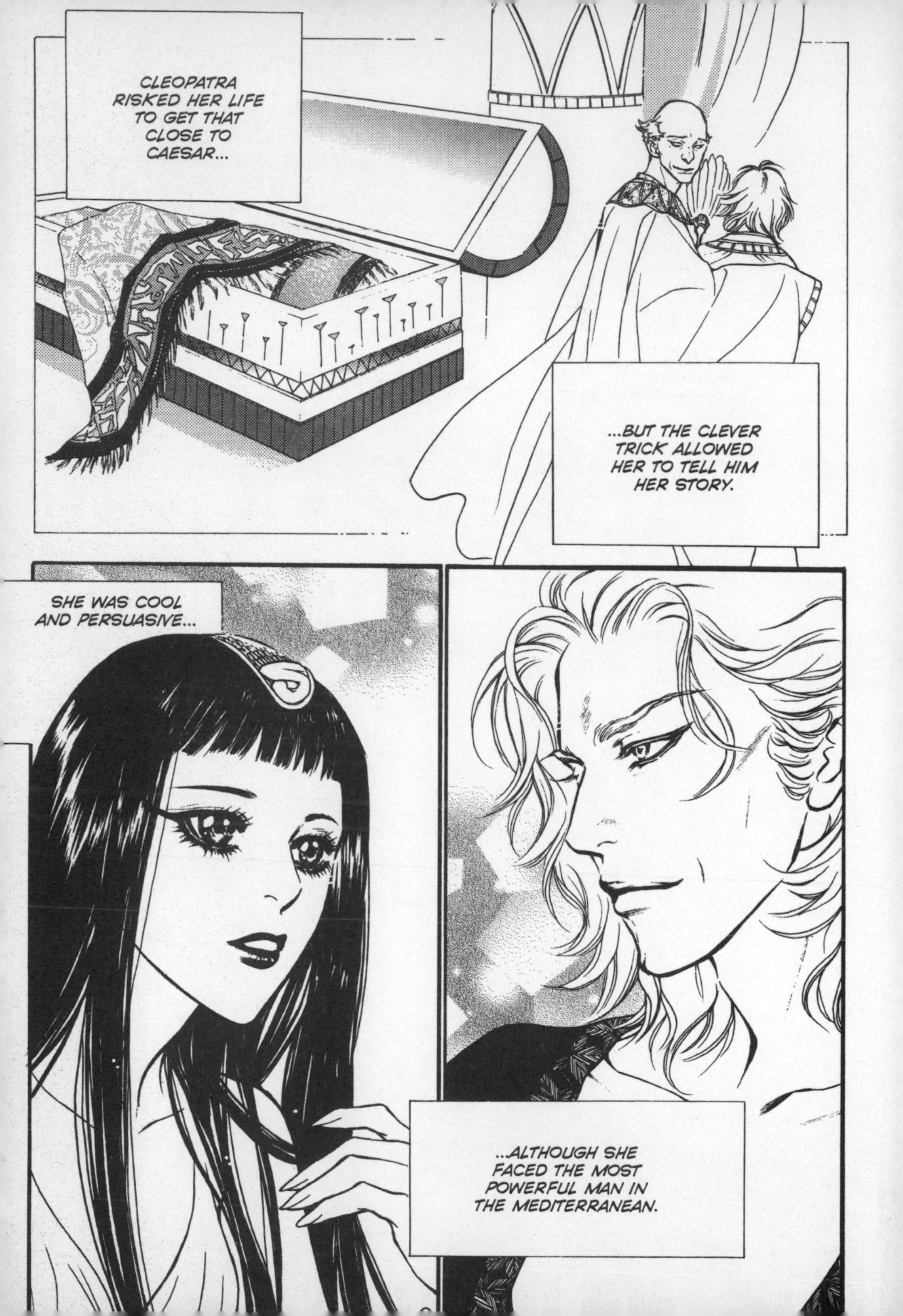
CLEOPATRA RISKED HER LIFE TO GET THAT CLOSE TO CAESAR...
...BUT THE CLEVER TRICK ALLOWED HER TO TELL HIM HER STORY.
SHE WAS COOL AND PERSUASIVE...
...ALTHOUGH SHE FACED THE MOST POWERFUL MAN IN THE MEDITERRANEAN.

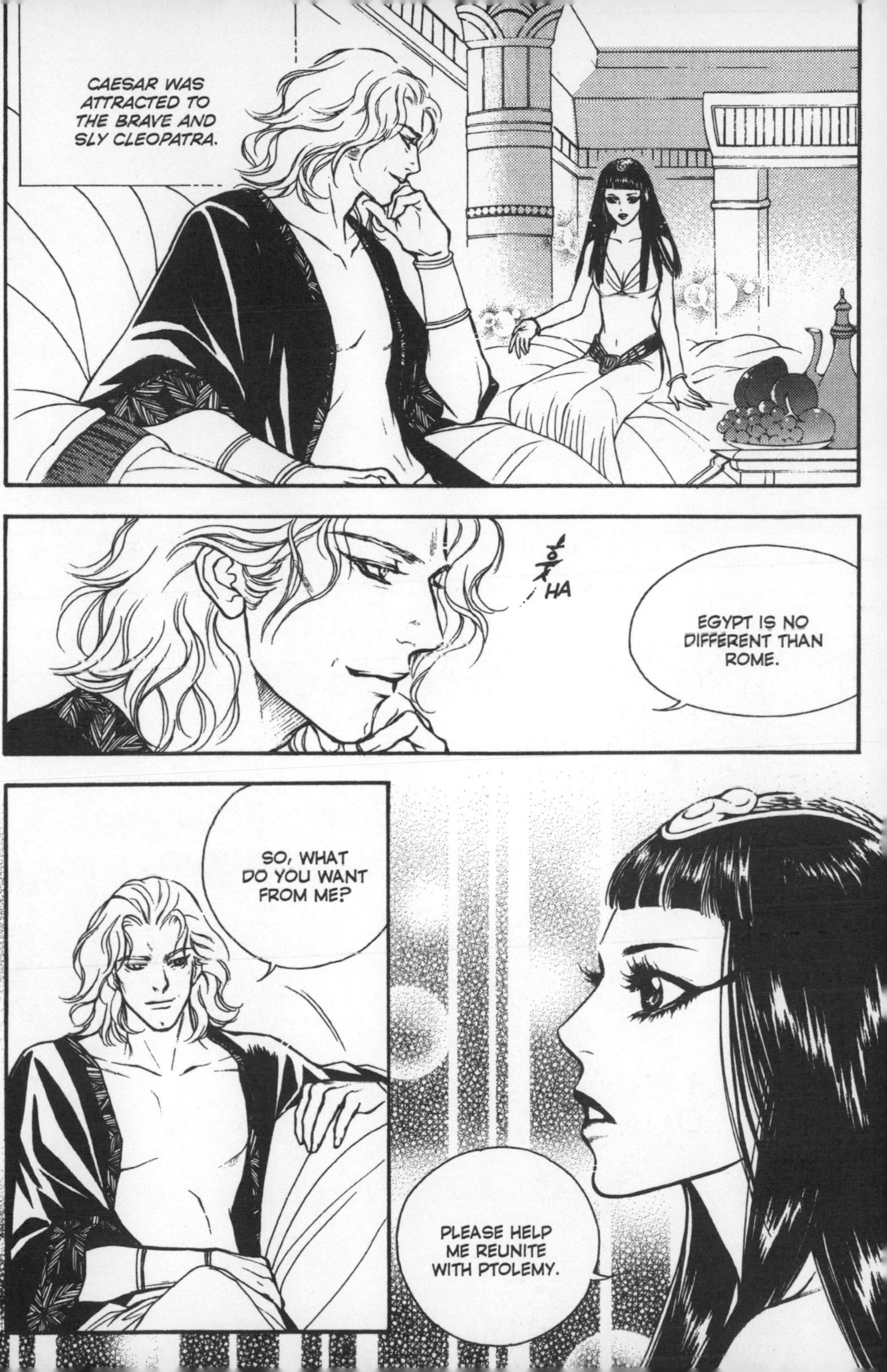
CAESAR WAS ATTRACTED TO THE BRAVE AND SLY CLEOPATRA.
훗 HA
EGYPT IS NO DIFFERENT THAN ROME.
SO, WHAT DO YOU WANT FROM ME?
PLEASE HELP ME REUNITE WITH PTOLEMY.

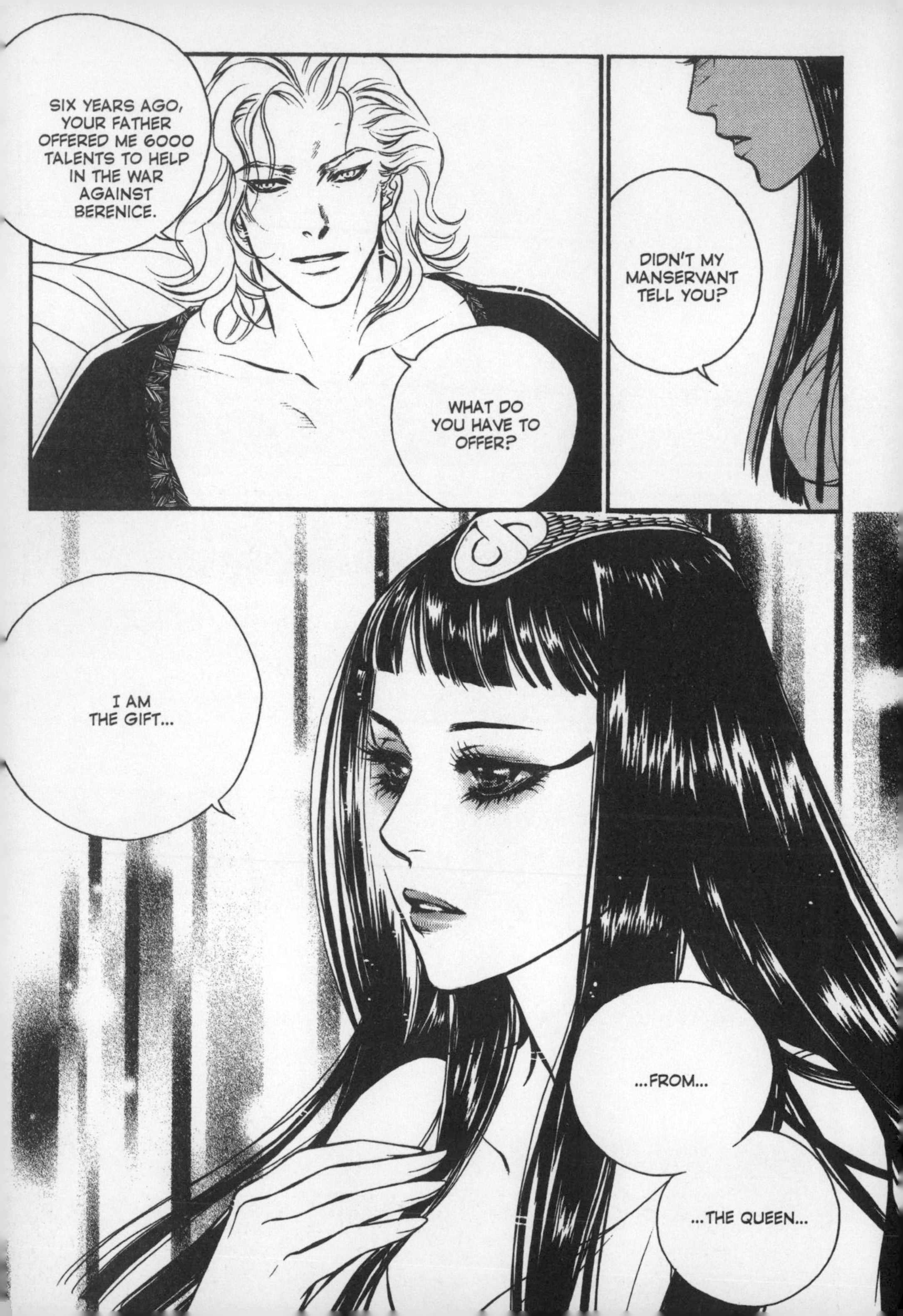
SIX YEARS AGO, YOUR FATHER OFFERED ME 6000 TALENTS TO HELP IN THE WAR AGAINST BERENICE.
WHAT DO YOU HAVE TO OFFER?
DIDN'T MY MANSERVANT TELL YOU?
I AM THE GIFT...
...FROM...
...THE QUEEN...

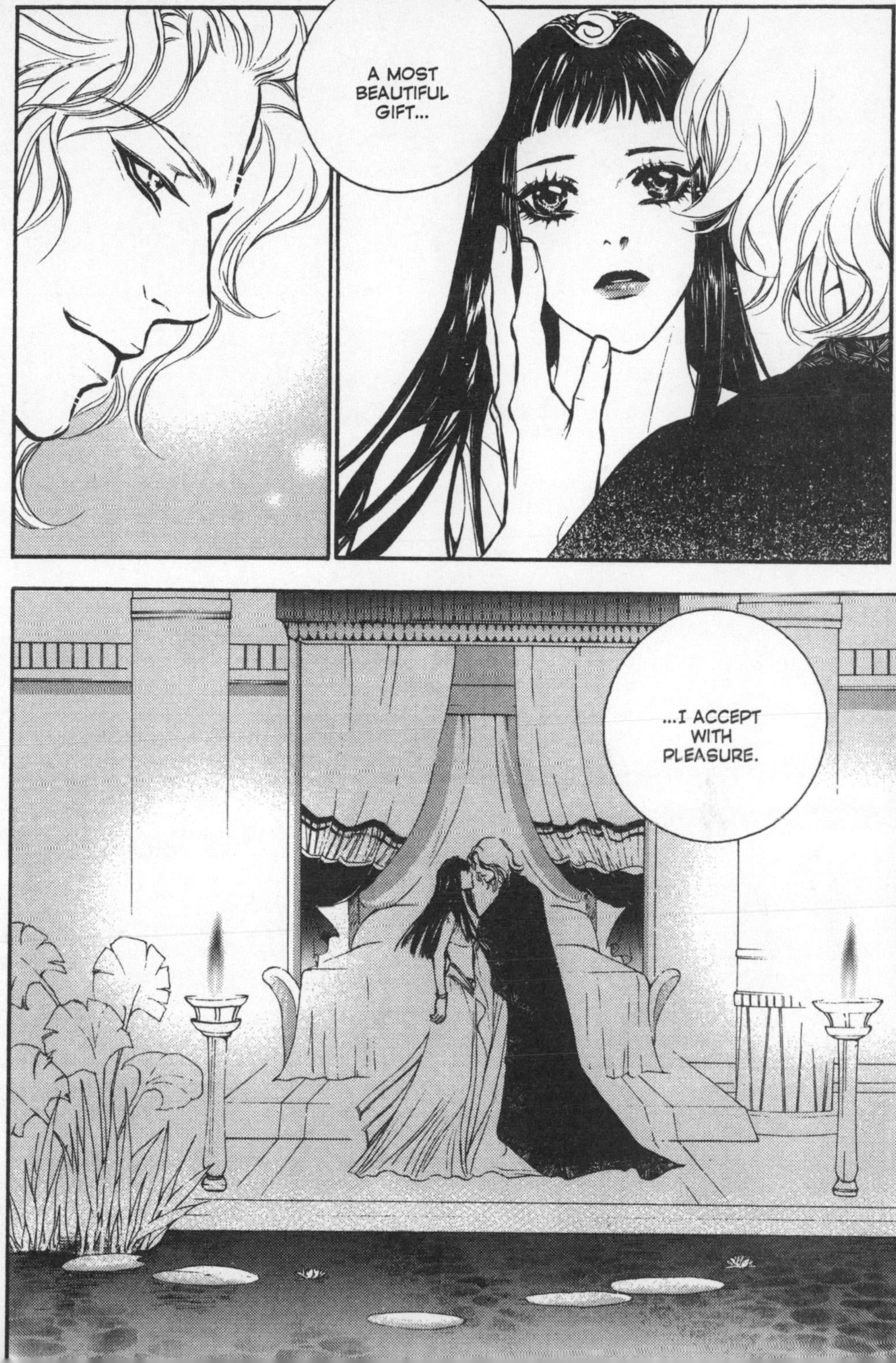
A MOST BEAUTIFUL GIFT...
...I ACCEPT WITH PLEASURE.

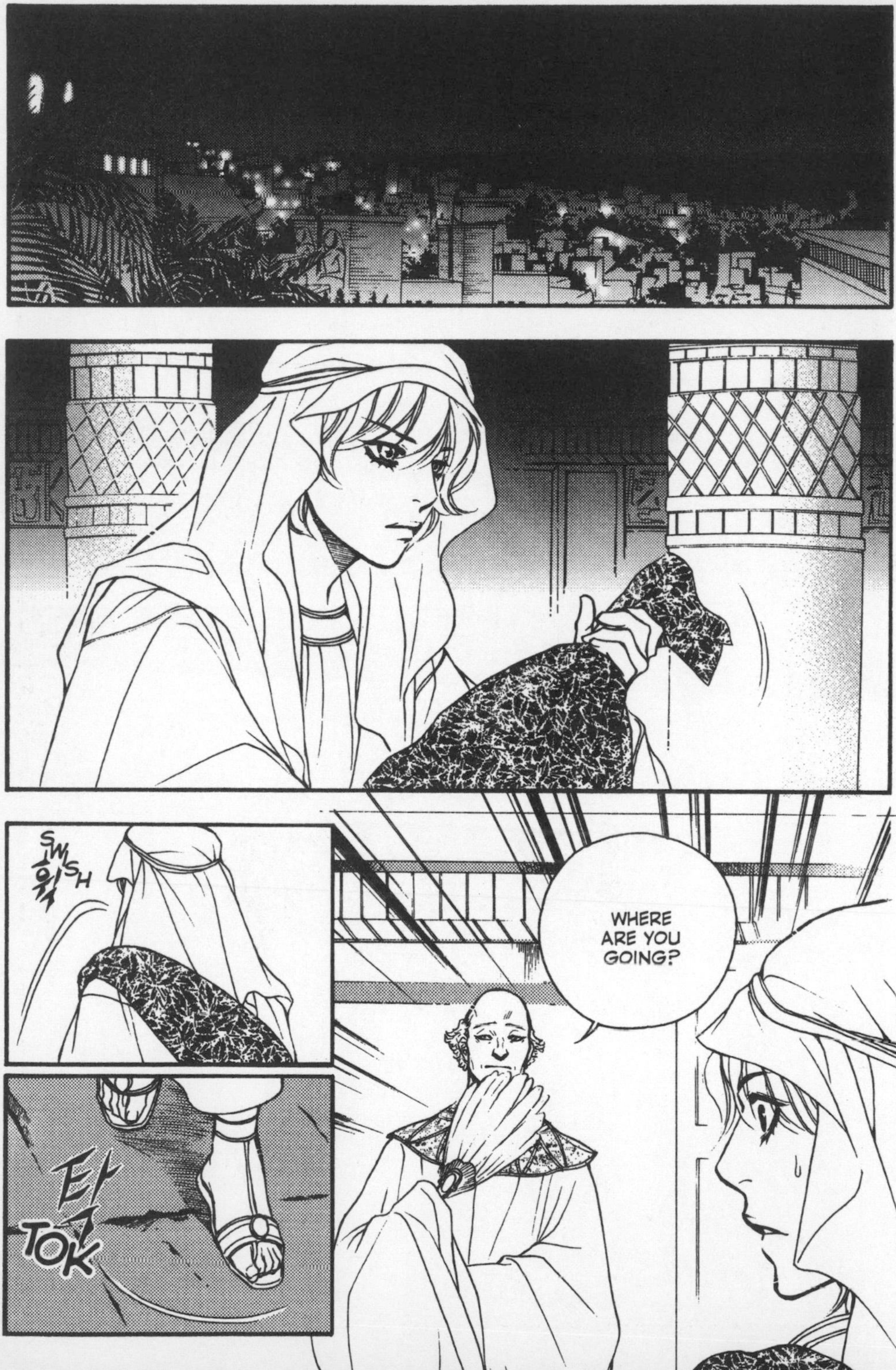
SWISH
TOK
WHERE ARE YOU GOING?

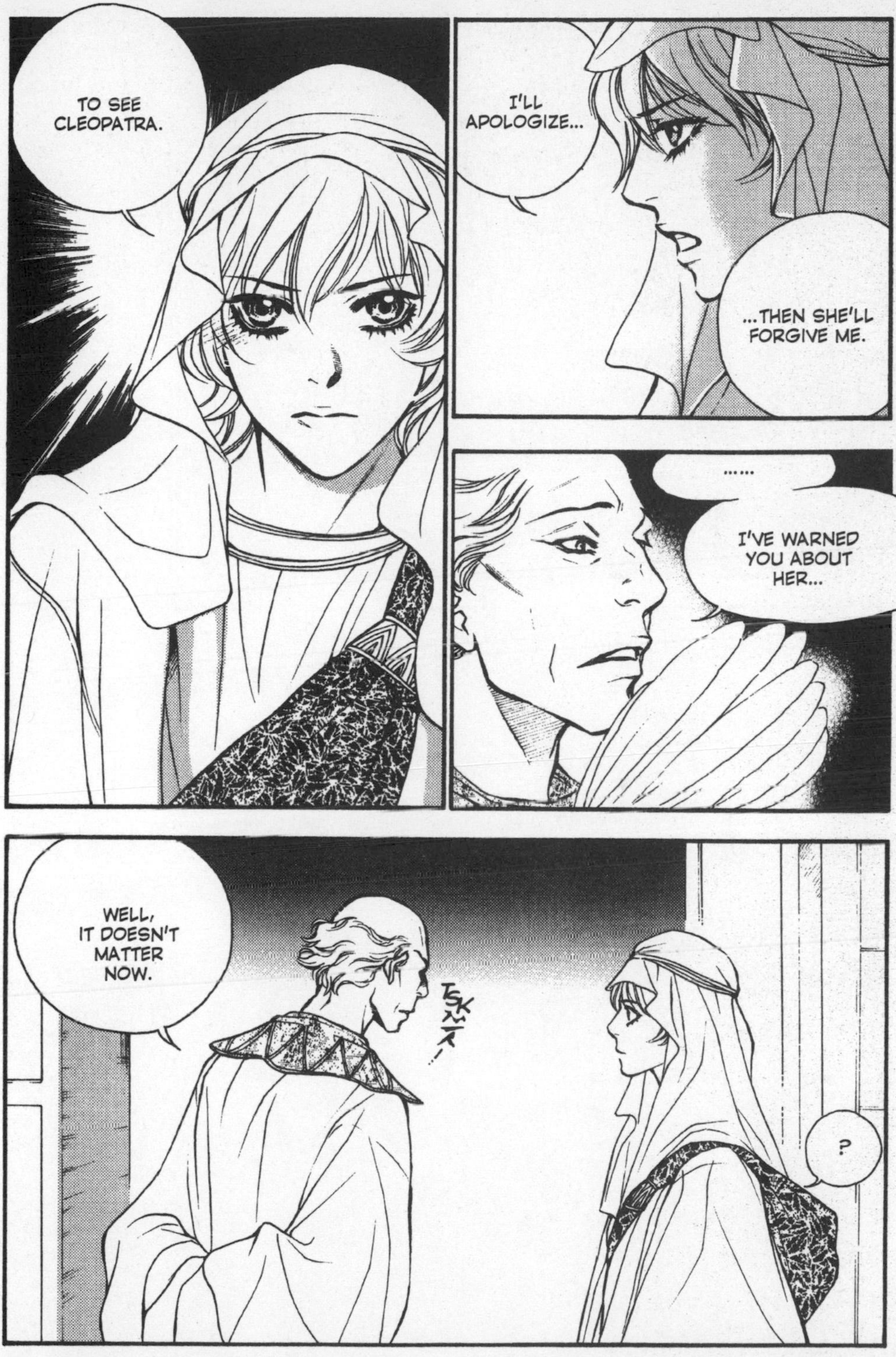
TO SEE CLEOPATRA.
I'LL APOLOGIZE...
...THEN SHE'LL FORGIVE ME.
......
I'VE WARNED YOU ABOUT HER...
WELL, IT DOESN'T MATTER NOW.
TSK
?

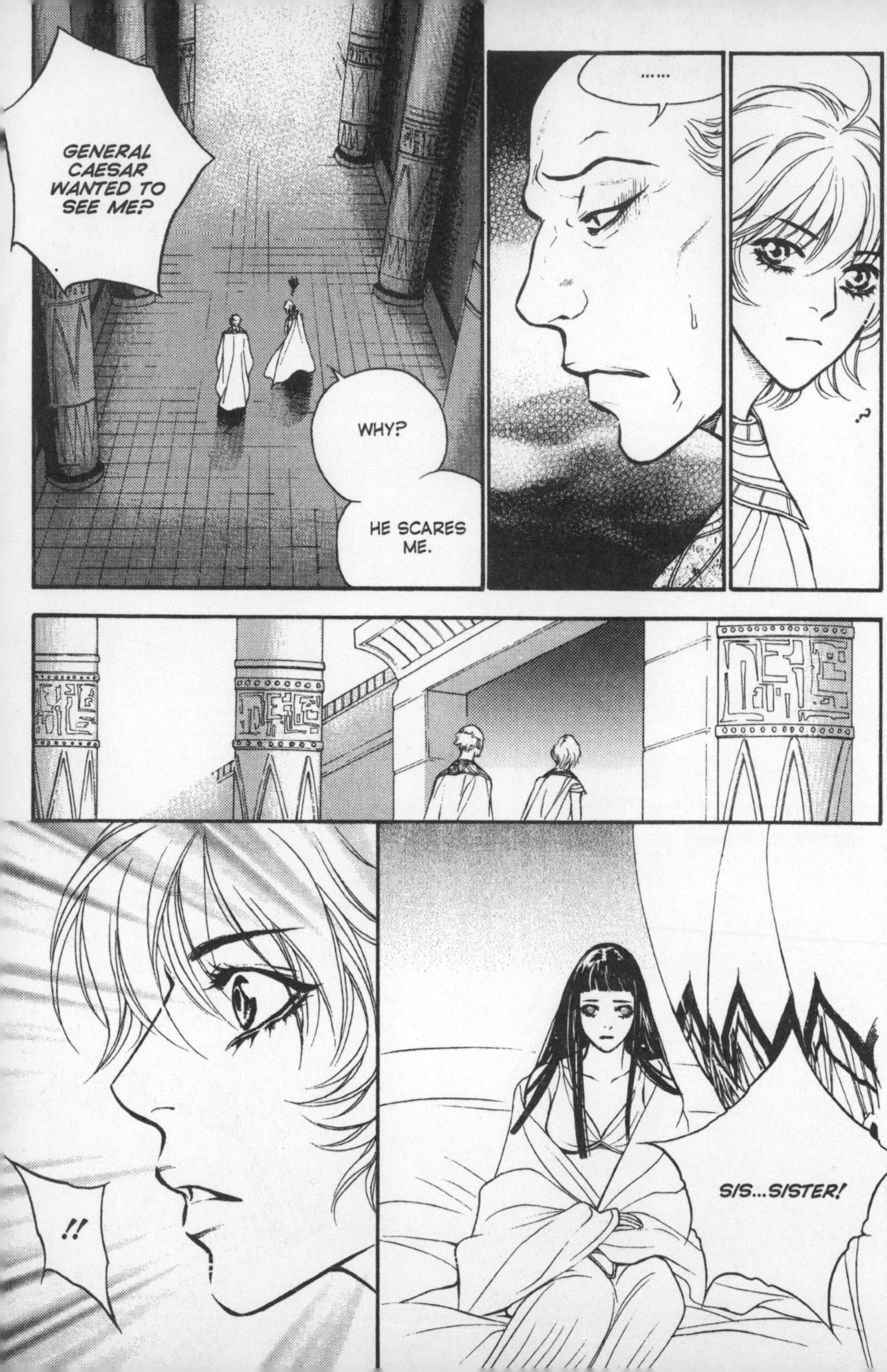
GENERAL CAESAR WANTED TO SEE ME?
WHY?
HE SCARES ME.
......
?
!!
SIS...SISTER!

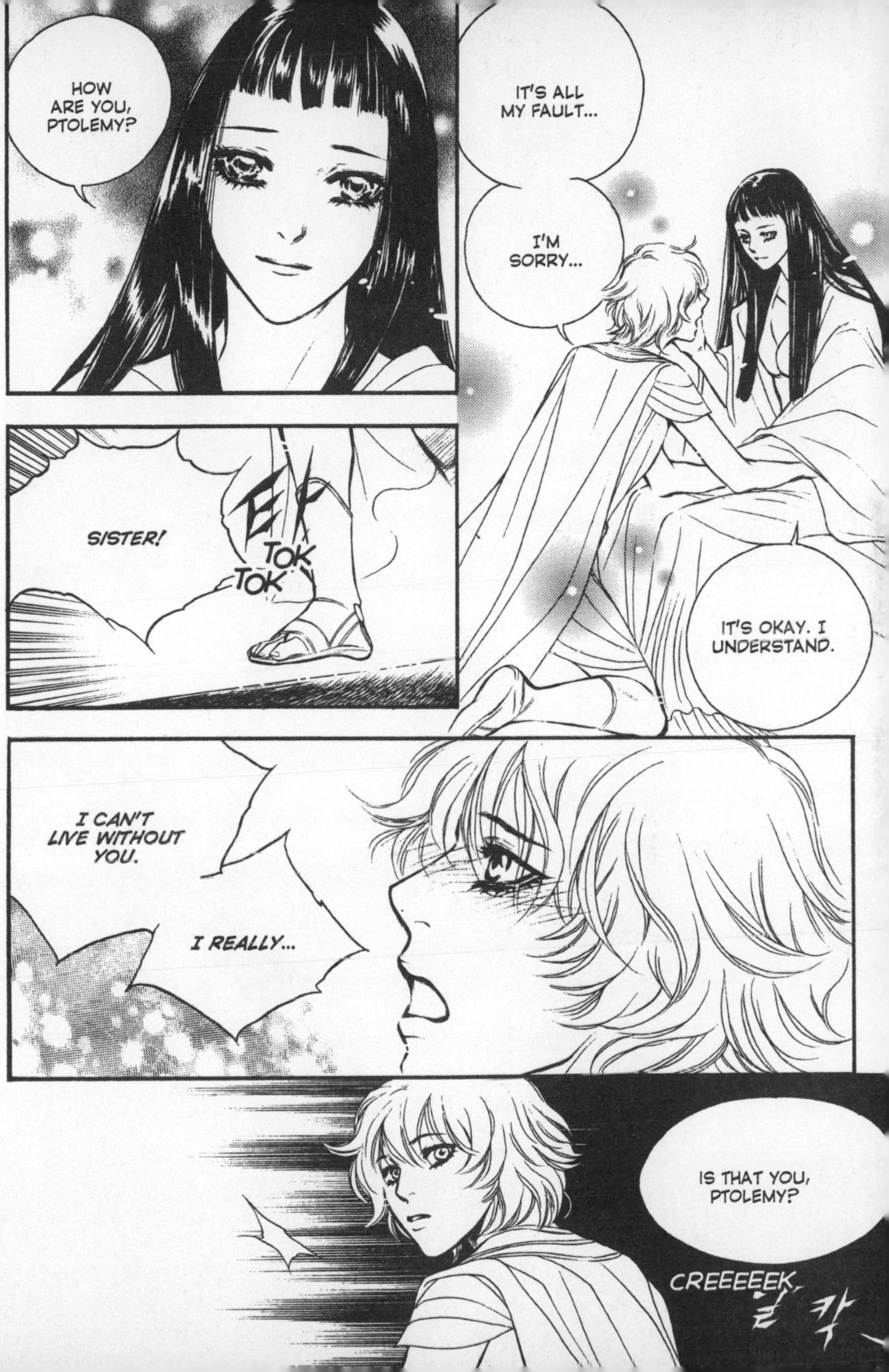

HOW ARE YOU, PTOLEMY?
SISTER!
TOK TOK
IT'S ALL MY FAULT...
I'M SORRY...
IT'S OKAY. I UNDERSTAND.
I CAN'T LIVE WITHOUT YOU.
I REALLY...
IS THAT YOU, PTOLEMY?
CREEEEEK

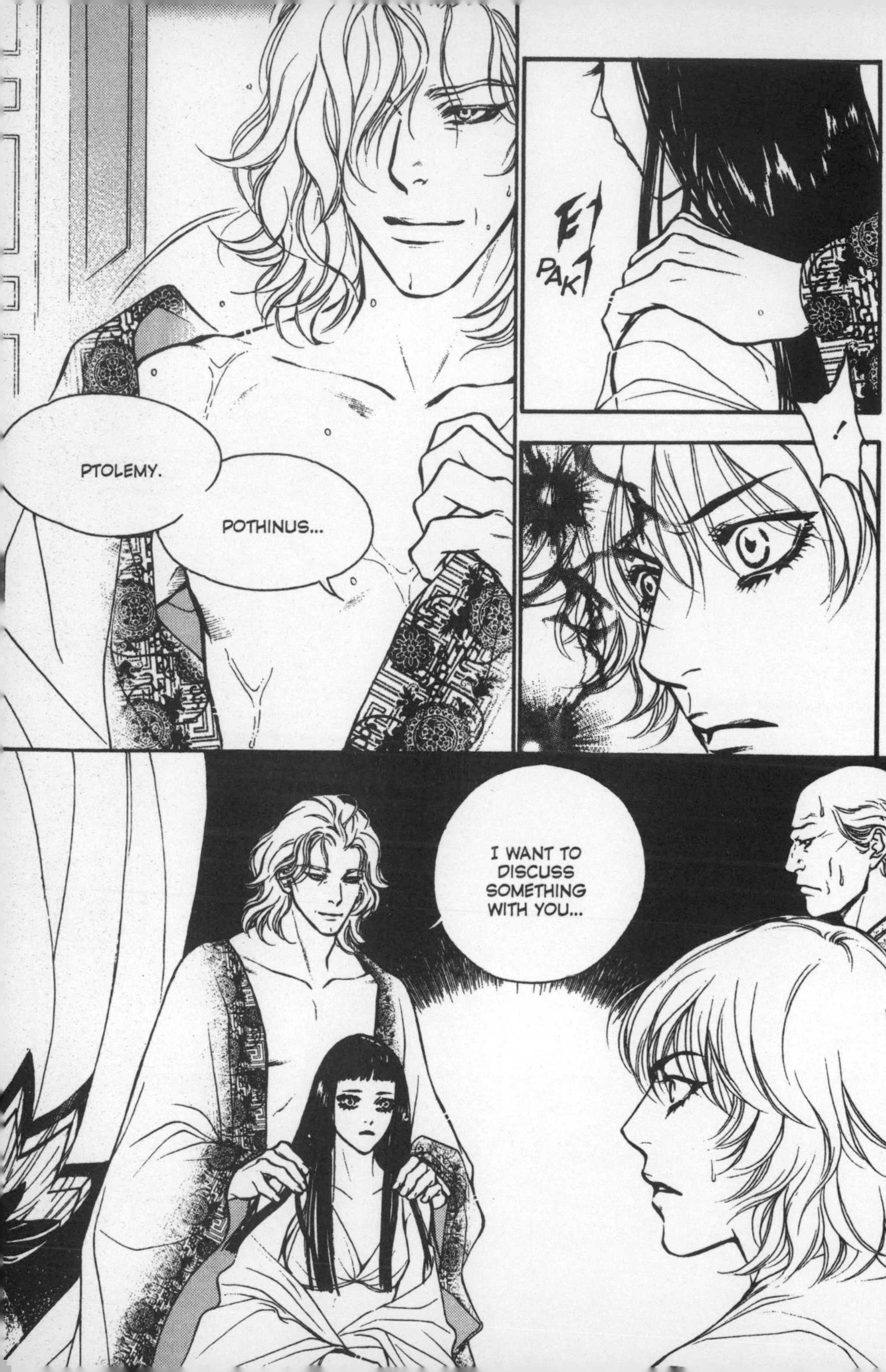
PTOLEMY.
POTHINUS...
PAK
!
I WANT TO DISCUSS SOMETHING WITH YOU...

One thousand
and one nights

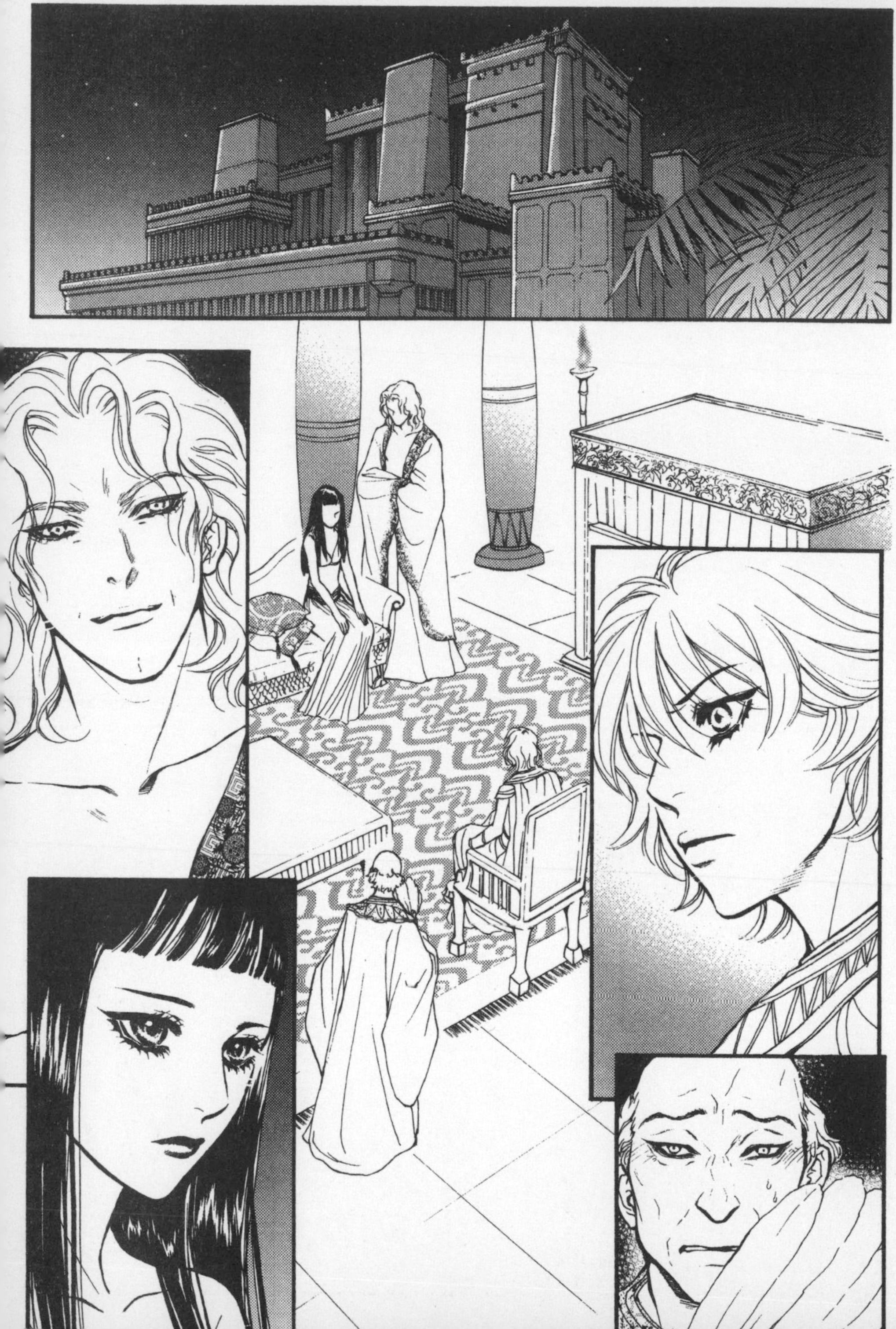

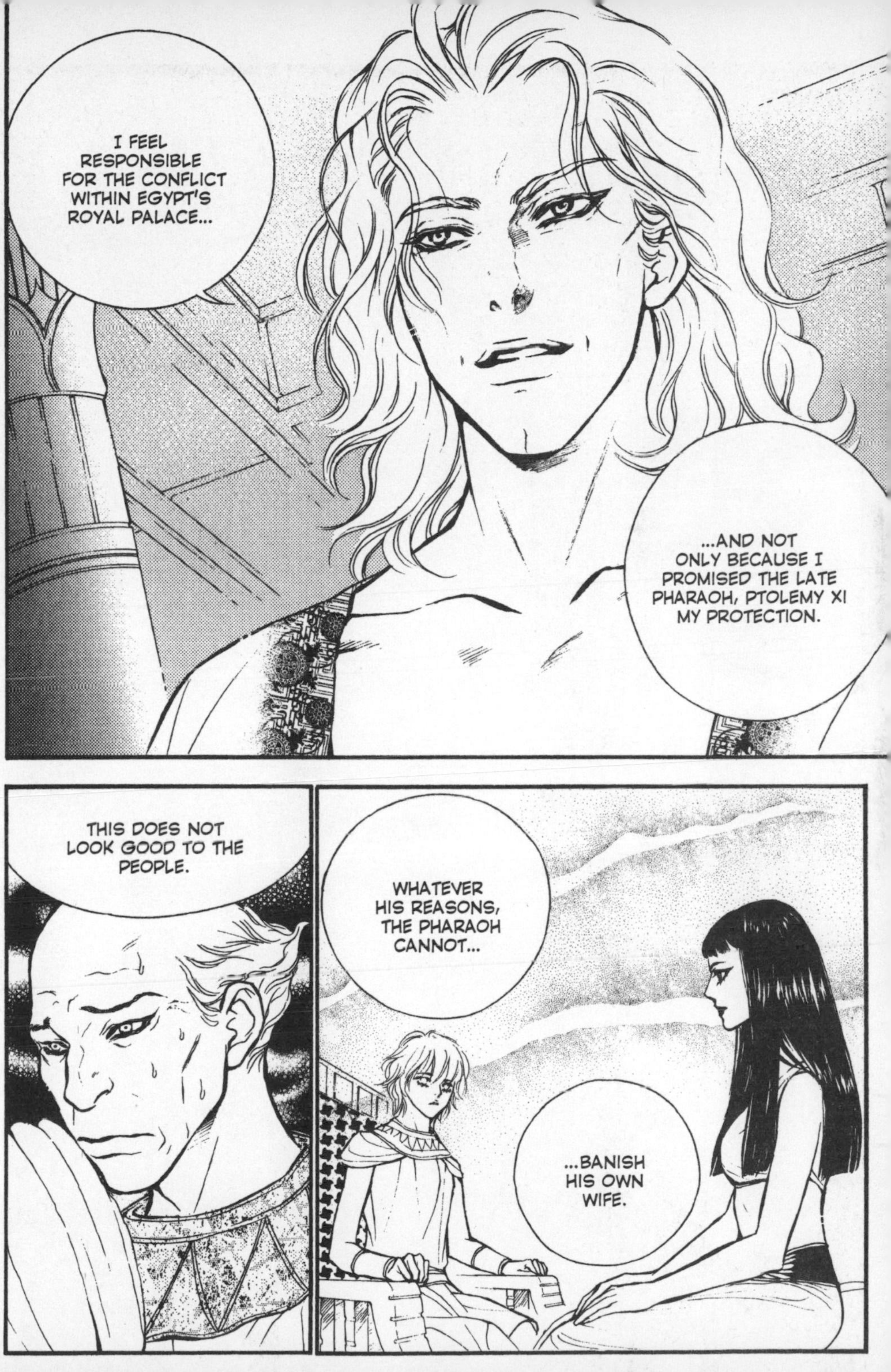
I FEEL RESPONSIBLE FOR THE CONFLICT WITHIN EGYPT'S ROYAL PALACE...
...AND NOT ONLY BECAUSE I PROMISED THE LATE PHARAOH, PTOLEMY XI MY PROTECTION.
THIS DOES NOT LOOK GOOD TO THE PEOPLE.
WHATEVER HIS REASONS, THE PHARAOH CANNOT...
...BANISH HIS OWN WIFE.

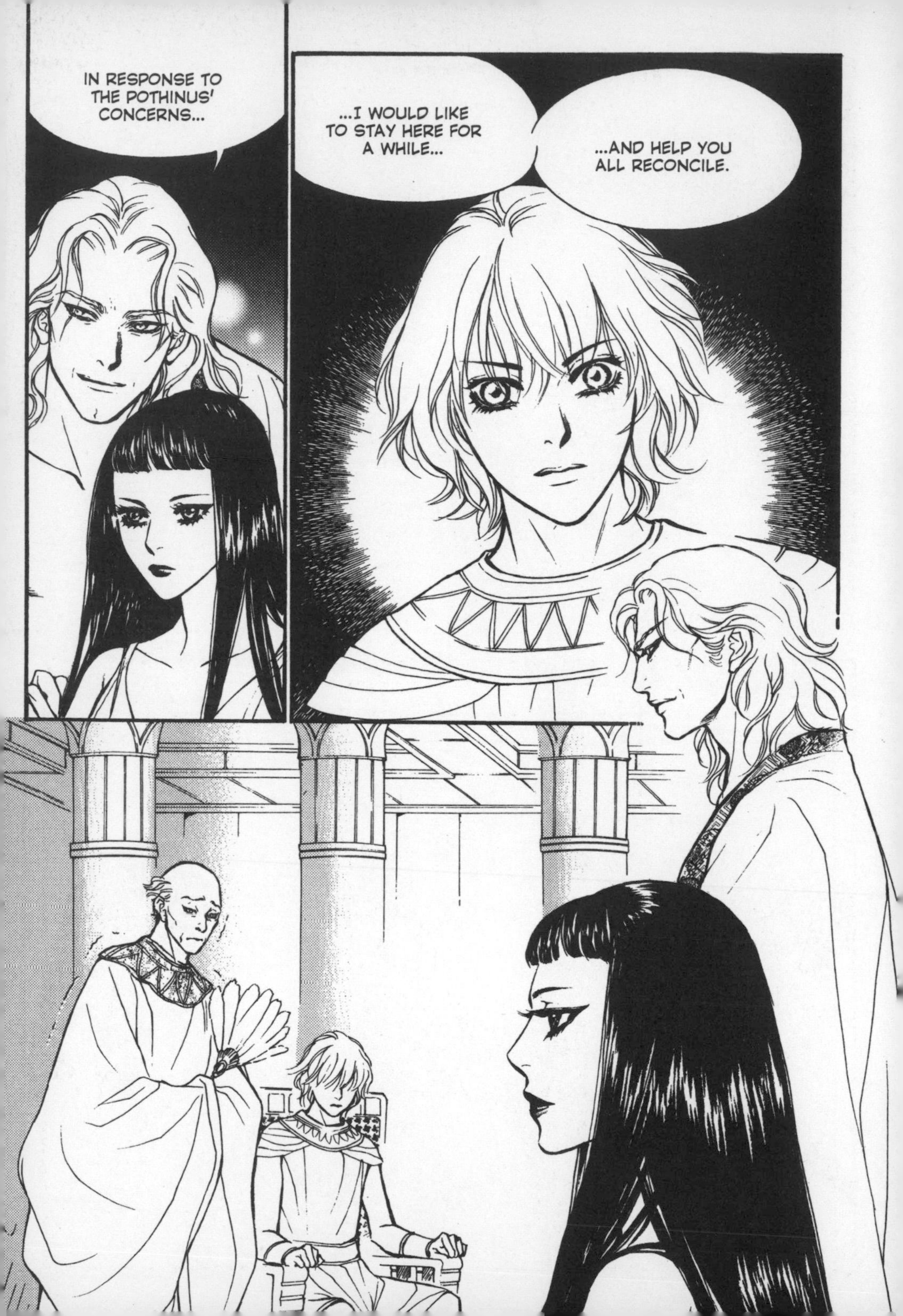
IN RESPONSE TO THE POTHINUS' CONCERNS...
...I WOULD LIKE TO STAY HERE FOR A WHILE...
...AND HELP YOU ALL RECONCILE.

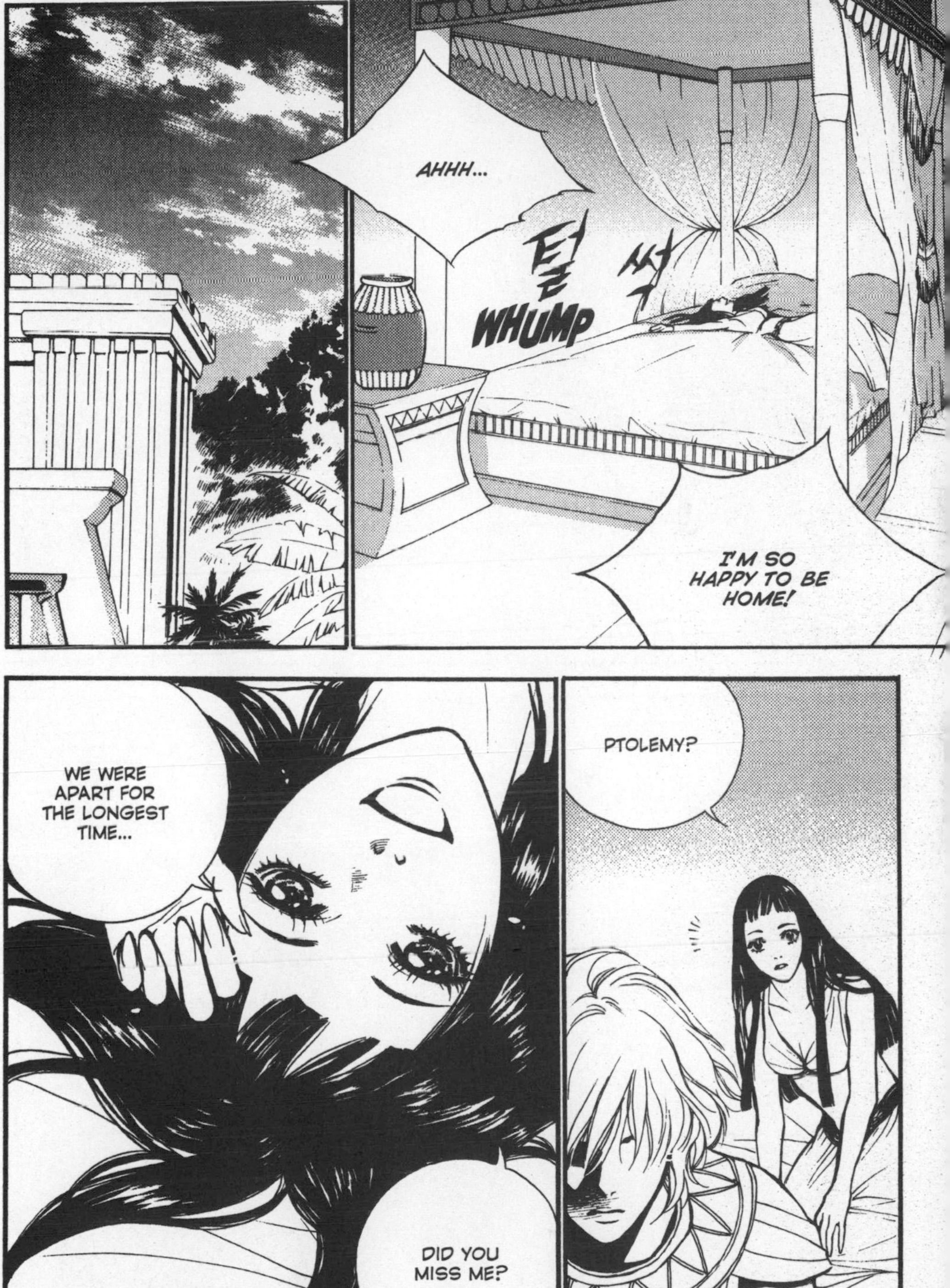
AHHH...
털썩
WHUMP
I'M SO HAPPY TO BE HOME!
WE WERE APART FOR THE LONGEST TIME...
DID YOU MISS ME?
PTOLEMY?

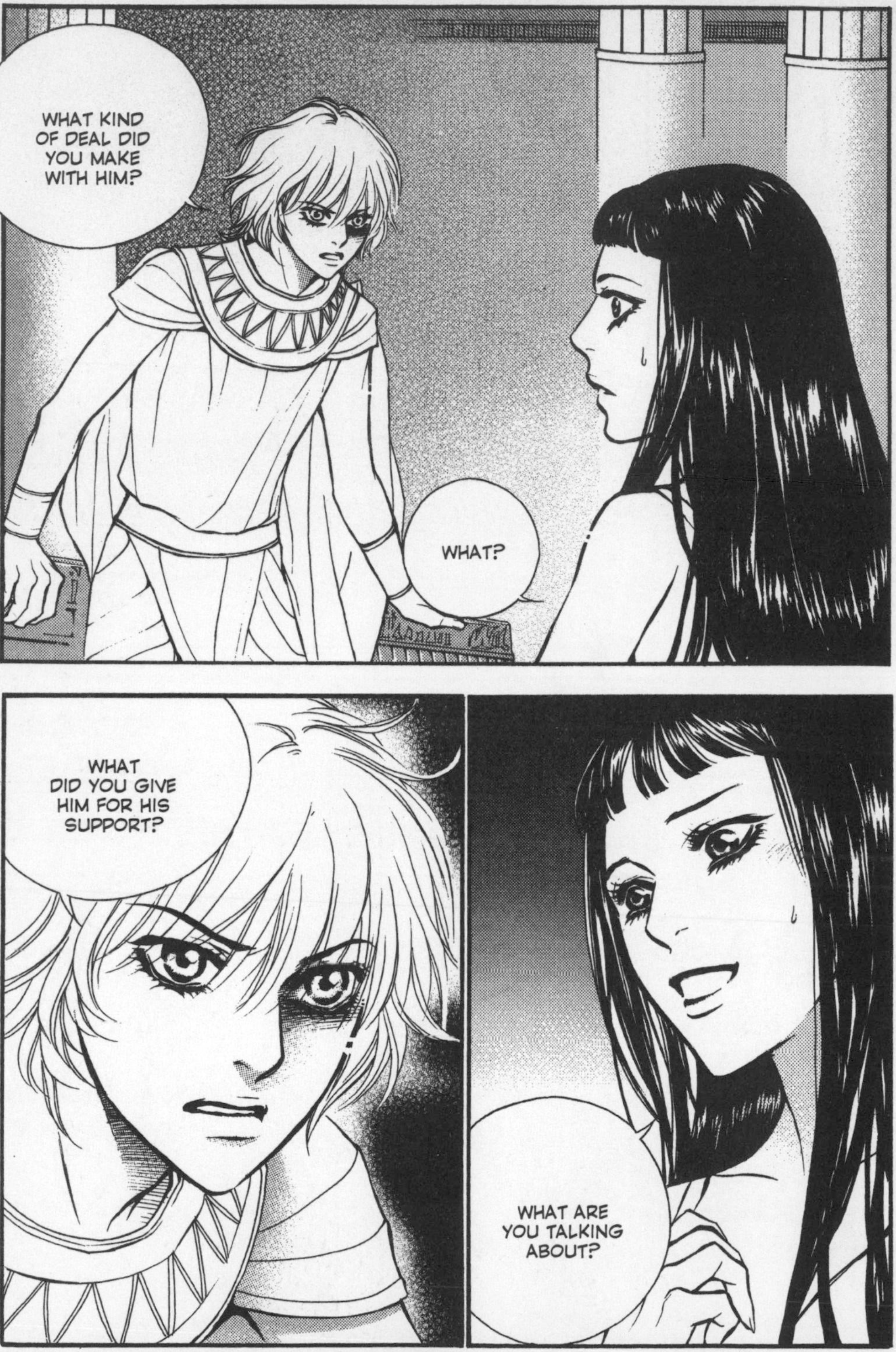
WHAT KIND OF DEAL DID YOU MAKE WITH HIM?
WHAT?
WHAT DID YOU GIVE HIM FOR HIS SUPPORT?
WHAT ARE YOU TALKING ABOUT?

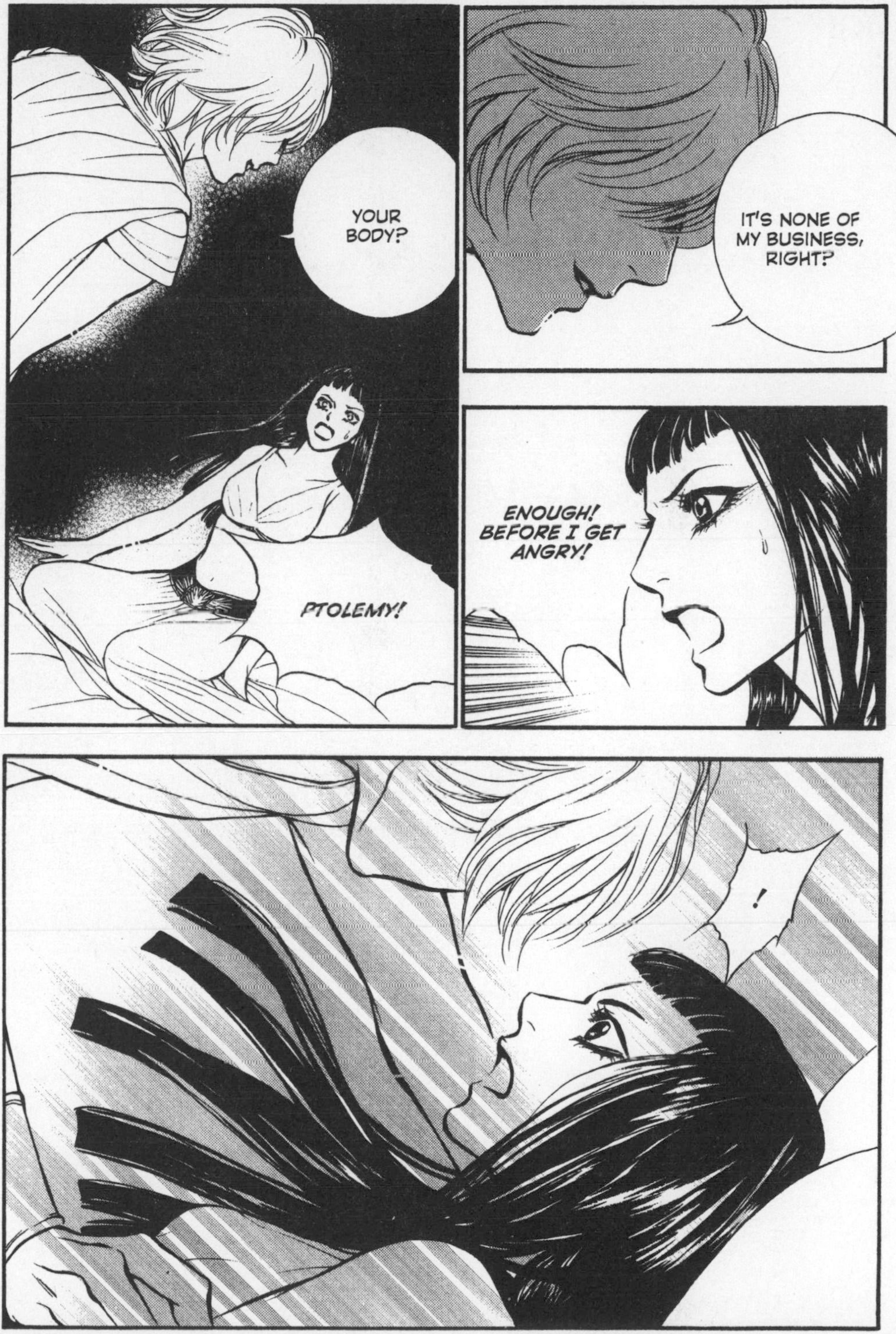
YOUR BODY?
PTOLEMY!
IT'S NONE OF MY BUSINESS, RIGHT?
ENOUGH! BEFORE I GET ANGRY!
!

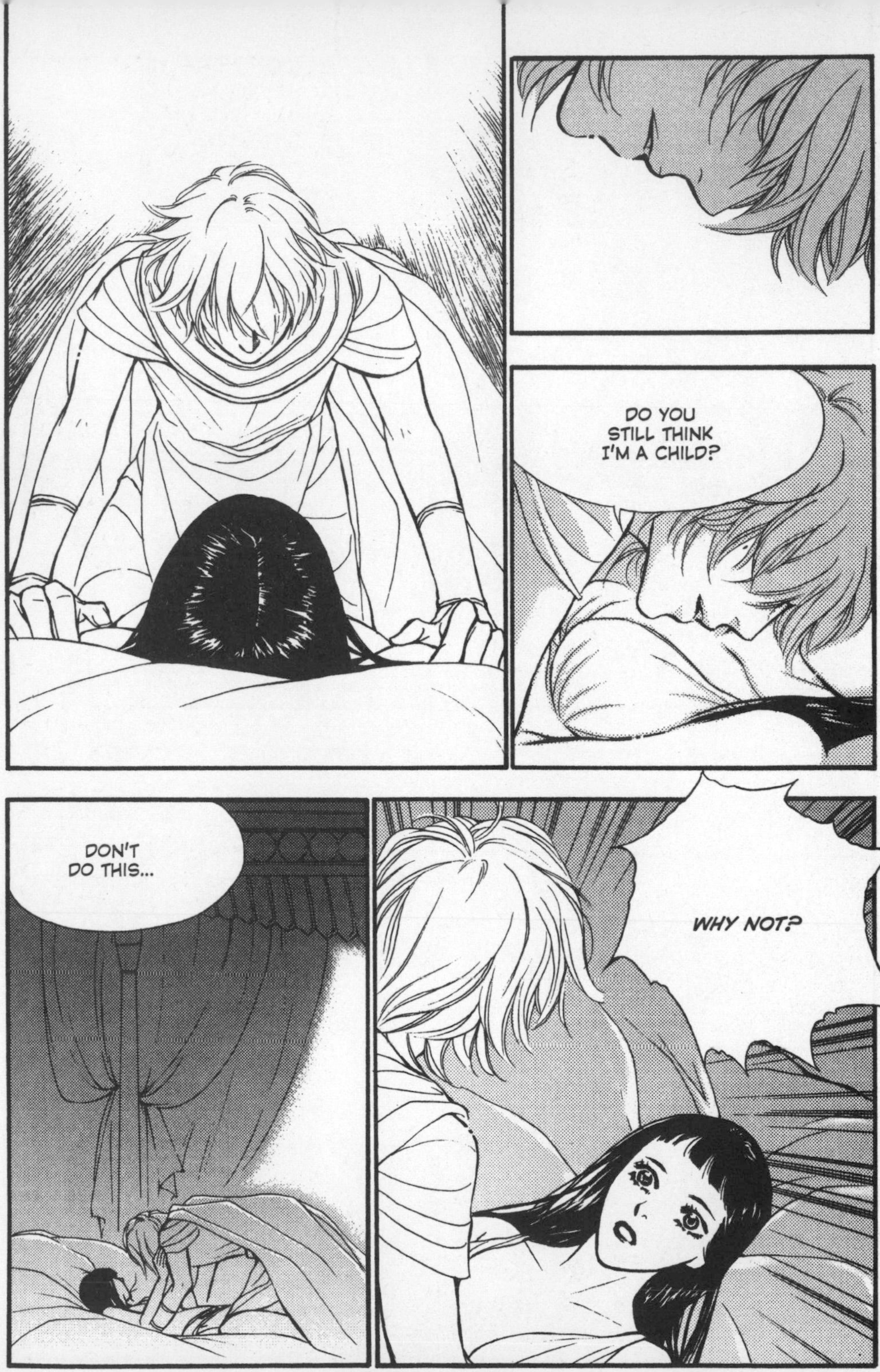
DO YOU STILL THINK I'M A CHILD?
DON'T DO THIS...
WHY NOT?

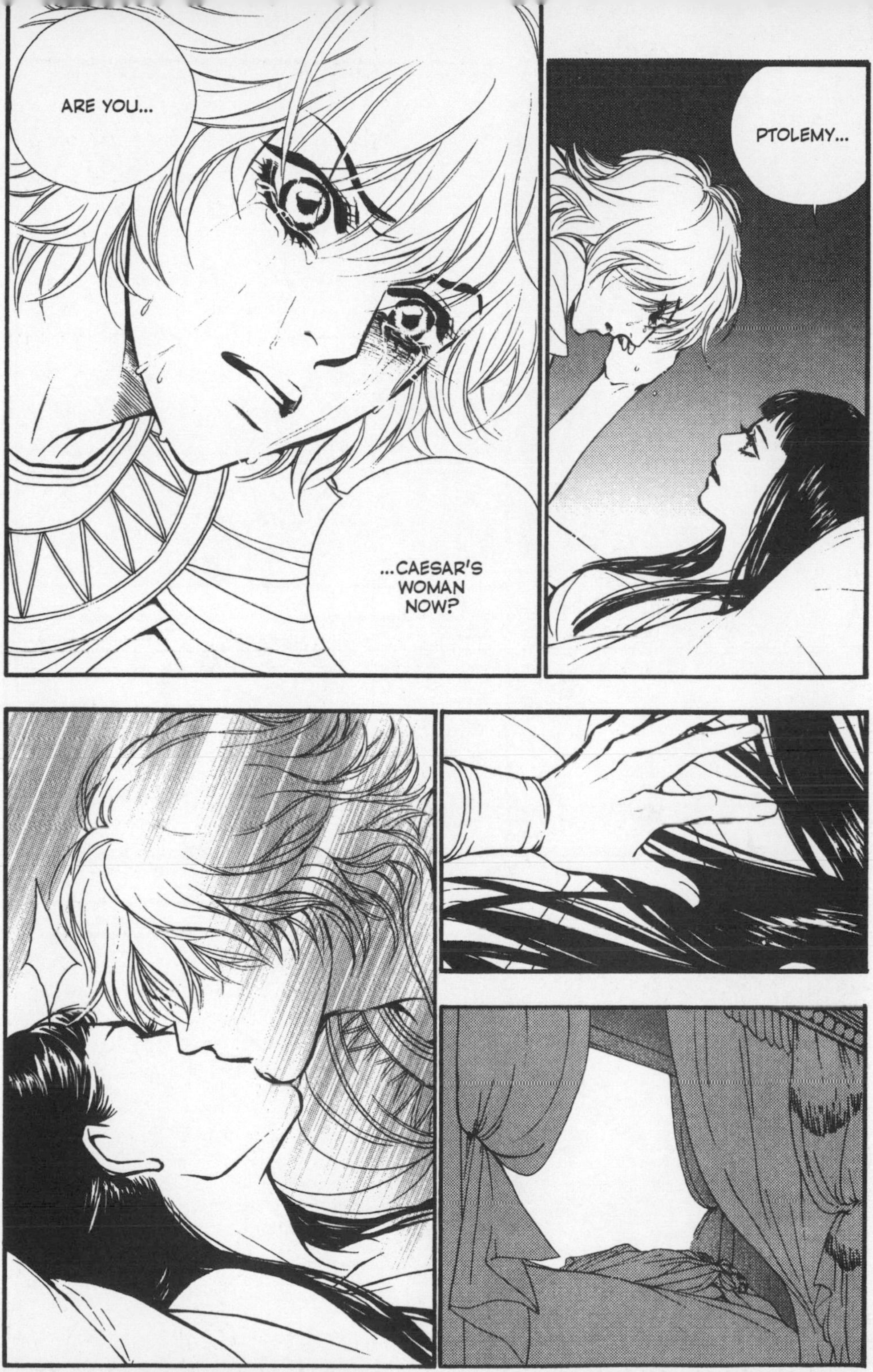
ARE YOU...
...CAESAR'S WOMAN NOW?
PTOLEMY...

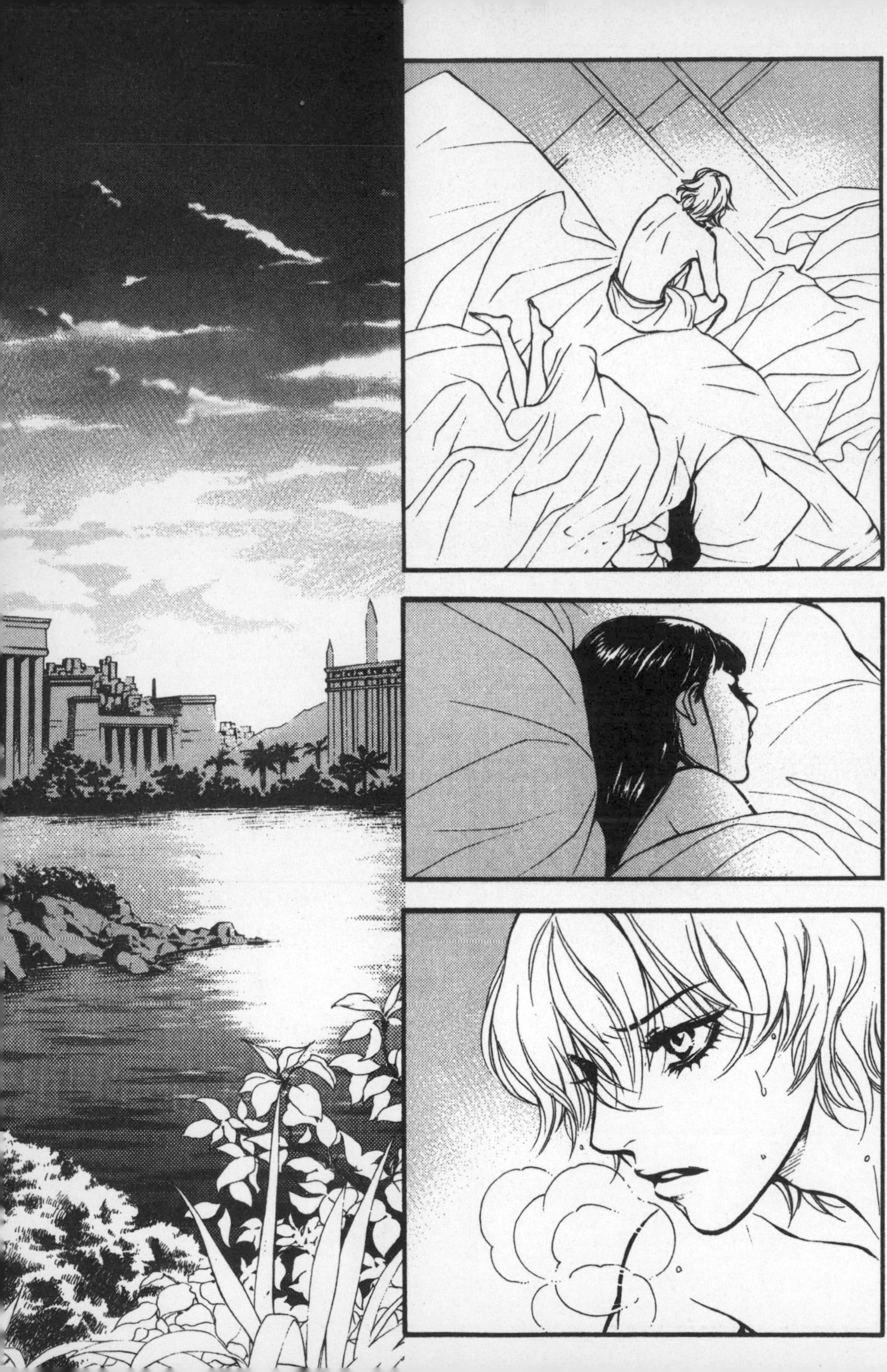

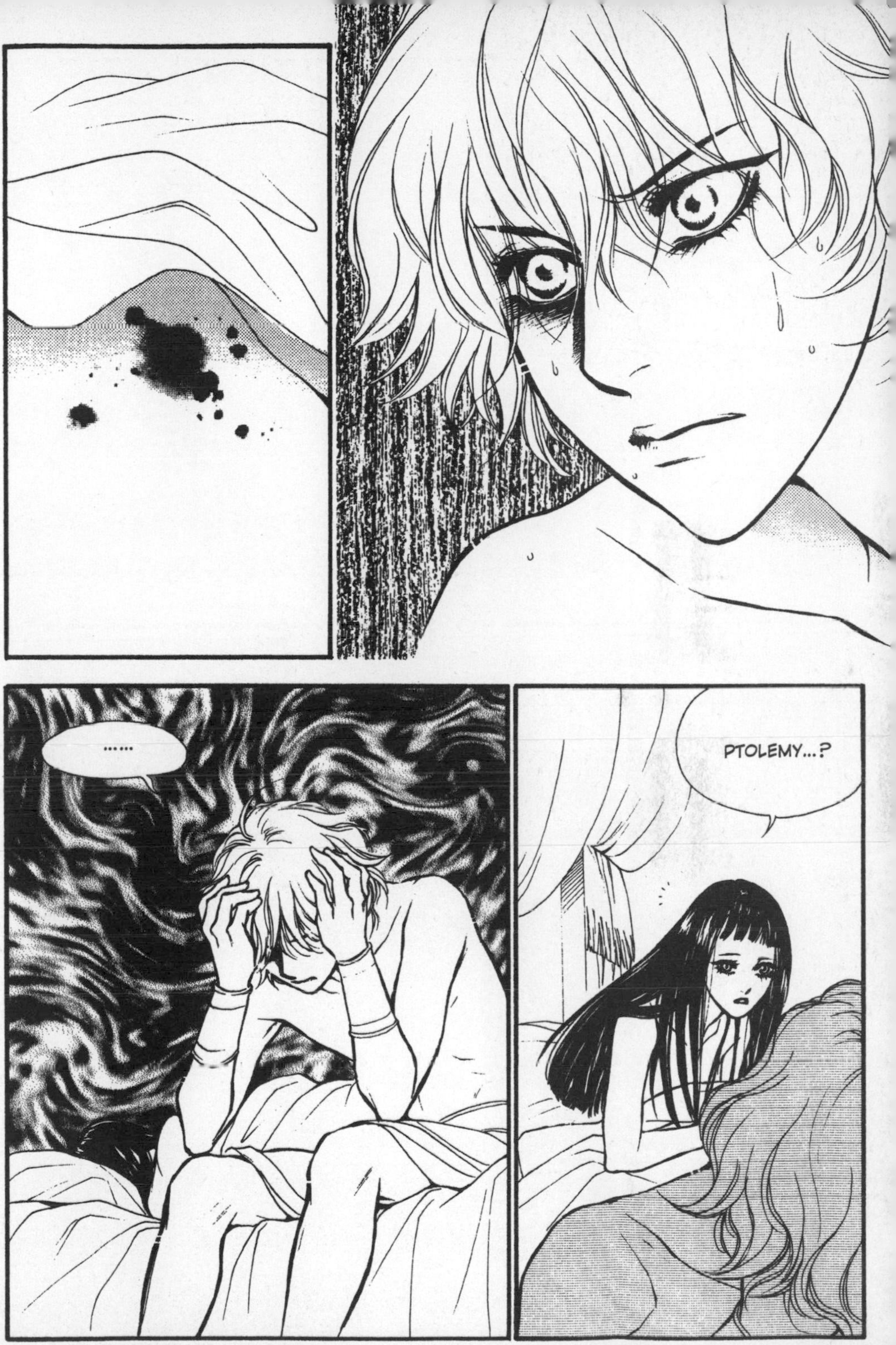
PTOLEMY...?
......

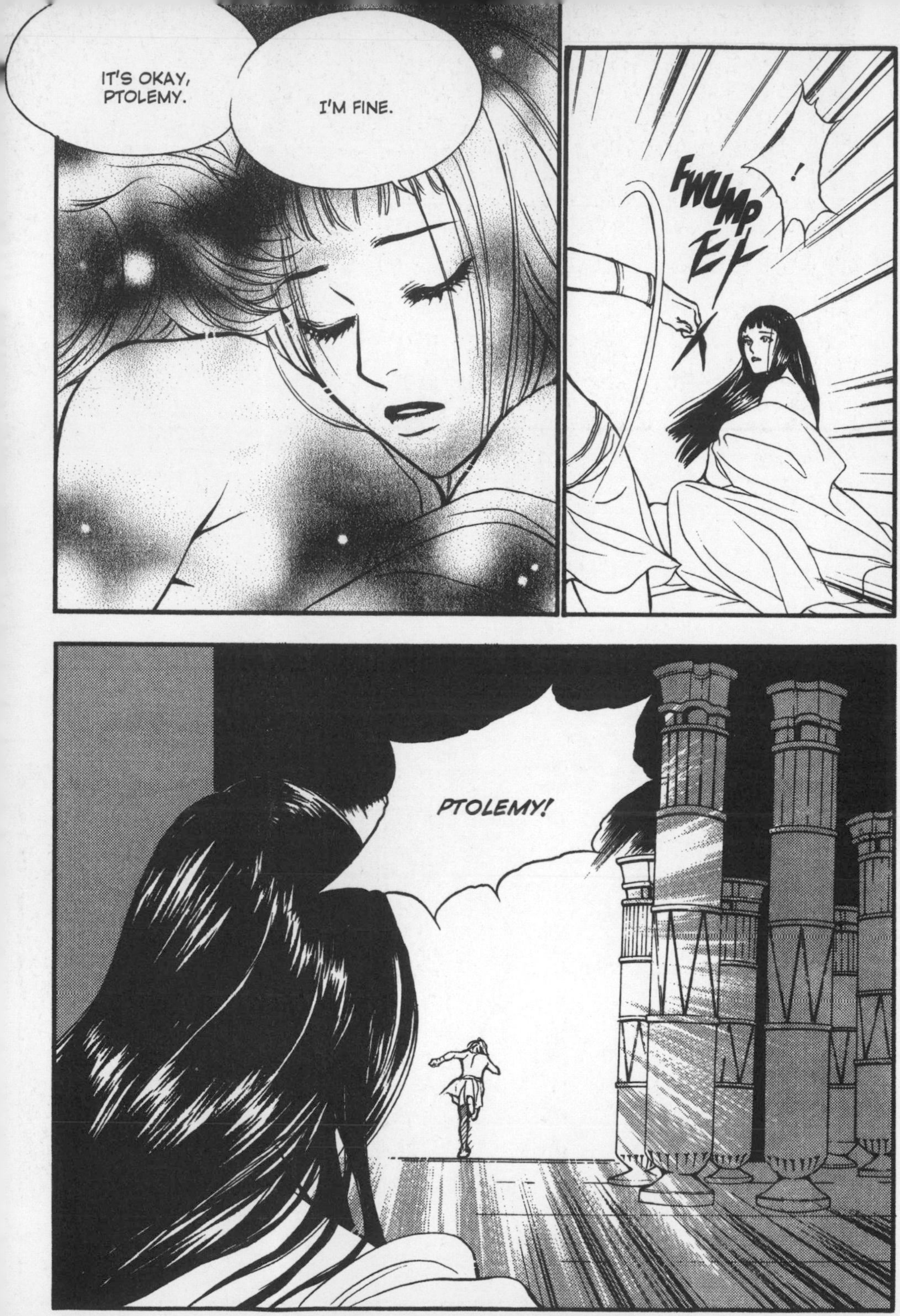
IT'S OKAY, PTOLEMY.
I'M FINE.
FWUMP
!
PTOLEMY!

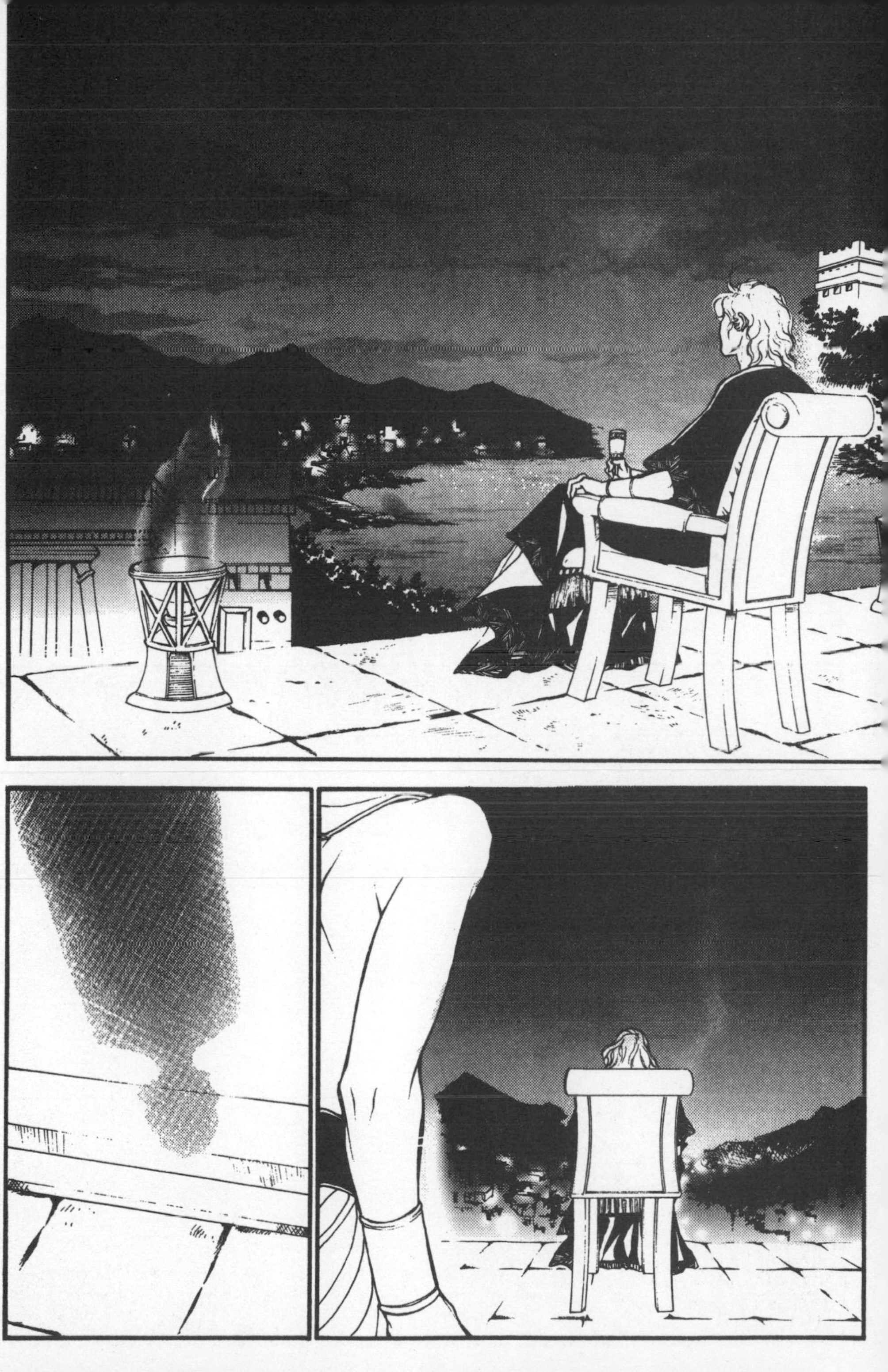

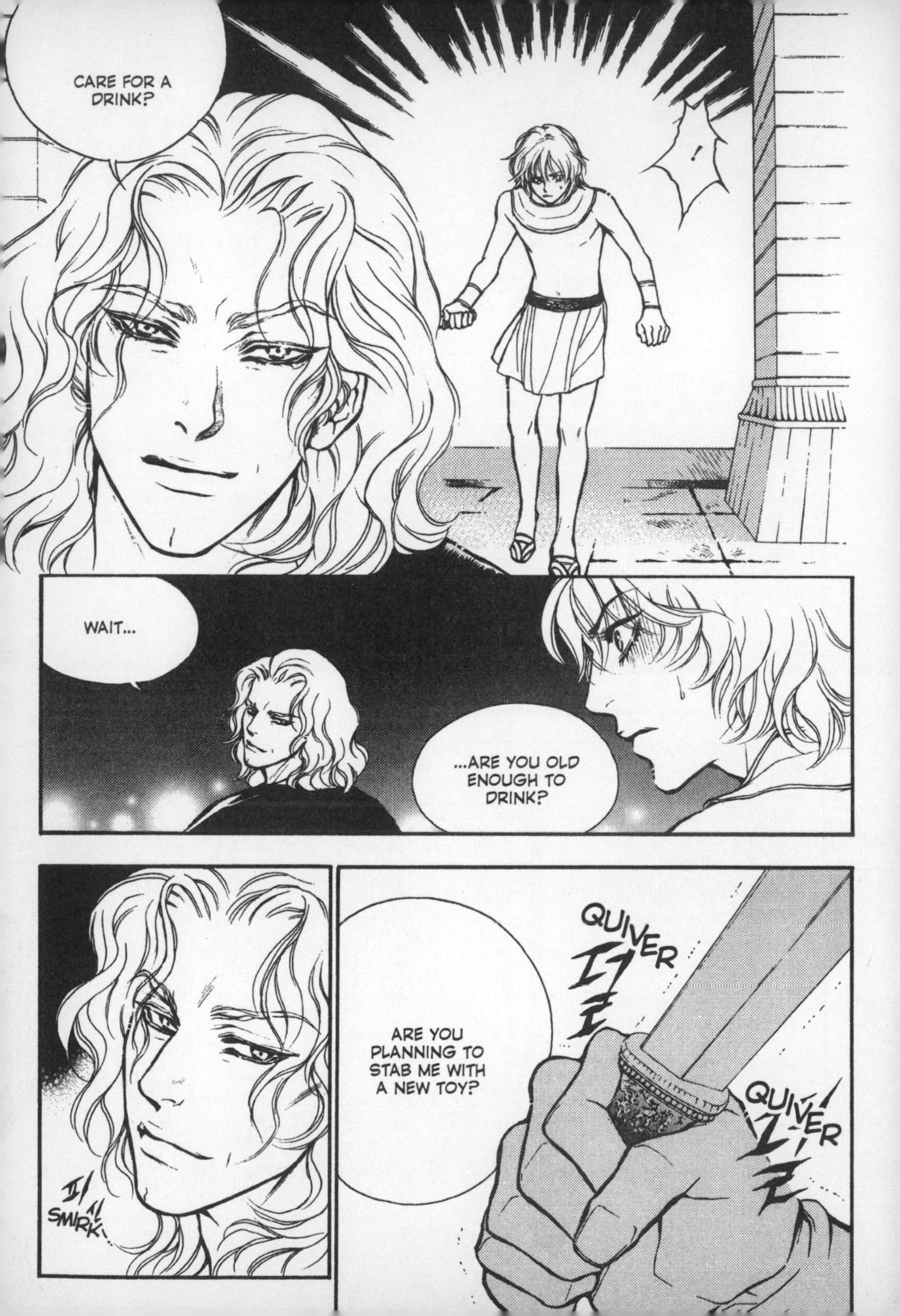
CARE FOR A DRINK?
!
WAIT...
...ARE YOU OLD ENOUGH TO DRINK?
SMIRK...
ARE YOU PLANNING TO STAB ME WITH A NEW TOY?
QUIVER
QUIVER

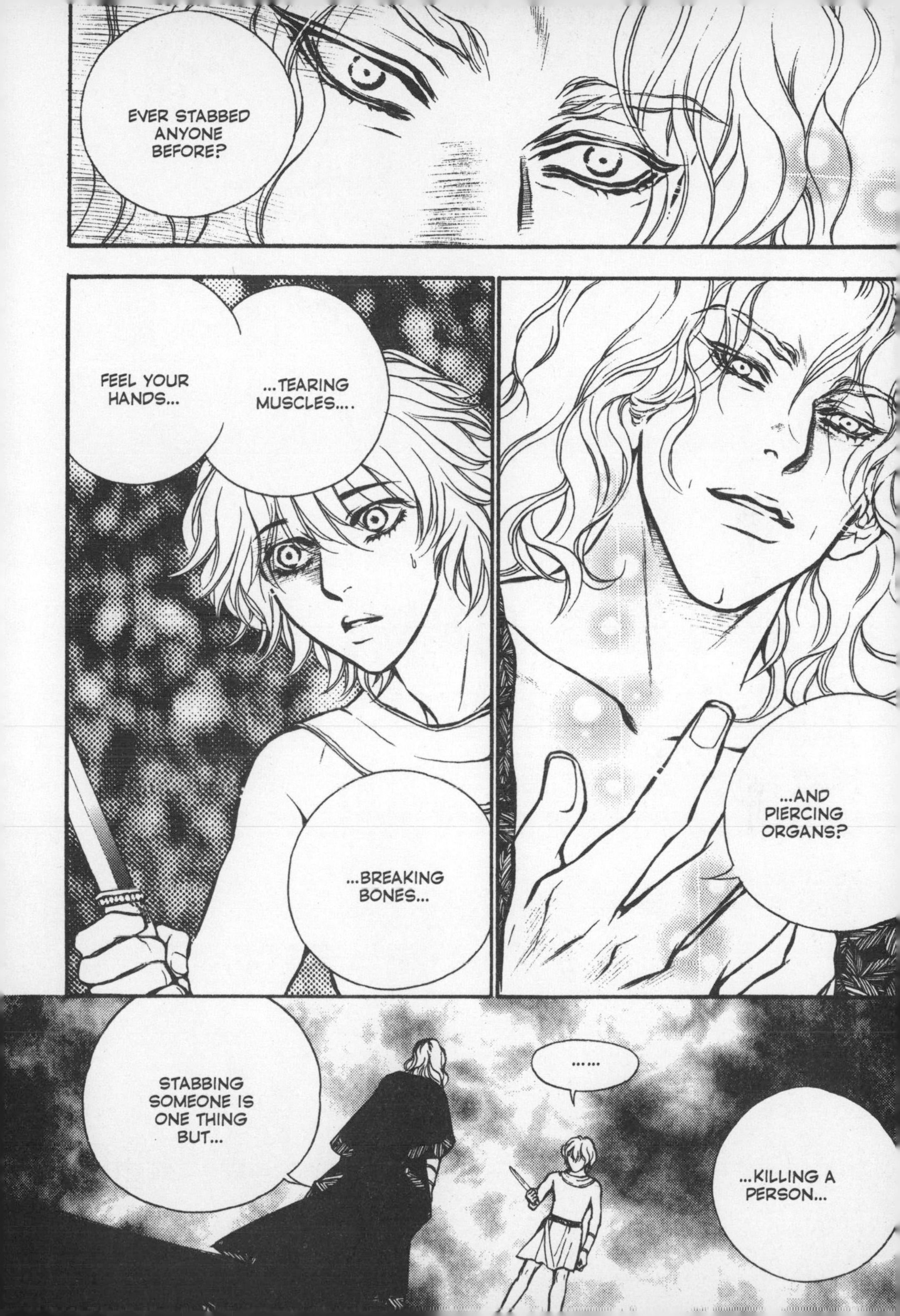
EVER STABBED ANYONE BEFORE?
FEEL YOUR HANDS...
...TEARING MUSCLES....
...BREAKING BONES...
...AND PIERCING ORGANS?
STABBING SOMEONE IS ONE THING BUT...
......
...KILLING A PERSON...

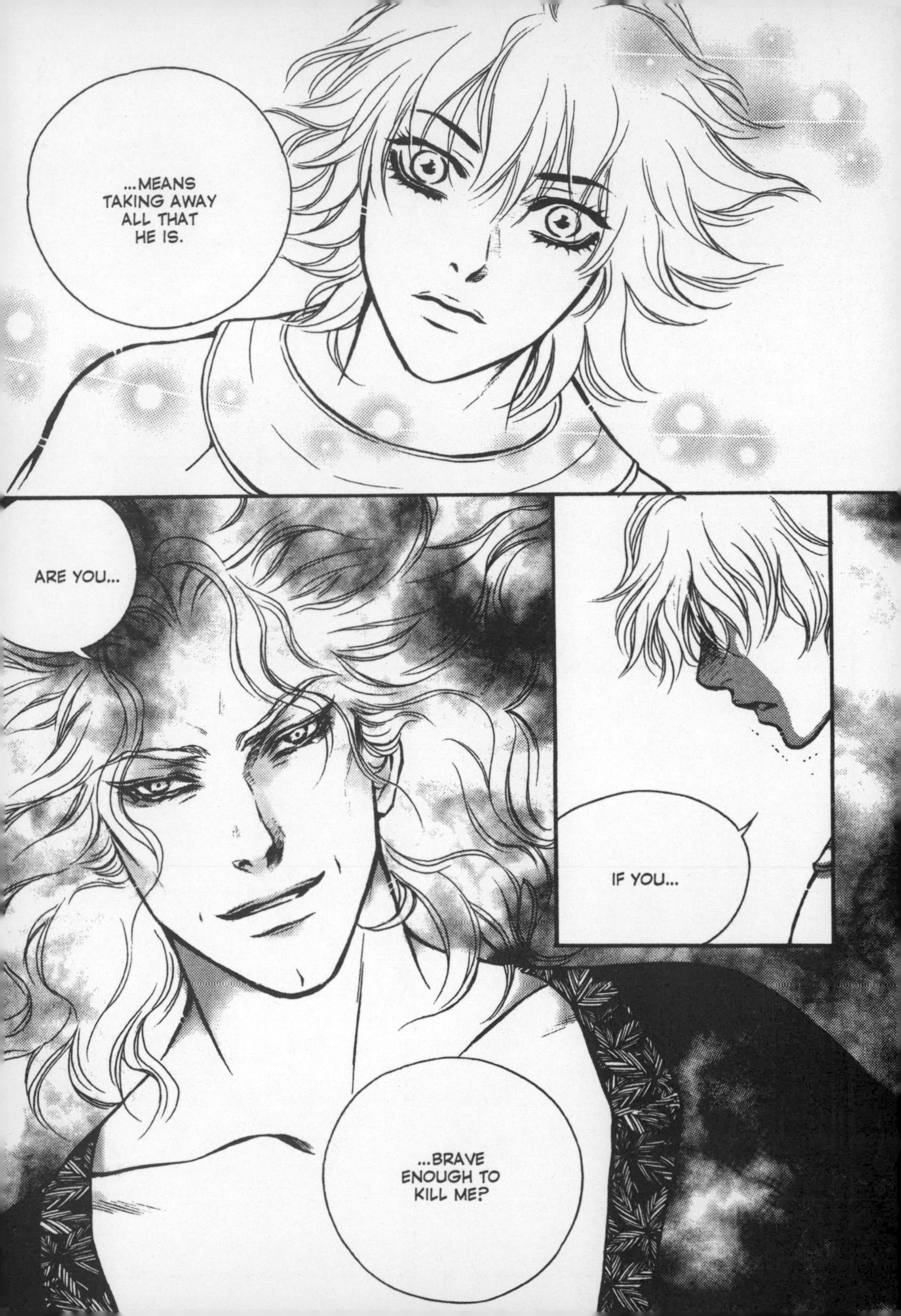
...MEANS TAKING AWAY ALL THAT HE IS.
ARE YOU...
...BRAVE ENOUGH TO KILL ME?
IF YOU...

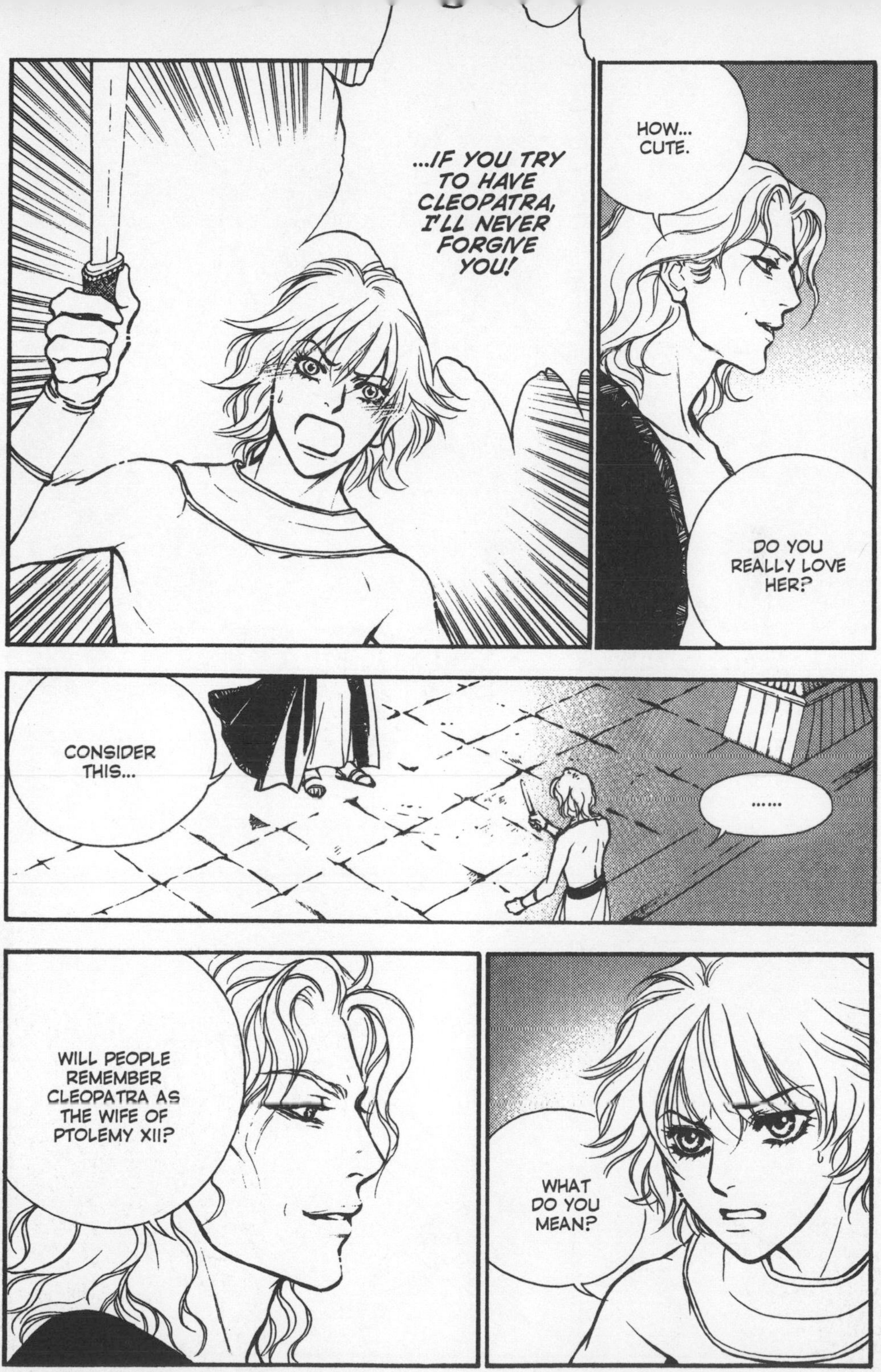
...IF YOU TRY TO HAVE CLEOPATRA, I'LL NEVER FORGIVE YOU!
HOW... CUTE.
DO YOU REALLY LOVE HER?
CONSIDER THIS...
......
WILL PEOPLE REMEMBER CLEOPATRA AS THE WIFE OF PTOLEMY XII?
WHAT DO YOU MEAN?

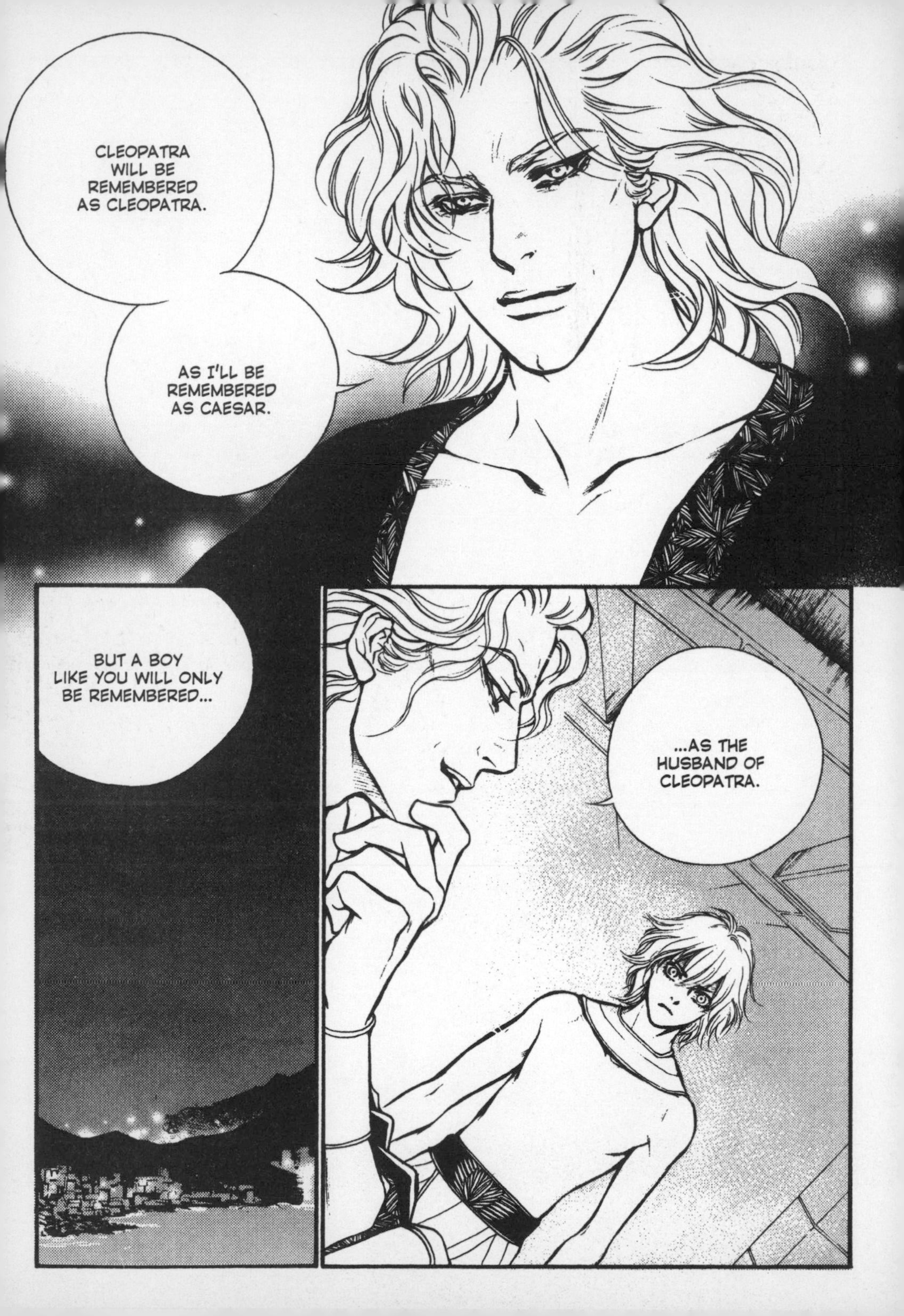
CLEOPATRA WILL BE REMEMBERED AS CLEOPATRA.
AS I'LL BE REMEMBERED AS CAESAR.
BUT A BOY LIKE YOU WILL ONLY BE REMEMBERED...
...AS THE HUSBAND OF CLEOPATRA.

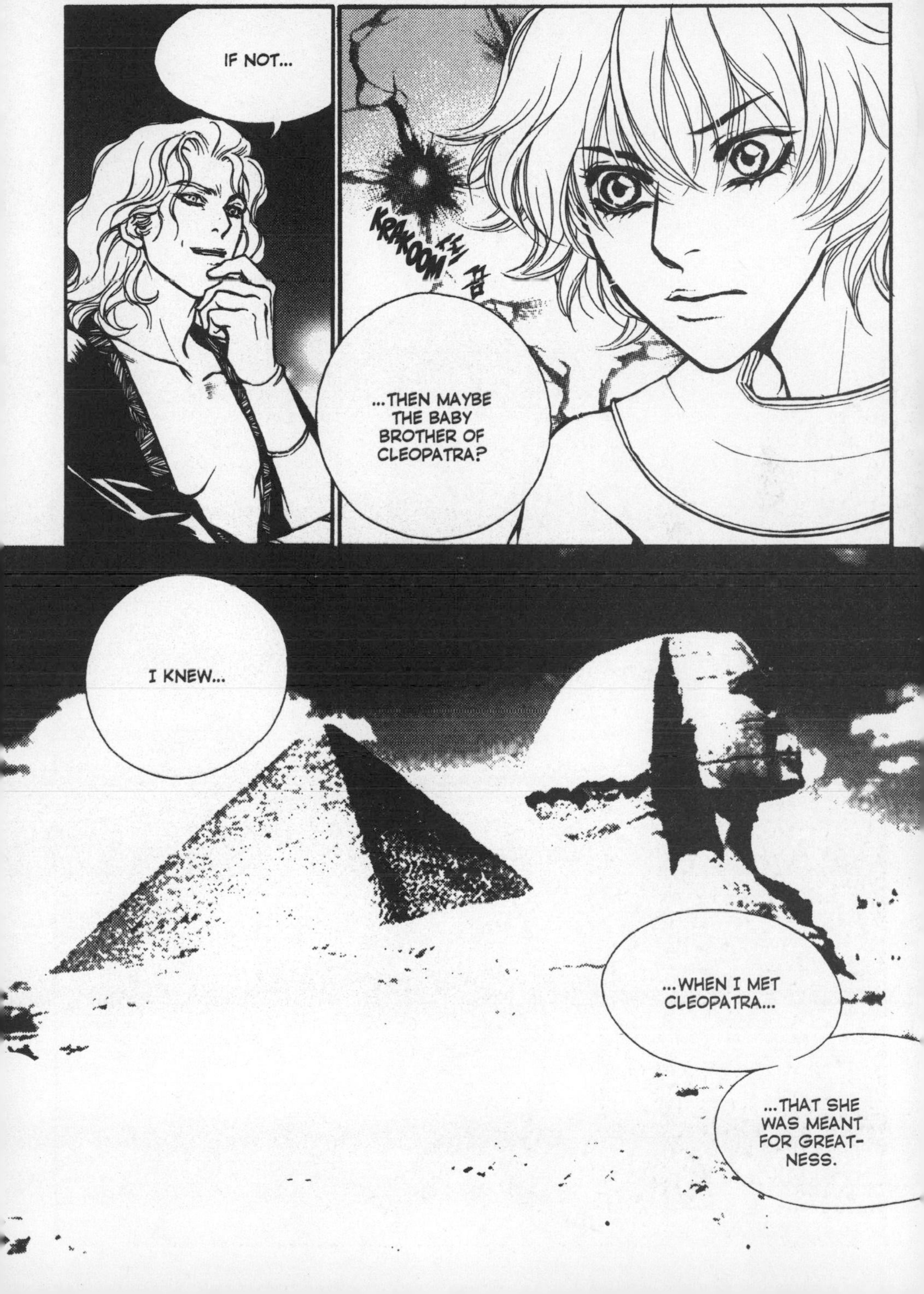
IF NOT...
KRAKOOM
...THEN MAYBE THE BABY BROTHER OF CLEOPATRA?
I KNEW...
...WHEN I MET CLEOPATRA...
...THAT SHE WAS MEANT FOR GREAT-NESS.

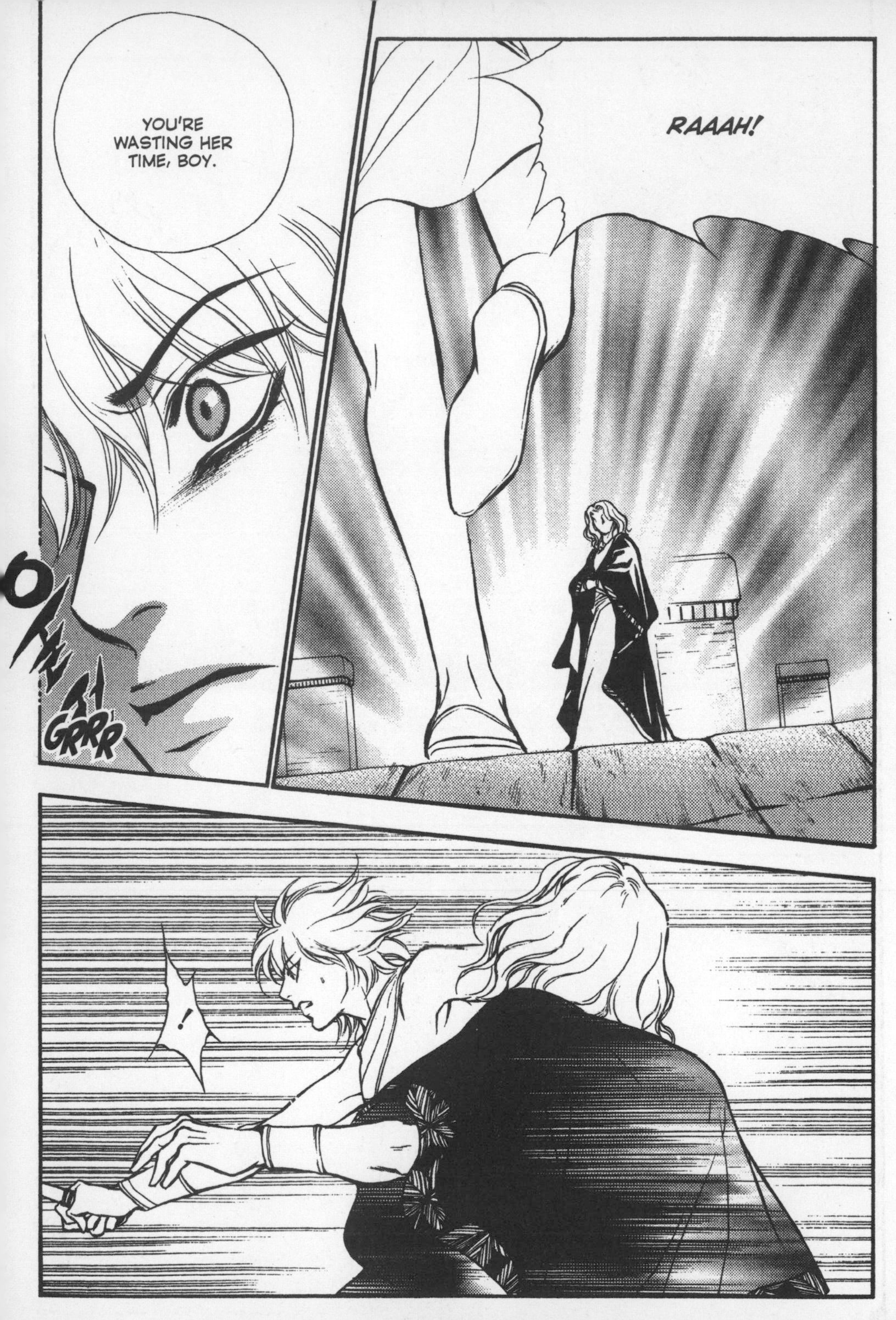
YOU'RE WASTING HER TIME, BOY.
GRRR
RAAAH!
!

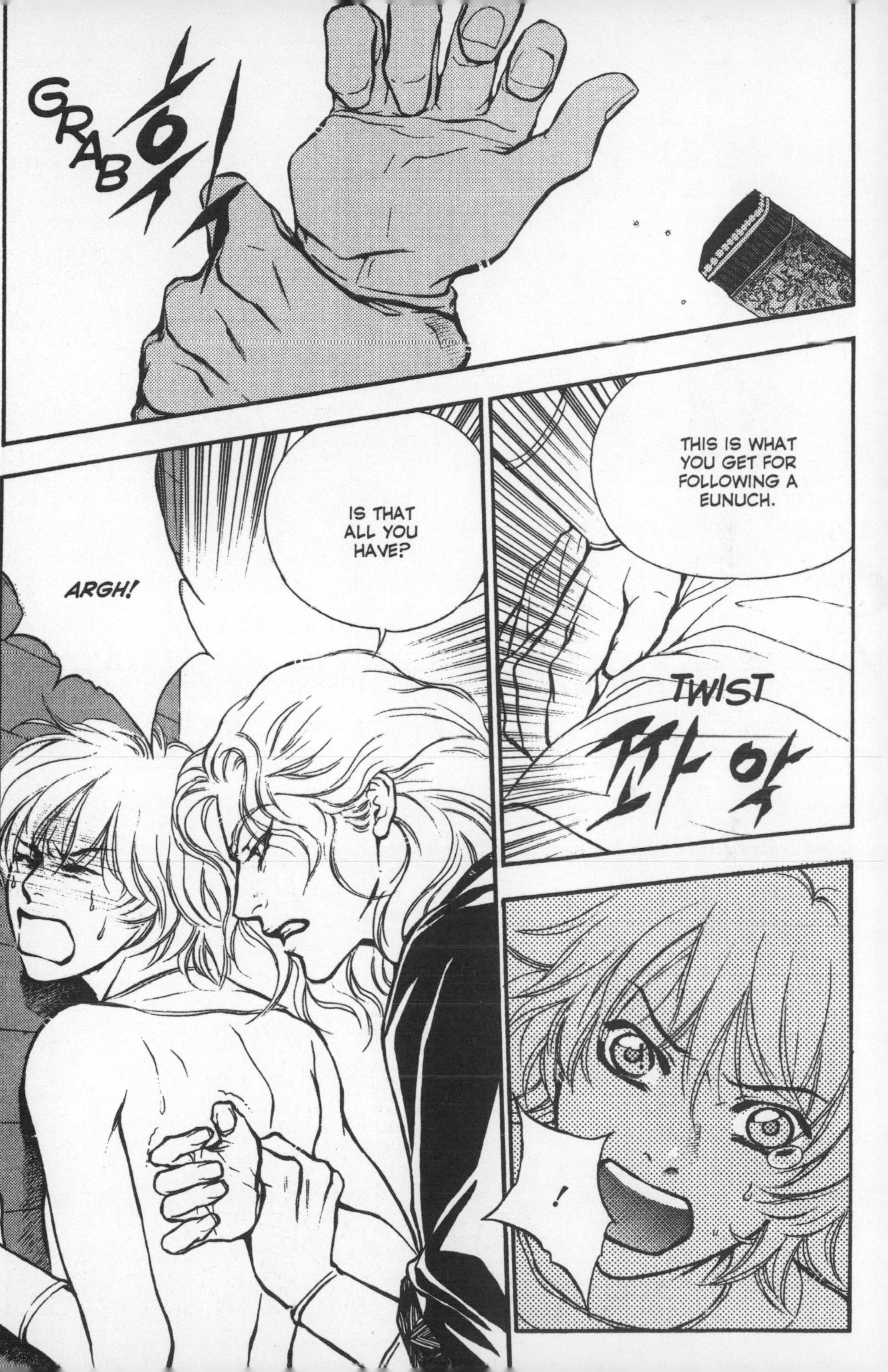
GRAB
IS THAT ALL YOU HAVE?
ARGH!
THIS IS WHAT YOU GET FOR FOLLOWING A EUNUCH.
TWIST
꽈악
!

THIS DELICATE NECK...

...IS ALL YOU HAVE IN COMMON WITH HER.

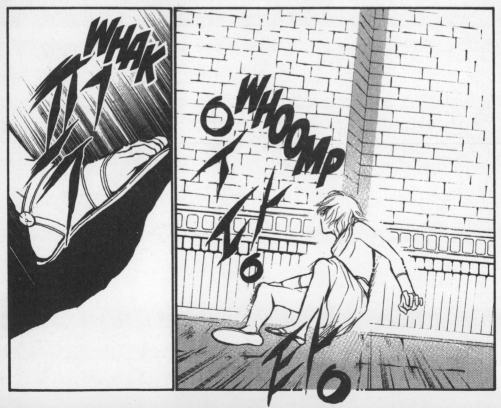

WHAK

WHOOMP

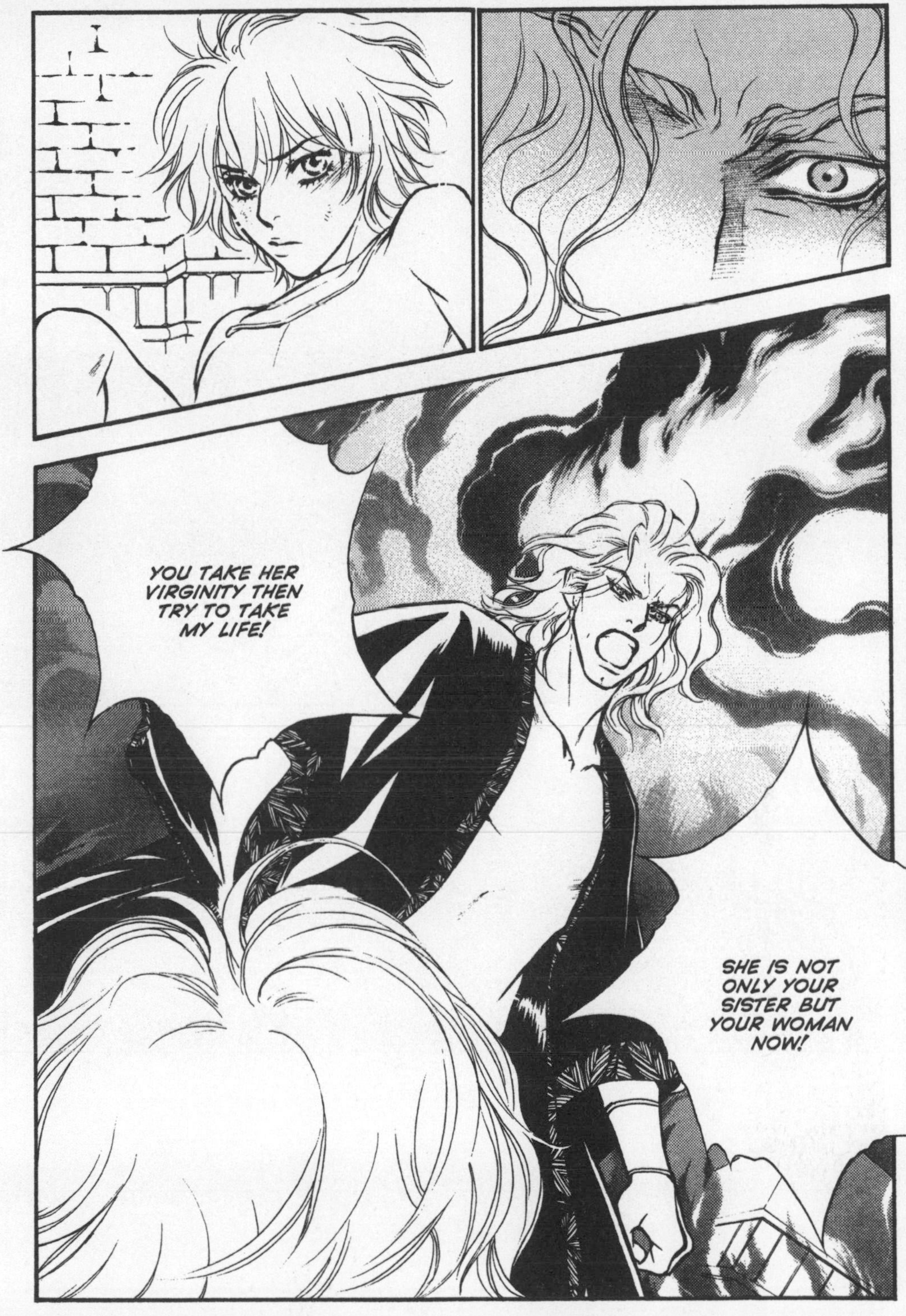
YOU TAKE HER VIRGINITY THEN TRY TO TAKE MY LIFE!
SHE IS NOT ONLY YOUR SISTER BUT YOUR WOMAN NOW!

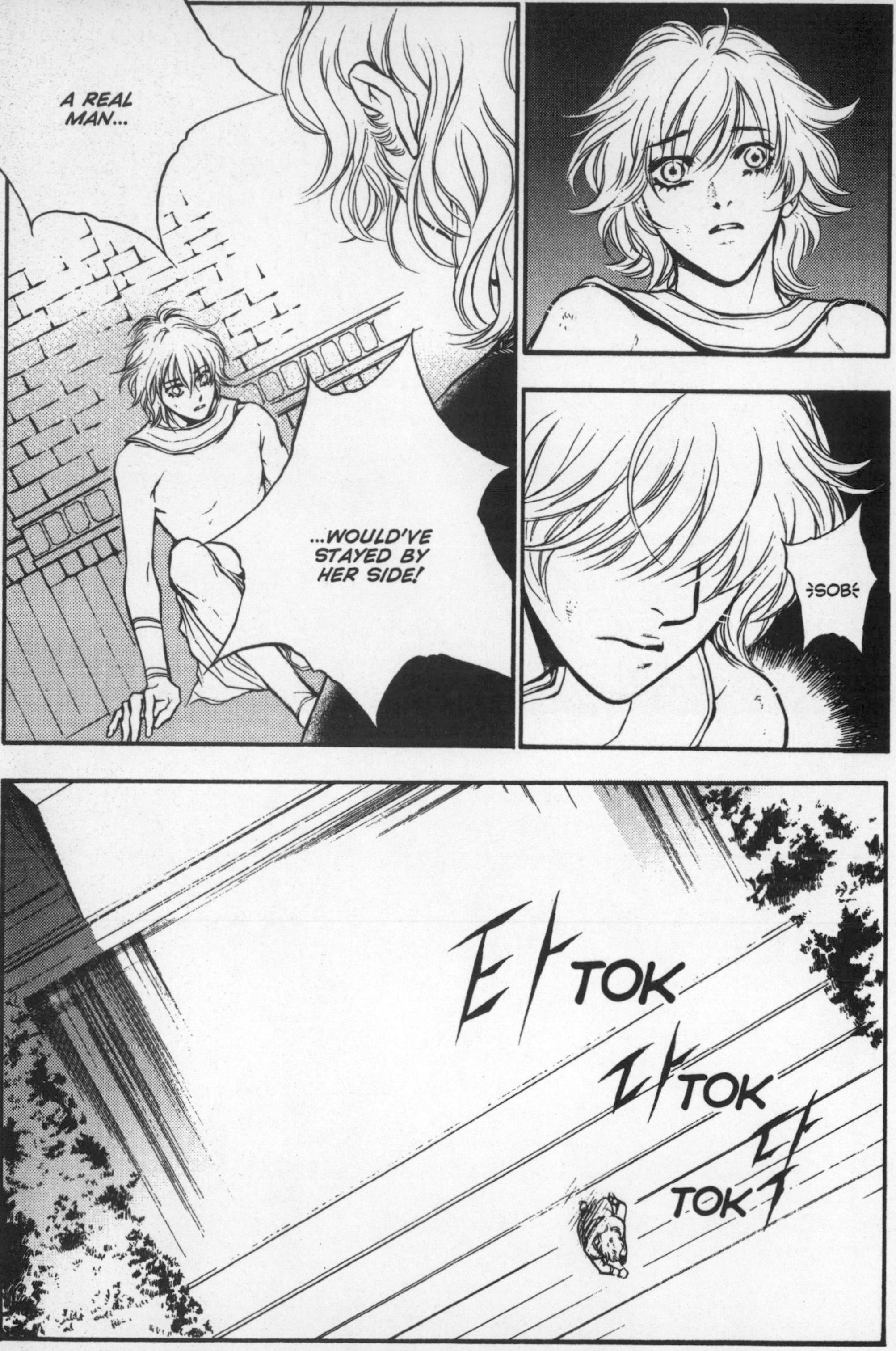
A REAL MAN...
...WOULD'VE STAYED BY HER SIDE!
SOB
TOK
TOK
TOK

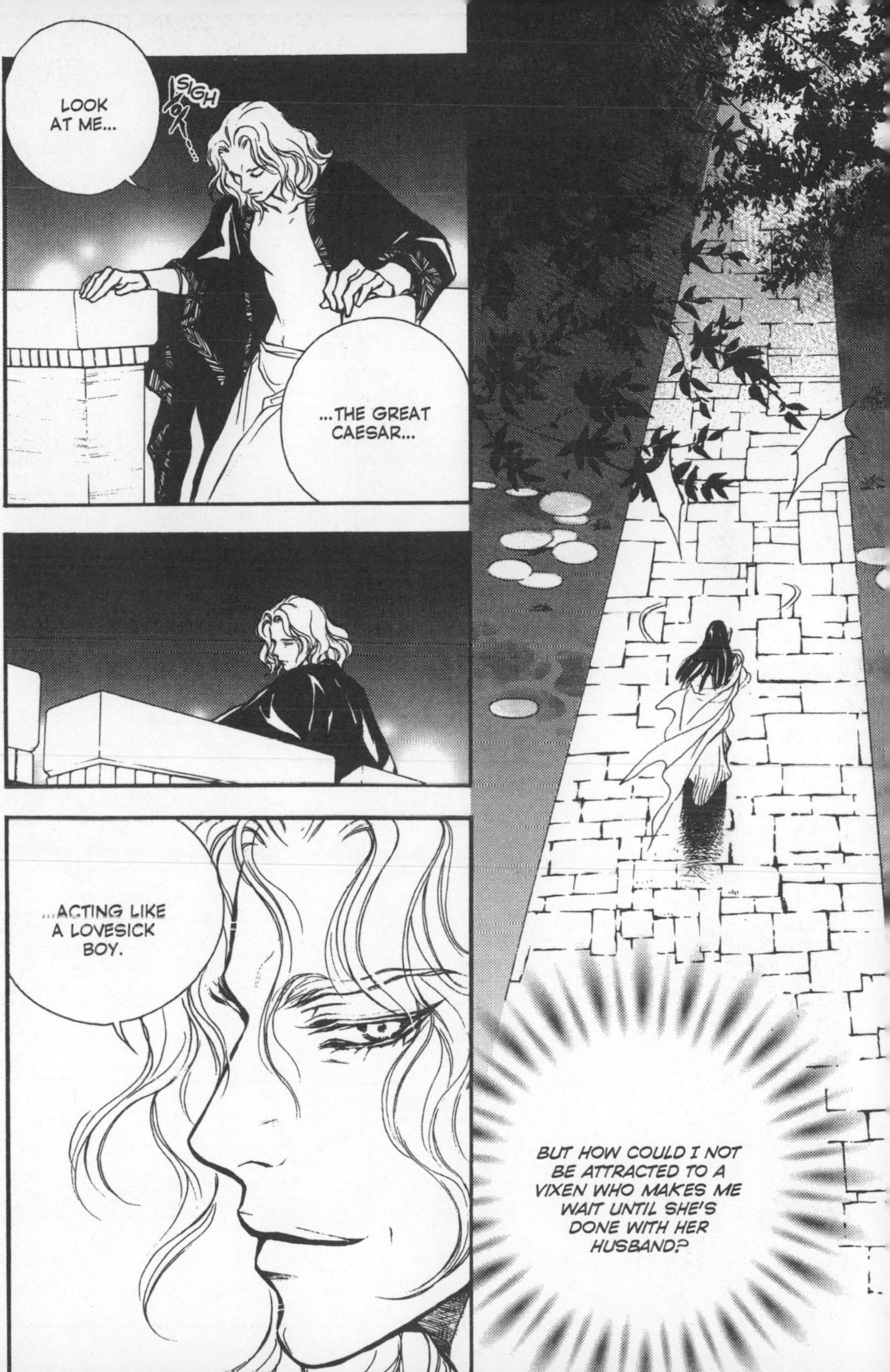
LOOK AT ME...
SIGH
...THE GREAT CAESAR...
...ACTING LIKE A LOVESICK BOY.
BUT HOW COULD I NOT BE ATTRACTED TO A VIXEN WHO MAKES ME WAIT UNTIL SHE'S DONE WITH HER HUSBAND?

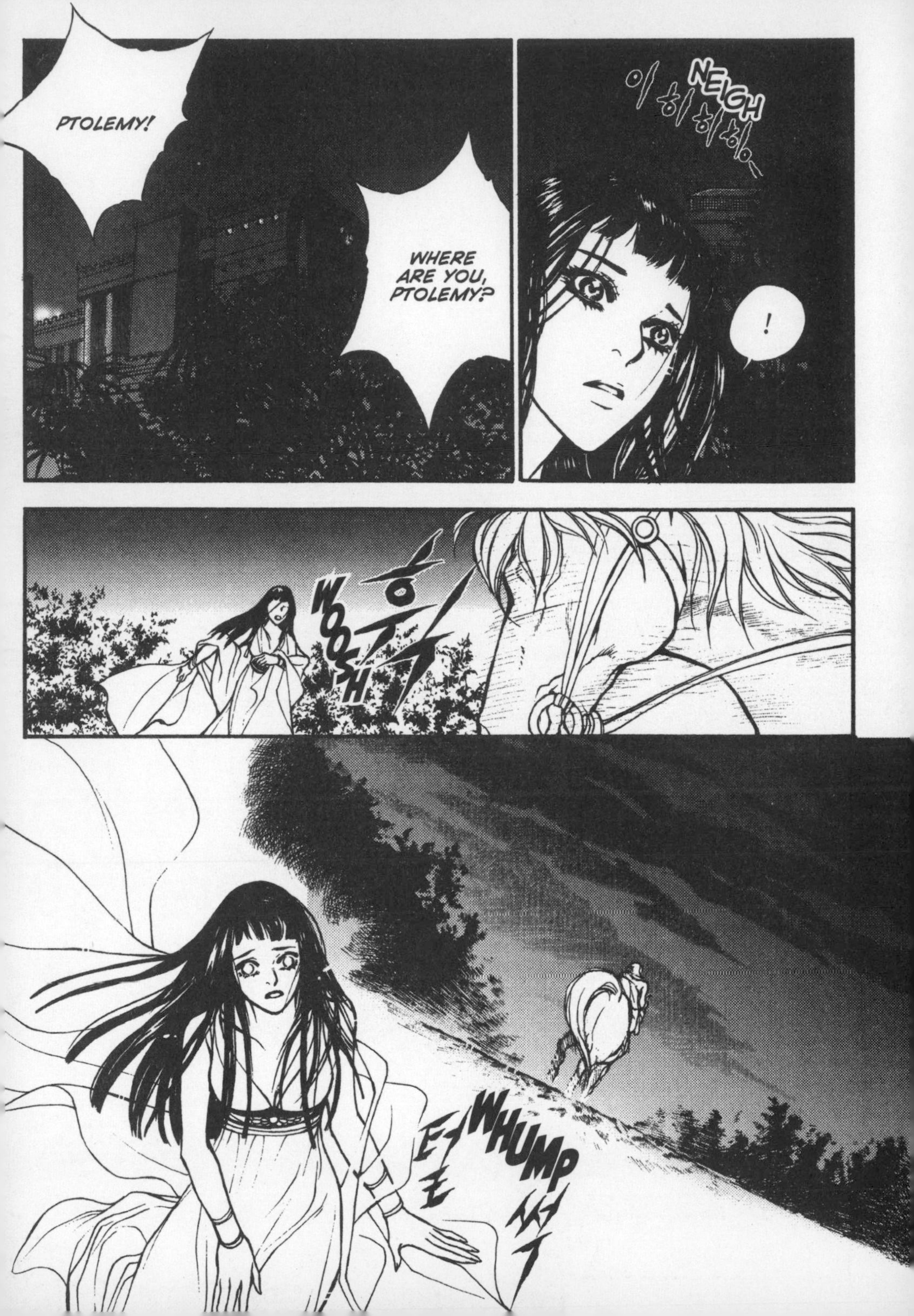
PTOLEMY!
WHERE ARE YOU, PTOLEMY?
NEIGH
!
WOOSH
WHUMP

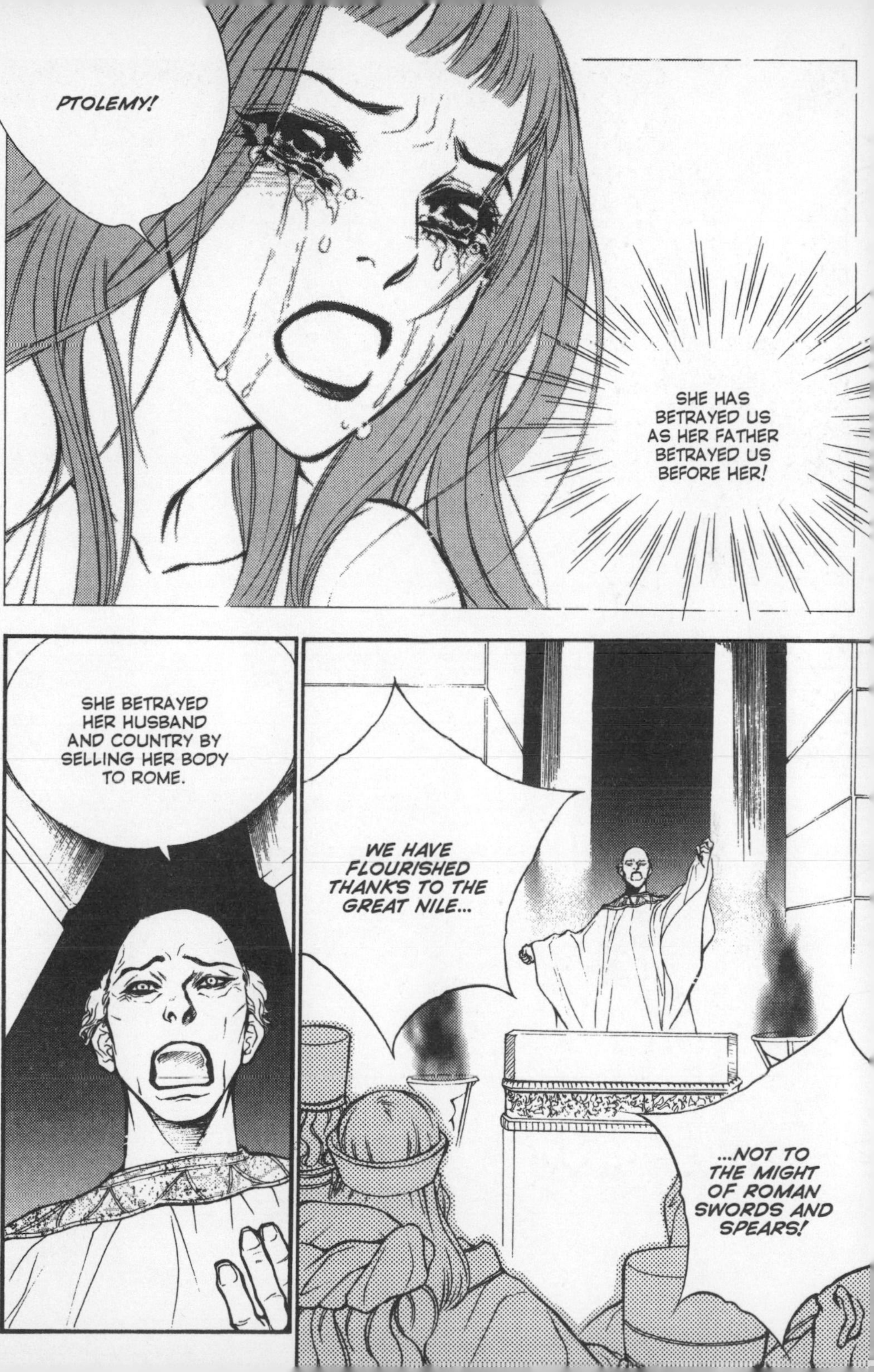
PTOLEMY!
SHE HAS BETRAYED US AS HER FATHER BETRAYED US BEFORE HER!
SHE BETRAYED HER HUSBAND AND COUNTRY BY SELLING HER BODY TO ROME.
WE HAVE FLOURISHED THANKS TO THE GREAT NILE...
...NOT TO THE MIGHT OF ROMAN SWORDS AND SPEARS!

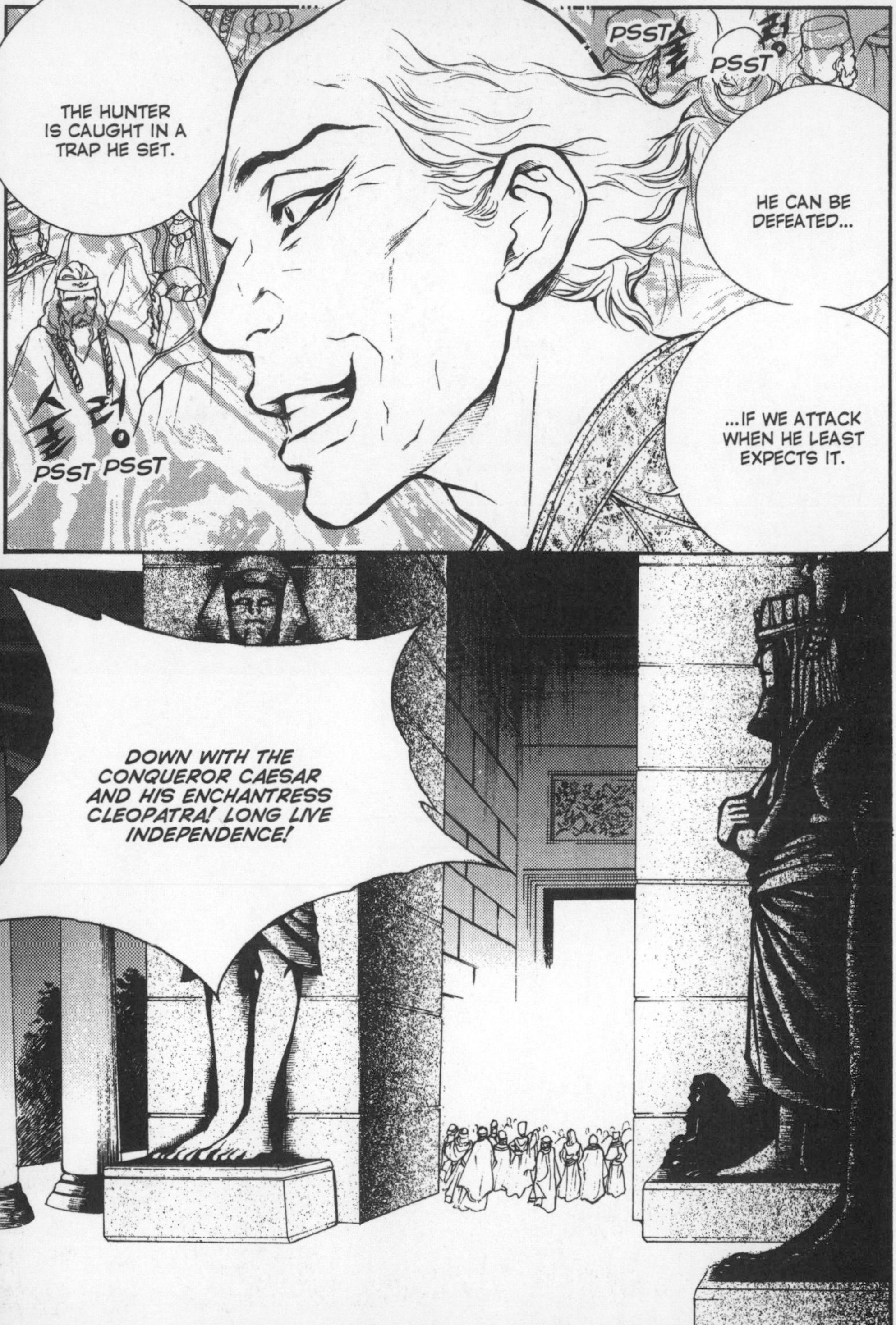
THE HUNTER IS CAUGHT IN A TRAP HE SET.
PSST
PSST
HE CAN BE DEFEATED...
...IF WE ATTACK WHEN HE LEAST EXPECTS IT.
PSST PSST
DOWN WITH THE CONQUEROR CAESAR AND HIS ENCHANTRESS CLEOPATRA! LONG LIVE INDEPENDENCE!

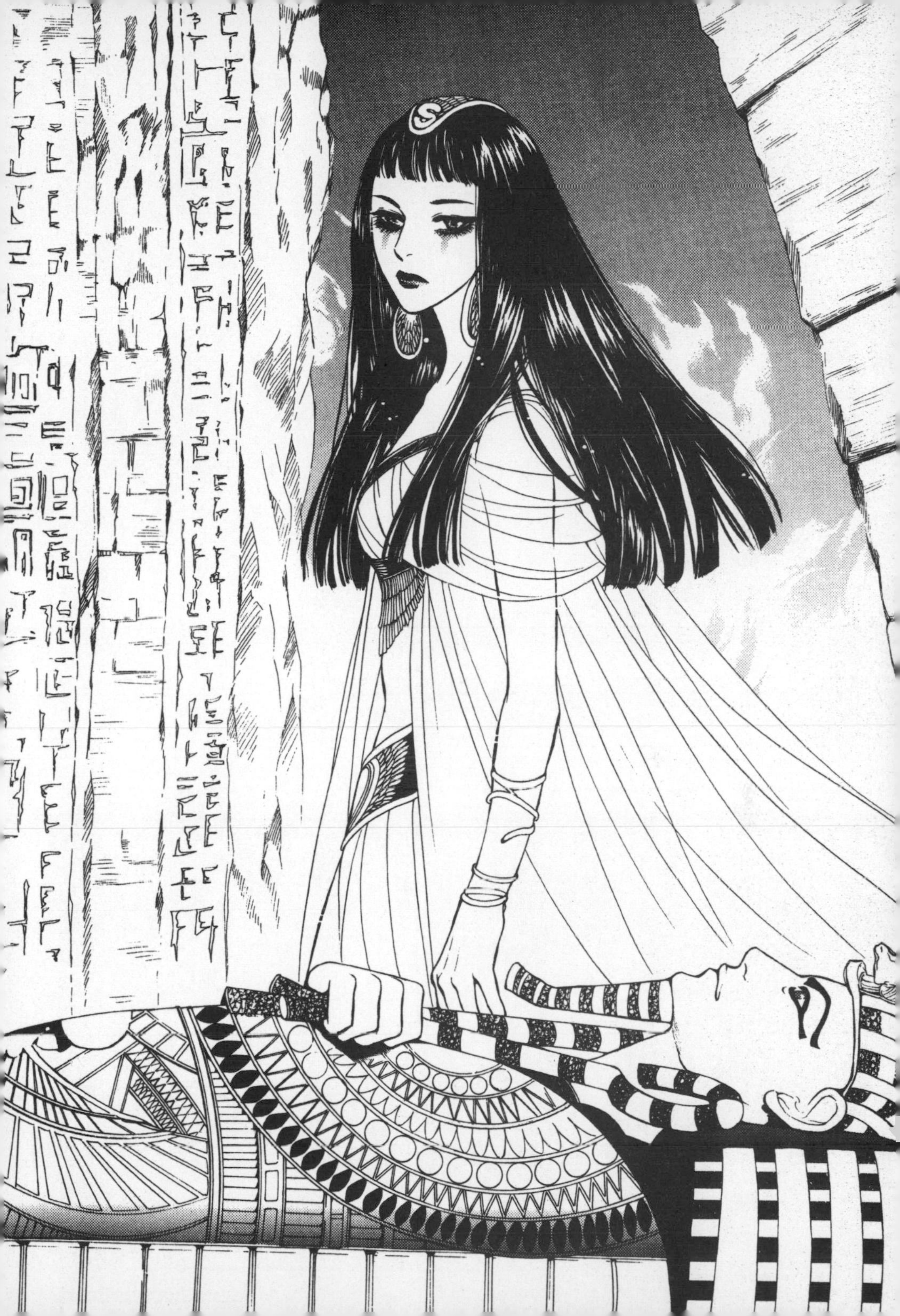

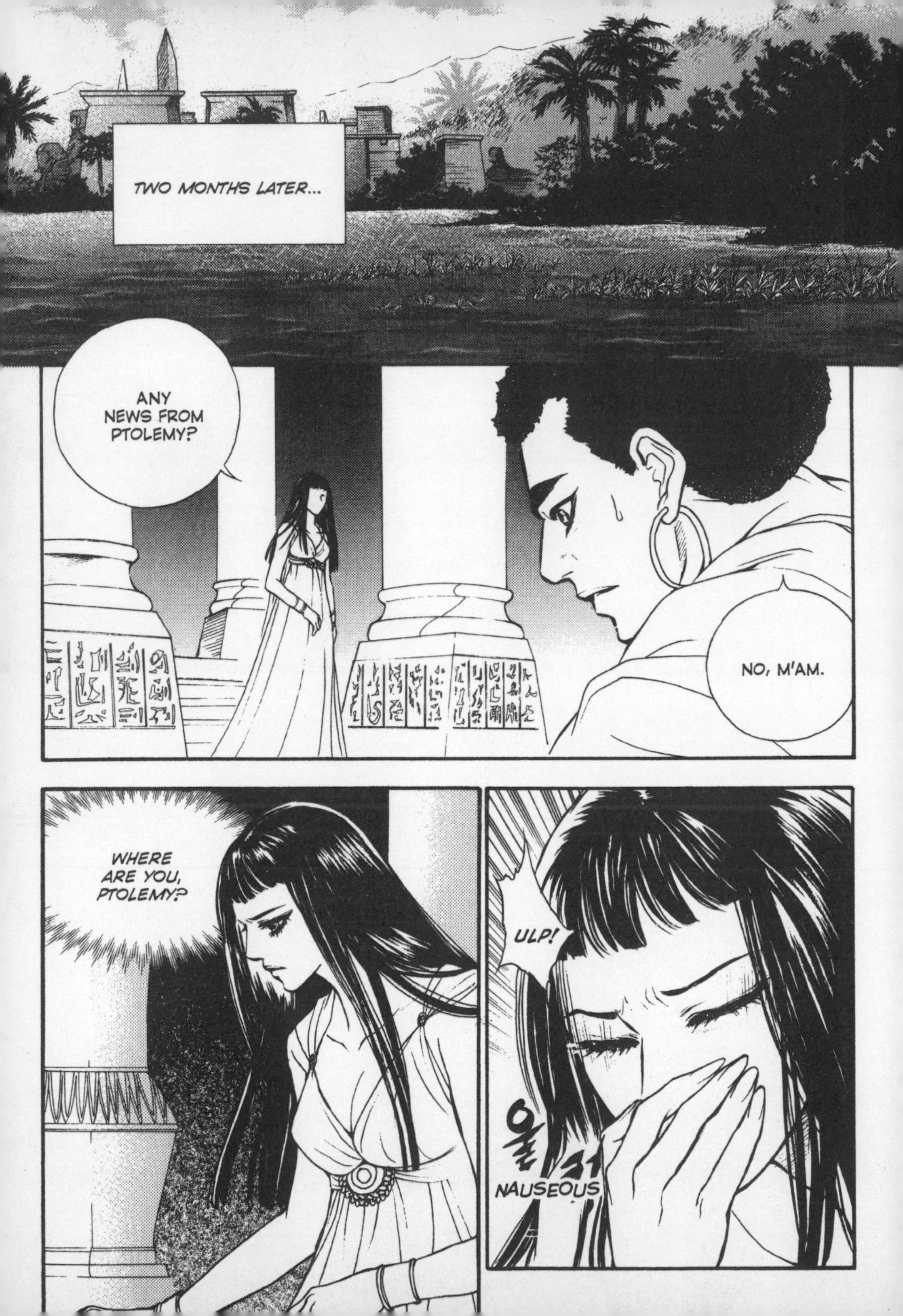
TWO MONTHS LATER...
ANY NEWS FROM PTOLEMY?
NO, M'AM.
WHERE ARE YOU, PTOLEMY?
ULP!
NAUSEOUS

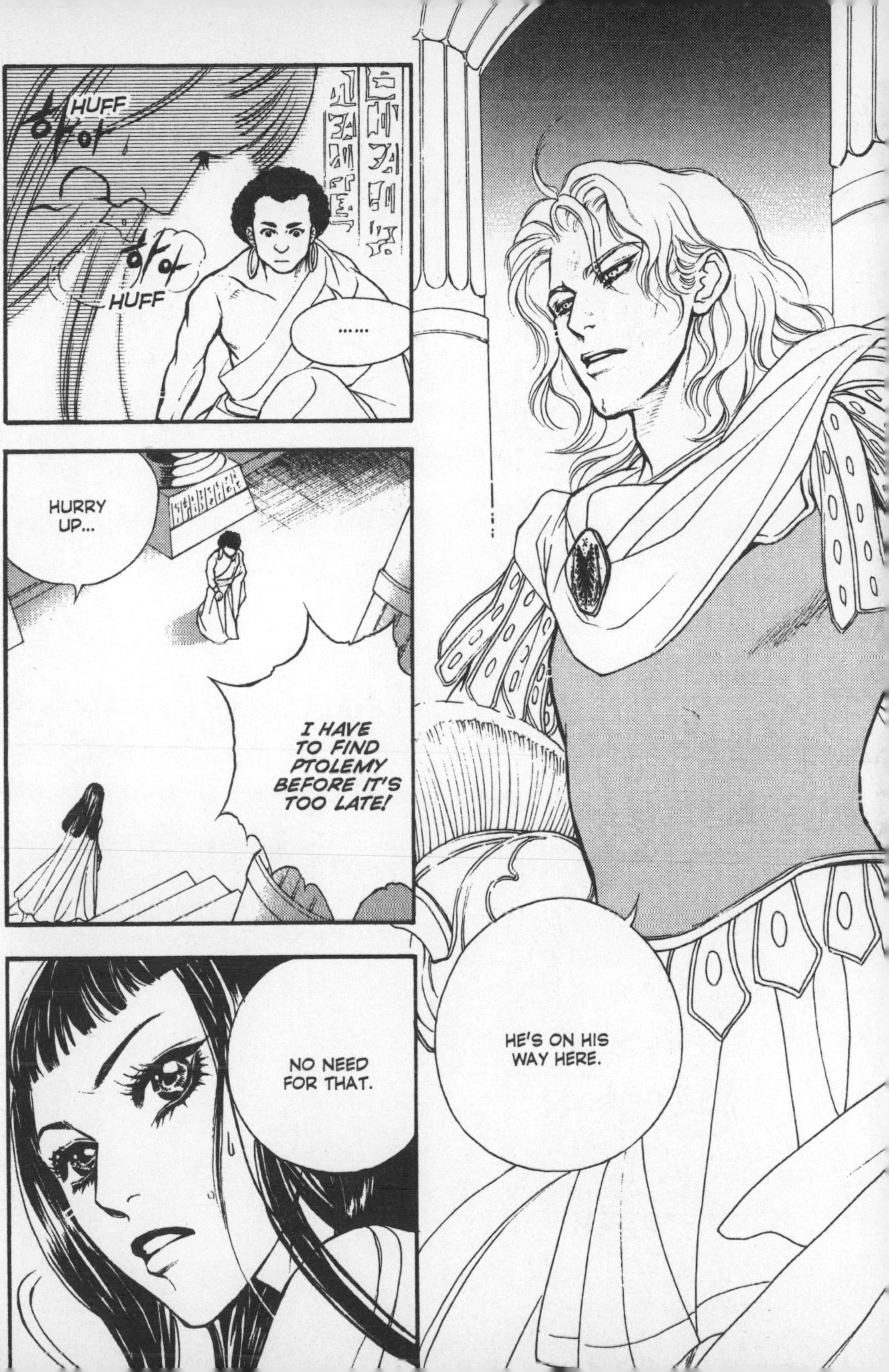
하아 HUFF
하아 HUFF
......
HURRY UP...
I HAVE TO FIND PTOLEMY BEFORE IT'S TOO LATE!
NO NEED FOR THAT.
HE'S ON HIS WAY HERE.

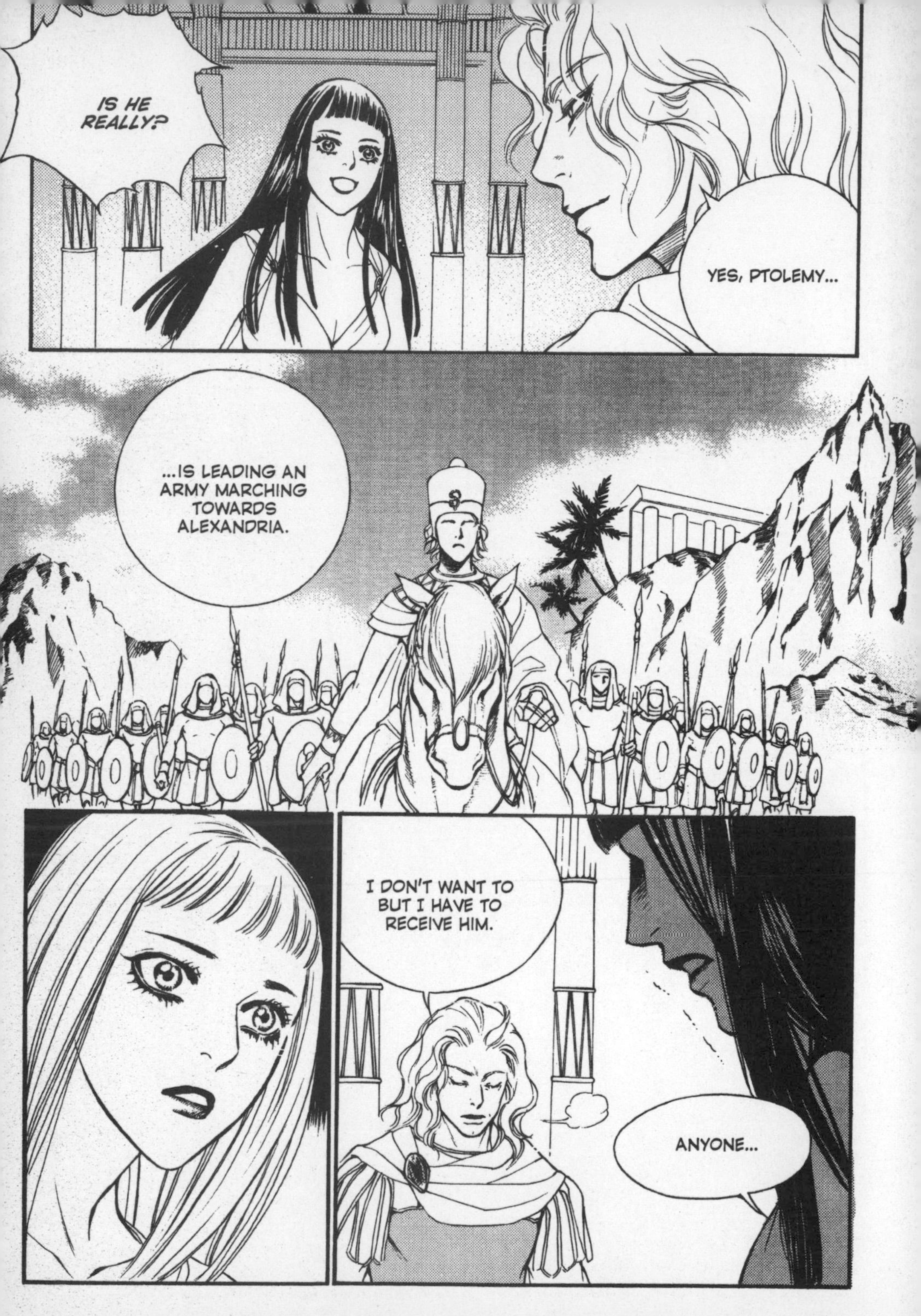
IS HE REALLY?
YES, PTOLEMY...
...IS LEADING AN ARMY MARCHING TOWARDS ALEXANDRIA.
I DON'T WANT TO BUT I HAVE TO RECEIVE HIM.
ANYONE...

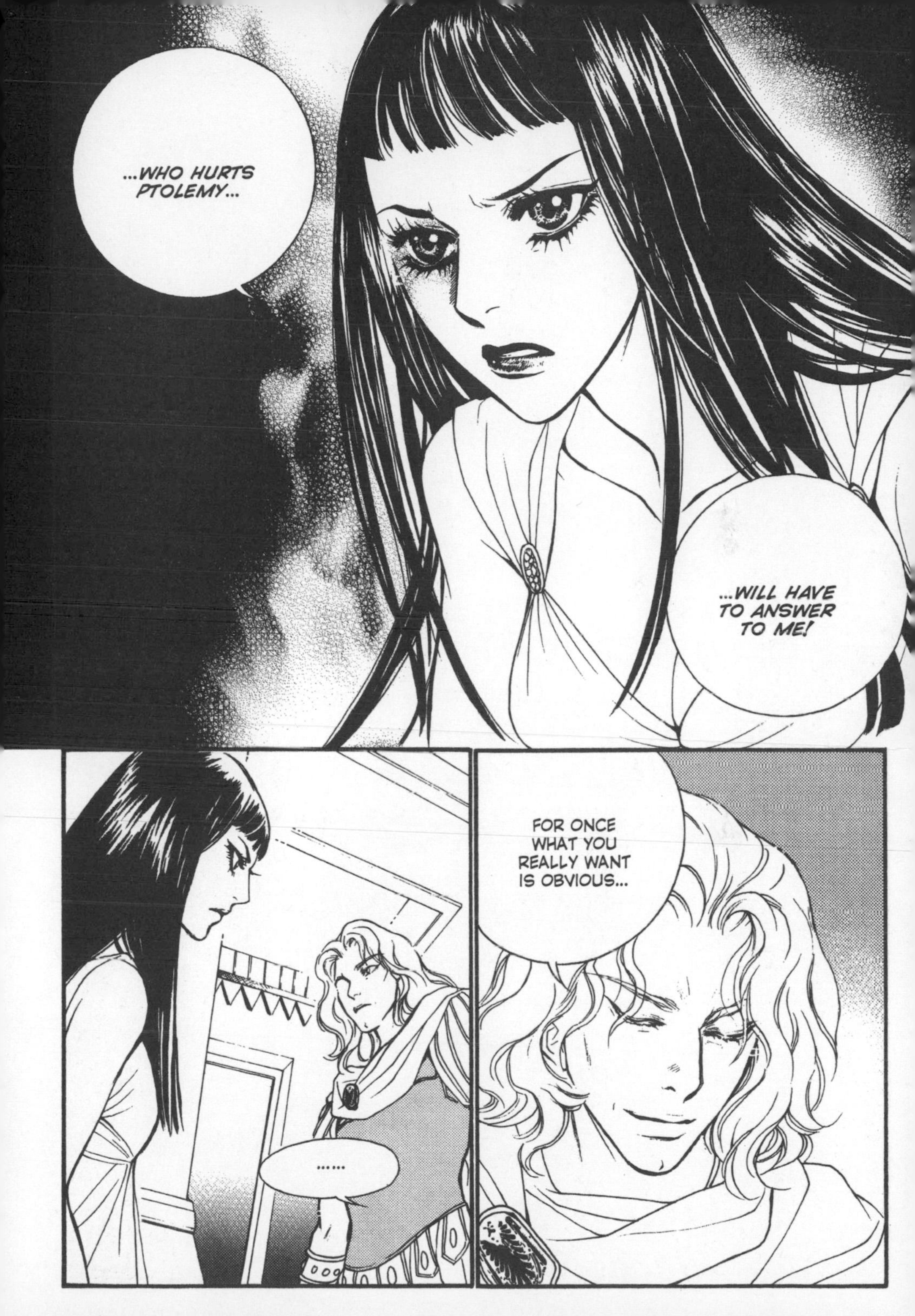
...WHO HURTS PTOLEMY...
...WILL HAVE TO ANSWER TO ME!
......
FOR ONCE WHAT YOU REALLY WANT IS OBVIOUS...

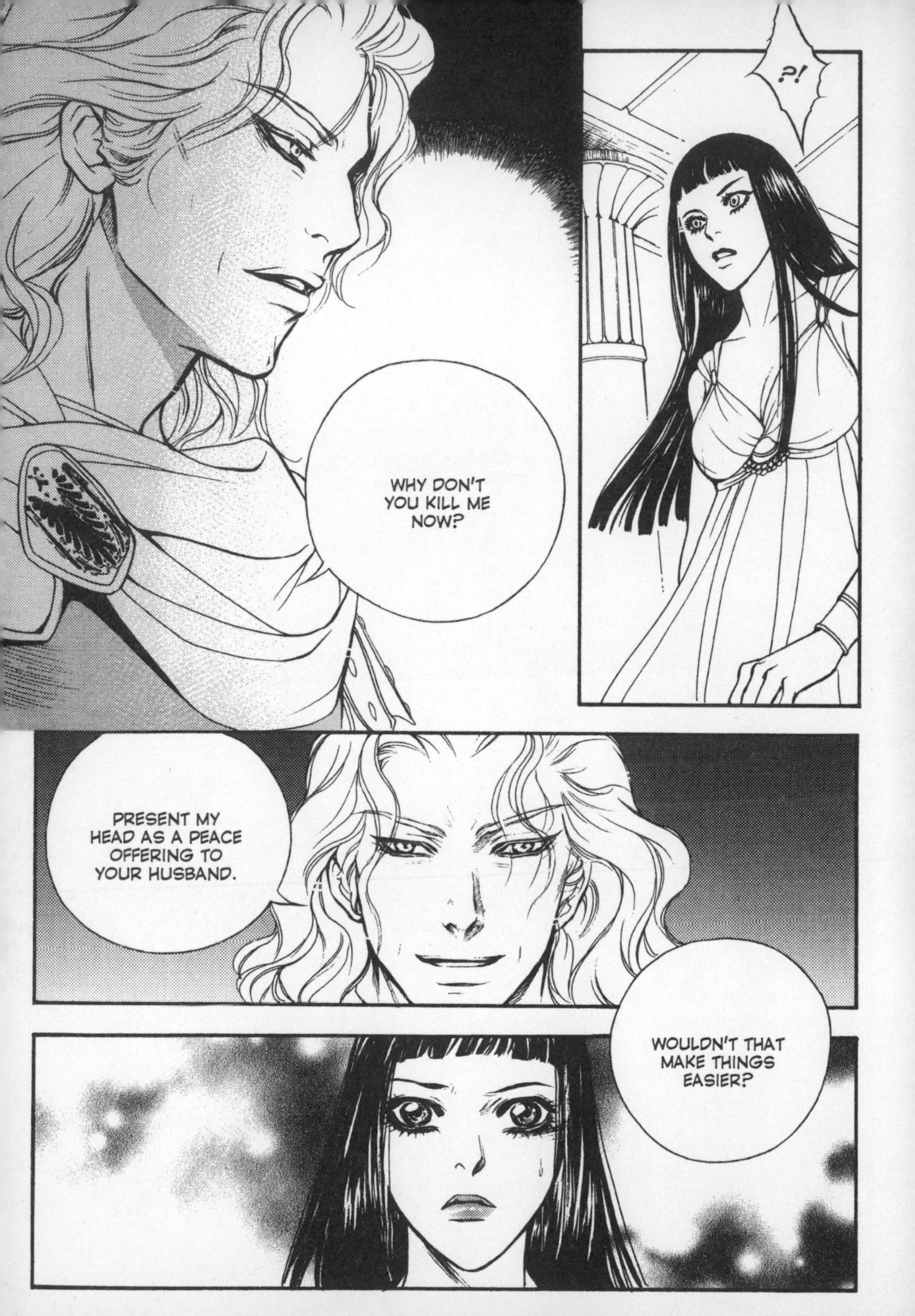
WHY DON'T YOU KILL ME NOW?
?!
PRESENT MY HEAD AS A PEACE OFFERING TO YOUR HUSBAND.
WOULDN'T THAT MAKE THINGS EASIER?

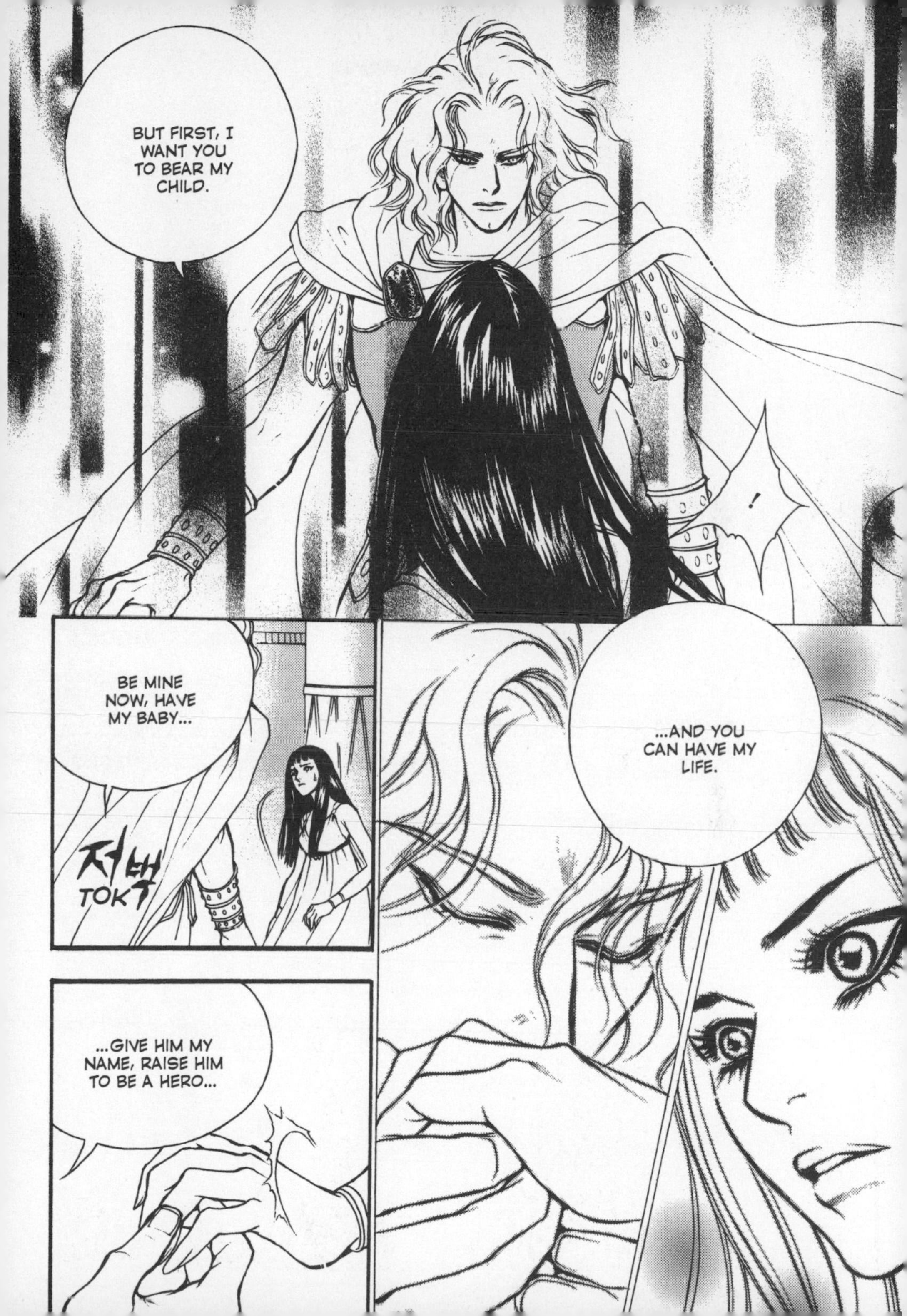
BUT FIRST, I WANT YOU TO BEAR MY CHILD.
!
BE MINE NOW, HAVE MY BABY...
저벅 TOK
...GIVE HIM MY NAME, RAISE HIM TO BE A HERO...
...AND YOU CAN HAVE MY LIFE.

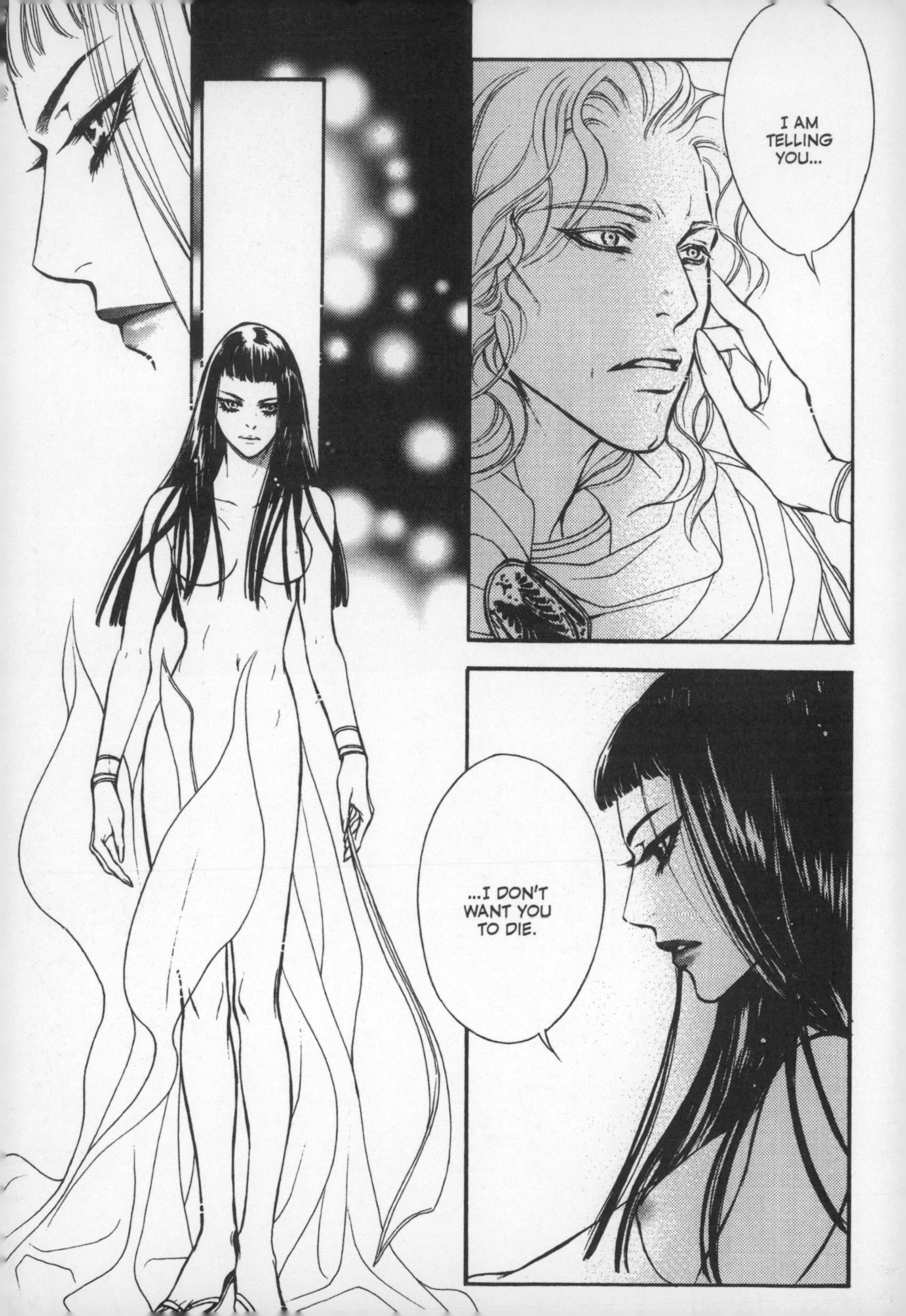
I AM TELLING YOU...
...I DON'T WANT YOU TO DIE.

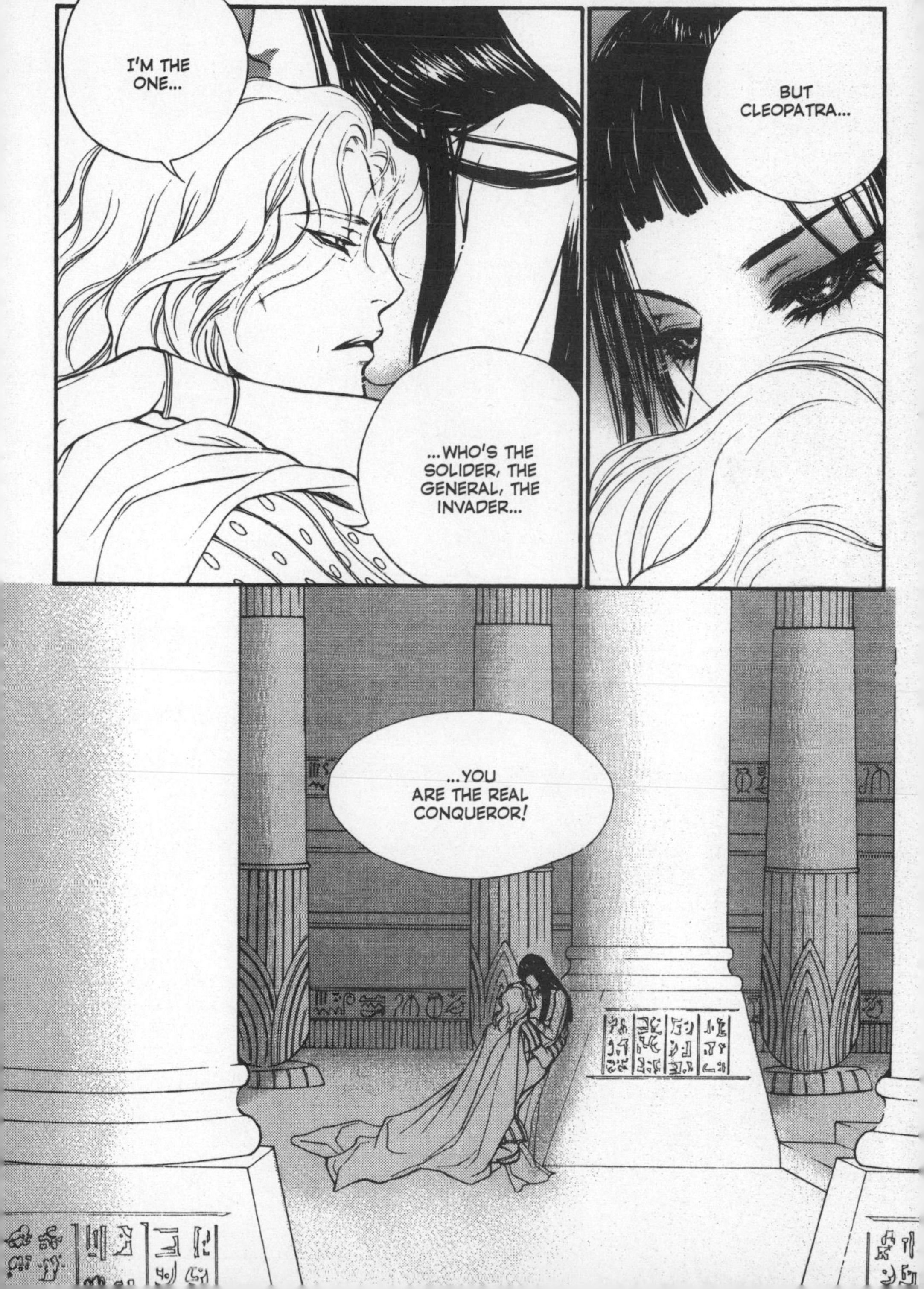
I'M THE ONE...
...WHO'S THE SOLIDER, THE GENERAL, THE INVADER...
BUT CLEOPATRA...
...YOU ARE THE REAL CONQUEROR!

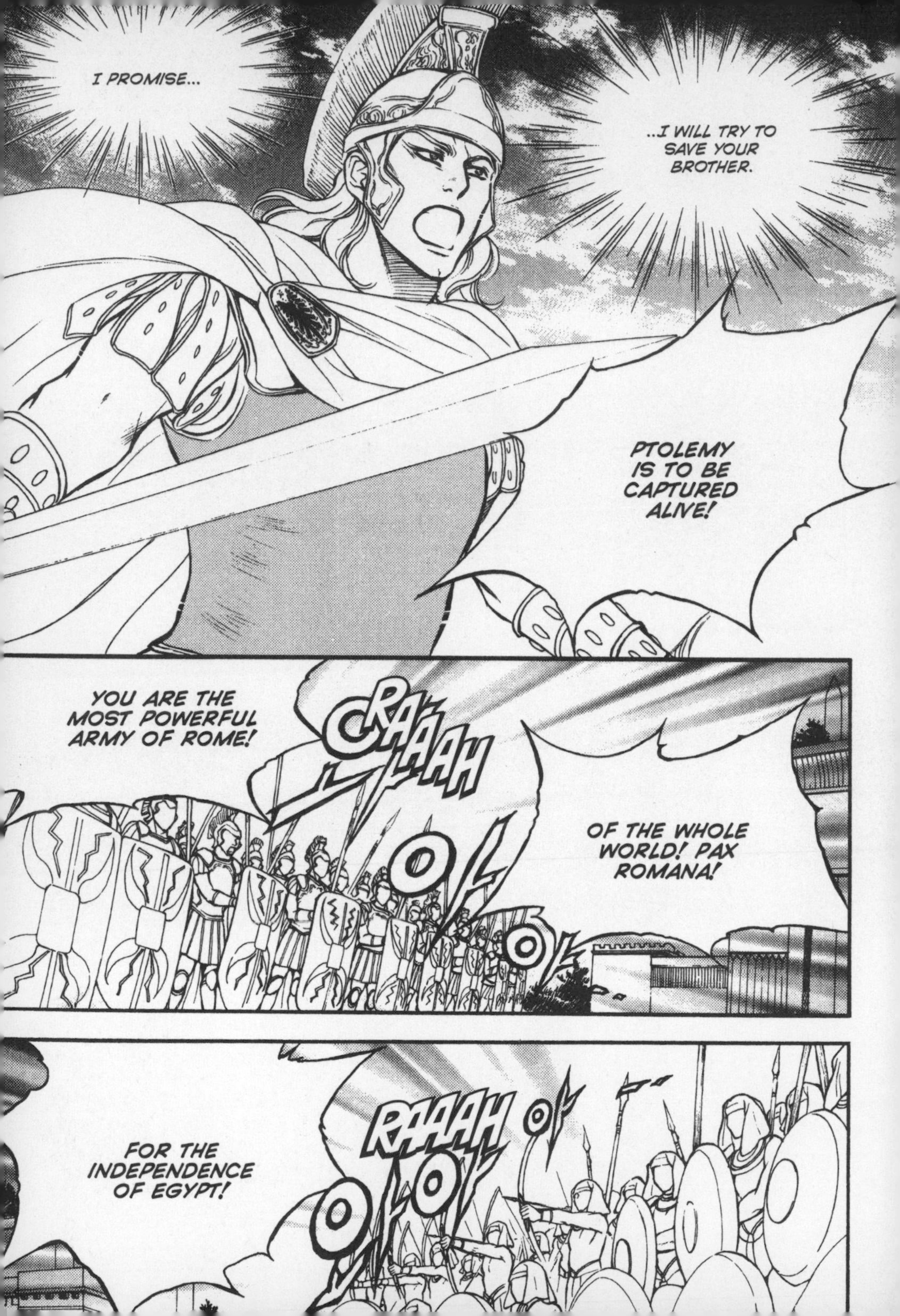
I PROMISE...
...I WILL TRY TO SAVE YOUR BROTHER.
PTOLEMY IS TO BE CAPTURED ALIVE!
YOU ARE THE MOST POWERFUL ARMY OF ROME!
CRAAAAH
OF THE WHOLE WORLD! PAX ROMANA!
FOR THE INDEPENDENCE OF EGYPT!
RAAAAH

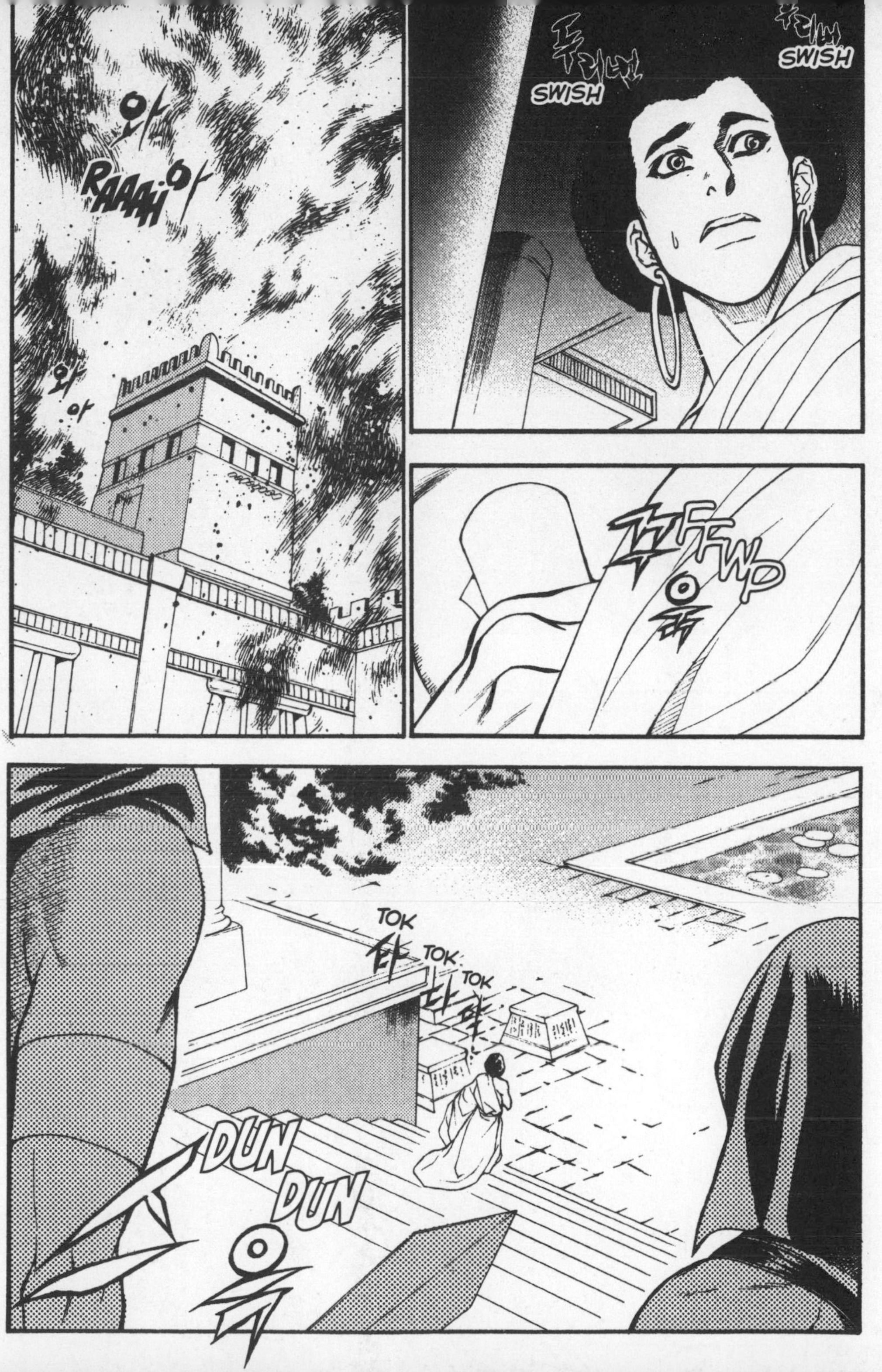
와아
RAAAH
와아
SWISH
SWISH
FFWP
TOK
TOK
TOK
DUN
DUN

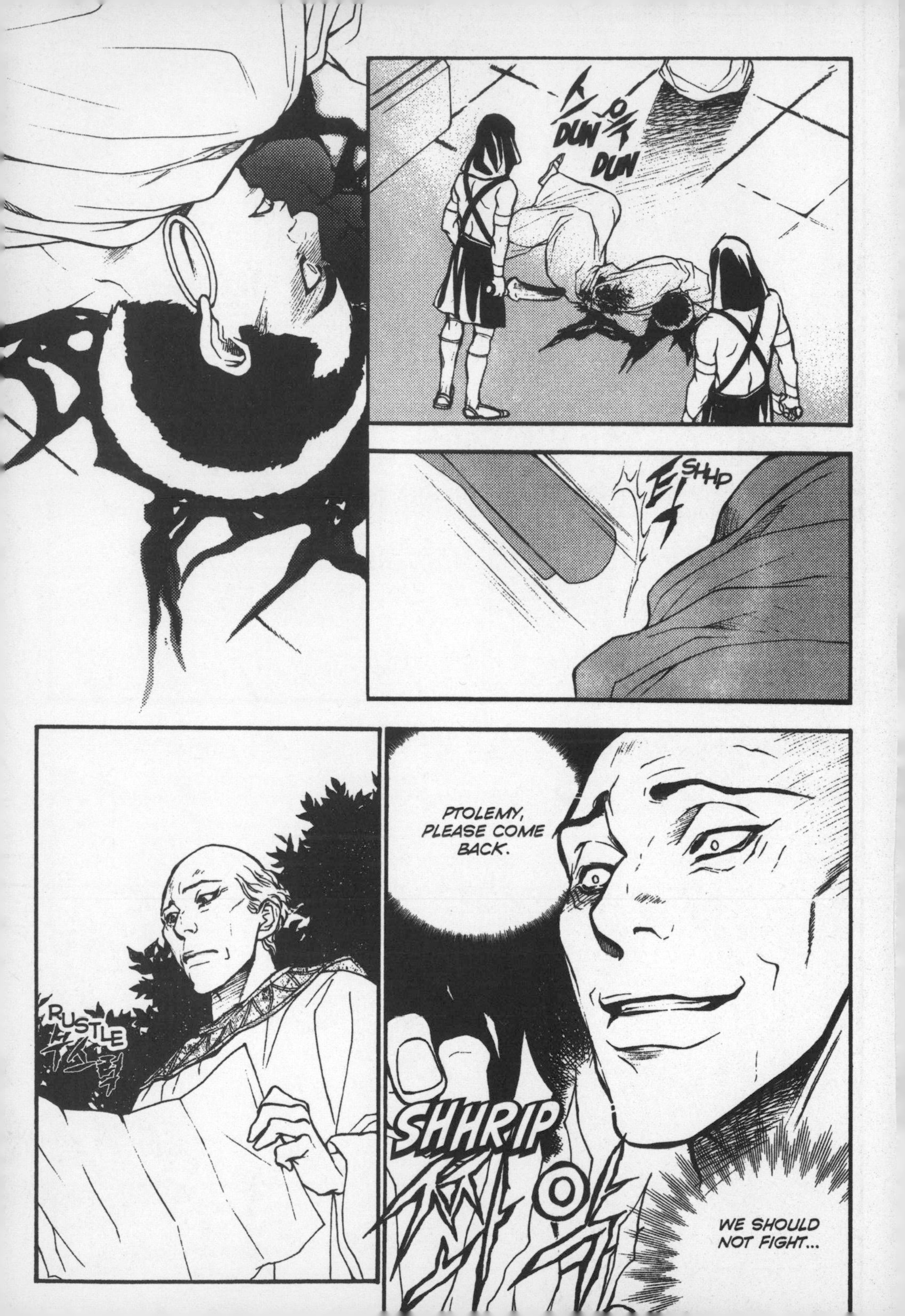
DUN
DUN
SHHP
RUSTLE
PTOLEMY, PLEASE COME BACK.
SHHRIP
WE SHOULD NOT FIGHT...

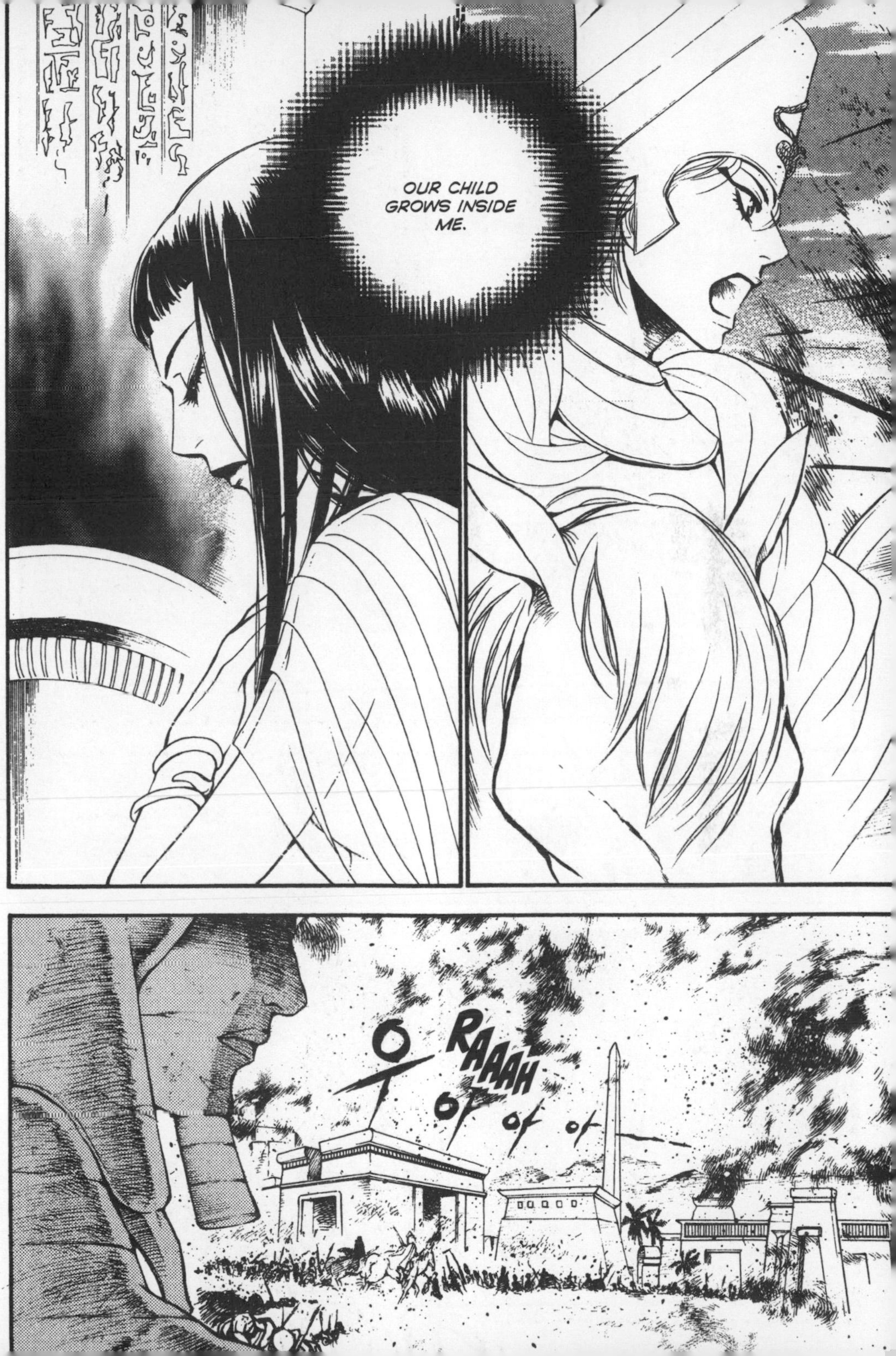
OUR CHILD GROWS INSIDE ME.
O RAAAH
OF OF OF

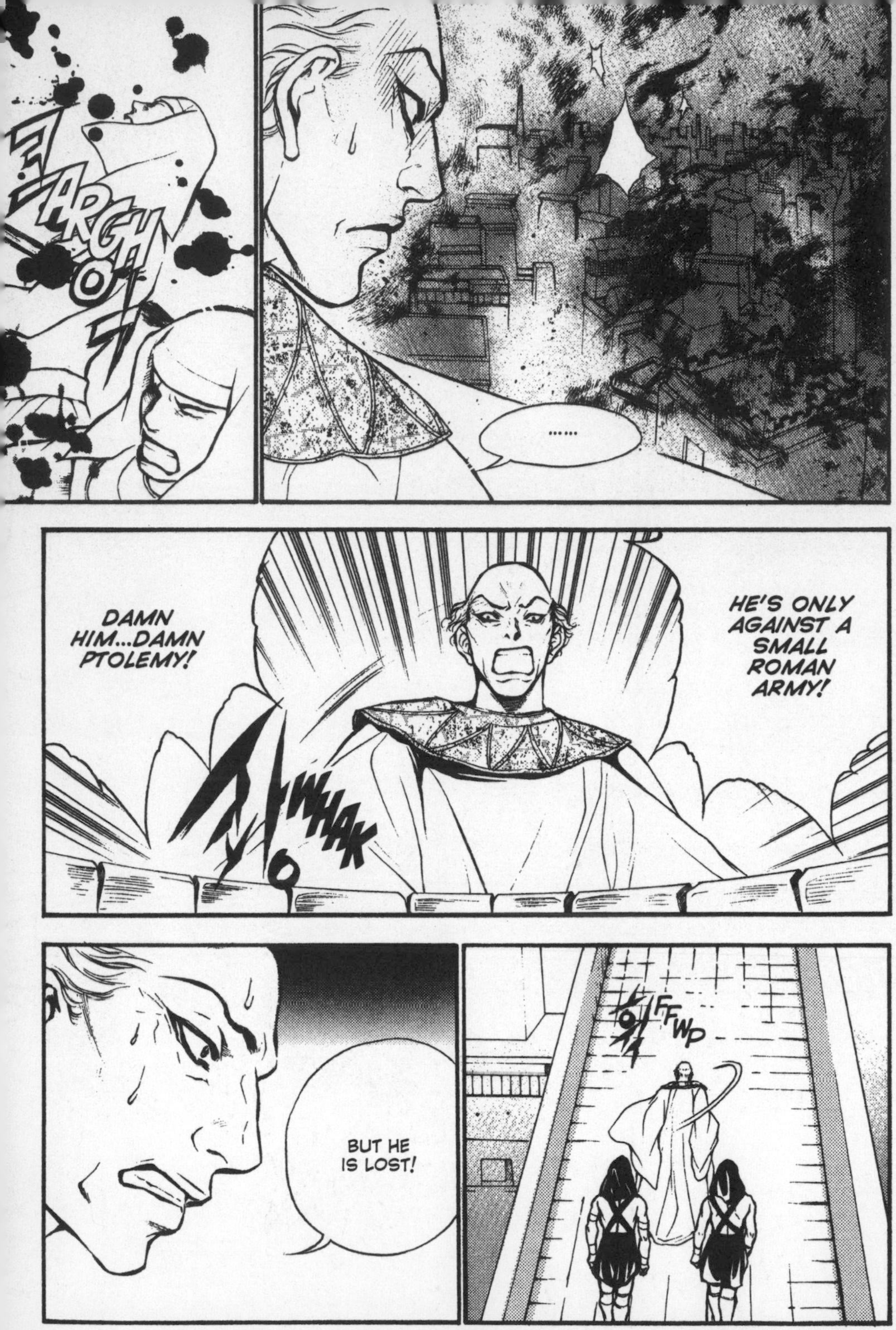
ARGH
......
DAMN HIM...DAMN PTOLEMY!
HE'S ONLY AGAINST A SMALL ROMAN ARMY!
WHAK
BUT HE IS LOST!
FFWP

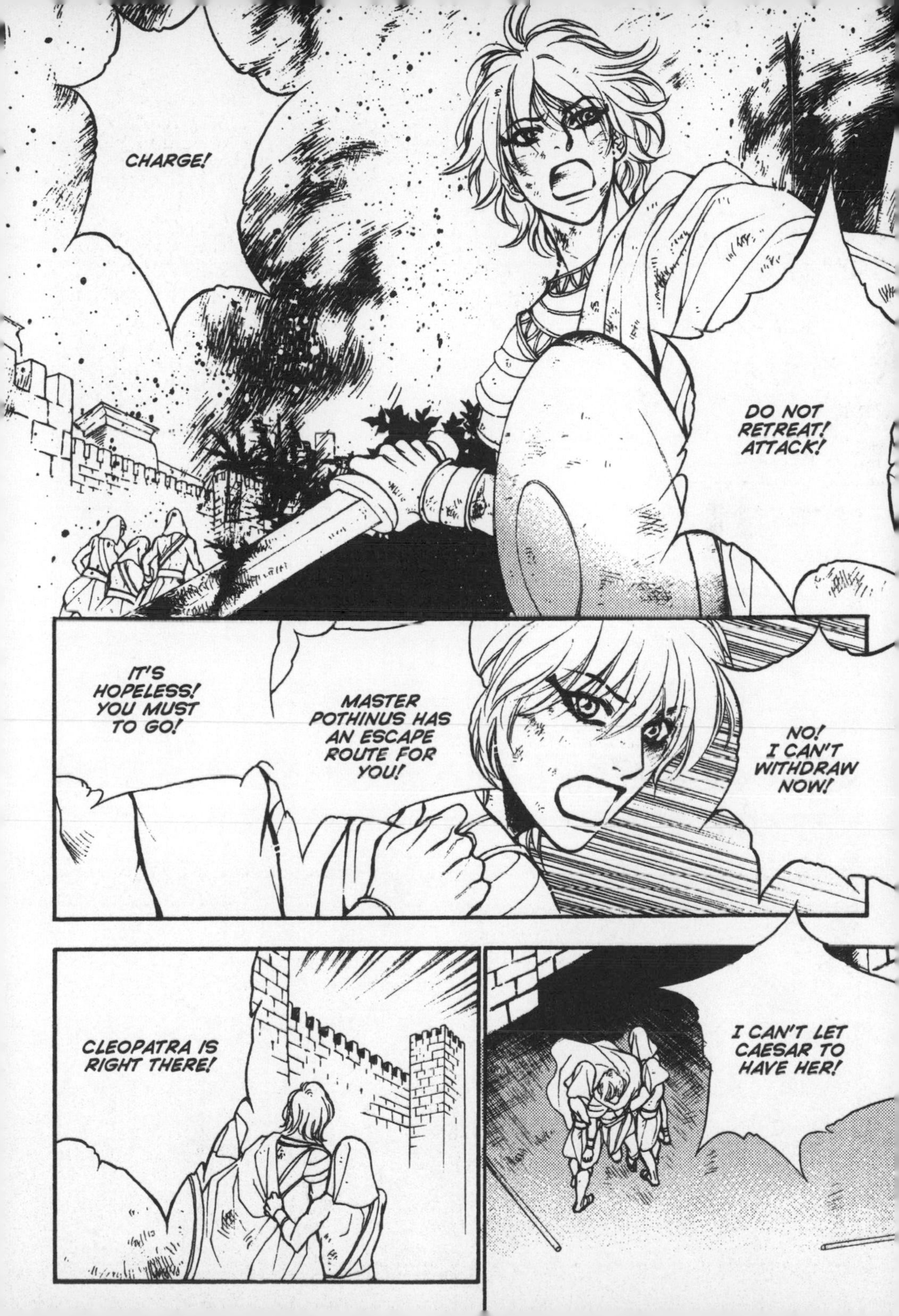
CHARGE!
DO NOT RETREAT! ATTACK!
IT'S HOPELESS! YOU MUST TO GO!
MASTER POTHINUS HAS AN ESCAPE ROUTE FOR YOU!
NO! I CAN'T WITHDRAW NOW!
CLEOPATRA IS RIGHT THERE!
I CAN'T LET CAESAR TO HAVE HER!

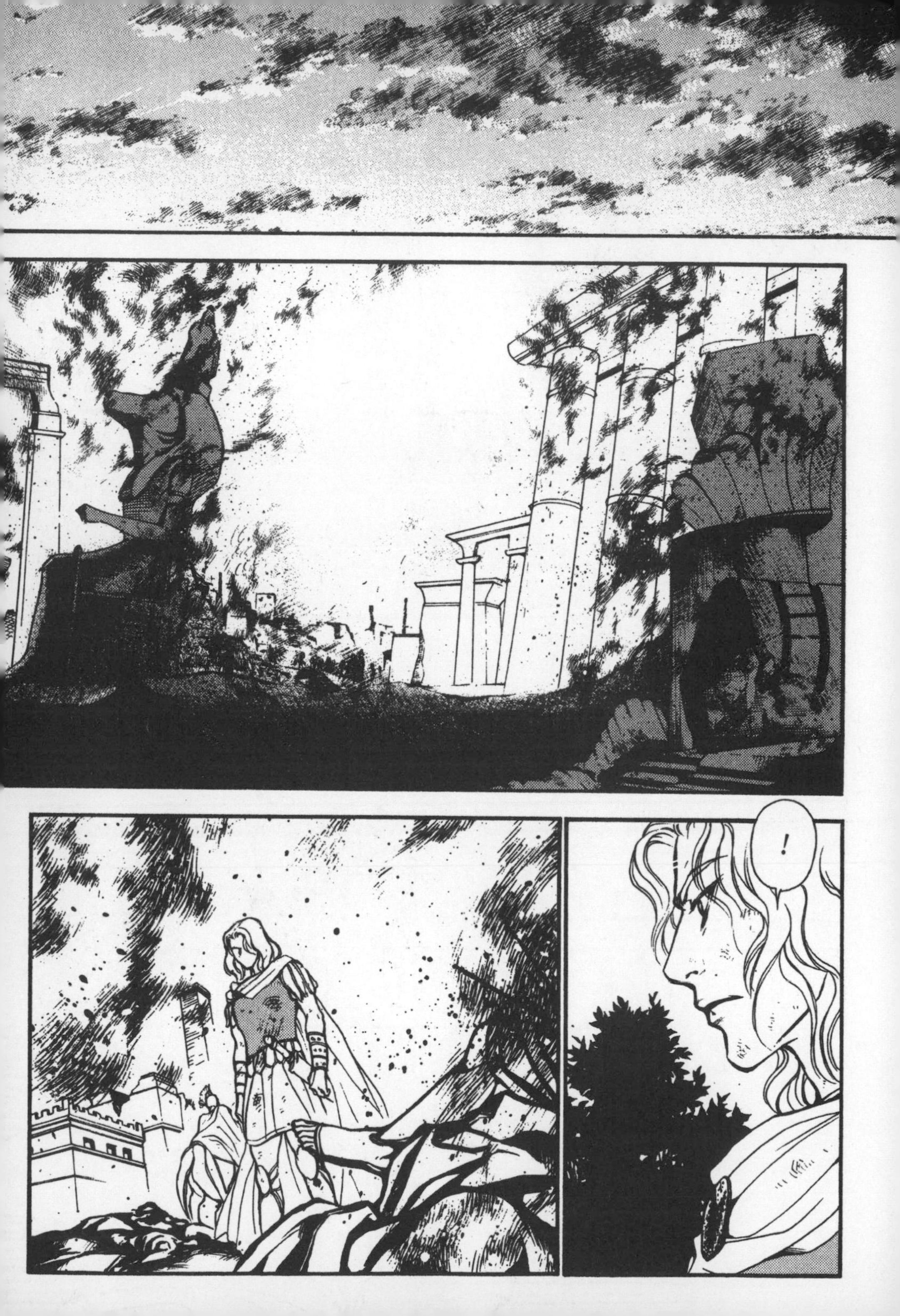
!

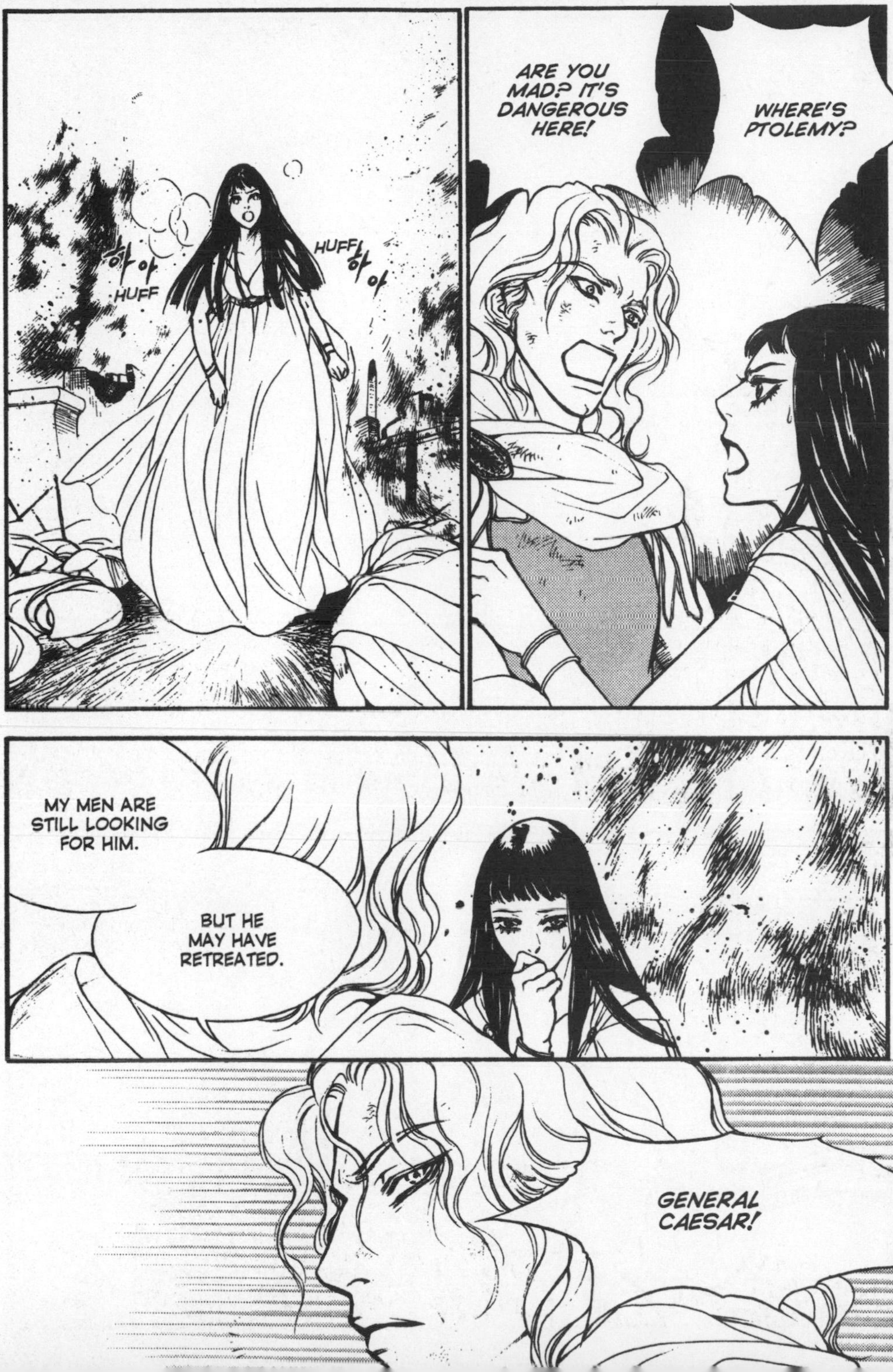
하아
HUFF
HUFF
하아
ARE YOU MAD? IT'S DANGEROUS HERE!
WHERE'S PTOLEMY?
MY MEN ARE STILL LOOKING FOR HIM.
BUT HE MAY HAVE RETREATED.
GENERAL CAESAR!

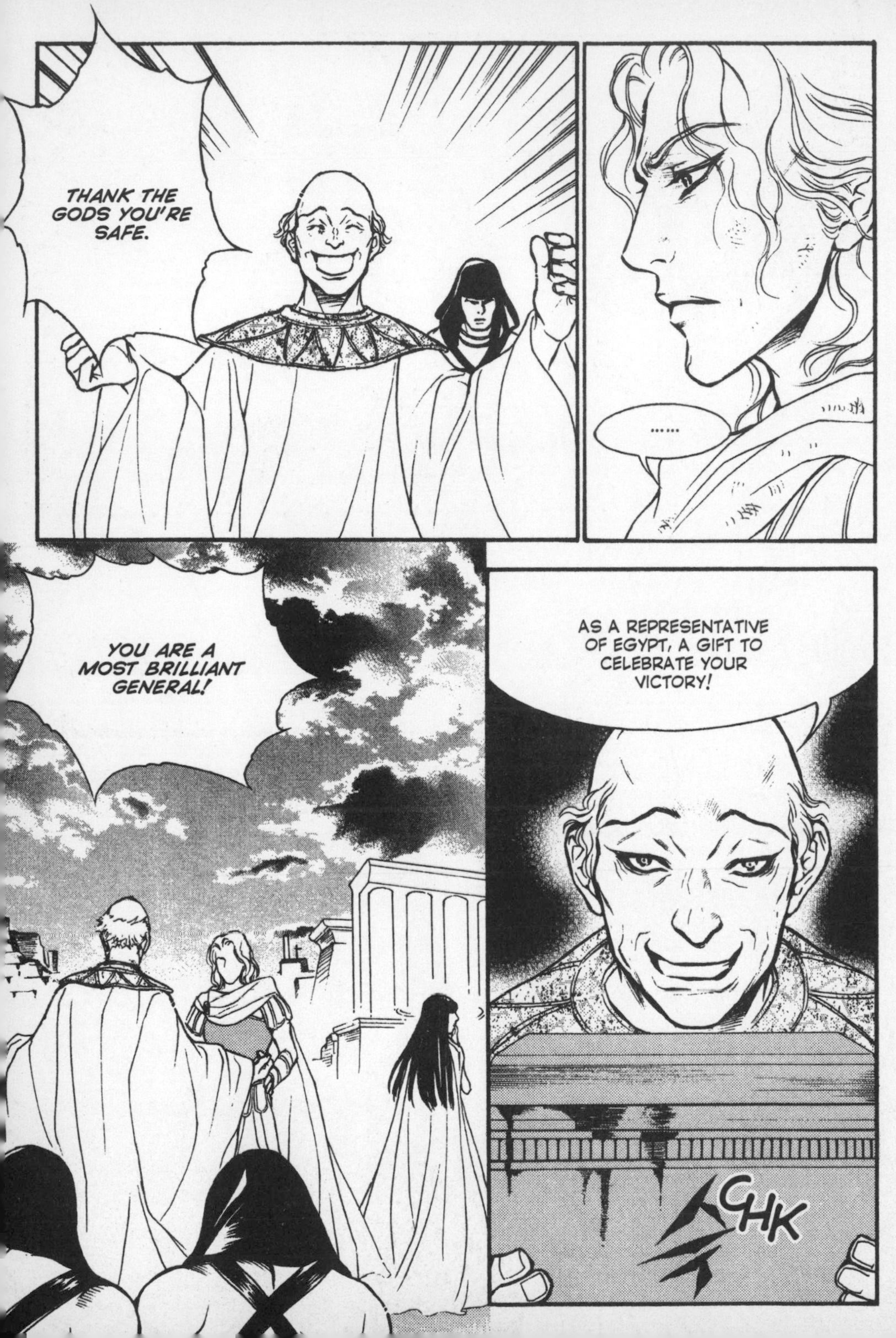
THANK THE GODS YOU'RE SAFE.
......
YOU ARE A MOST BRILLIANT GENERAL!
AS A REPRESENTATIVE OF EGYPT, A GIFT TO CELEBRATE YOUR VICTORY!
CHK

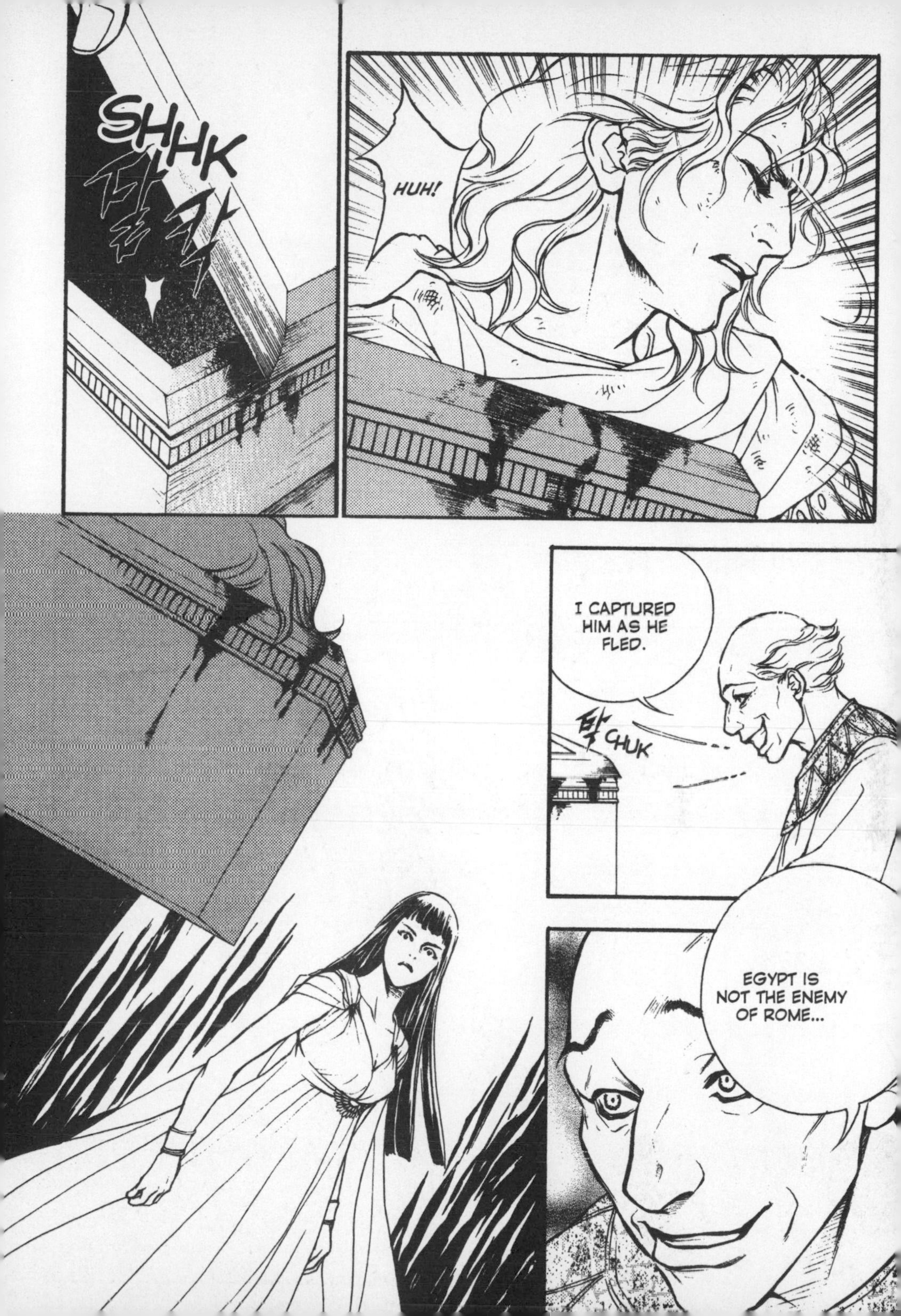
SHHK
HUH!
I CAPTURED HIM AS HE FLED.
탁 CHUK
EGYPT IS NOT THE ENEMY OF ROME...

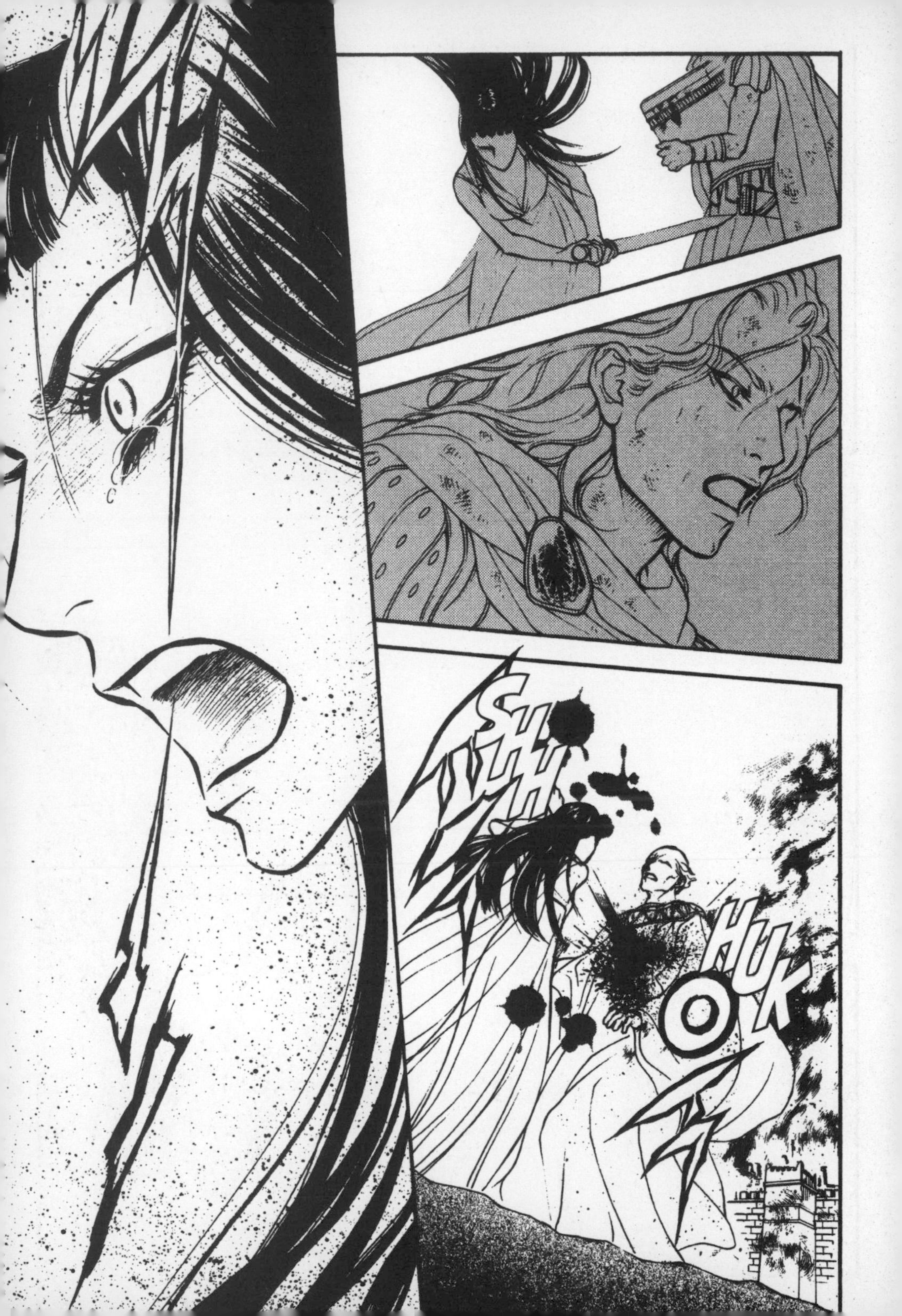
SHHH
HUOK

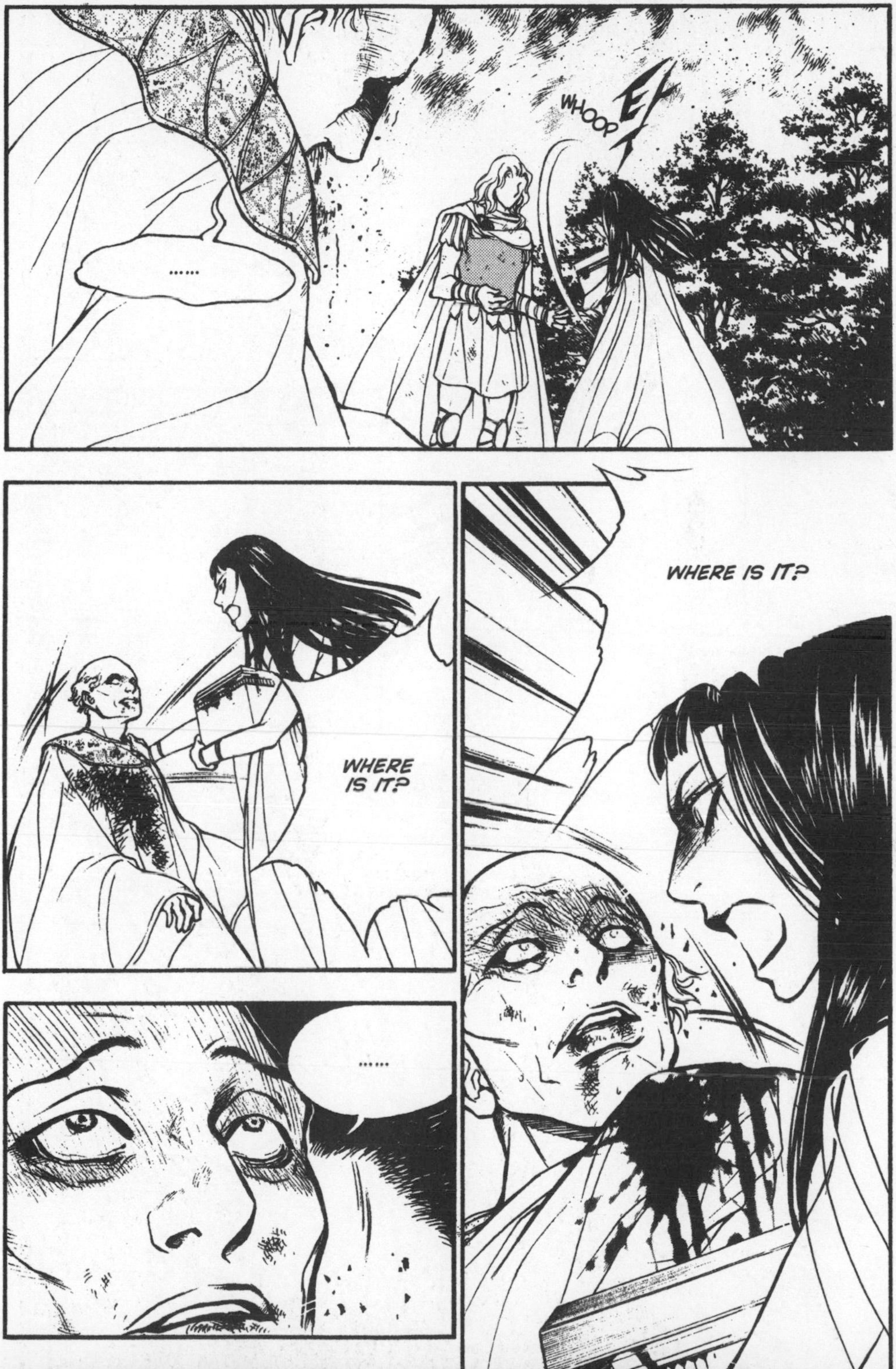
……
WHOOPE
WHERE IS IT?
……
WHERE IS IT?

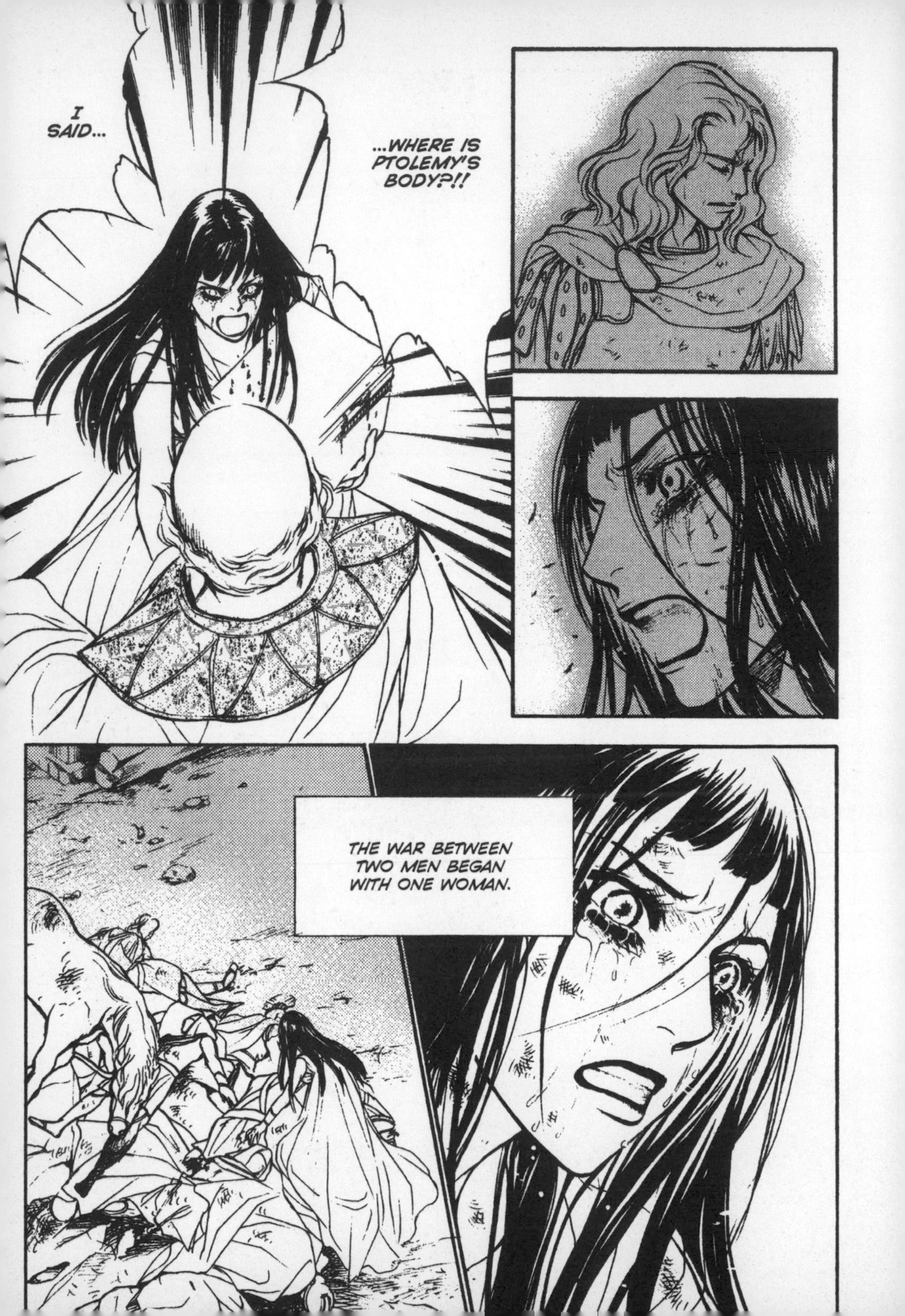
I SAID...
...WHERE IS PTOLEMY'S BODY?!!
THE WAR BETWEEN TWO MEN BEGAN WITH ONE WOMAN.

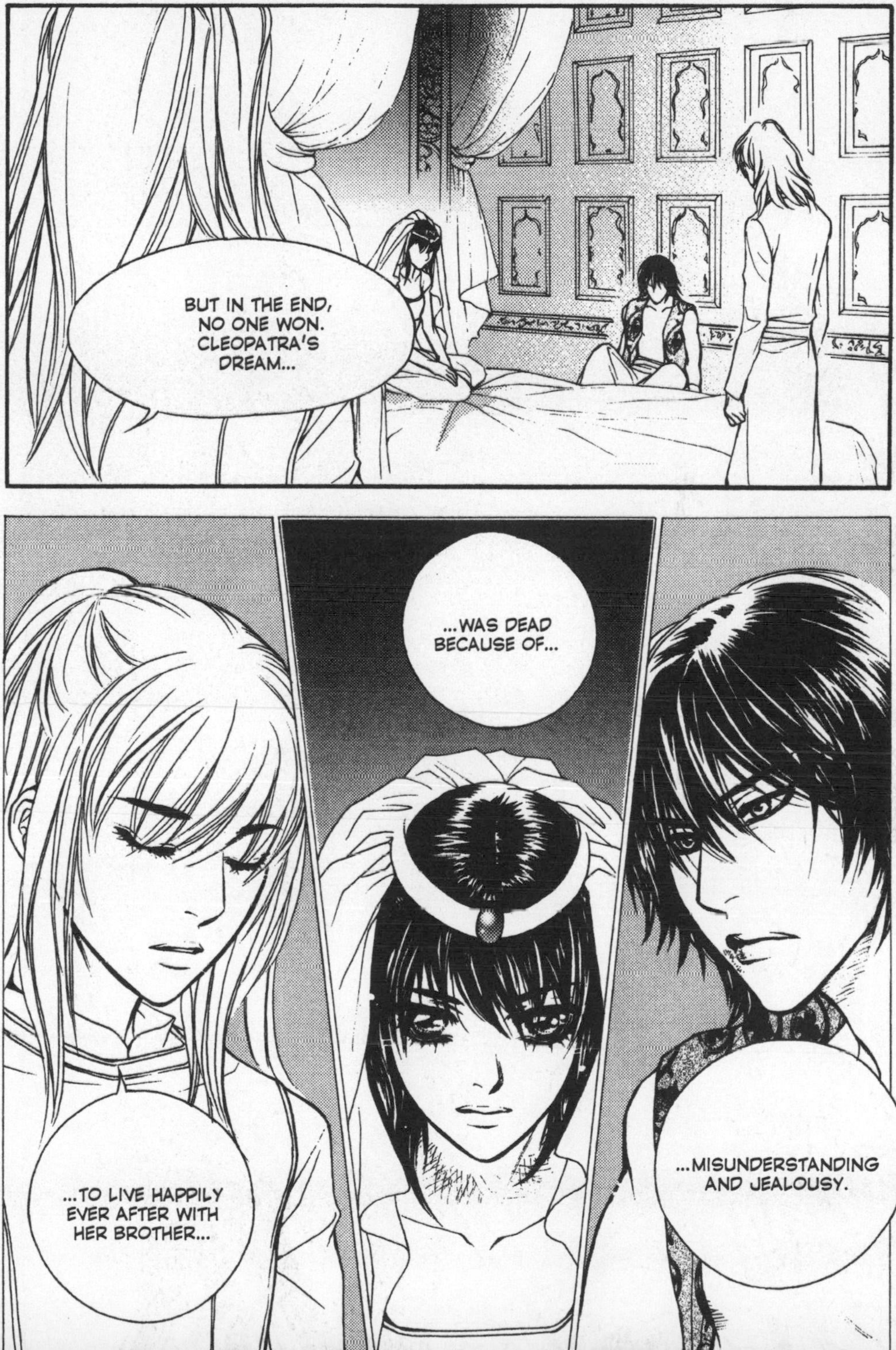
BUT IN THE END, NO ONE WON. CLEOPATRA'S DREAM...
...TO LIVE HAPPILY EVER AFTER WITH HER BROTHER...
...WAS DEAD BECAUSE OF...
...MISUNDERSTANDING AND JEALOUSY.

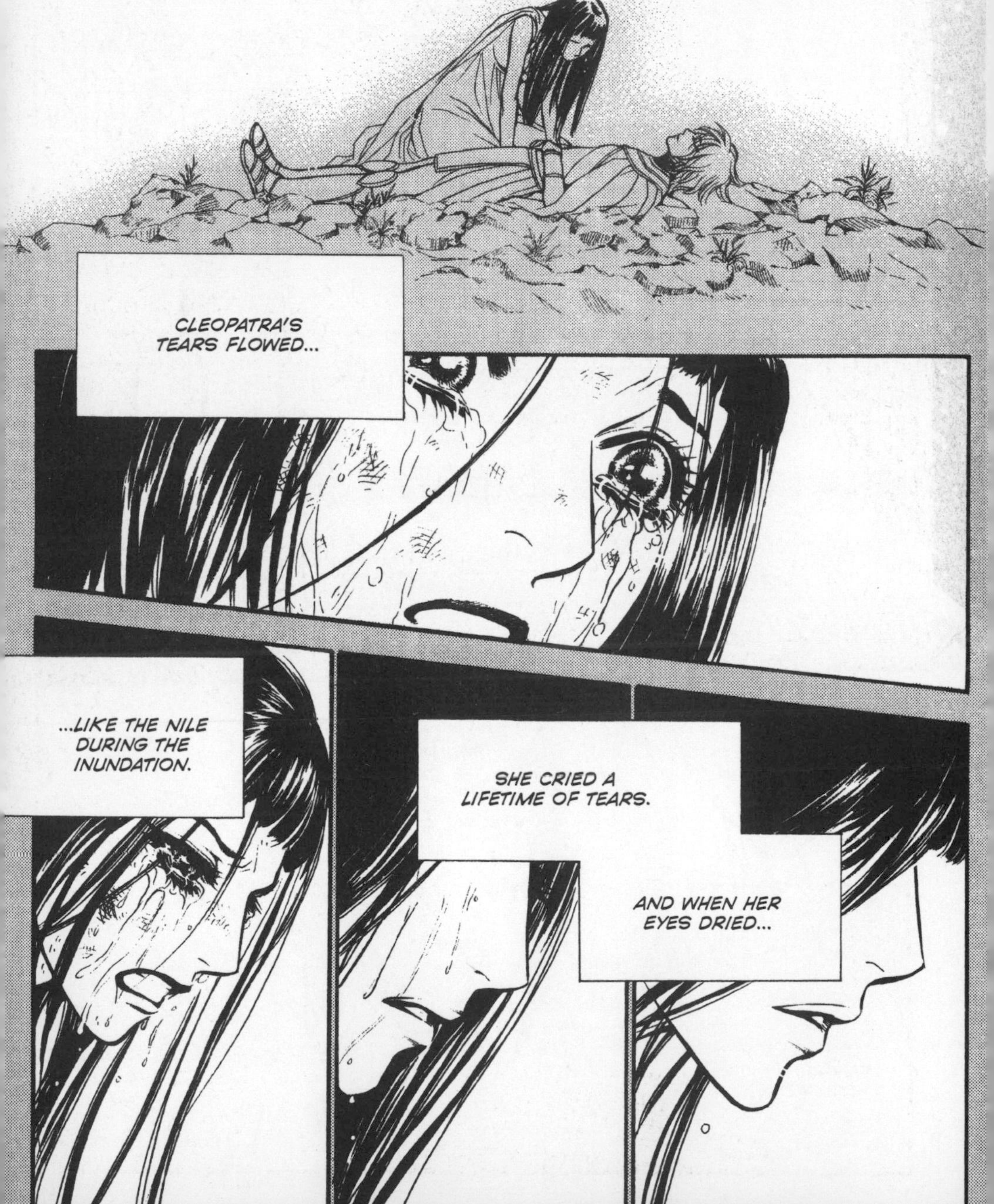
CLEOPATRA'S TEARS FLOWED...
...LIKE THE NILE DURING THE INUNDATION.
SHE CRIED A LIFETIME OF TEARS.
AND WHEN HER EYES DRIED...

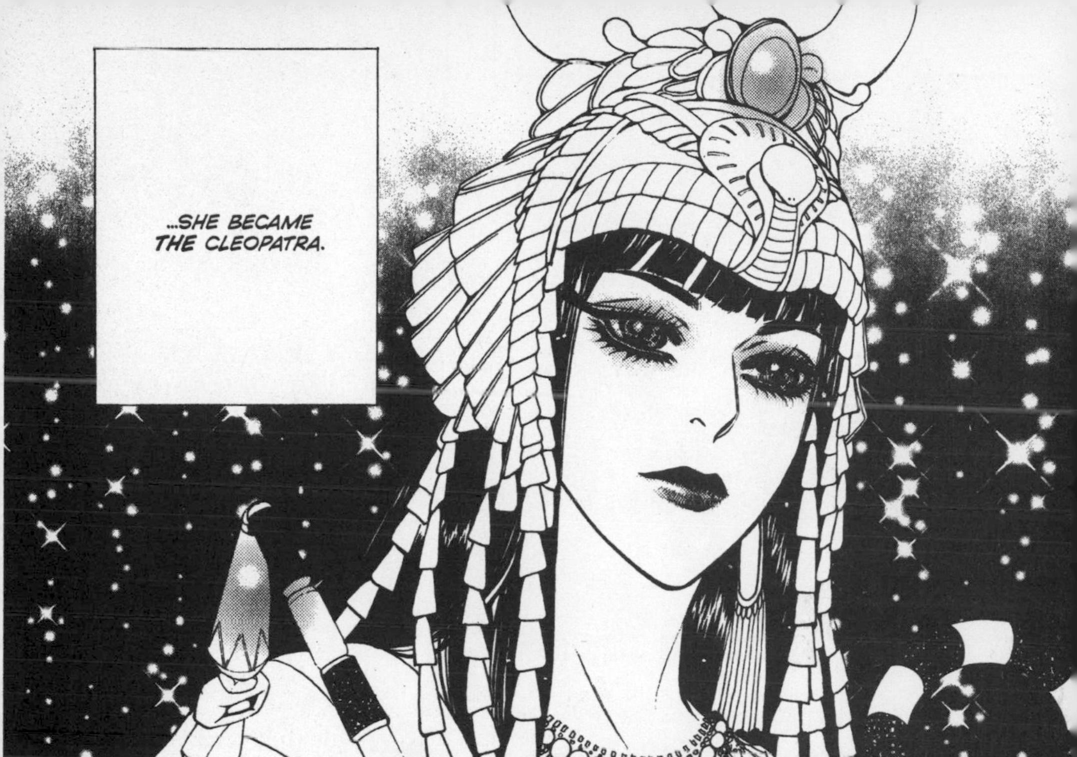
...SHE BECAME THE CLEOPATRA.

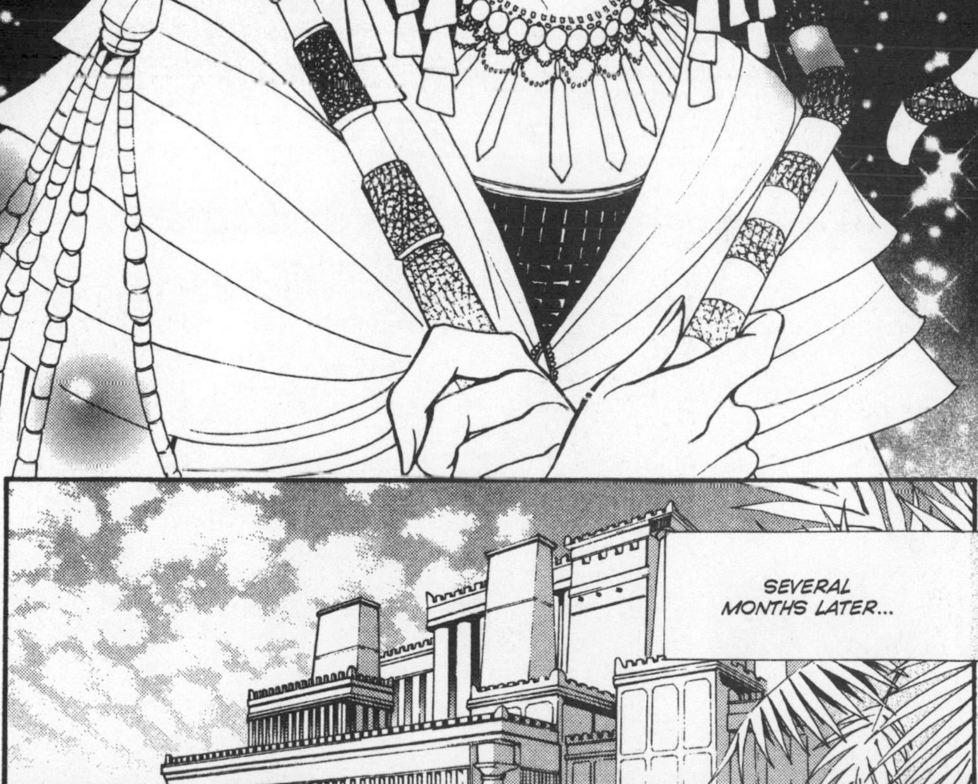
SEVERAL MONTHS LATER...

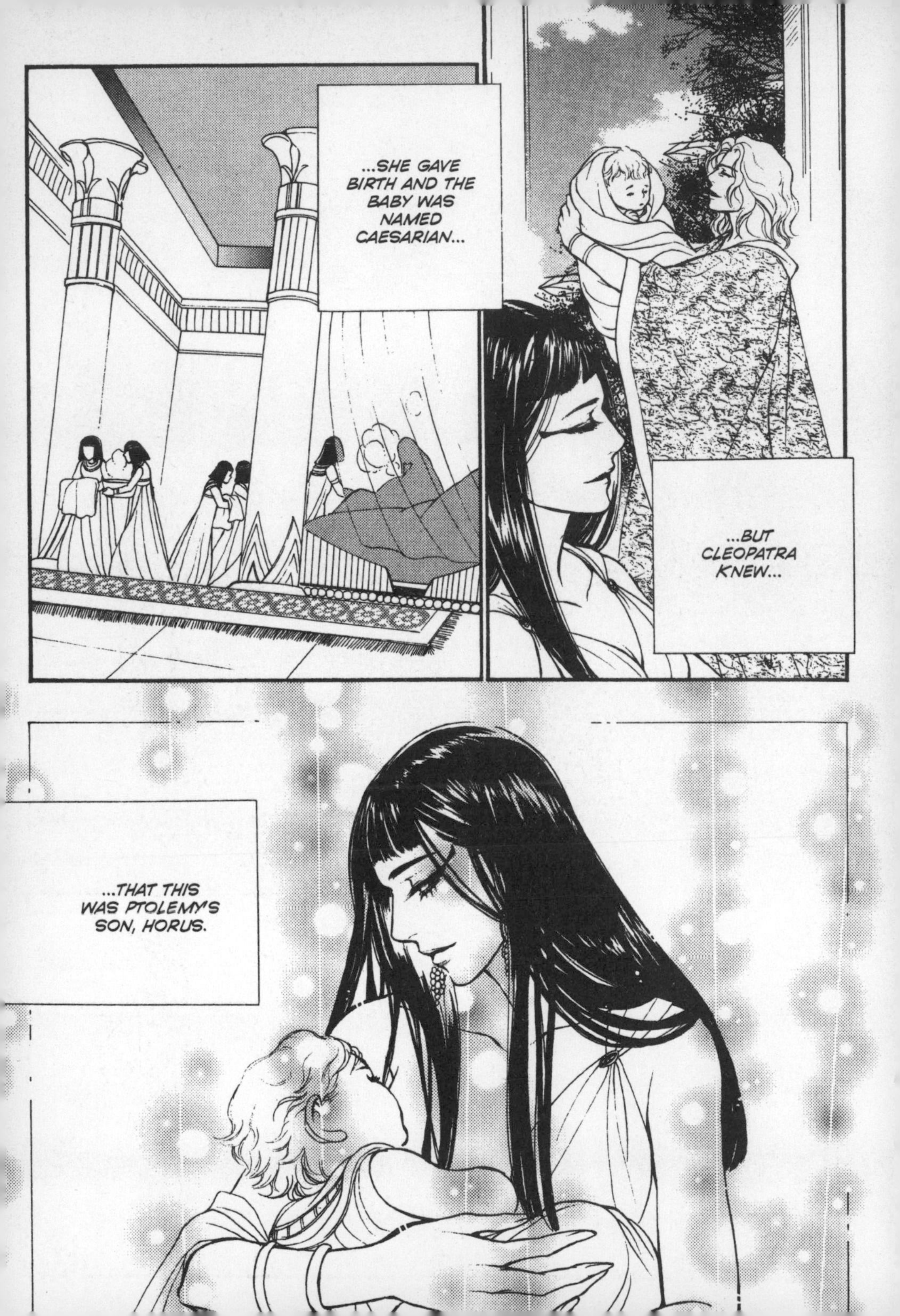
...SHE GAVE BIRTH AND THE BABY WAS NAMED CAESARIAN...
...BUT CLEOPATRA KNEW...
...THAT THIS WAS PTOLEMY'S SON, HORUS.

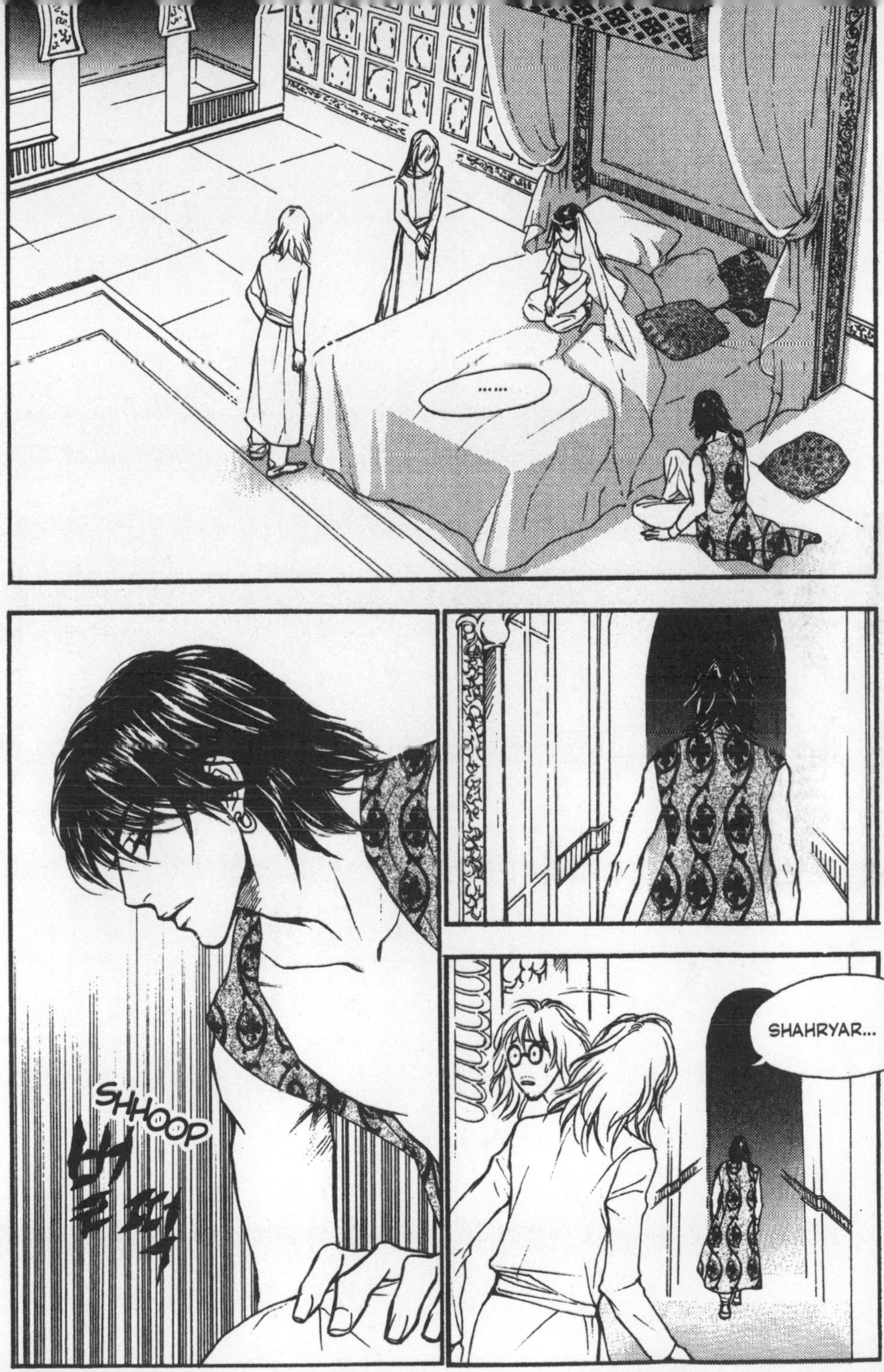
……
SHHOOP
벌떡
SHAHRYAR...

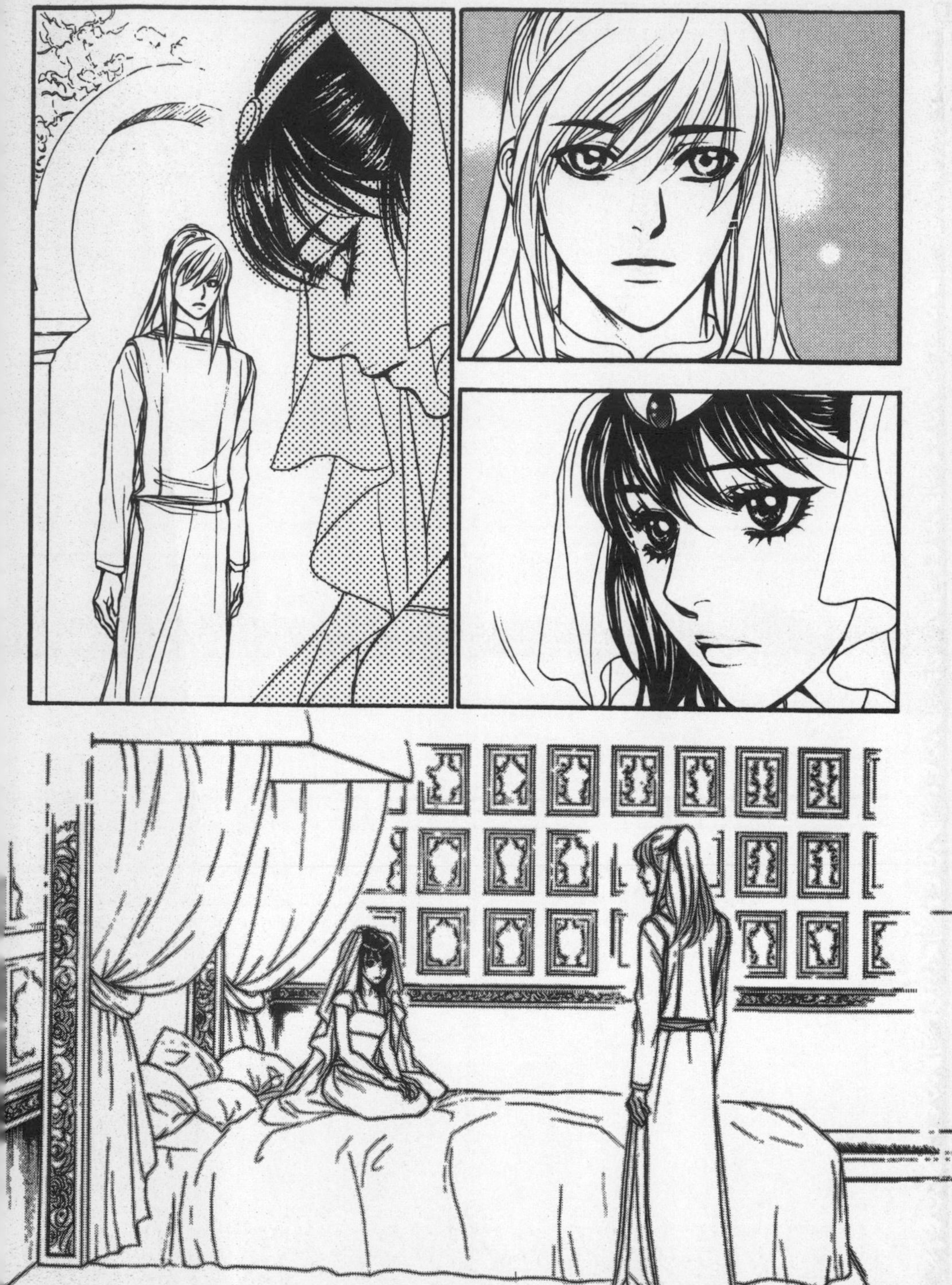

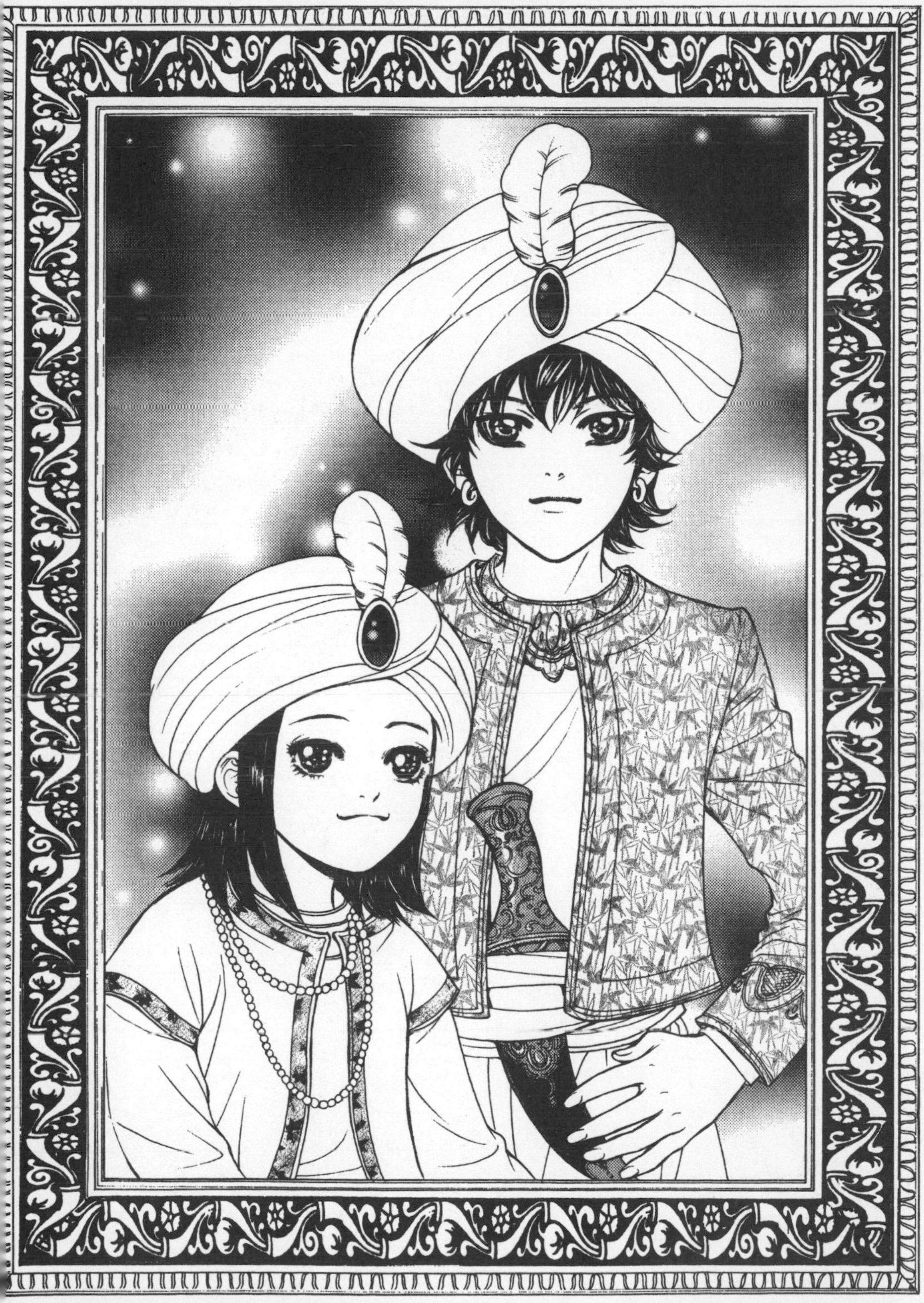

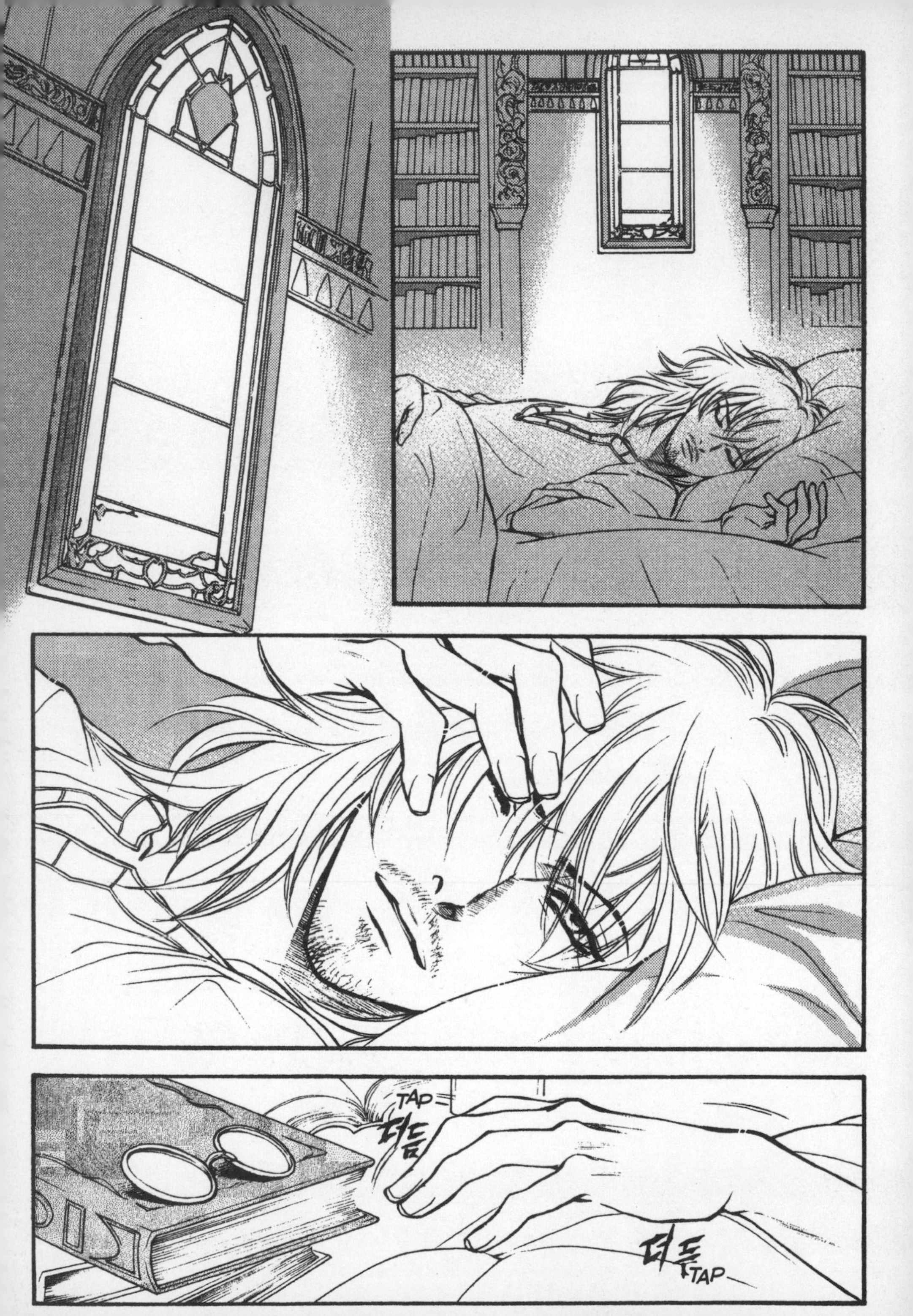
TAP
더듬
더듬
TAP

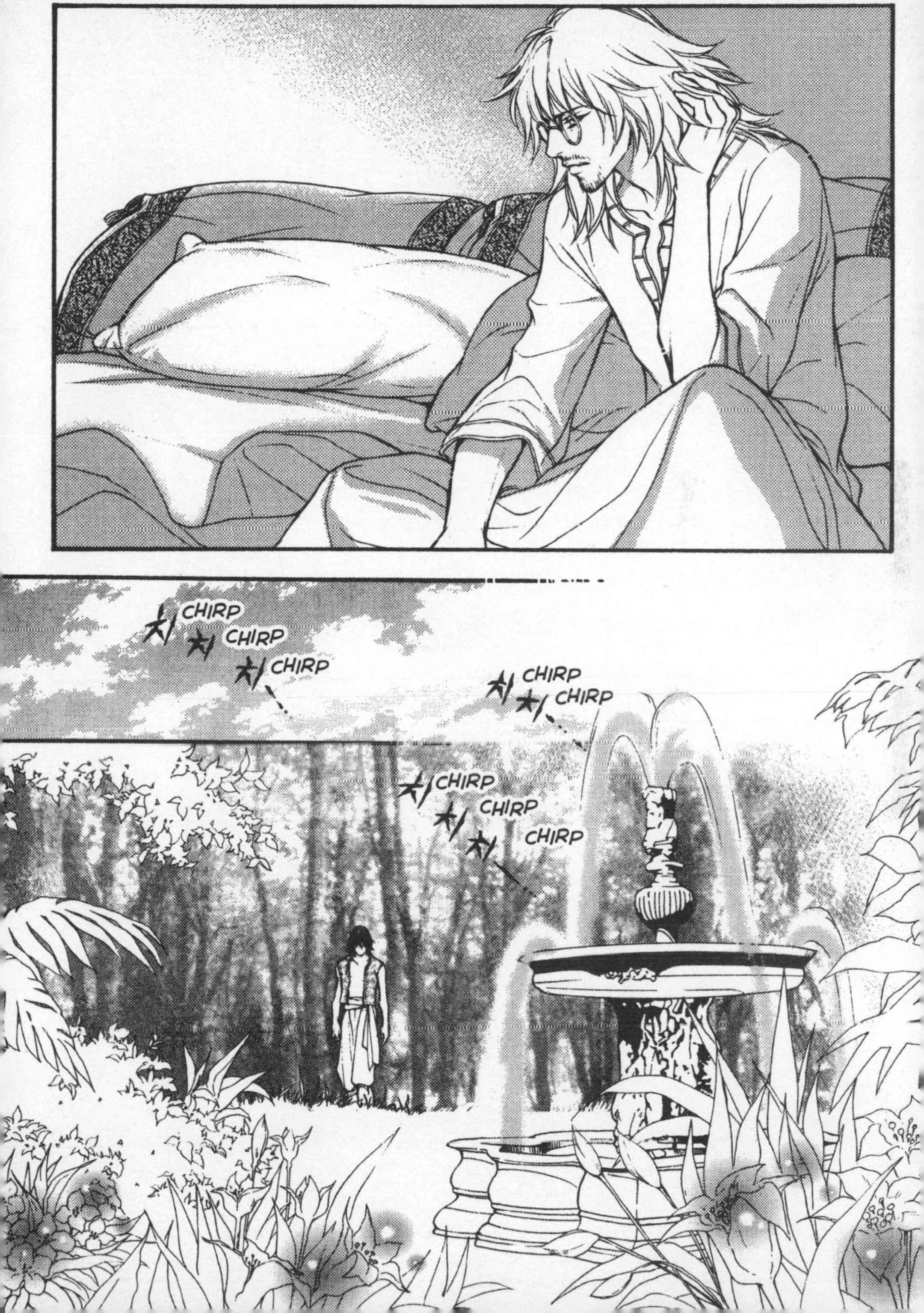
치 CHIRP
치 CHIRP
치 CHIRP
치 CHIRP
치 CHIRP
치 CHIRP
치 CHIRP
치 CHIRP

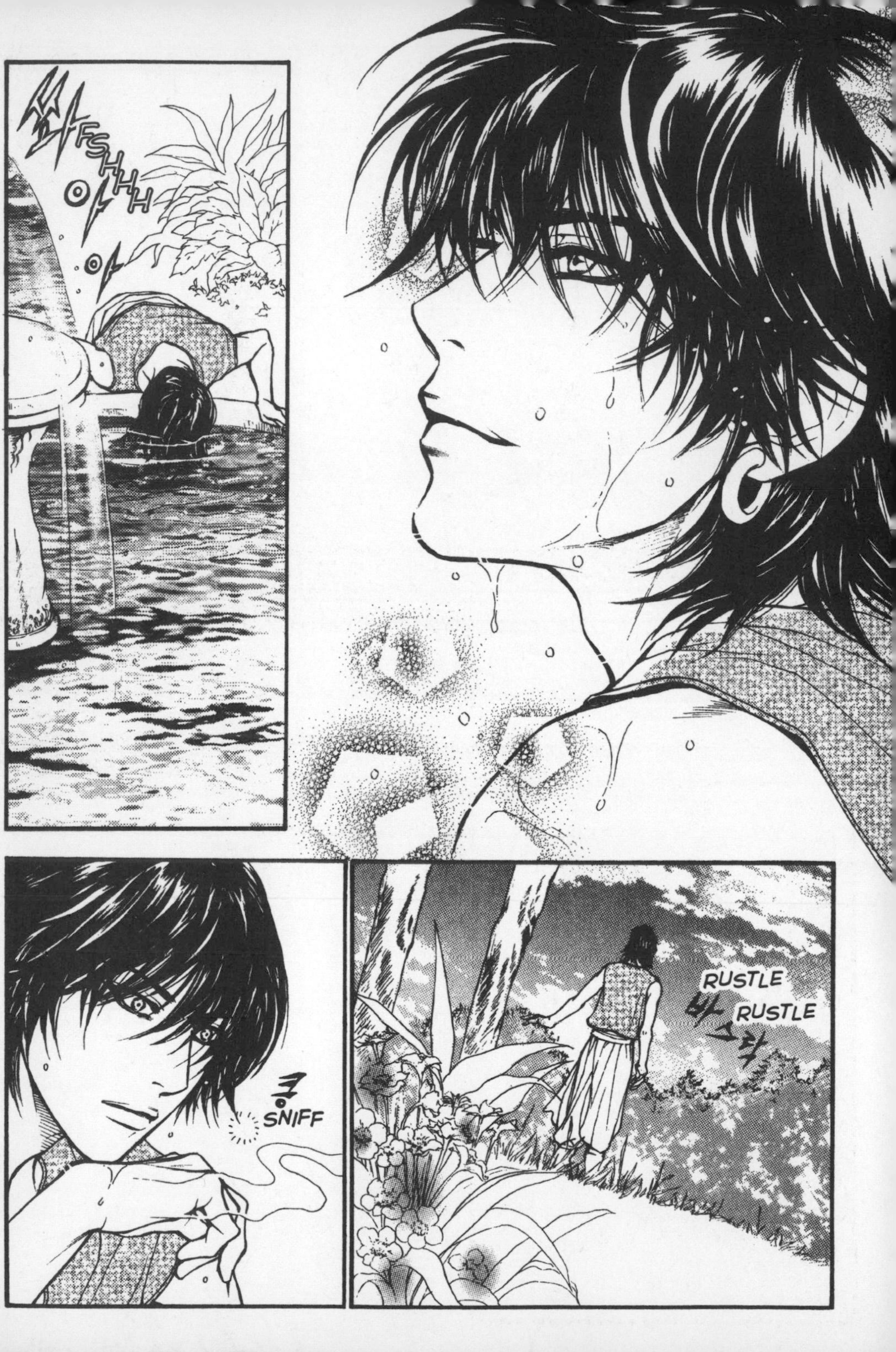
FSHHH
킁
SNIFF
RUSTLE
바스락
RUSTLE

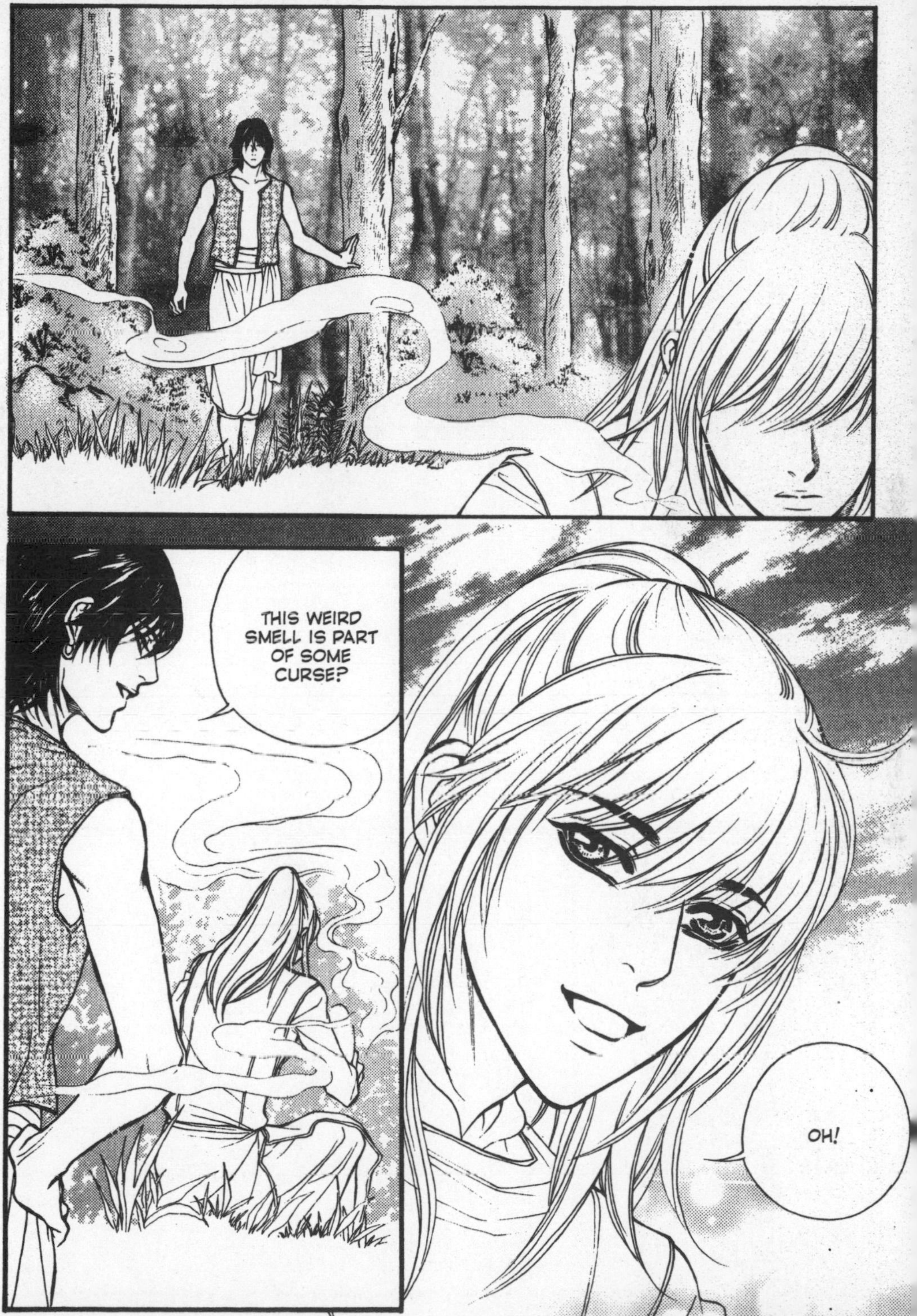
THIS WEIRD SMELL IS PART OF SOME CURSE?
OH!

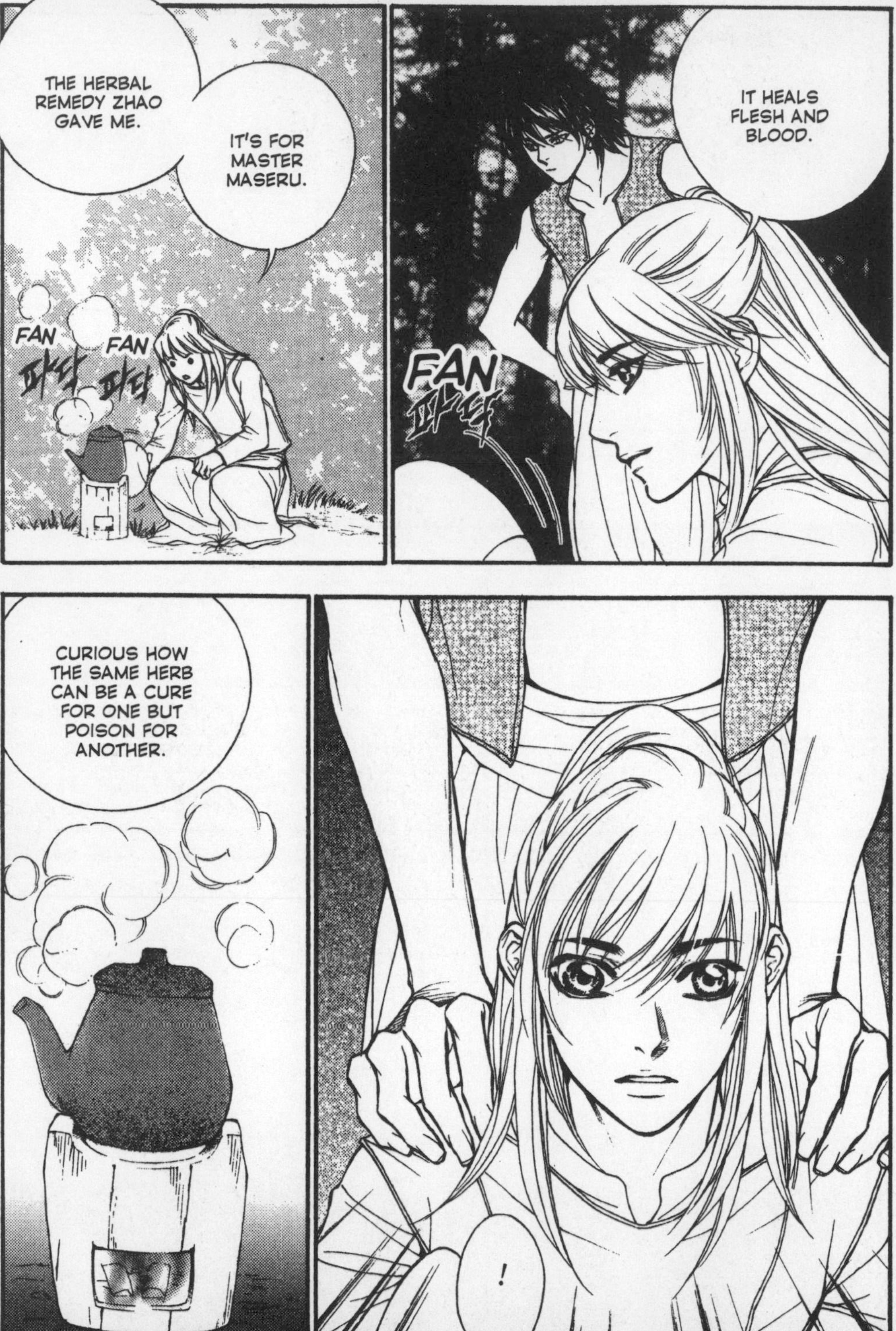
THE HERBAL REMEDY ZHAO GAVE ME.
IT'S FOR MASTER MASERU.
FAN
파닥
FAN
파닥
IT HEALS FLESH AND BLOOD.
FAN
파닥
CURIOUS HOW THE SAME HERB CAN BE A CURE FOR ONE BUT POISON FOR ANOTHER.
!

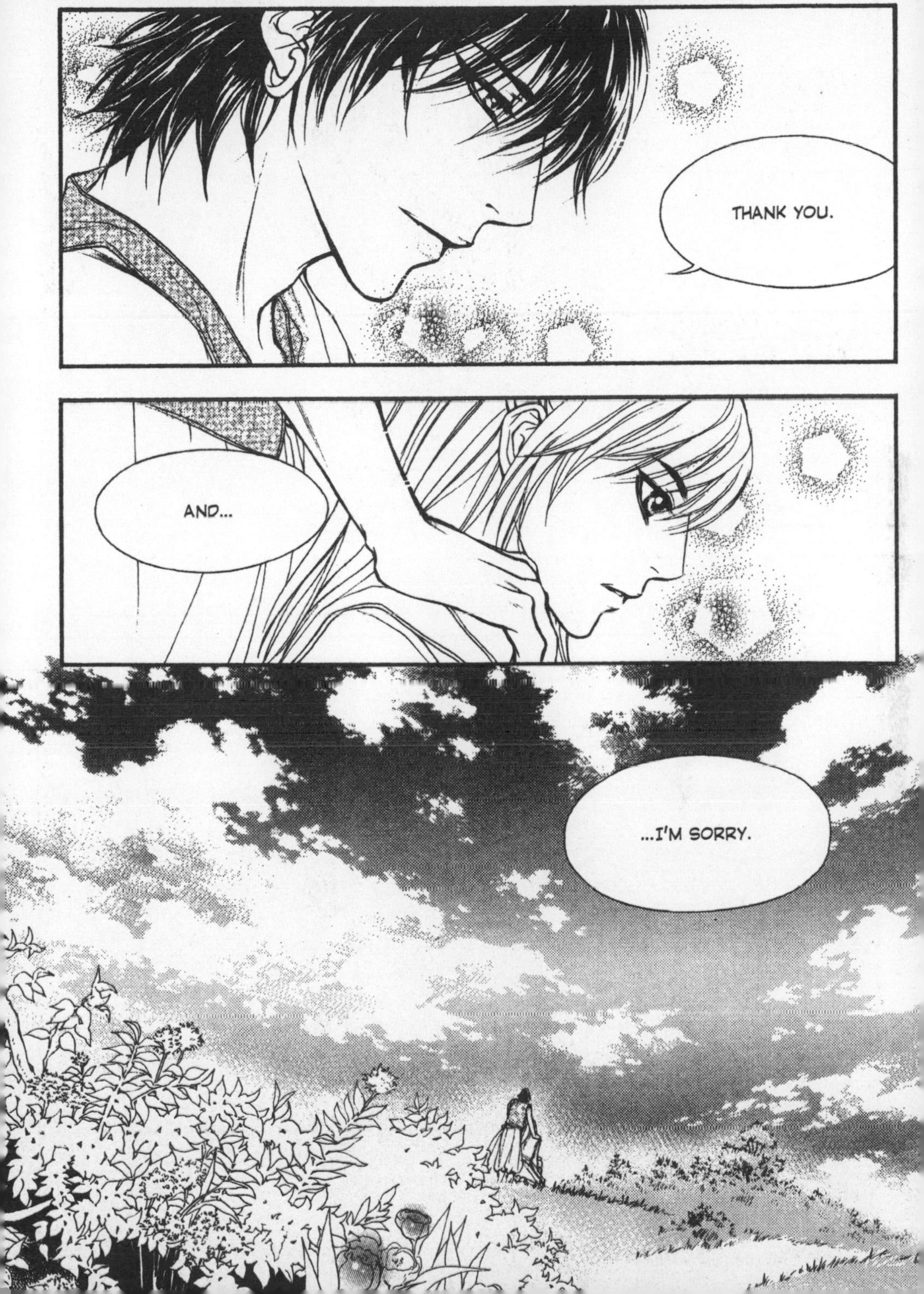
THANK YOU.
AND...
...I'M SORRY.

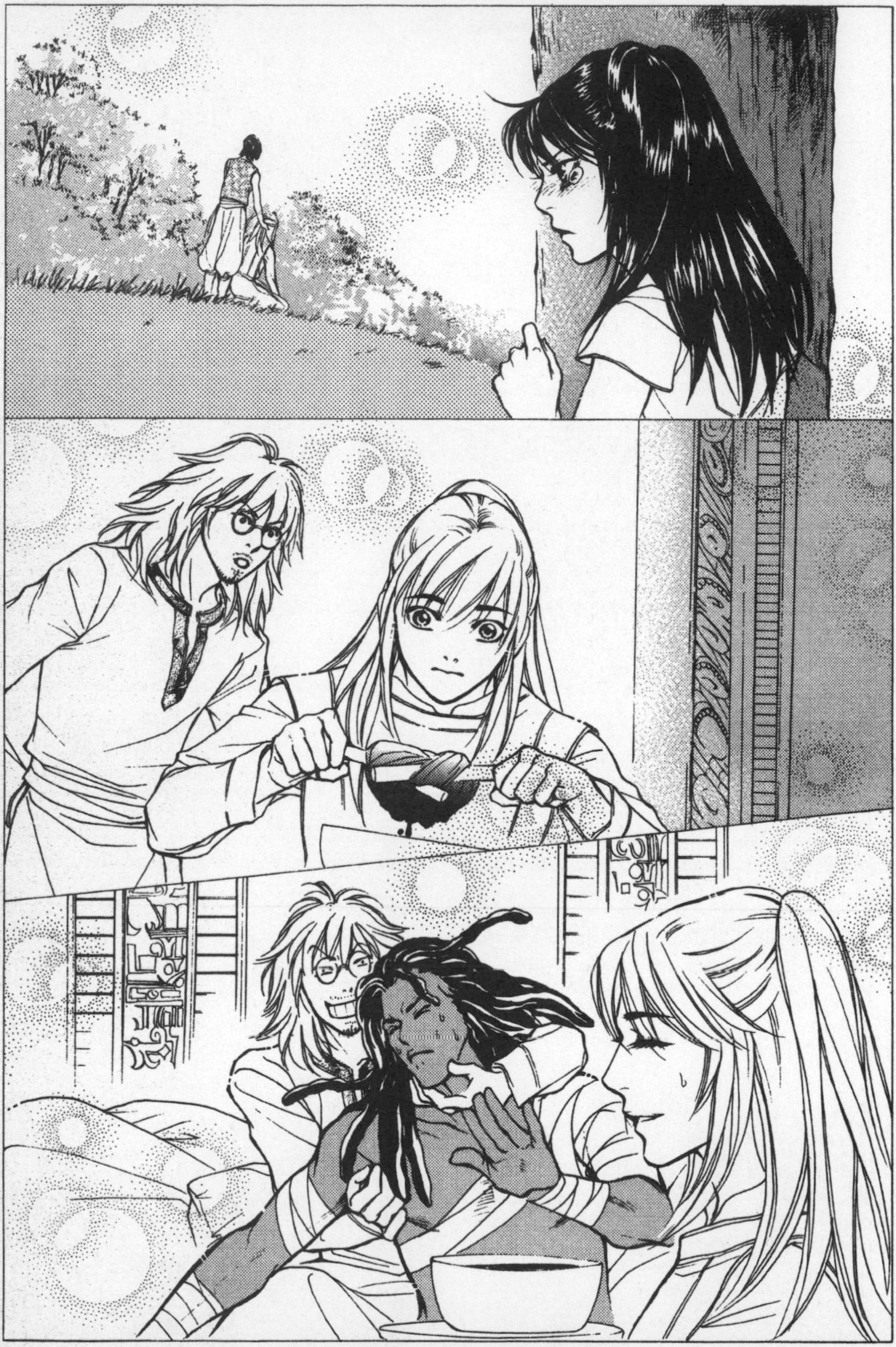

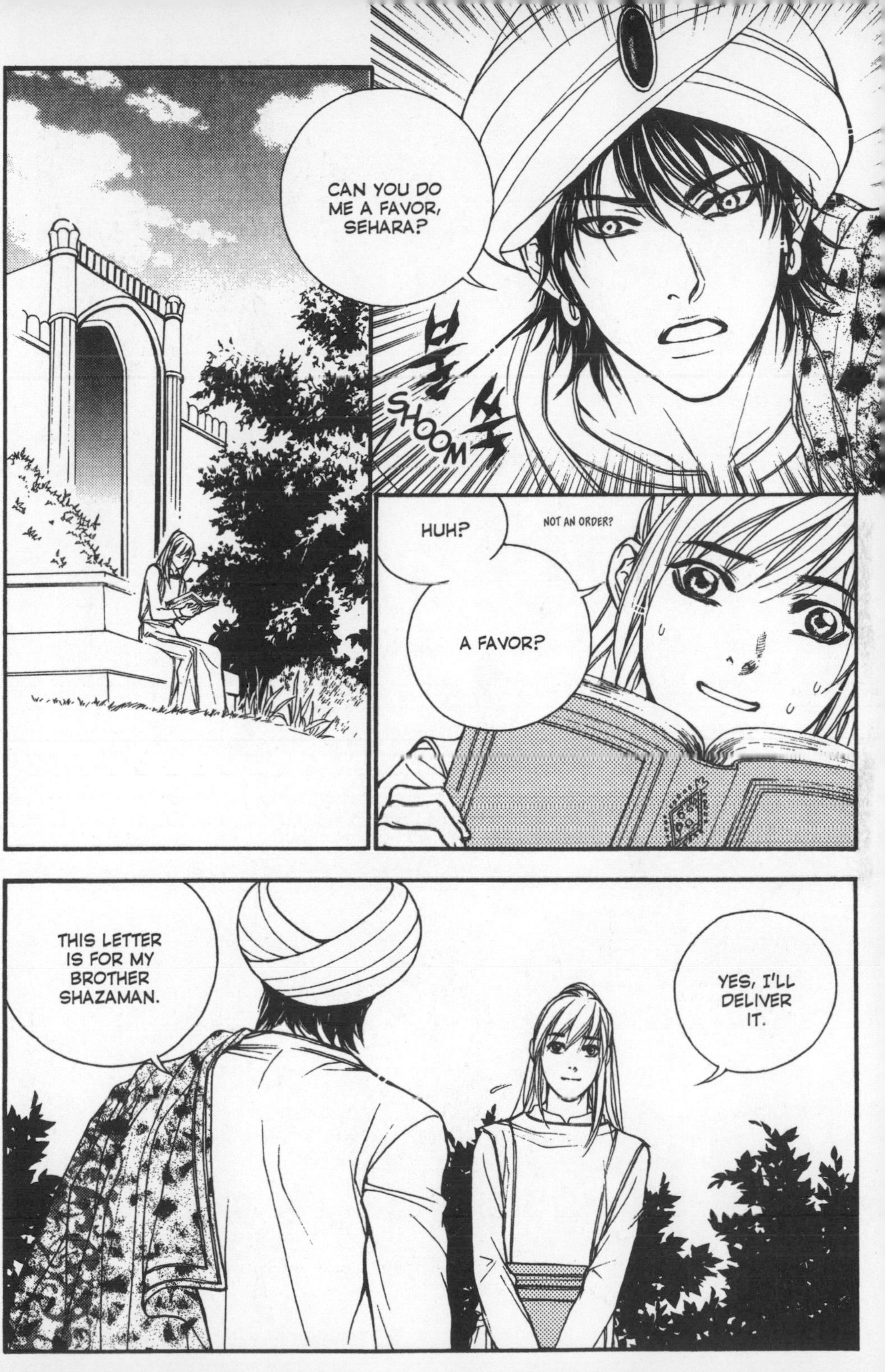
CAN YOU DO ME A FAVOR, SEHARA?
불쑥
SHOOM
HUH?
NOT AN ORDER?
A FAVOR?
THIS LETTER IS FOR MY BROTHER SHAZAMAN.
YES, I'LL DELIVER IT.

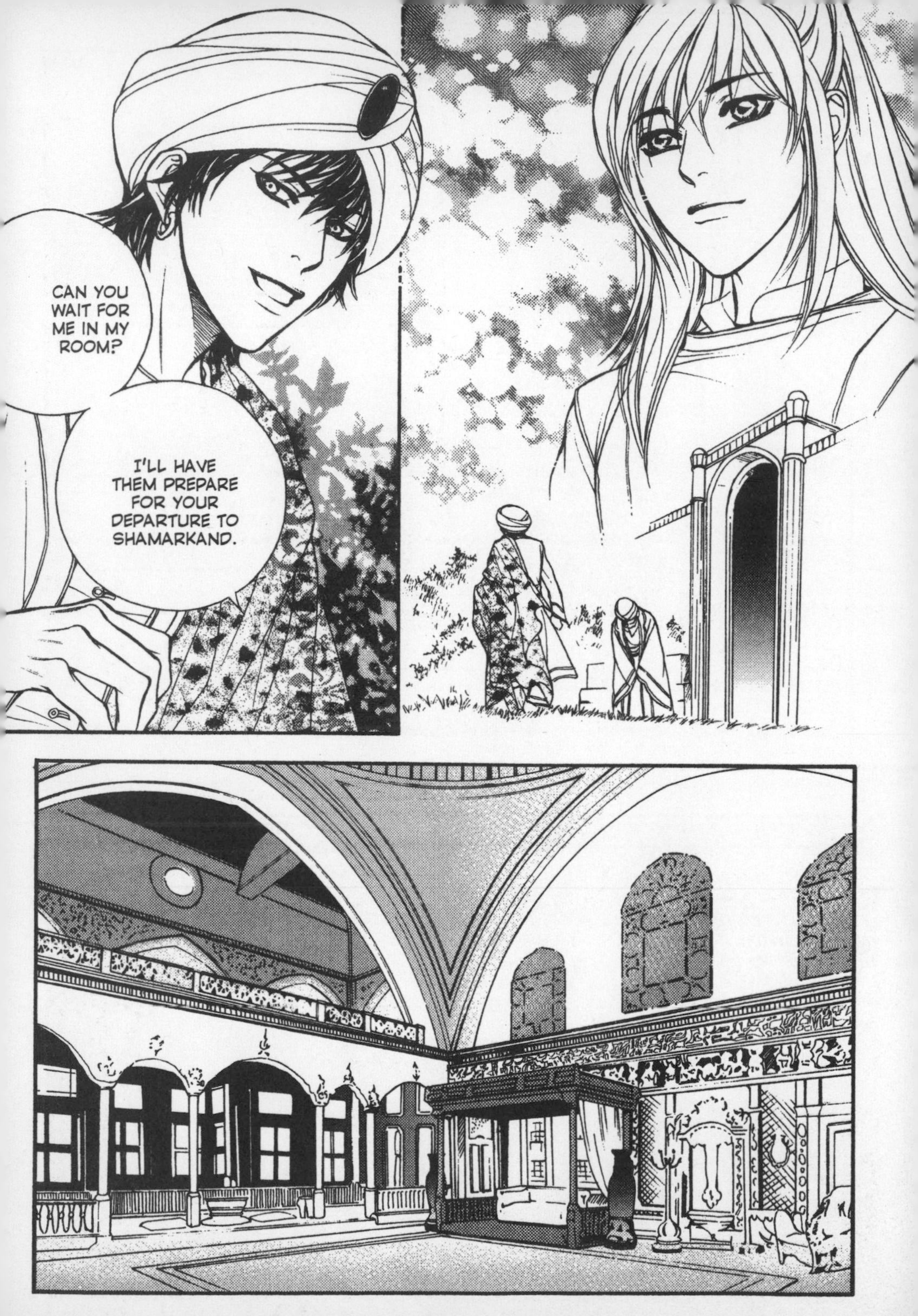
CAN YOU WAIT FOR ME IN MY ROOM?
I'LL HAVE THEM PREPARE FOR YOUR DEPARTURE TO SHAMARKAND.

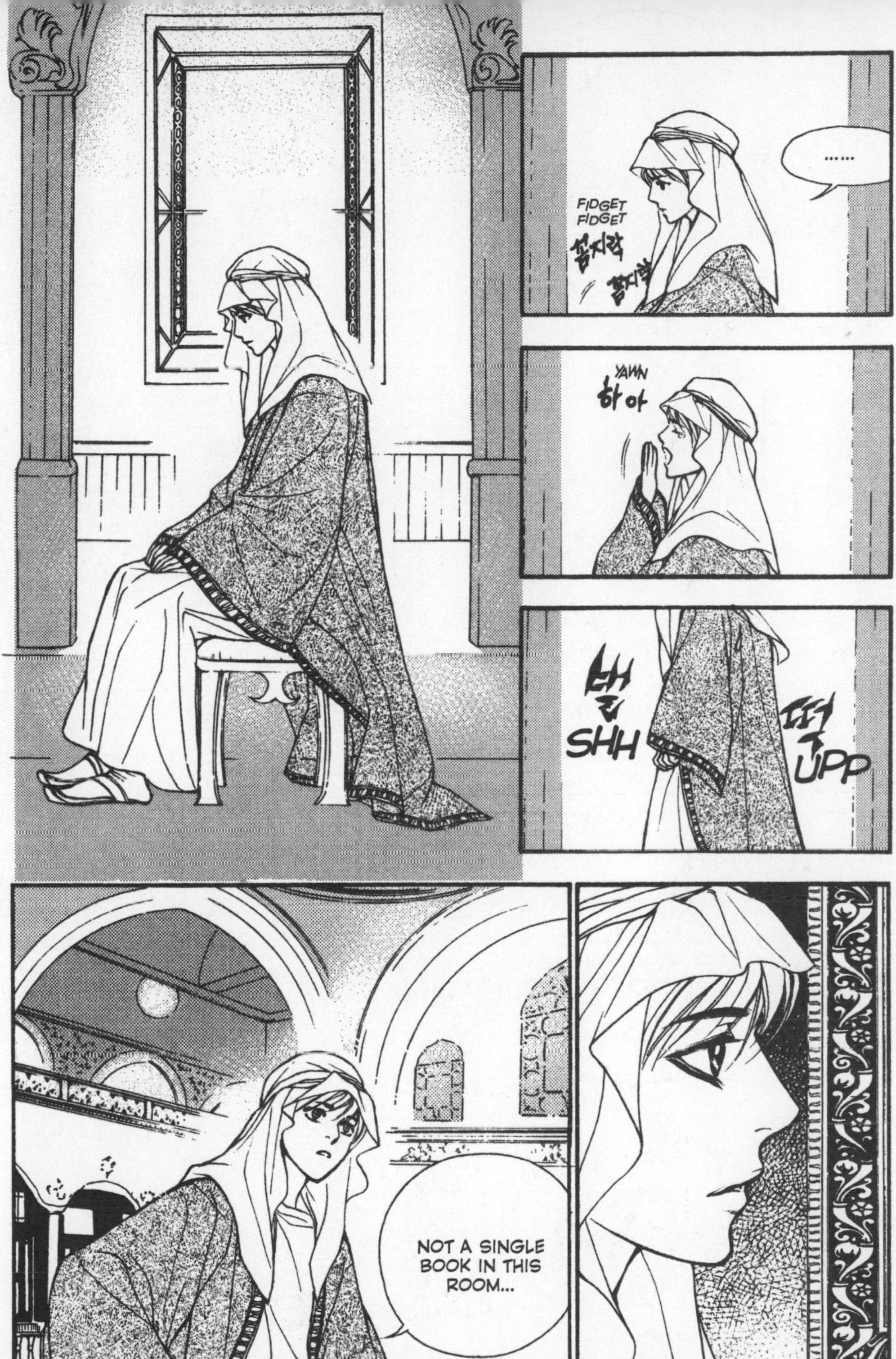
FIDGET
FIDGET
꼼지락
꼼지락
……
YAWN
하아
벌
SHH
떡
UPP
NOT A SINGLE BOOK IN THIS ROOM...

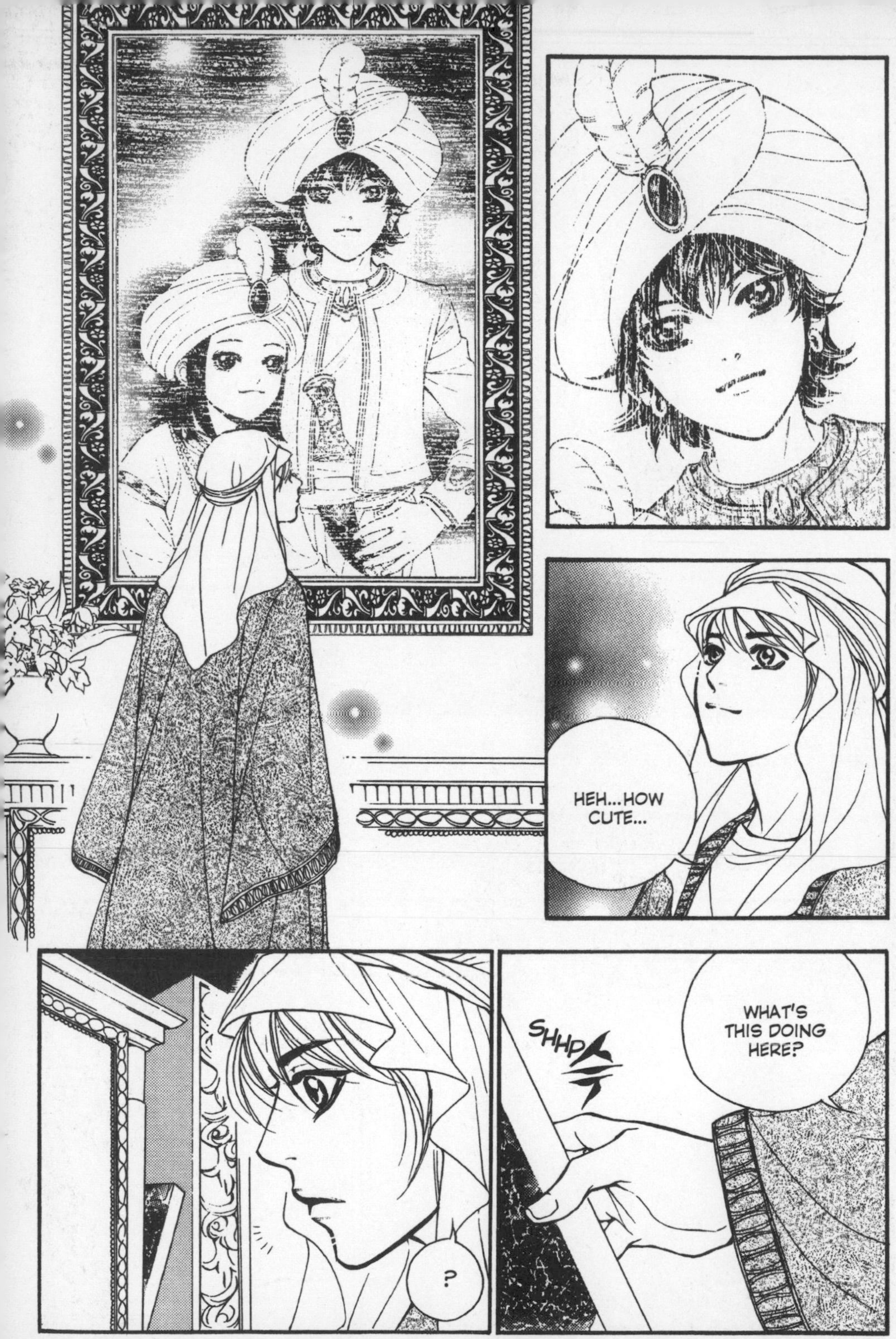
HEH...HOW CUTE...
?
SHHP
WHAT'S THIS DOING HERE?

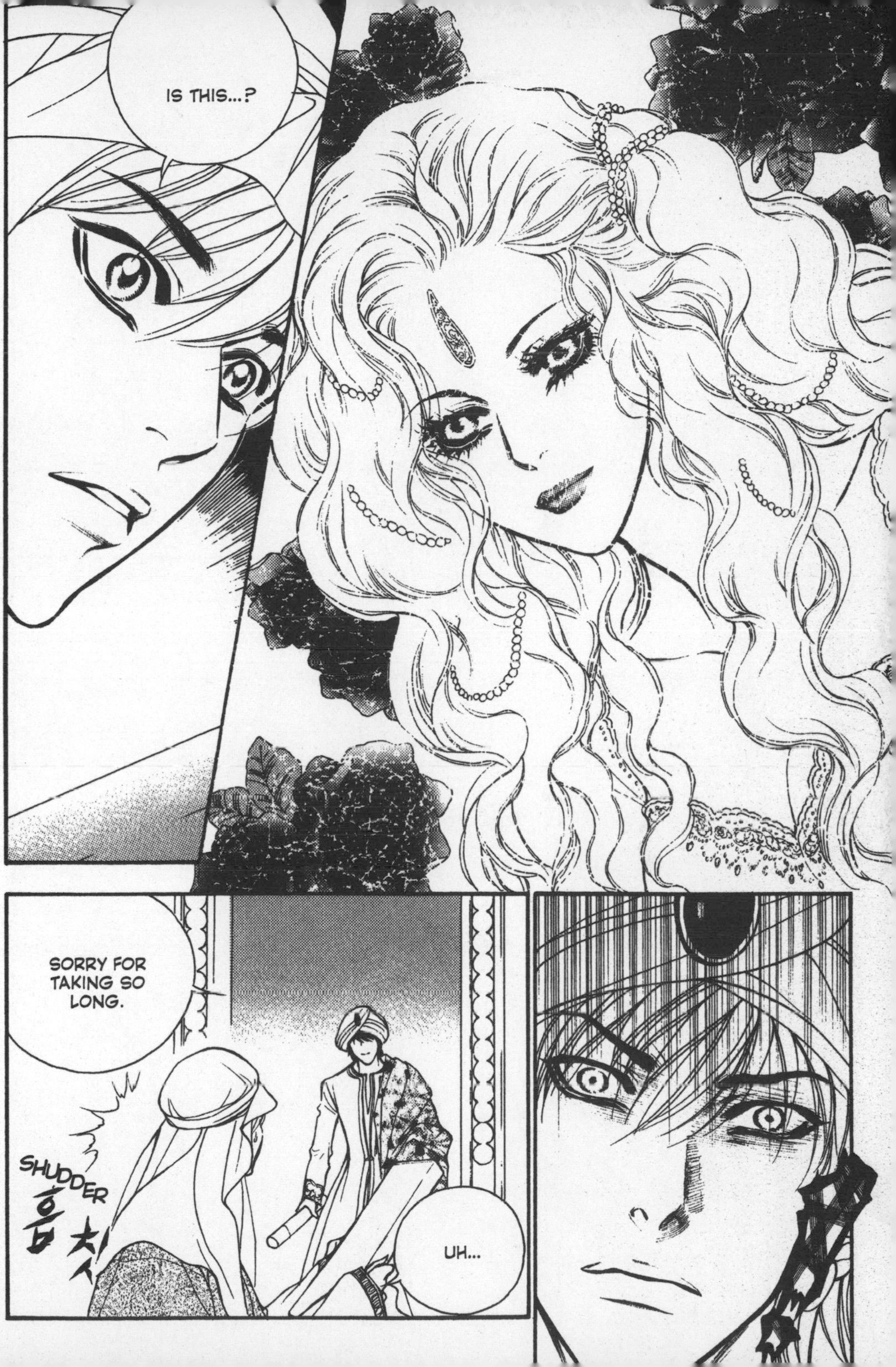
IS THIS...?
SORRY FOR TAKING SO LONG.
SHUDDER
흠칫
UH...

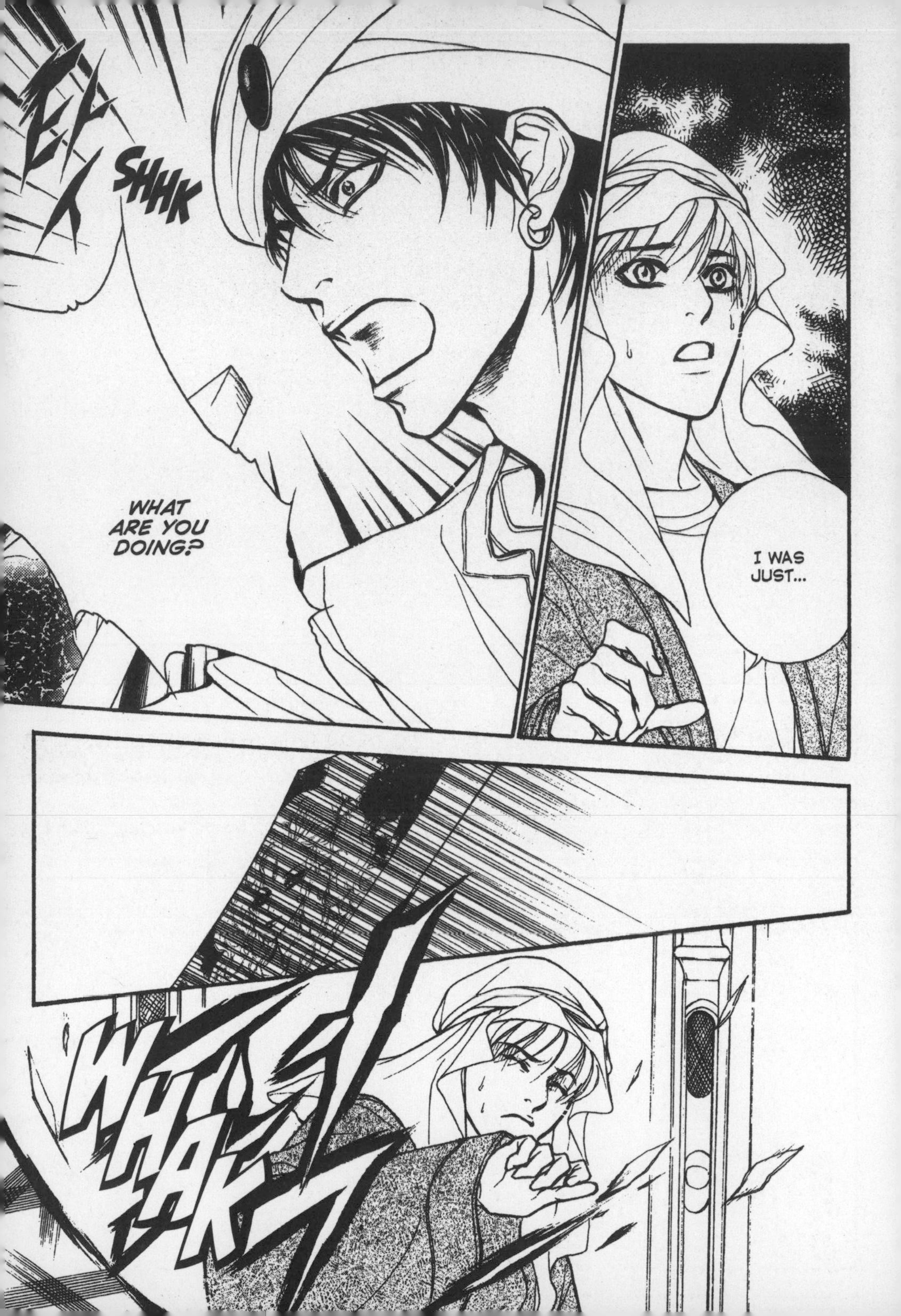
SHHK
WHAT ARE YOU DOING?
I WAS JUST...

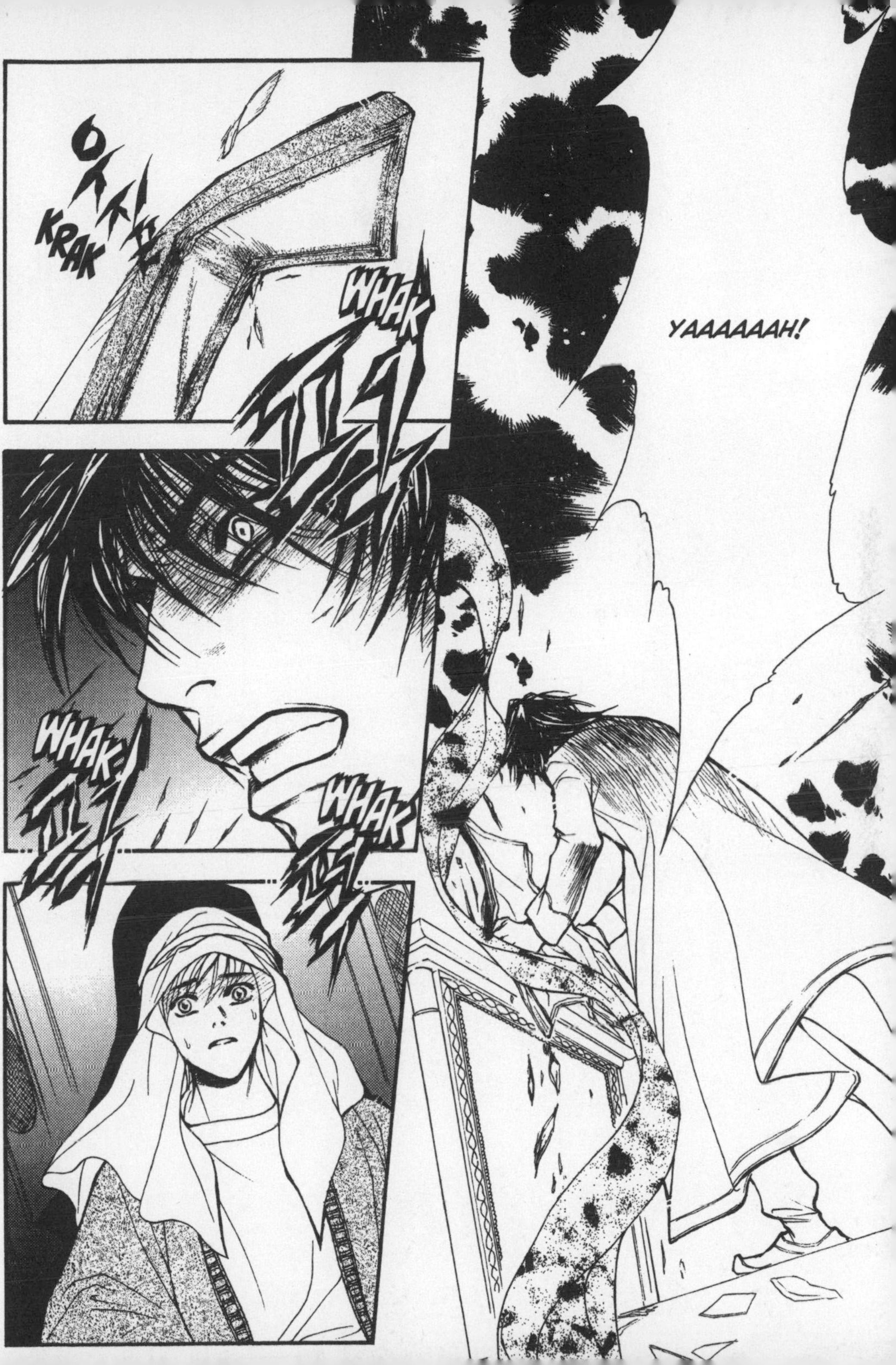
KRAK
WHAK
WHAK
WHAK
YAAAAAAH!

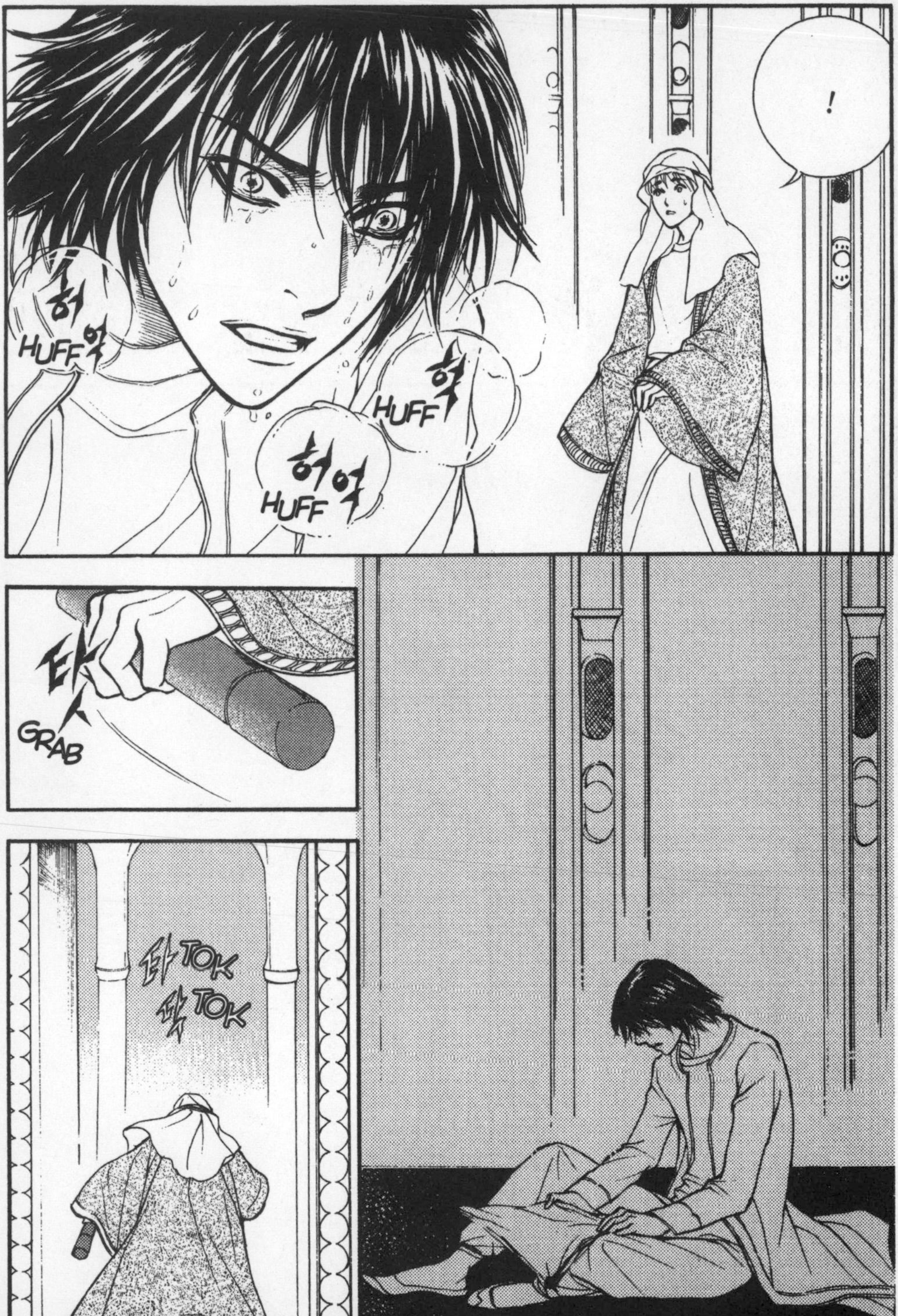
허억 HUFF
헉 HUFF
허억 HUFF
!
탁 GRAB
탁 TOK
탁 TOK

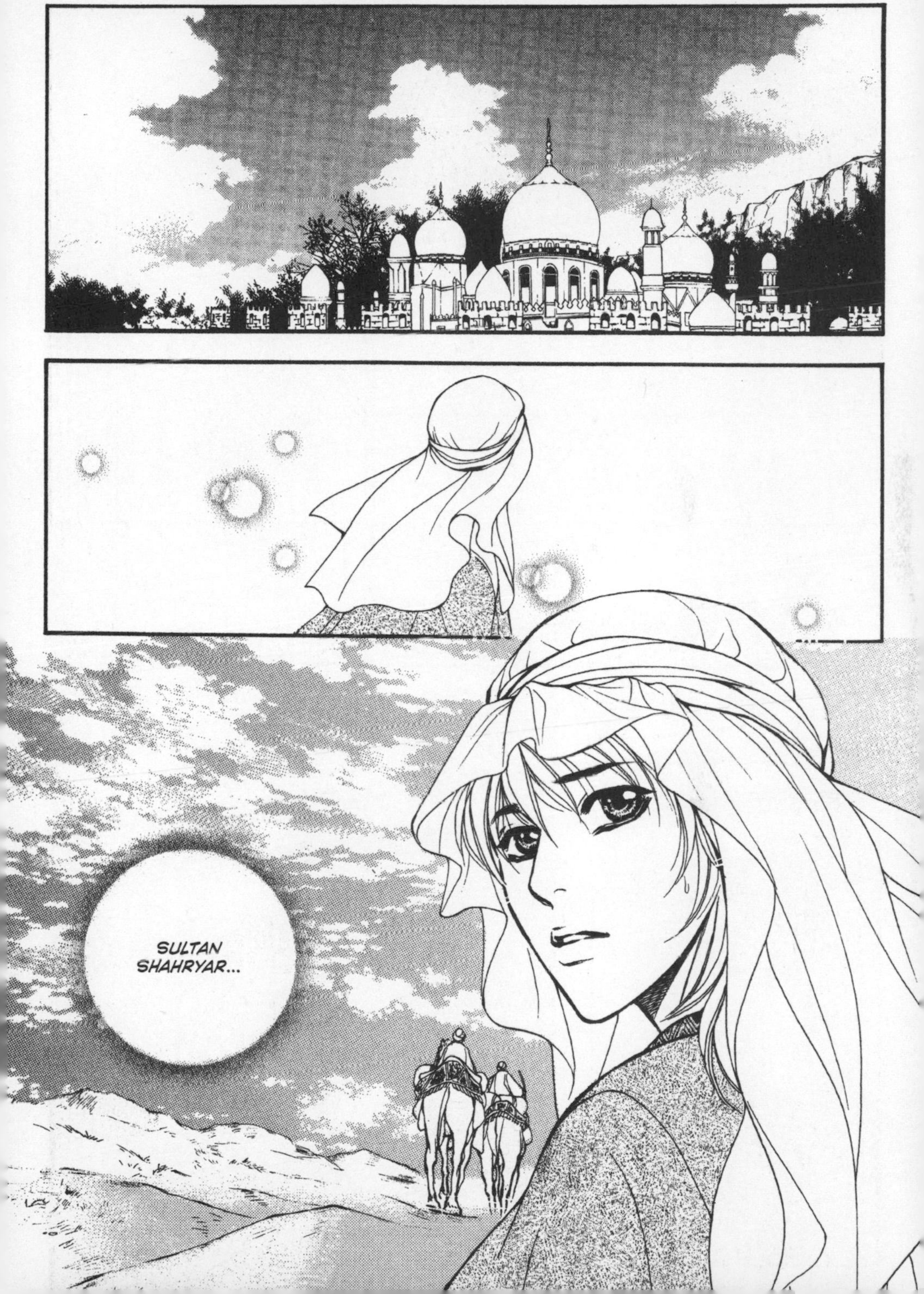
SULTAN SHAHRYAR...

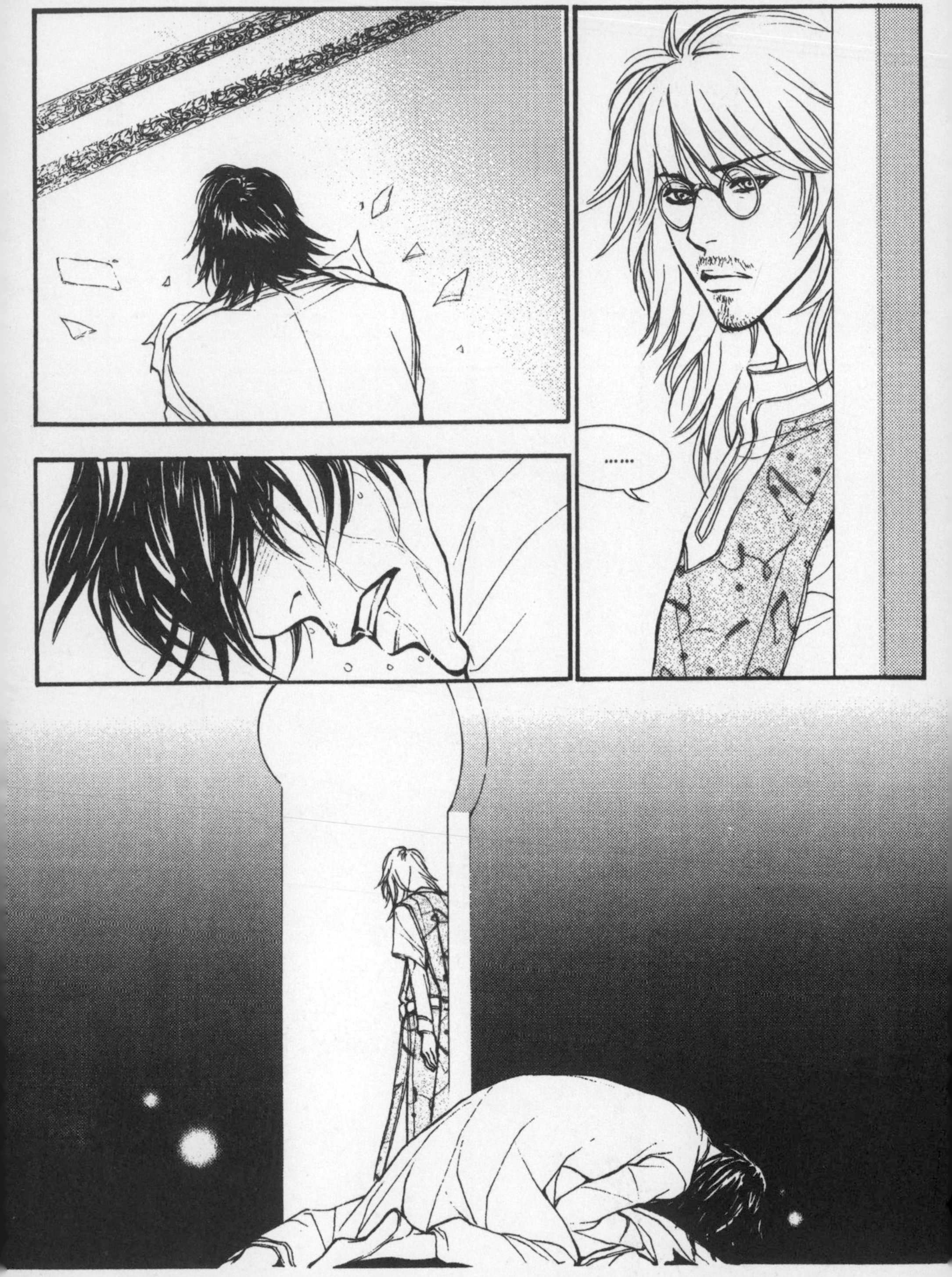
……

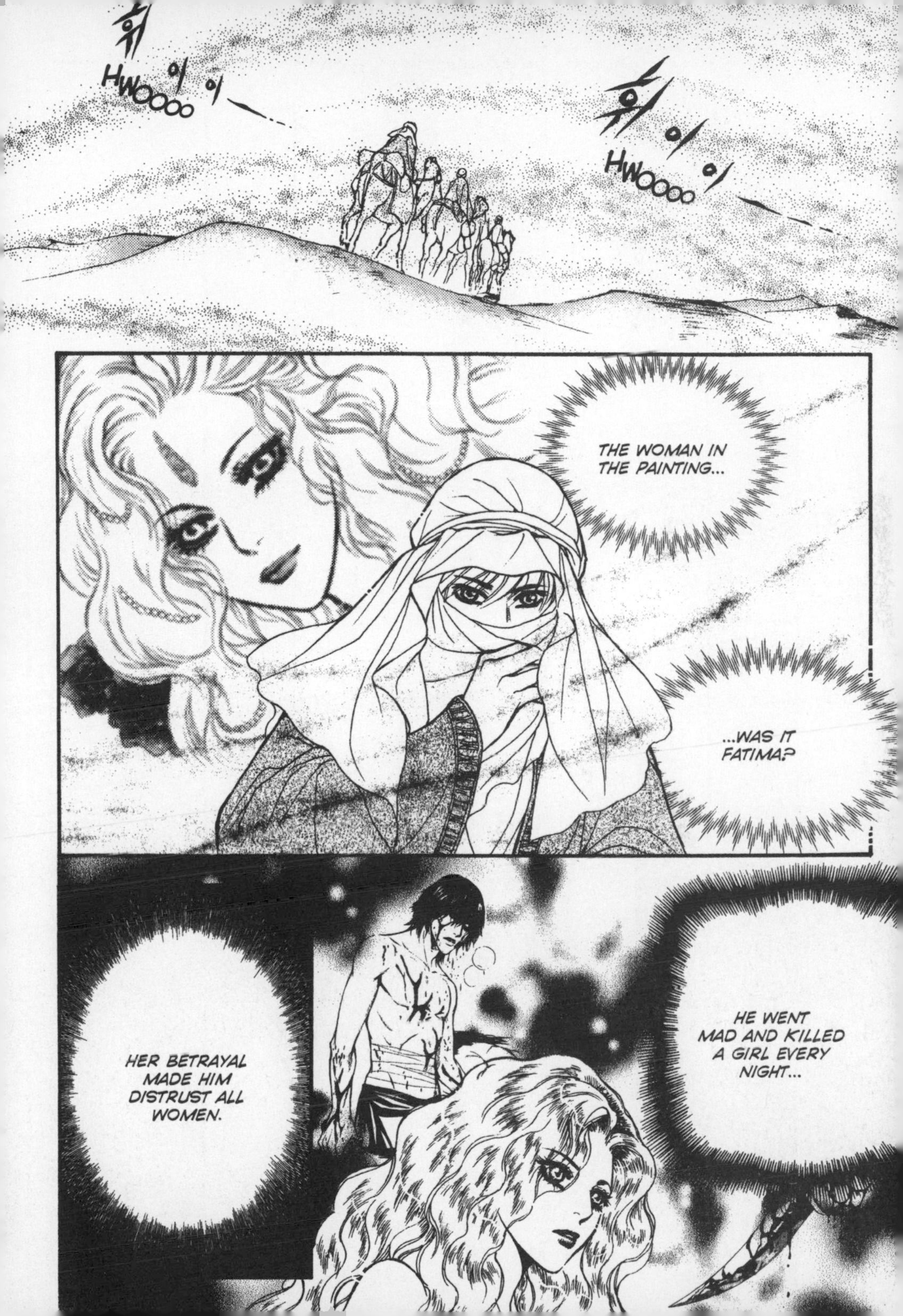
휘이이
HWOOOO
휘이이
HWOOOO
THE WOMAN IN THE PAINTING...
...WAS IT FATIMA?
HER BETRAYAL MADE HIM DISTRUST ALL WOMEN.
HE WENT MAD AND KILLED A GIRL EVERY NIGHT...

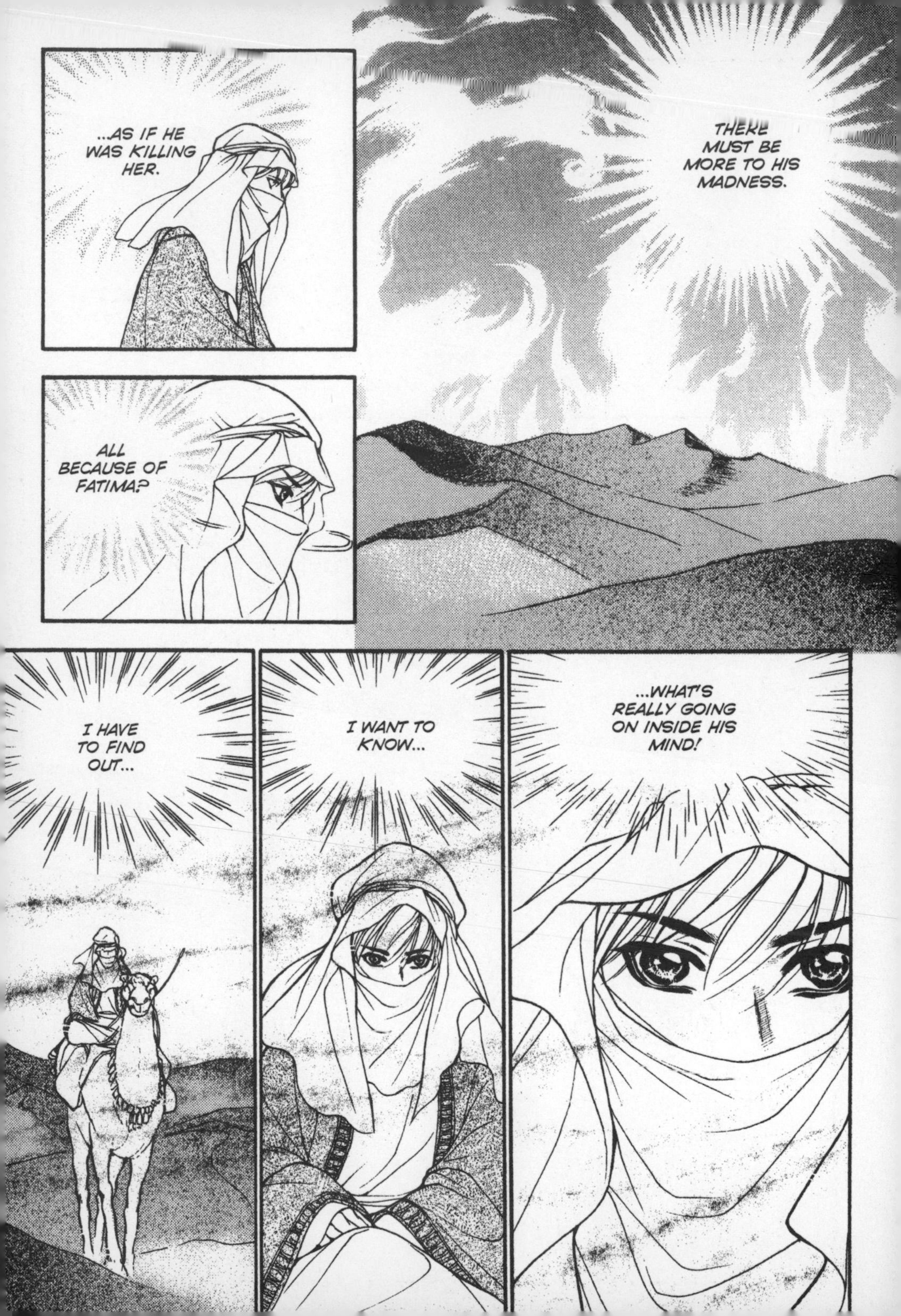
...AS IF HE WAS KILLING HER.
ALL BECAUSE OF FATIMA?
THERE MUST BE MORE TO HIS MADNESS.
I HAVE TO FIND OUT...
I WANT TO KNOW...
...WHAT'S REALLY GOING ON INSIDE HIS MIND!

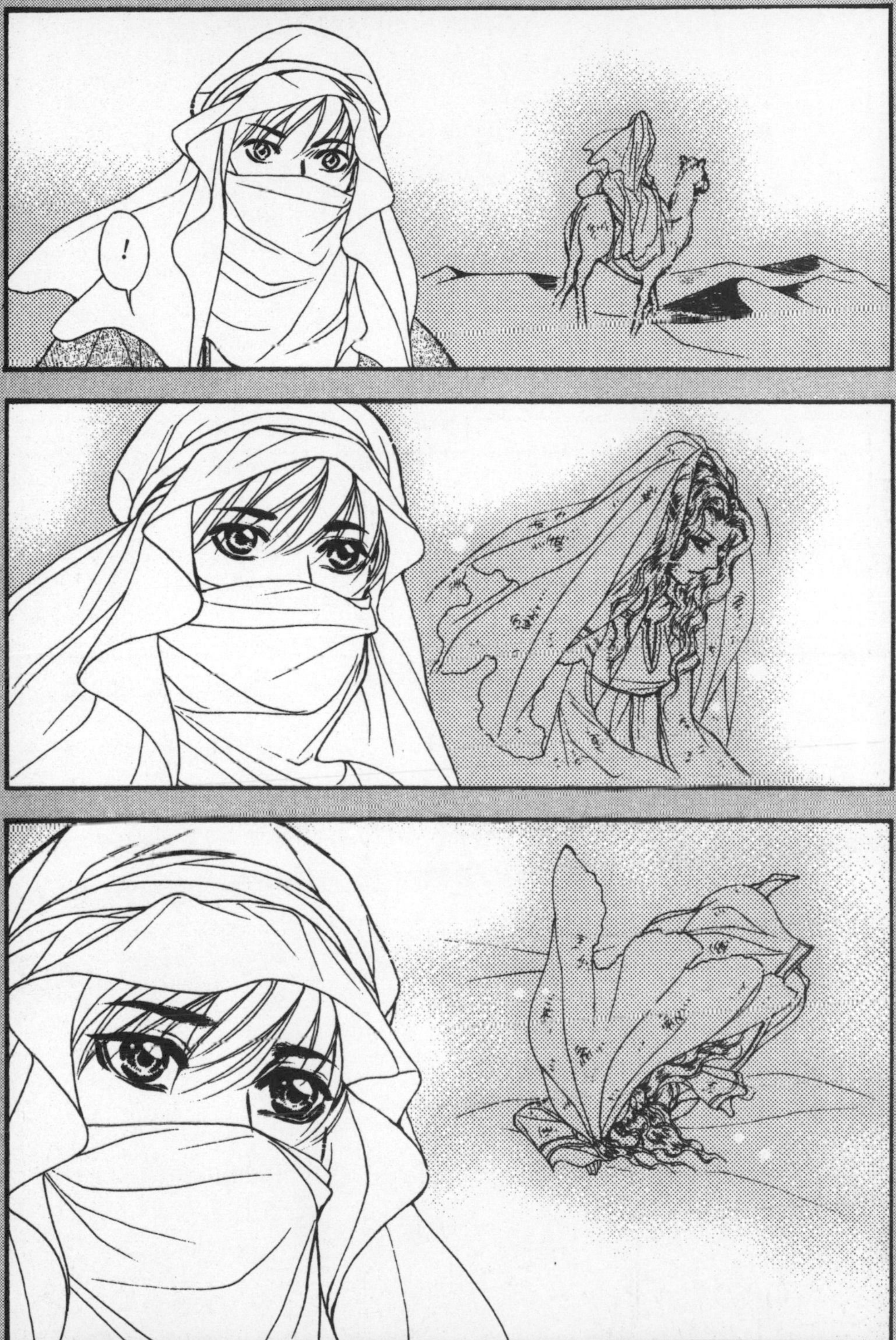
!

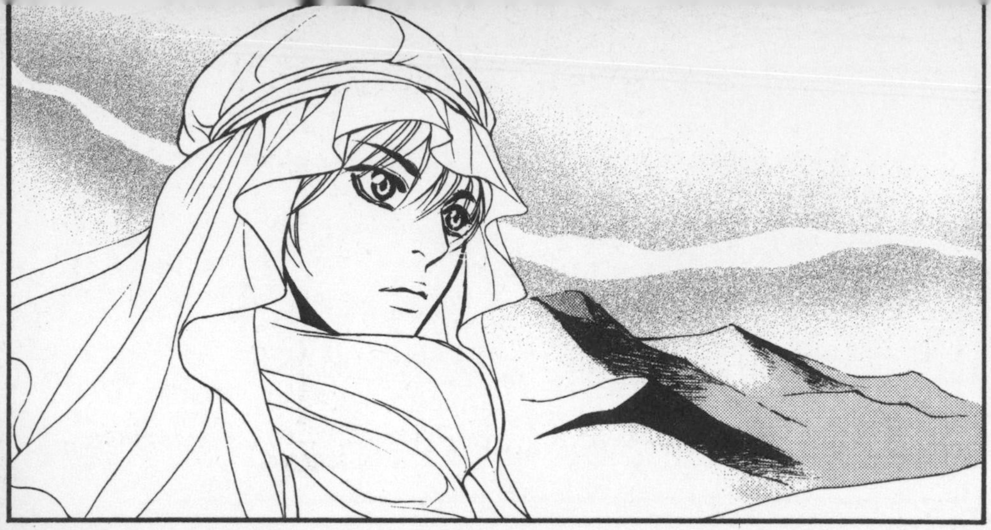

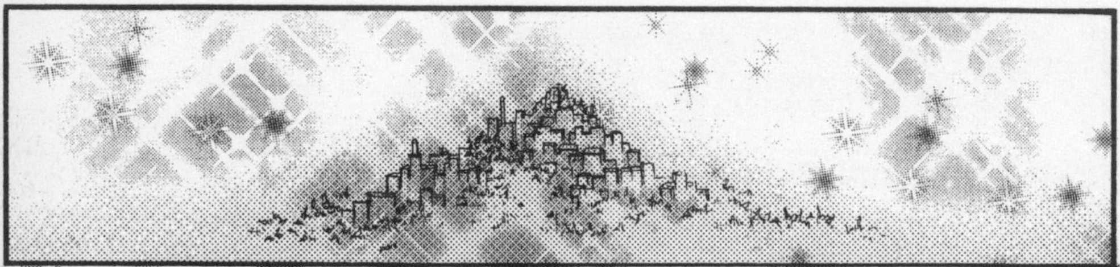

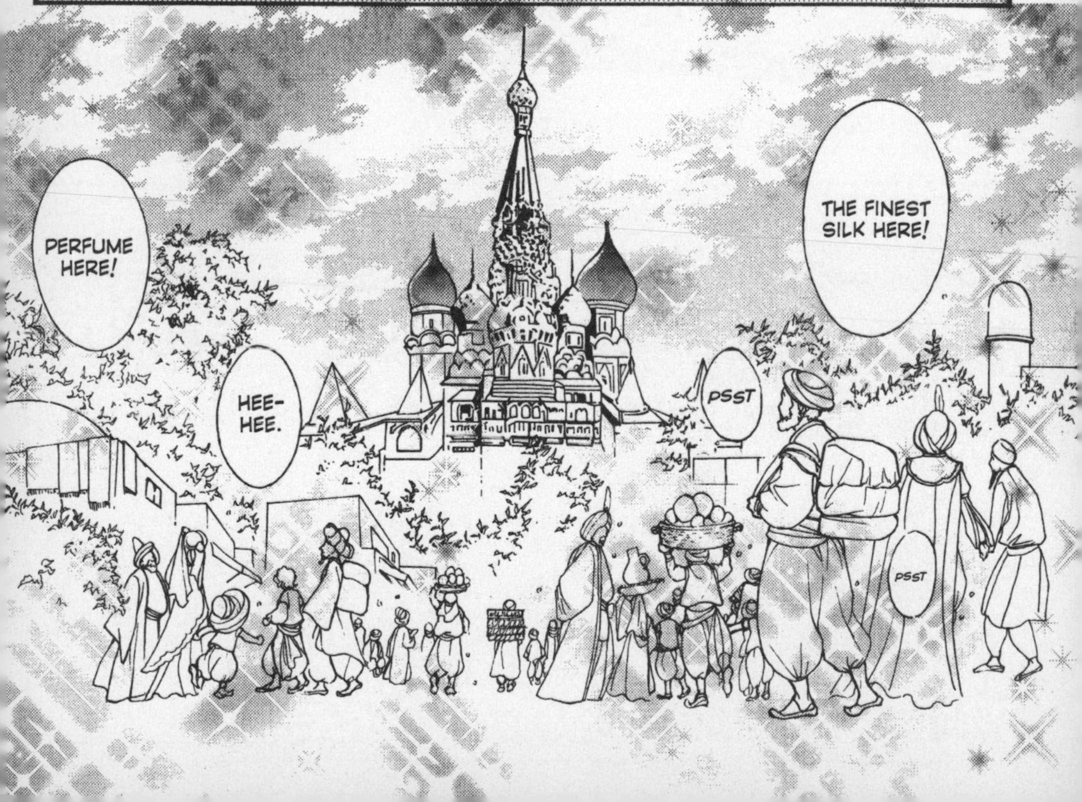
PERFUME HERE!
HEE-HEE.
PSST
THE FINEST SILK HERE!
PSST

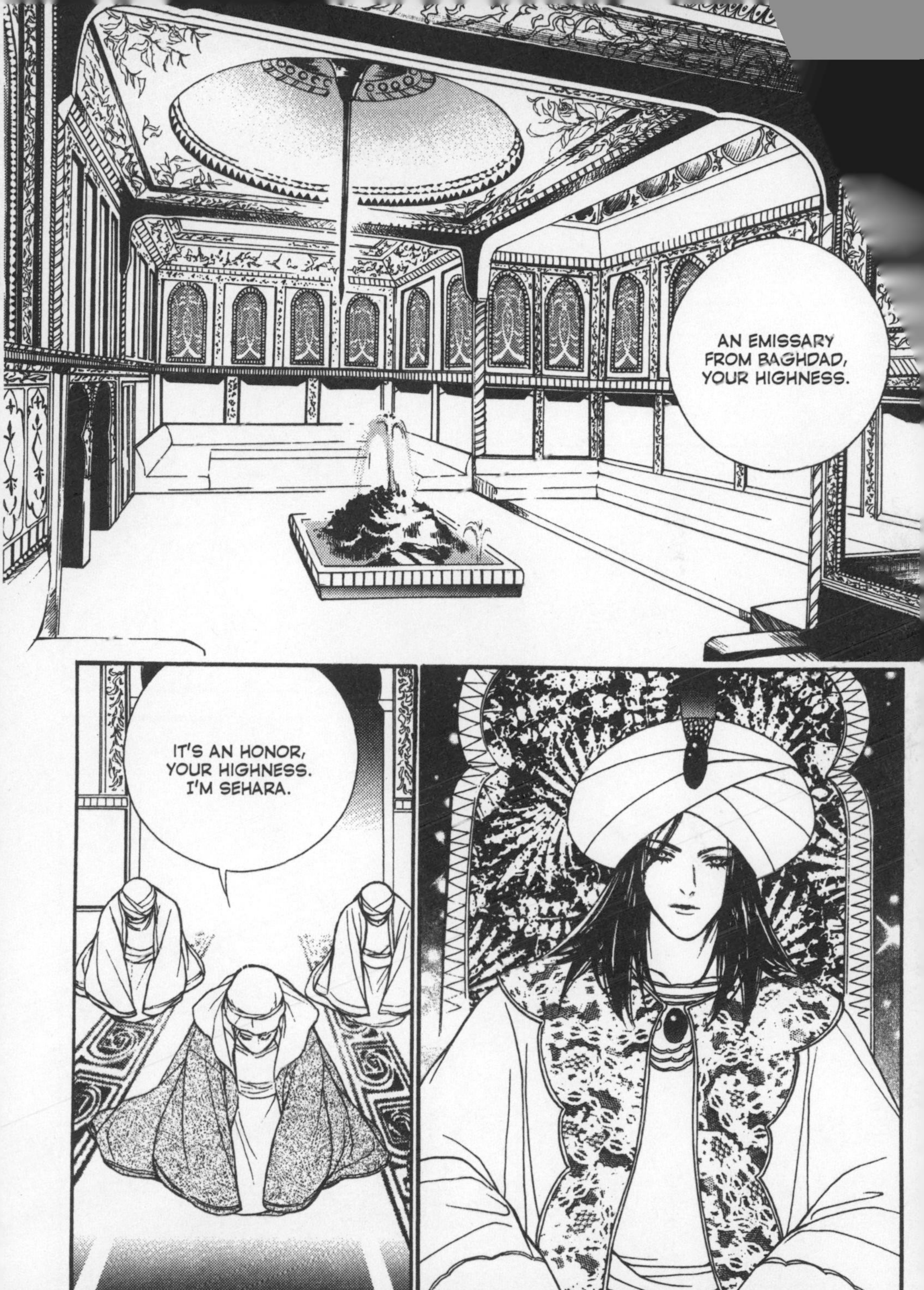
AN EMISSARY FROM BAGHDAD, YOUR HIGHNESS.
IT'S AN HONOR, YOUR HIGHNESS. I'M SEHARA.

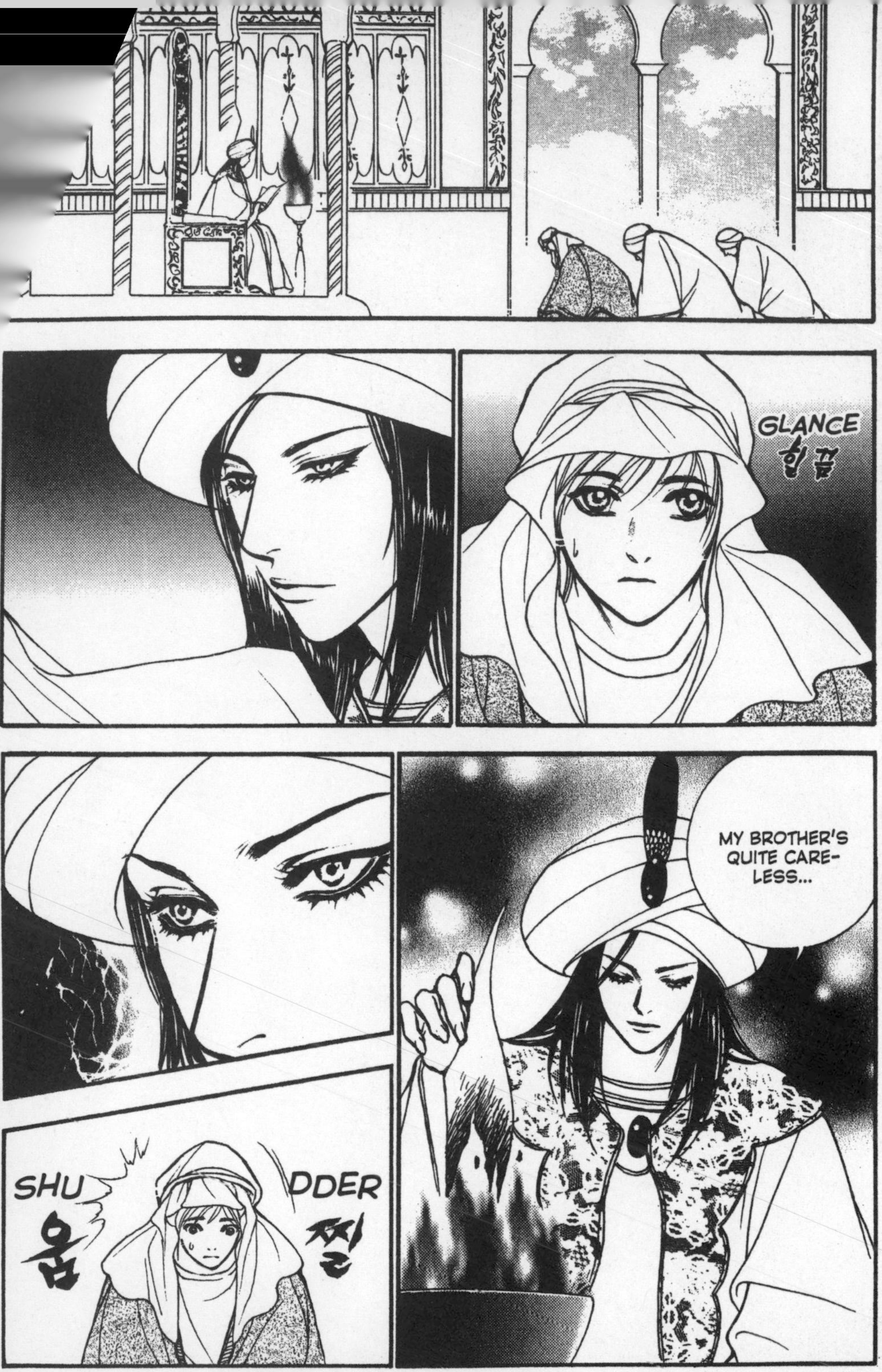
GLANCE
힐끔
SHU
움
DDER
찔
MY BROTHER'S QUITE CARE-LESS...

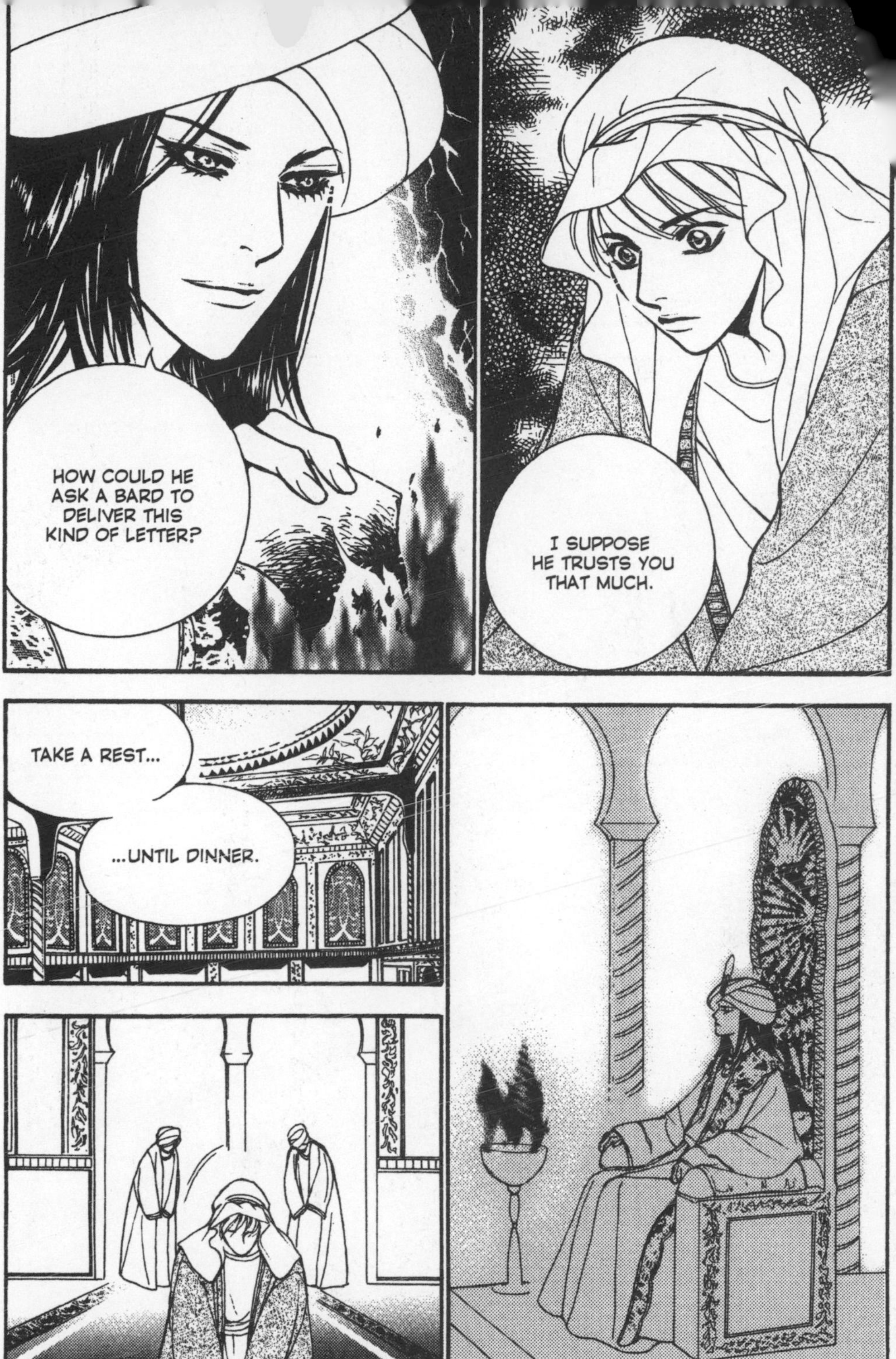
HOW COULD HE ASK A BARD TO DELIVER THIS KIND OF LETTER?
I SUPPOSE HE TRUSTS YOU THAT MUCH.
TAKE A REST...
...UNTIL DINNER.

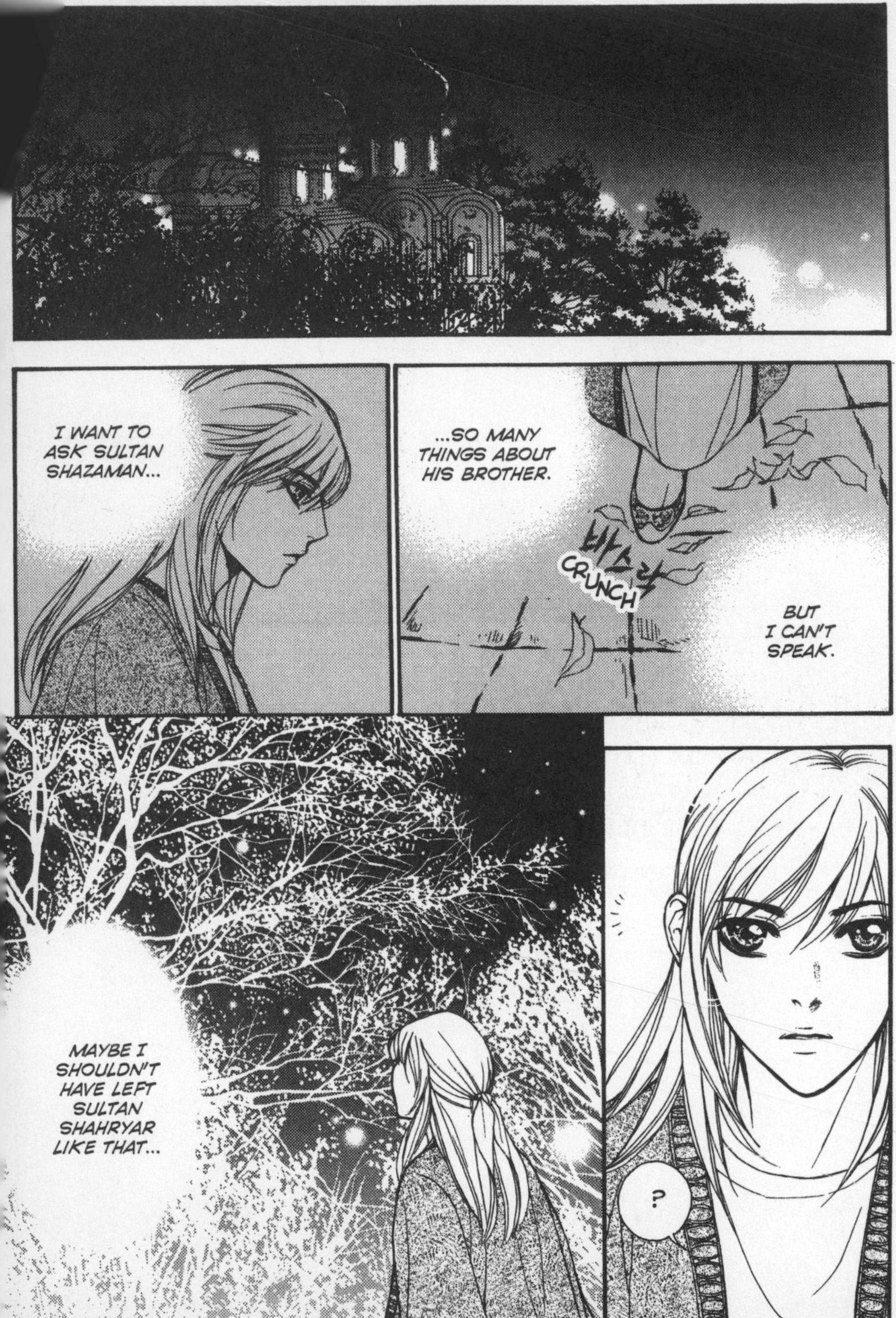
I WANT TO ASK SULTAN SHAZAMAN...
...SO MANY THINGS ABOUT HIS BROTHER.
바스락
CRUNCH
BUT I CAN'T SPEAK.
MAYBE I SHOULDN'T HAVE LEFT SULTAN SHAHRYAR LIKE THAT...
?

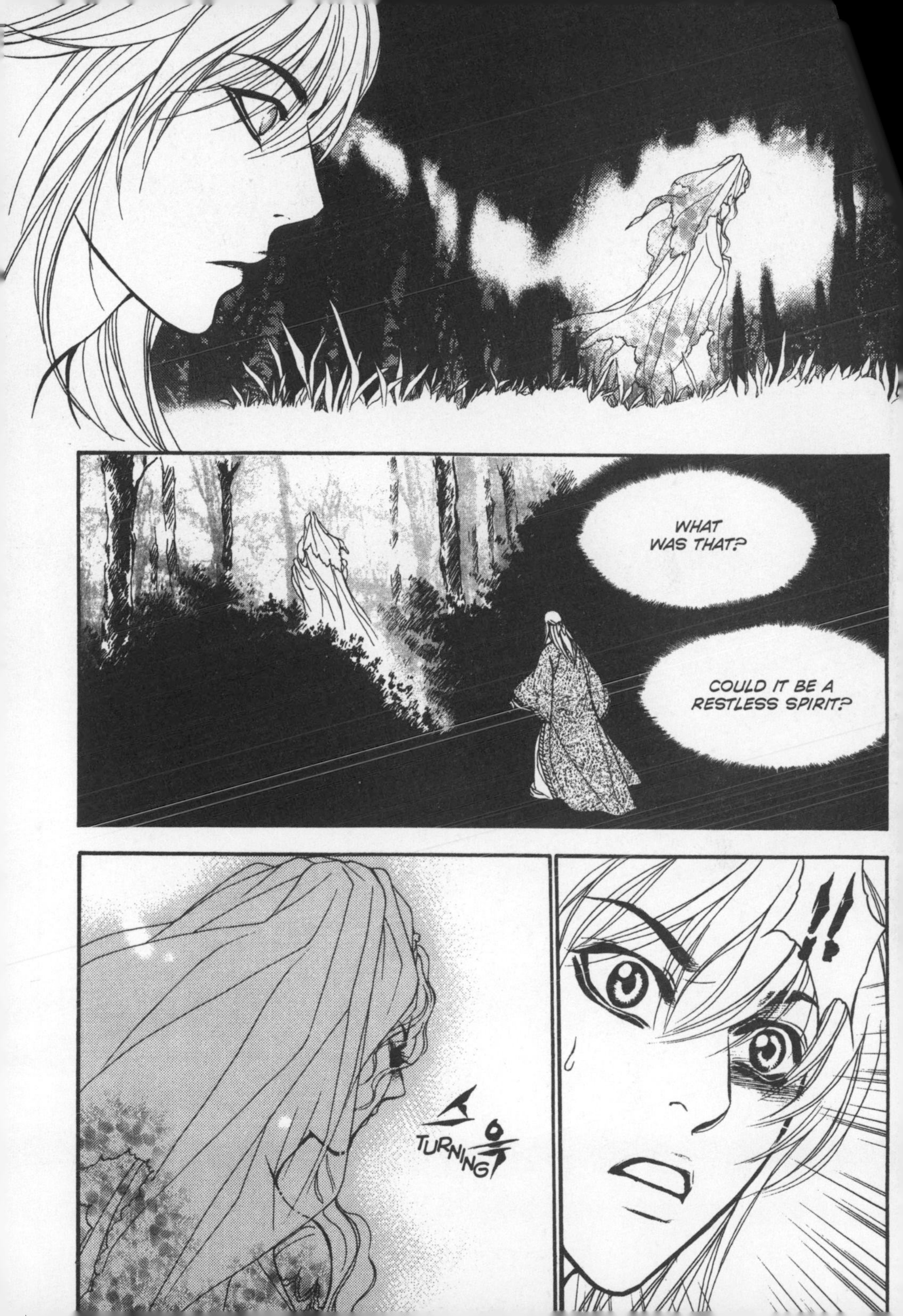
WHAT WAS THAT?
COULD IT BE A RESTLESS SPIRIT?
TURNING
!!

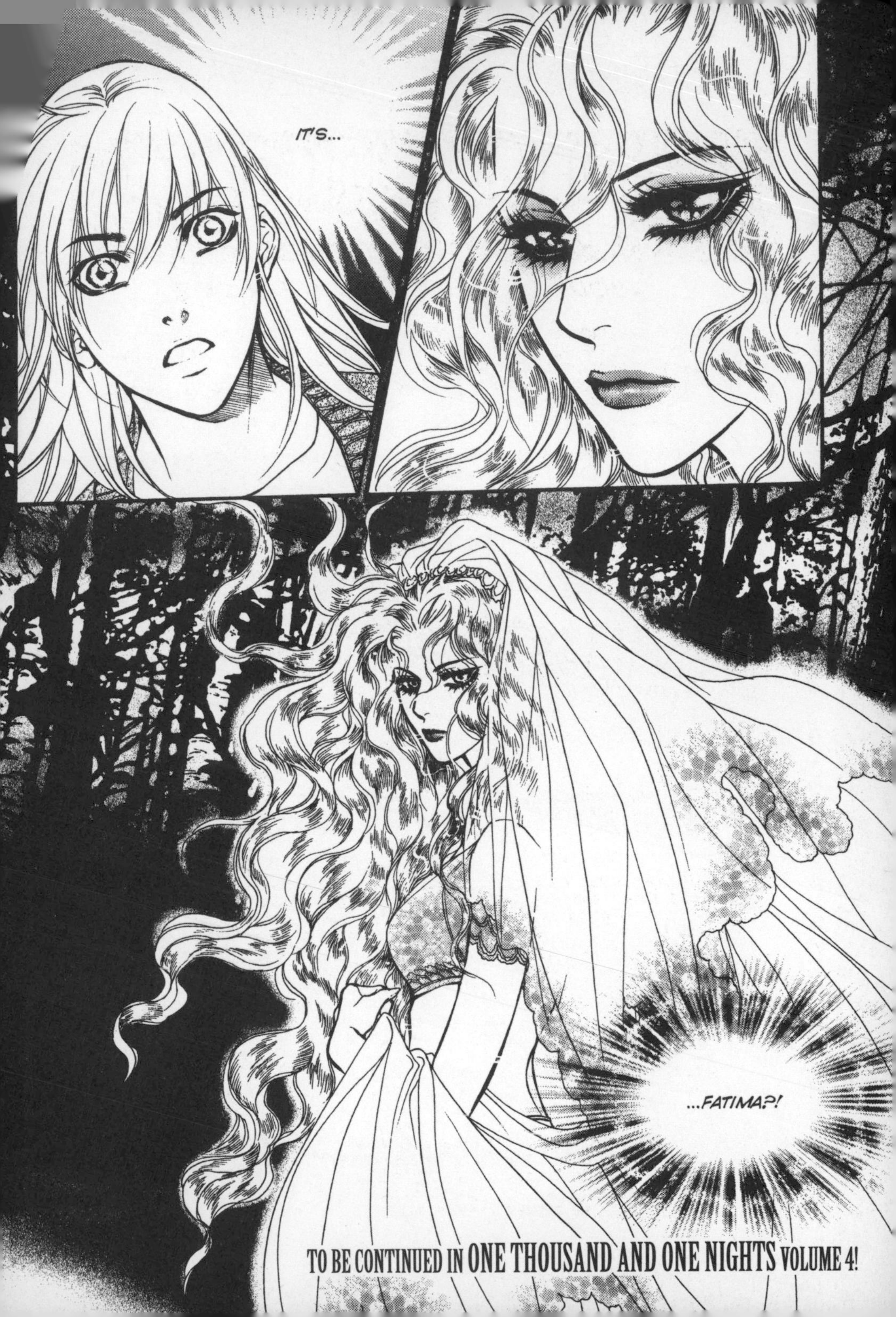
IT'S...
...FATIMA?!
TO BE CONTINUED IN ONE THOUSAND AND ONE NIGHTS VOLUME 4!

Special Commentary From The Writer Jin-seok Jeon

ONE — ABOUT CLEOPATRA'S APPEARANCE

THE EXPRESSION GOES: "IF CLEOPATRA'S NOSE HAD BEEN SHORTER, THE WHOLE FACE OF THE WORLD WOULD HAVE CHANGED." SOME SAY SHE WAS SIMPLY A BEAUTIFUL WOMAN WHOSE LOOKS ENCHANTED POWERFUL MEN. OTHER HISTORIANS EMPHASIZE THAT SHE WAS AN AMAZING POLITICIAN WHO WAS "SHORT, CHUBBY, AND HAD A CROCKED NOSE." BUT SHE WAS ARTICULATE, SPOKE TEN LANGUAGES, AND WAS ABLE TO APPEAL TO PEOPLE.

SHE FELL IN LOVE WITH HEROES AND SET HER PLACE IN HISTORY ALONGSIDE THOSE MEN. I FIND IT UNFORTUNATE WHEN PEOPLE CHARACTERIZE CLEOPATRA AS GREEDY AND CORRUPT BASICALLY BECAUSE THEY CAN'T OTHERWISE FATHOM A WOMAN WITH SUCH POWER. IT'S SAD THAT WE HAVE TO INSIST THAT SHE WASN'T BEAUTIFUL IN ORDER TO EMPHASIZE HER GREAT ACHIEVEMENTS.

WHY CAN'T A WOMAN HAVE BOTH BEAUTY AND POWER? IF CLEOPATRA WERE A MAN, WOULD HER ACHIEVEMENTS EVEN BE QUESTIONED?

TWO — THE PREJUDICE TOWARDS CLEOPATRA AND HOW MEN LOOK AT WOMEN

"EVE" NOT ONLY ATE THE APPLE GOD TOLD HER NOT TO, BUT ALSO MADE ADAM EAT IT.

"PANDORA" OPENED THE BOX THAT ZEUS WARNED HER NOT TO, AND UNLEASHED BAD THINGS INTO THE WORLD.

BLAMING WOMEN FOR THE HARDSHIPS OF LIFE IS NOT EXCLUSIVE TO RELIGION AND MYTHOLOGY. PEOPLE TRY TO PORTRAY CLEOPATRA, ONE OF THE MOST AMAZING WOMEN IN HISTORY, AS ONE OF THE MOST EVIL WOMEN IN HISTORY.

ROME DECLARED WAR ON CLEOPATRA AND NOT ANTONY BECAUSE ROMANS KNEW THAT SHE WAS THE REAL LEADER BEHIND THEIR UNITED ARMY. THE ROMANS TRIED HARD TO BLAME CLEOPATRA FOR EVERYTHING. BUT WHY...?

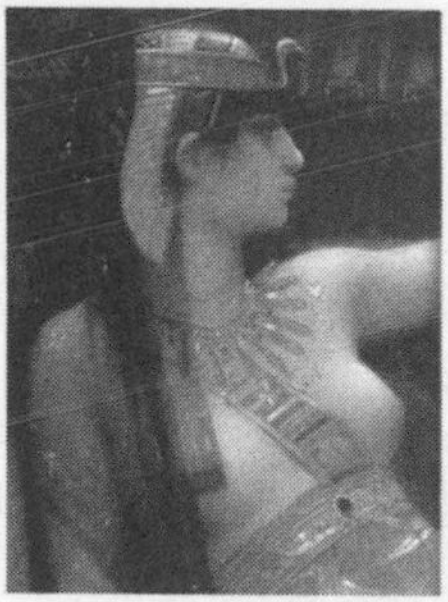

BEFORE THE BATTLE OF ACTIUM, OCTAVIUS WAS QUOTED AS SAYING THAT IF THE ROMANS, THE RULERS OF THE BIGGEST AND THE RICHEST EMPIRE IN THE WORLD, WERE DEFEATED BY A MERE EGYPTIAN WOMAN, THEY SHOULD BE ASHAMED TO MEET THEIR ANCESTORS AND DEAD HEROES IN THE AFTERLIFE.

ROMANS COULD NOT STAND THAT THEIR GREATEST HEROES WERE CONTROLLED BY A WOMAN, THAT THEIR DESTINY WAS IN THE HANDS OF A WOMAN. THE WAR BETWEEN ROME AND EGYPT, WHICH WAS A WAR BETWEEN MEN AND WOMEN, ENDED WITH CLEOPATRA'S DEFEAT. CLEOPATRA KILLED HERSELF WITH A SNAKE BITE. AND THE SNAKE IS THE SYMBOL OF THE GODDESS, ISIS. CLEOPATRA IS DEAD, BUT SHE'LL BE REMEMBERED FOREVER.

STUDIO DIARY?

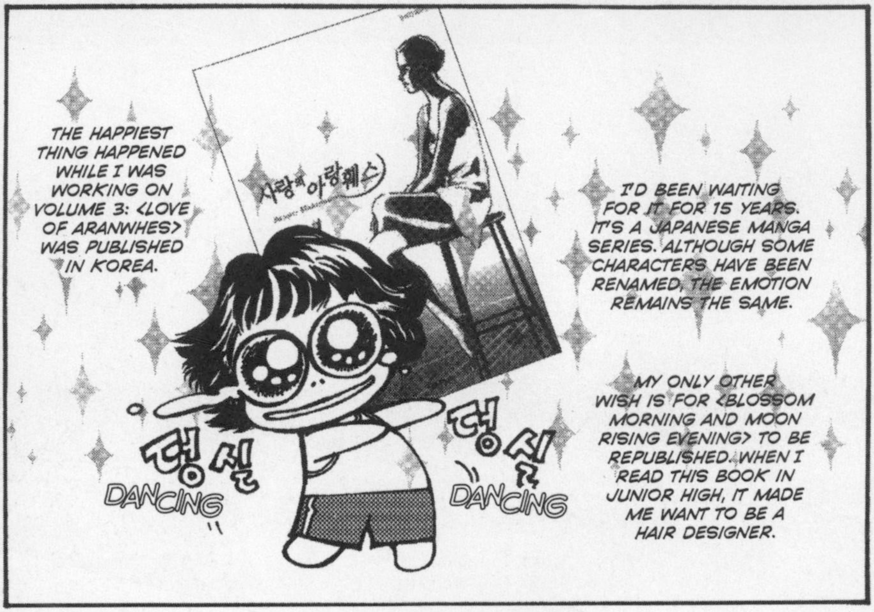
THE HAPPIEST THING HAPPENED WHILE I WAS WORKING ON VOLUME 3: <LOVE OF ARANWHES> WAS PUBLISHED IN KOREA.
I'D BEEN WAITING FOR IT FOR 15 YEARS. IT'S A JAPANESE MANGA SERIES. ALTHOUGH SOME CHARACTERS HAVE BEEN RENAMED, THE EMOTION REMAINS THE SAME.
MY ONLY OTHER WISH IS FOR <BLOSSOM MORNING AND MOON RISING EVENING> TO BE REPUBLISHED. WHEN I READ THIS BOOK IN JUNIOR HIGH, IT MADE ME WANT TO BE A HAIR DESIGNER.
DANCING
DANCING

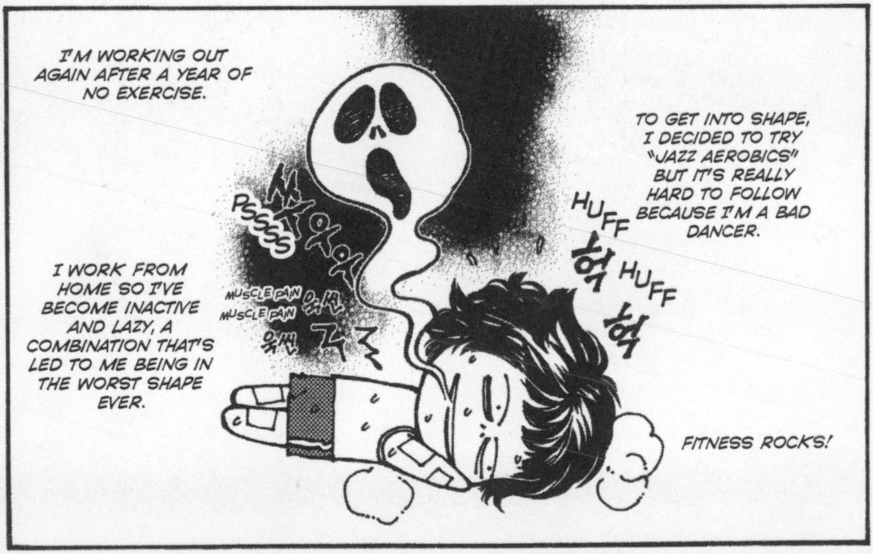
I'M WORKING OUT AGAIN AFTER A YEAR OF NO EXERCISE.
TO GET INTO SHAPE, I DECIDED TO TRY "JAZZ AEROBICS" BUT IT'S REALLY HARD TO FOLLOW BECAUSE I'M A BAD DANCER.
PSSSSS
HUFF
HUFF
MUSCLE PAIN
MUSCLE PAIN
I WORK FROM HOME SO I'VE BECOME INACTIVE AND LAZY, A COMBINATION THAT'S LED TO ME BEING IN THE WORST SHAPE EVER.
FITNESS ROCKS!

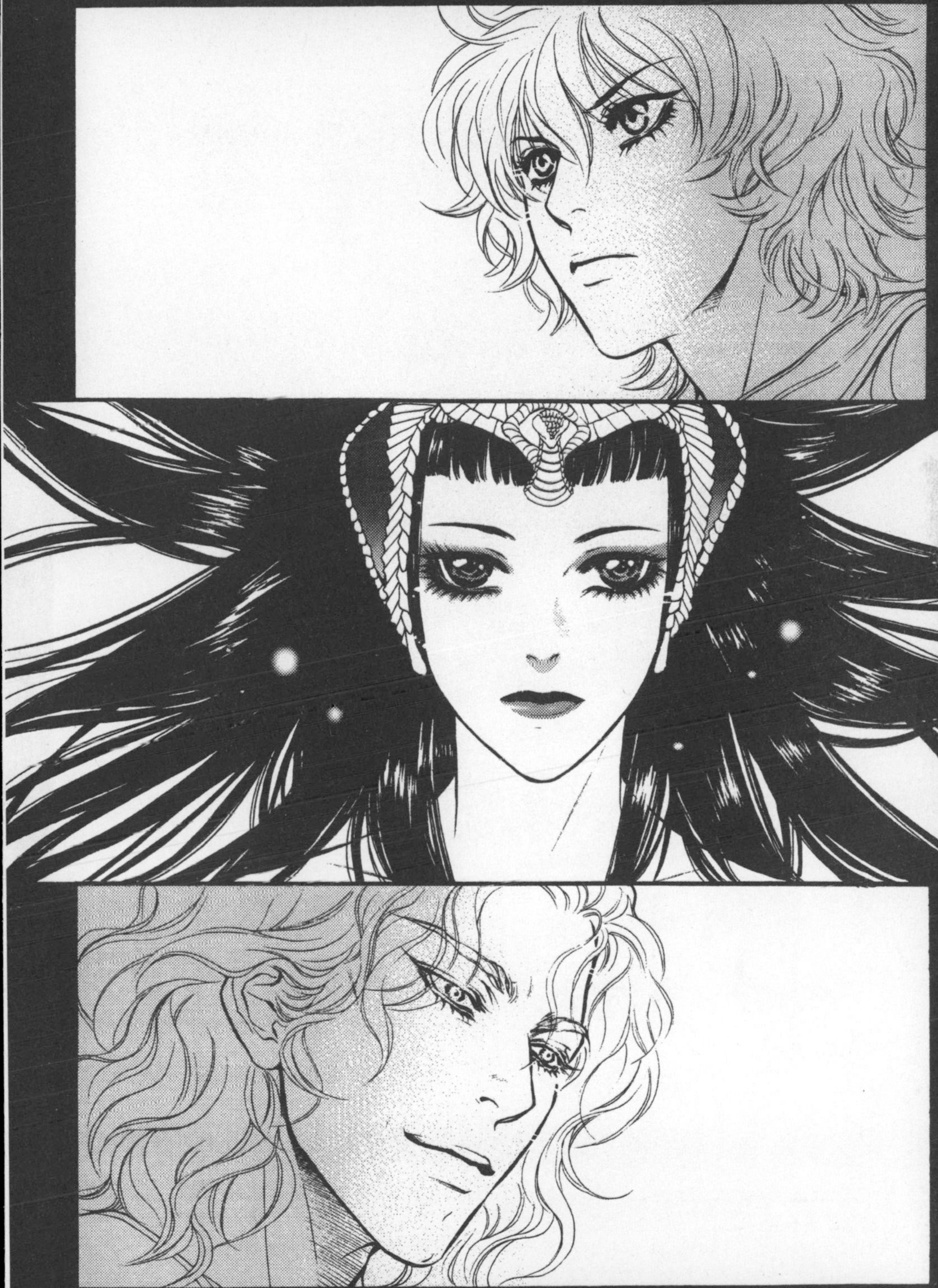

Preview

The Antique Gift Shop

vol.3

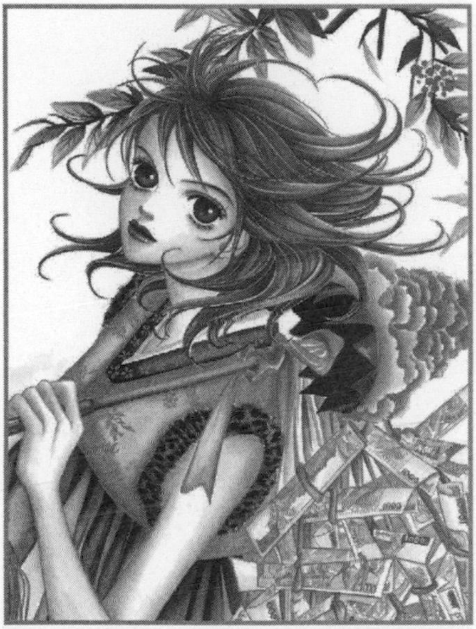

Lee Eun

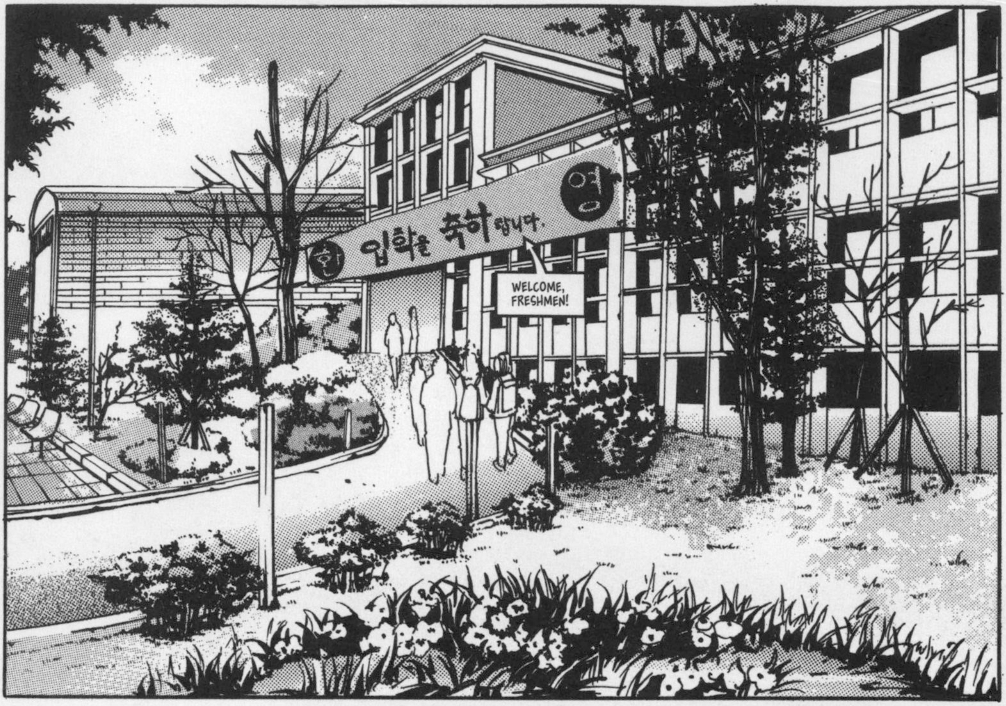
입학을 축하합니다.
WELCOME, FRESHMEN!

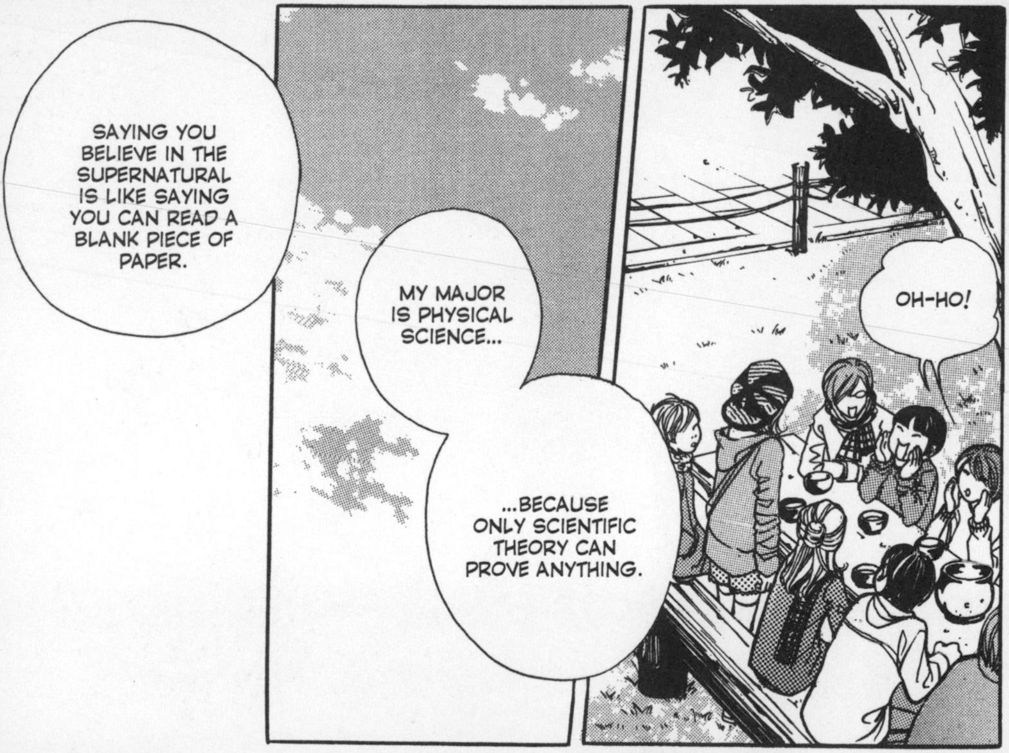
SAYING YOU BELIEVE IN THE SUPERNATURAL IS LIKE SAYING YOU CAN READ A BLANK PIECE OF PAPER.
MY MAJOR IS PHYSICAL SCIENCE...
...BECAUSE ONLY SCIENTIFIC THEORY CAN PROVE ANYTHING.
OH-HO!

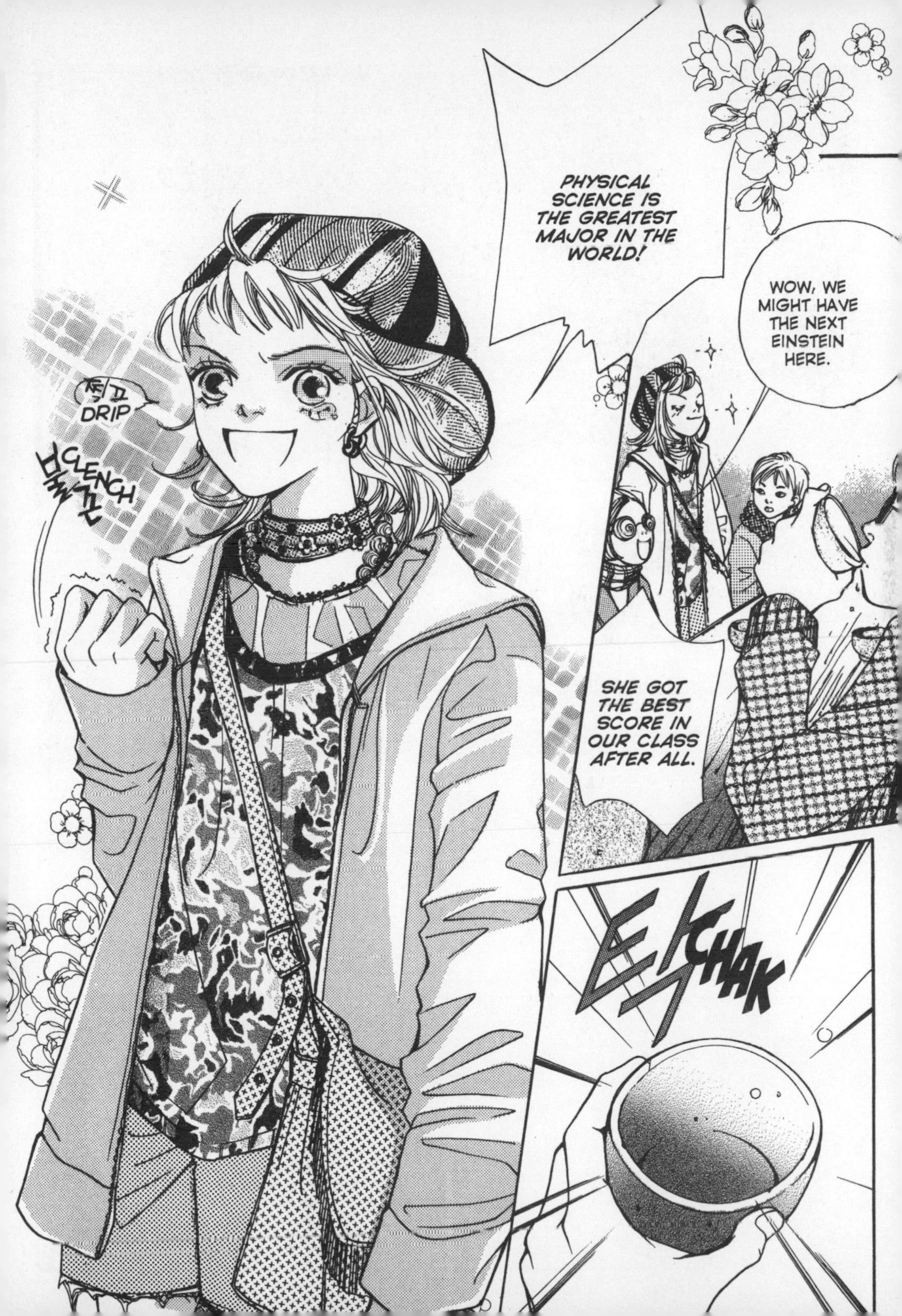
DRIP
CLENCH
PHYSICAL SCIENCE IS THE GREATEST MAJOR IN THE WORLD!
WOW, WE MIGHT HAVE THE NEXT EINSTEIN HERE.
SHE GOT THE BEST SCORE IN OUR CLASS AFTER ALL.
CHAK

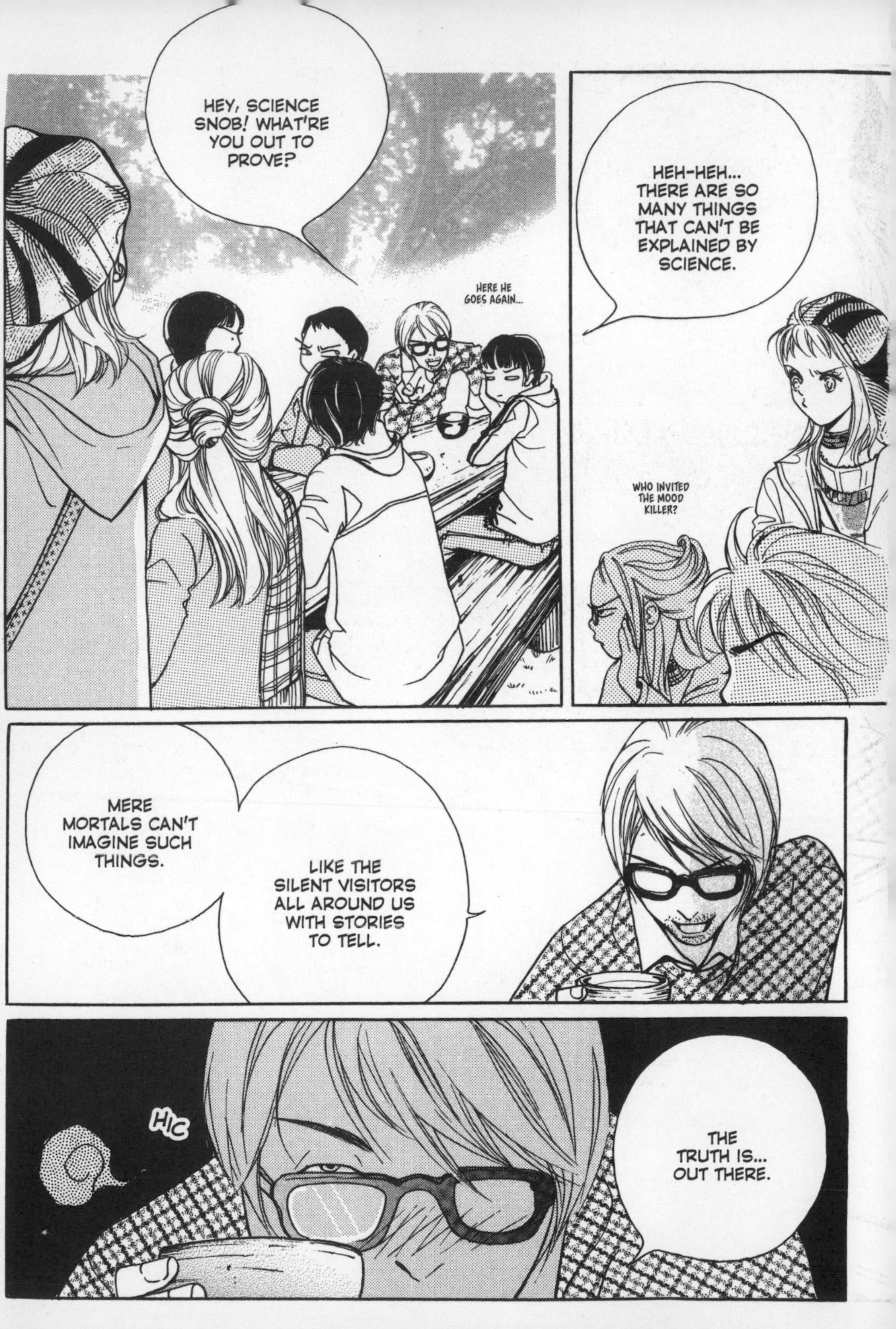
HEY, SCIENCE SNOB! WHAT'RE YOU OUT TO PROVE?
HERE HE GOES AGAIN...
HEH-HEH... THERE ARE SO MANY THINGS THAT CAN'T BE EXPLAINED BY SCIENCE.
WHO INVITED THE MOOD KILLER?
MERE MORTALS CAN'T IMAGINE SUCH THINGS.
LIKE THE SILENT VISITORS ALL AROUND US WITH STORIES TO TELL.
HIC
THE TRUTH IS... OUT THERE.

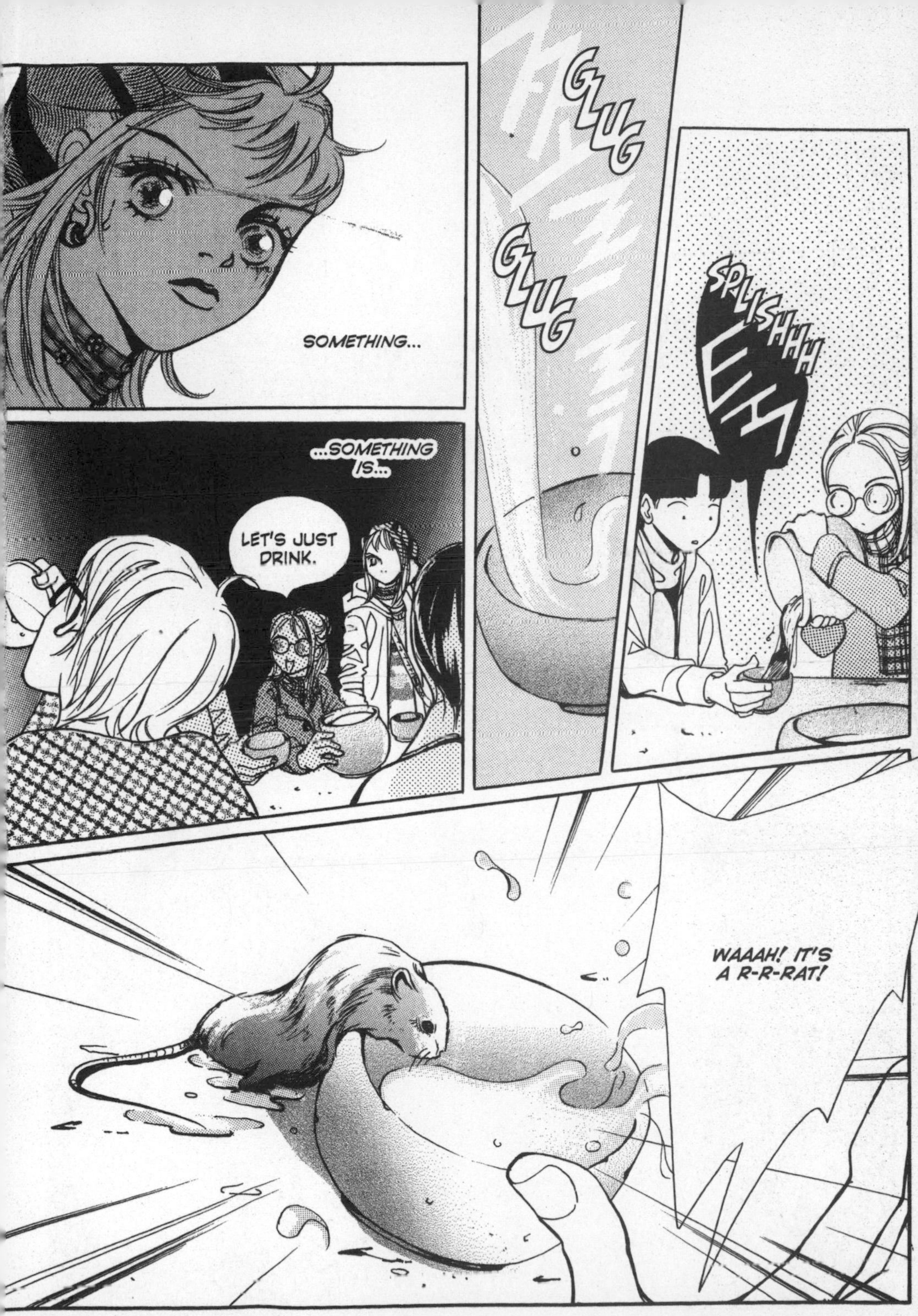
SOMETHING...
...SOMETHING IS...
LET'S JUST DRINK.
GLUG
GLUG
SPLISHHH
WAAAH! IT'S A R-R-RAT!

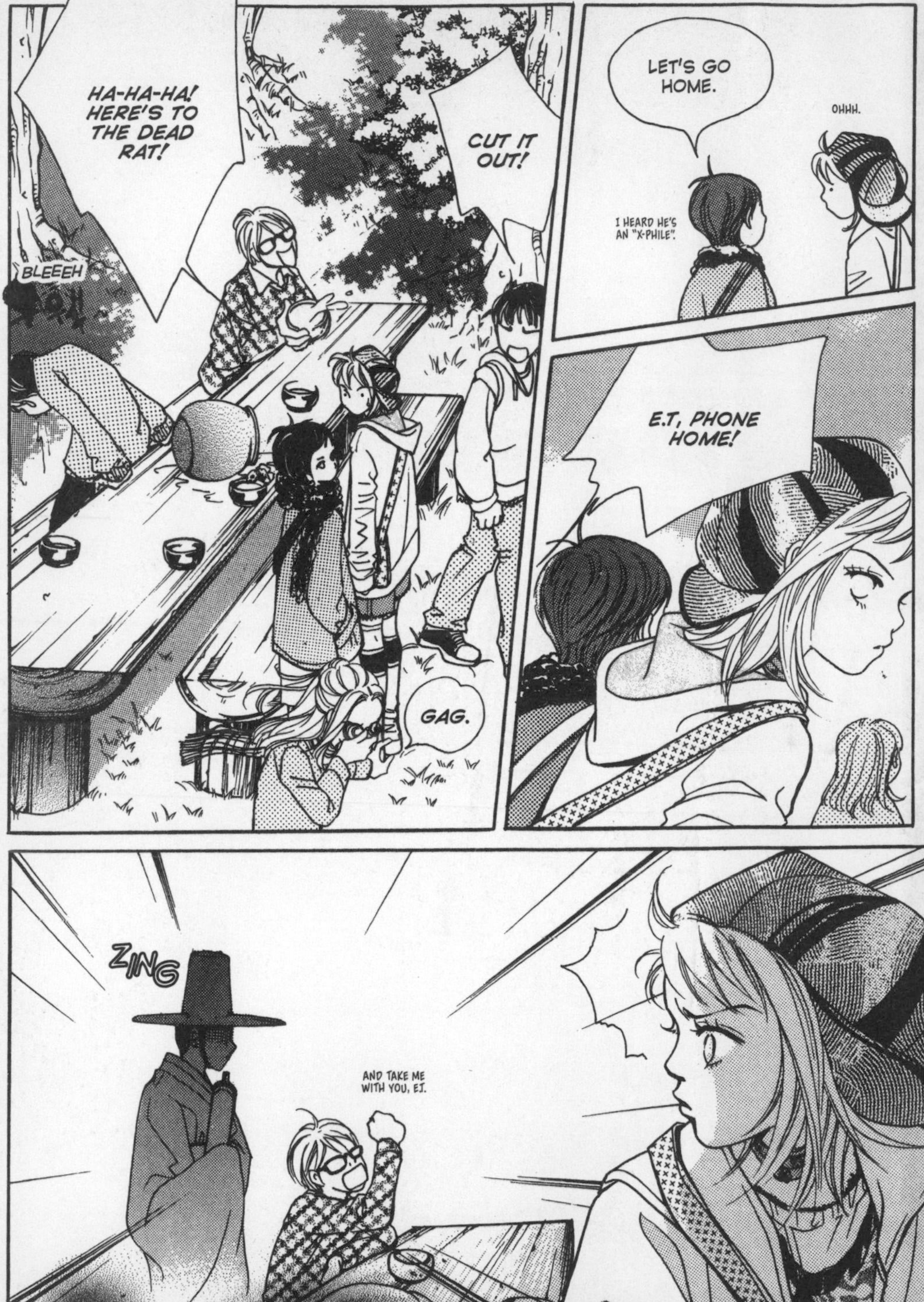
BLEEEH
HA-HA-HA! HERE'S TO THE DEAD RAT!
CUT IT OUT!
GAG.
LET'S GO HOME.
I HEARD HE'S AN "X-PHILE".
OHHH.
E.T, PHONE HOME!
ZING
AND TAKE ME WITH YOU, E.T.

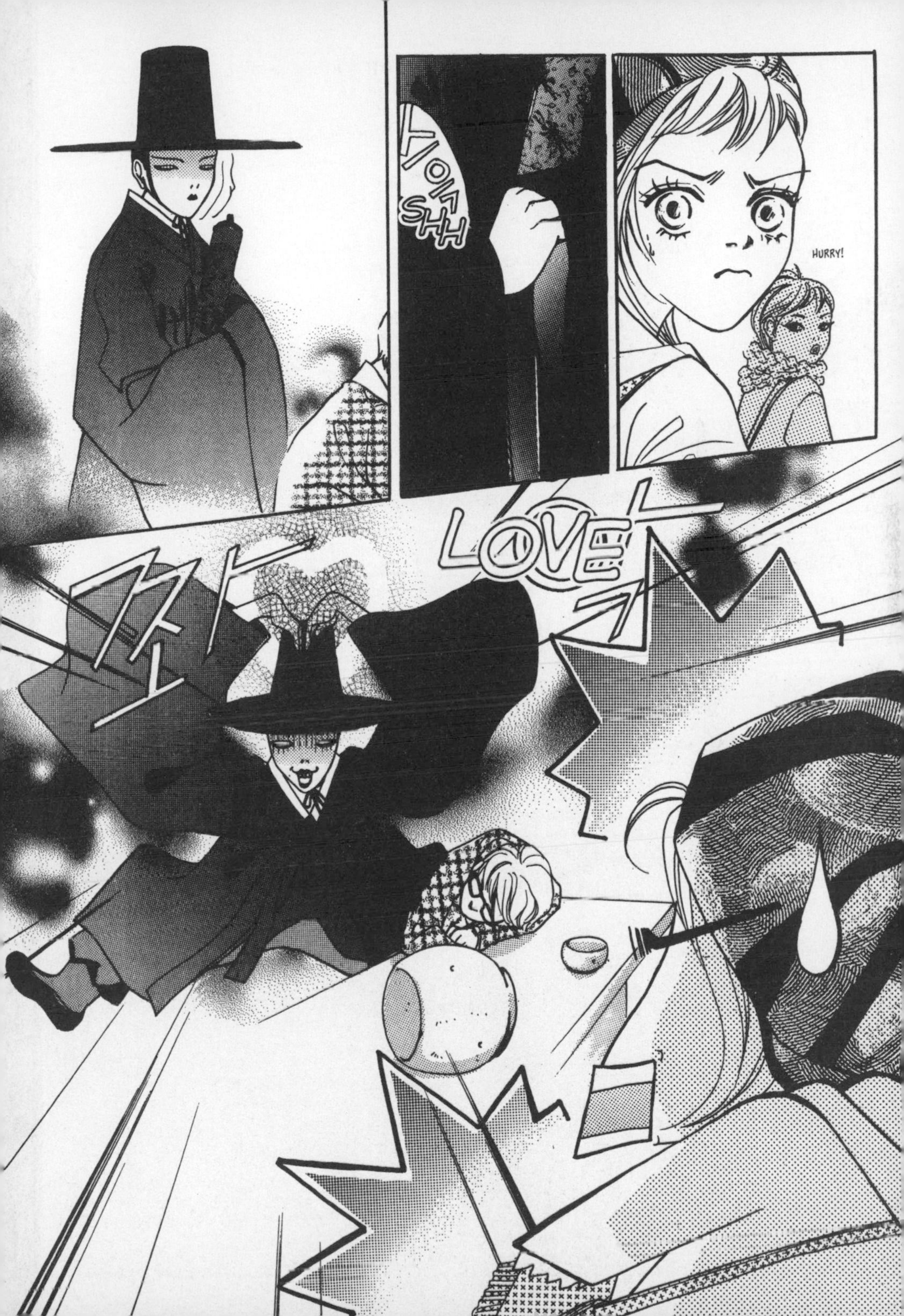
SHH
HURRY!
LOVE

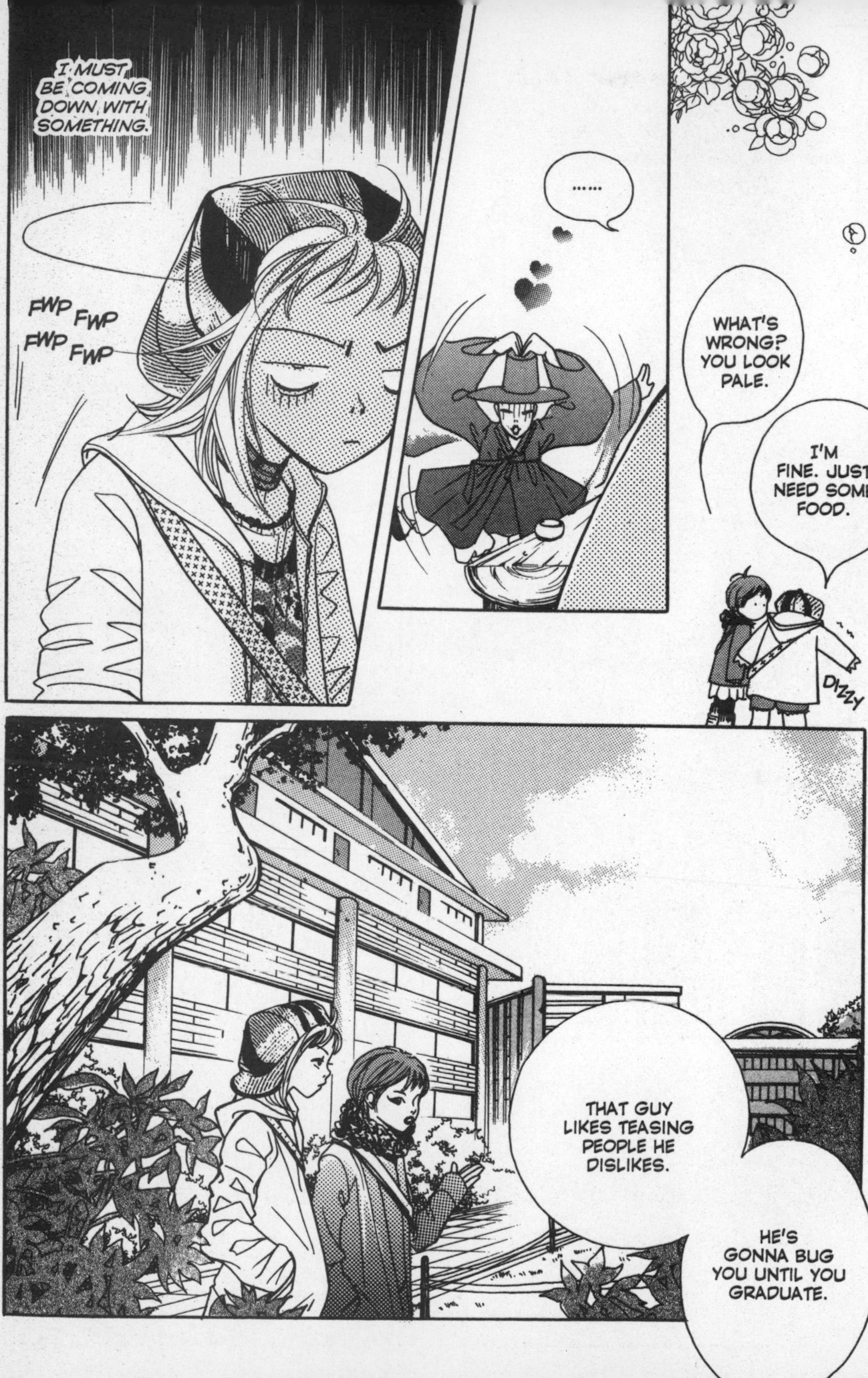
I MUST BE COMING DOWN WITH SOMETHING.
FWP FWP FWP FWP
......
WHAT'S WRONG? YOU LOOK PALE.
I'M FINE. JUST NEED SOME FOOD.
DIZZY
THAT GUY LIKES TEASING PEOPLE HE DISLIKES.
HE'S GONNA BUG YOU UNTIL YOU GRADUATE.

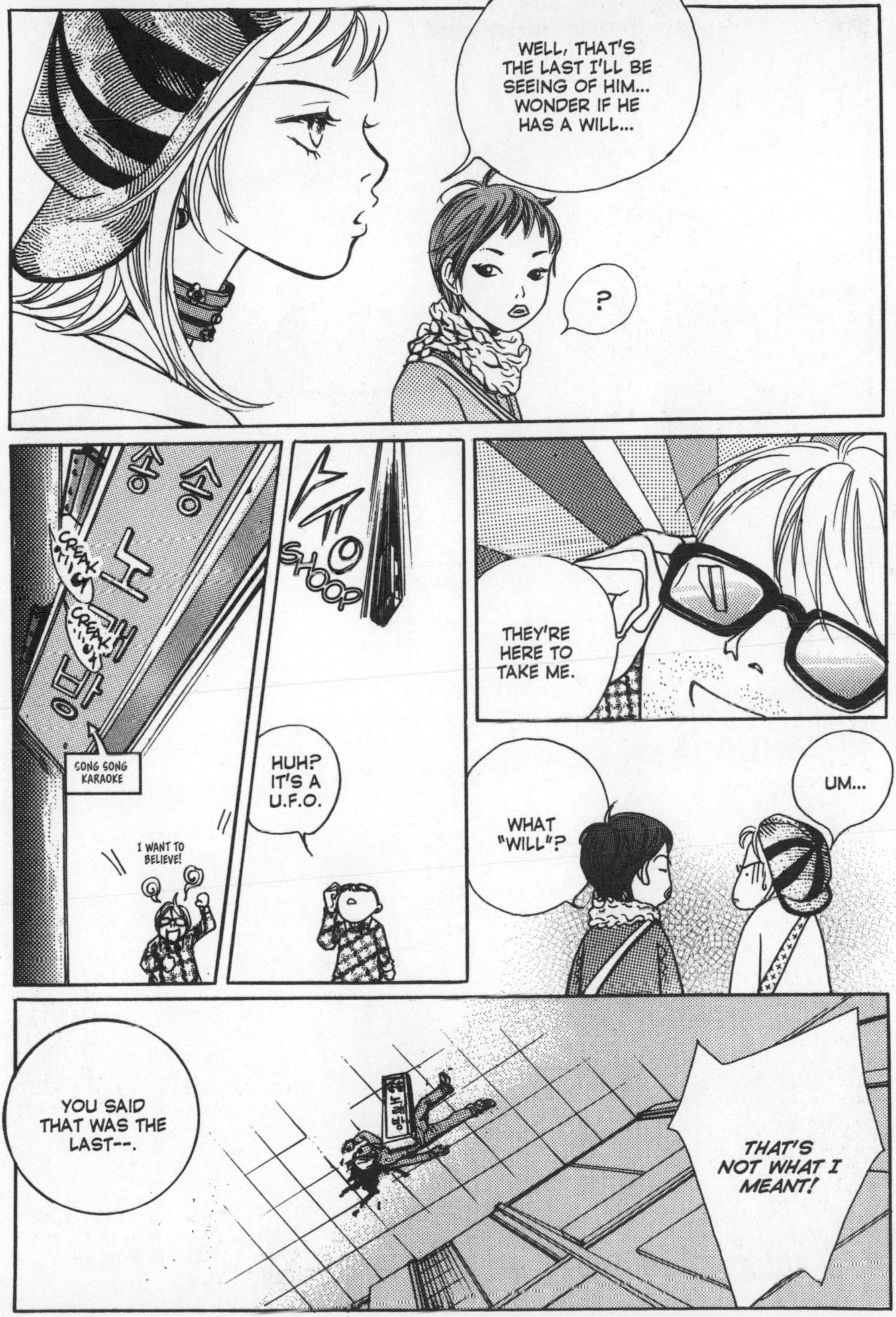
WELL, THAT'S THE LAST I'LL BE SEEING OF HIM... WONDER IF HE HAS A WILL...
?
송송 노래방
CREAK
CREAK
SONG SONG KARAOKE
I WANT TO BELIEVE!
SHOOP
HUH? IT'S A U.F.O.
THEY'RE HERE TO TAKE ME.
WHAT "WILL"?
UM...
YOU SAID THAT WAS THE LAST--.
THAT'S NOT WHAT I MEANT!

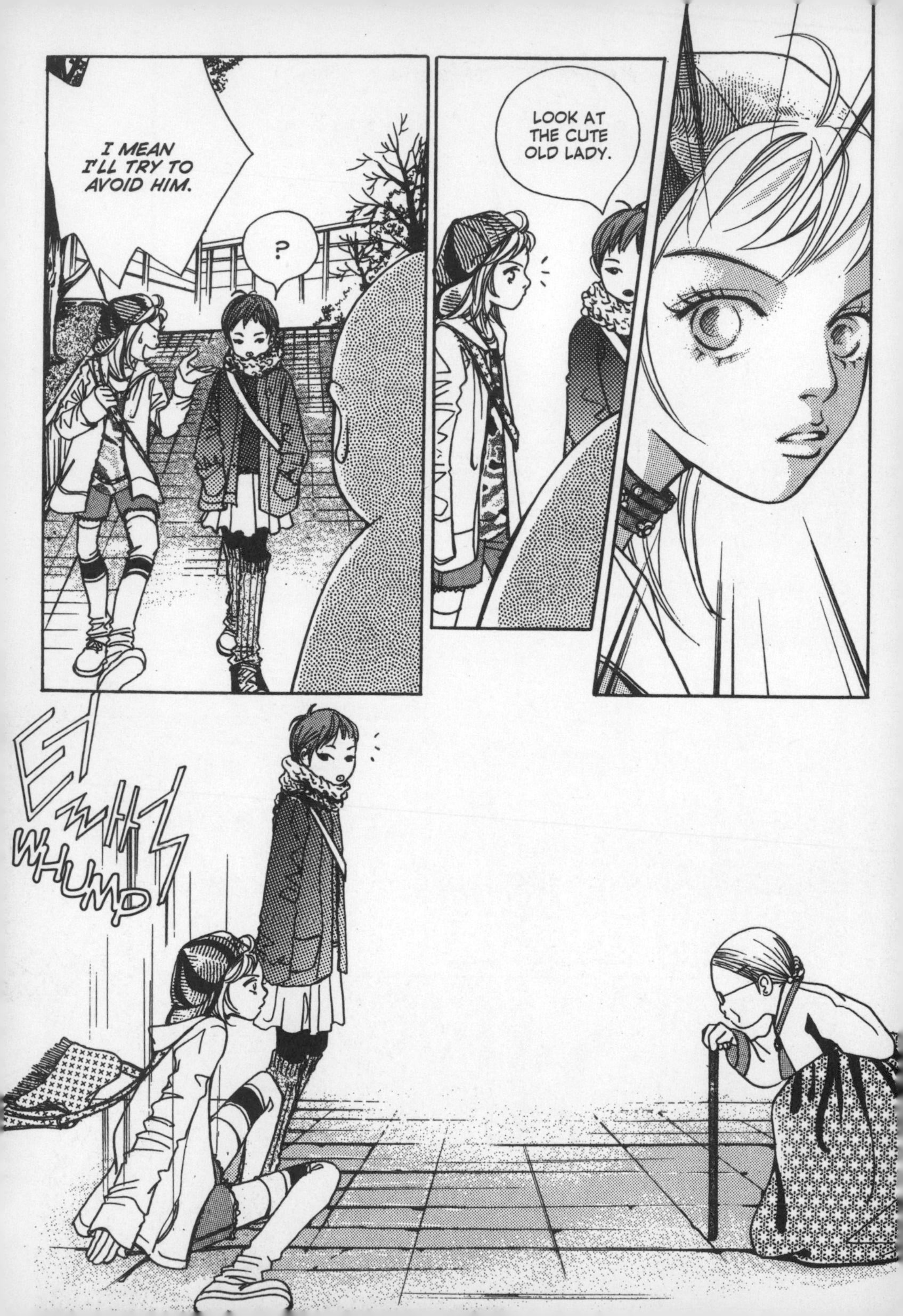
I MEAN I'LL TRY TO AVOID HIM.
?
LOOK AT THE CUTE OLD LADY.
WHUMP

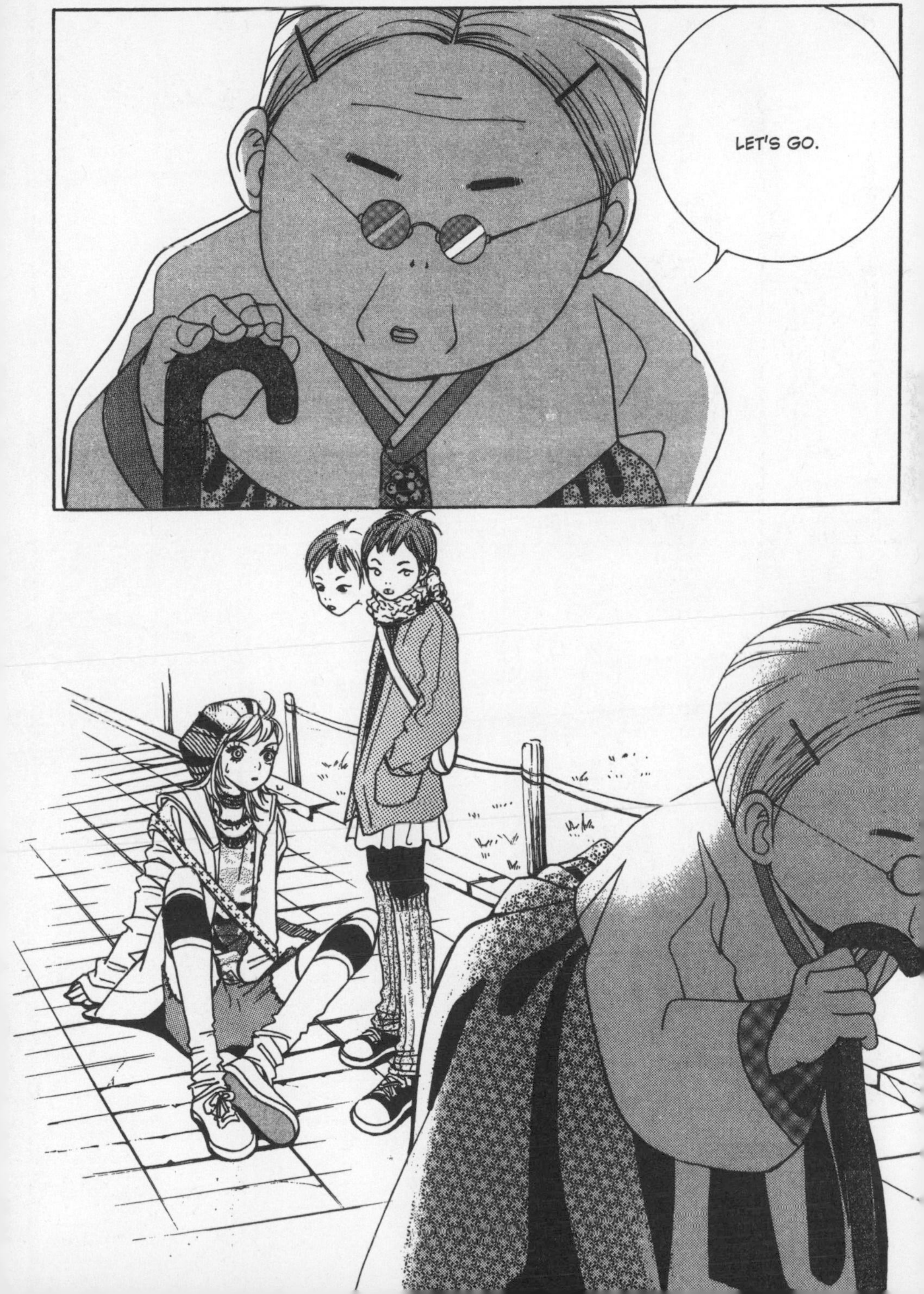
LET'S GO.

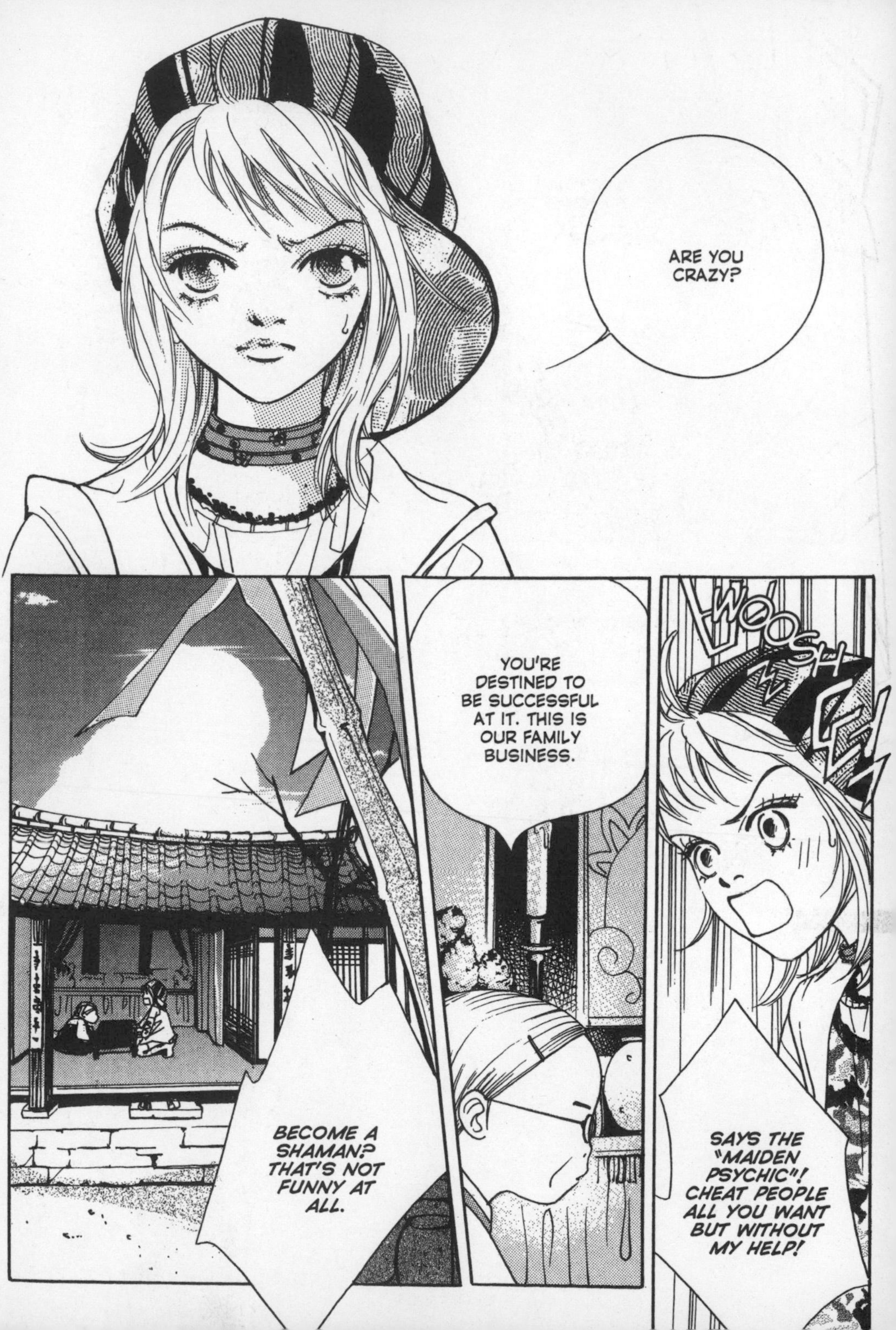
ARE YOU CRAZY?
BECOME A SHAMAN? THAT'S NOT FUNNY AT ALL.
YOU'RE DESTINED TO BE SUCCESSFUL AT IT. THIS IS OUR FAMILY BUSINESS.
WOOSH
SAYS THE "MAIDEN PSYCHIC"! CHEAT PEOPLE ALL YOU WANT BUT WITHOUT MY HELP!

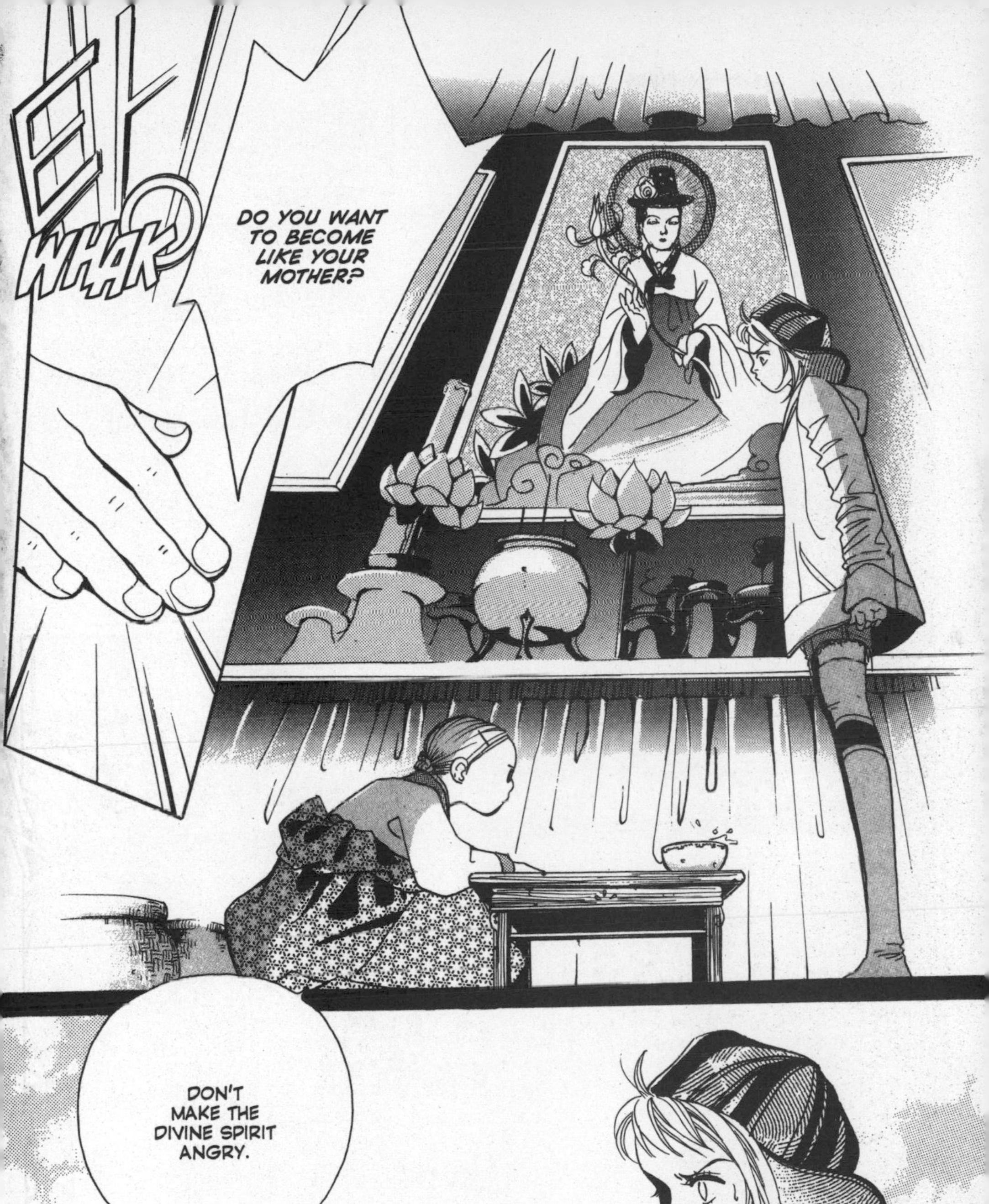
WHAK
DO YOU WANT TO BECOME LIKE YOUR MOTHER?
DON'T MAKE THE DIVINE SPIRIT ANGRY.
THE END OF THE PREVIEW FOR
THE ANTIQUE GIFT SHOP VOL 3!
ON SALE NOW!

Danbi Original

One thousand and one nights vol.3

Story by JinSeok Jeon
Art by SeungHee Han

Translation HyeYoung Im
English Adaptation J. Torres
Touch-up and Lettering Terri Delgado · Marshall Dillon
Graphic Design EunKyung Kim

ICE Kunion

English Adaptation Editor HyeYoung Im · J. Torres
Managing Editor Marshall Dillon
Marketing Manager Erik Ko
Senior Editor JuYoun Lee
Editorial Director MoonJung Kim
Managing Director Jackie Lee
Publisher and C.E.O. JaeKook Chun

One thousand and one nights © 2005 SeungHee Han · JinSeok Jeon
First published in Korea in 2005 by SEOUL CULTURAL PUBLISHERS, Inc.
English text translation rights arranged by SEOUL CULTURAL PUBLISHERS, Inc.
English text © 2005 ICE KUNION

Published by ICE Kunion.
SIGONGSA 2F Yeil Bldg. 1619-4, Seocho-dong, Seocho-gu, Seoul, 137-878, Korea

ISBN : 89-527-4493-4

First printing, October 2006
10 9 8 7 6 5 4 3 2 1
Printed in Canada

www.icekunion.com/www.koreanmanhwa.com